'A timely, important, and impressive book that provides a tremendous new examination of Alexander the Great. Ferguson and Worthington establish convincingly that civilization's advances have not made war less complex or less taxing on the human condition. As the world evolves from an era of benign globalization to one of renewed great power rivalries, *The Military Legacy of Alexander the Great* is a compelling exploration of the timeless and often brutal nature of war'.

– **General David Petraeus** *(U.S. Army, Ret.), former Commander of the Surge in Iraq, U.S. Central Command, and NATO/US Forces in Afghanistan and co-author (with Andrew Roberts) of* Conflict: The Evolution of Warfare from 1945 to Ukraine.

'Ferguson and Worthington's book is a bold effort that integrates a history from antiquity with contemporary insights on leadership. A well-designed project of no small amount of intellectual ambition, it is brilliantly executed with nuance and good deal of classical scholarship. Professional students of the art of war will benefit from this historically grounded study that serves as a unique guide to anyone aspiring to master the complexities of strategic leadership'.

– **Frank Hoffman, Ph.D.**, *U.S. National Defense University*

'A much needed, didactic reexamination of the unique ways in which Alexander the Great overcame daunting challenges of logistics, geography, numbers, culture, and politics that should have guaranteed his failure – and the lessons that ancient history offers. A rare, scholarly, and pragmatic guide to the unchanging principles of conducting war by authors who are as versed with wars of the past as they are familiar with conflict in the present'.

– **Victor Davis Hanson,** *the Hoover Institution, Stanford University. Author of* A War Like No Other; The Second World Wars.

'Michael P. Ferguson and Ian Worthington have presented an excellent account and analysis of Alexander's campaigns, detailing his strengths and weaknesses across the different levels and components of strategy. Moreover, the book identifies a range of valuable insights for the modern practitioner of strategy. Perhaps most importantly, the book determines that, despite our ever-changing world, war and strategy remain fundamentally human endeavours in which leadership and strategic judgement remain paramount'.

– **David J. Lonsdale**, *author of* Alexander the Great: Lessons in Strategy.

'Leadership, strategy, perseverance, individual will . . . these characteristics are the legacy of Alexander the Great, and they are why we have studied him and his campaigns over the centuries. His ability to push his army beyond normal limits and reach the fullest possible potential of his soldiers are what is expected of every modern leader today'.

– **Lt. Gen. Ben Hodges**, *US Army (Retired).*

Designed cover image: Credit line: Matthias Kestel/Alamy Stock Photo and AFP/US Air Force

First published 2024
by Routledge
4 Park Square, Milton Park, Abingdon, Oxon OX14 4RN

and by Routledge
605 Third Avenue, New York, NY 10158

Routledge is an imprint of the Taylor & Francis Group, an informa business

© 2024 Michael P. Ferguson and Ian Worthington

The right of Michael P. Ferguson and Ian Worthington to be identified as authors of this work has been asserted in accordance with sections 77 and 78 of the Copyright, Designs and Patents Act 1988.

All rights reserved. No part of this book may be reprinted or reproduced or utilised in any form or by any electronic, mechanical, or other means, now known or hereafter invented, including photocopying and recording, or in any information storage or retrieval system, without permission in writing from the publishers.

Trademark notice: Product or corporate names may be trademarks or registered trademarks, and are used only for identification and explanation without intent to infringe.

British Library Cataloguing-in-Publication Data
A catalogue record for this book is available from the British Library

Library of Congress Cataloging-in-Publication Data
Names: Ferguson, Michael P., author. | Worthington, Ian, author.
Title: The military legacy of Alexander the Great : lessons for the information age / Michael P. Ferguson and Ian Worthington ; conclusion by Lt. Gen. H. R. McMaster, U.S. Army (retired).
Description: Abingdon, Oxon ; New York, NY : Routledge, 2024. | Includes bibliographical references and index.
Identifiers: LCCN 2023024833 (print) | LCCN 2023024834 (ebook) | ISBN 9780367482435 (hardback) | ISBN 9780367512323 (paperback) | ISBN 9781003052951 (ebook)
Subjects: LCSH: Alexander, the Great, 356 B.C.-323 B.C.—Military leadership. | Alexander, the Great, 356 B.C.-323 B.C.—Influence. | Greece—History—Macedonian Expansion, 359–323 B.C.
Classification: LCC DF234.2 .F388 2024 (print) | LCC DF234.2 (ebook) | DDC 938/.07092—dc23/eng/20230526
LC record available at https://lccn.loc.gov/2023024833
LC ebook record available at https://lccn.loc.gov/2023024834

ISBN: 978-0-367-48243-5 (hbk)
ISBN: 978-0-367-51232-3 (pbk)
ISBN: 978-1-003-05295-1 (ebk)

DOI: 10.4324/9781003052951

Typeset in Times New Roman
by Apex CoVantage, LLC

The Military Legacy of Alexander the Great
Lessons for the Information Age

Michael P. Ferguson and Ian Worthington

Conclusion by
Lt. Gen. H. R. McMaster, U.S. Army (retired)

LONDON AND NEW YORK

The Military Legacy of Alexander the Great

Placing Alexander the Great's leadership, command skills, and grand strategy within the context of twenty-first century military challenges, and thus showing continuities in leadership and warfare since his time, this volume demonstrates how and why Alexander is relevant to the modern world by emphasizing the need for human leadership in our digital era.

Not only does this volume explore Alexander's rich military history, but also it provides a robust exploration of the twenty-first century security environment. Theorists and policy-makers will gain insight into how Alexander's story informs our thinking about peace, war, and strategy, while practitioners and educators will encounter ways to improve their approaches to leader development and building curricula. Ferguson and Worthington set forth these lessons in a thematic framework that organises Alexander's reign into distinct parts, together with chapters discussing the lessons and warnings he brings to the modern world. Twenty-fifth National Security Advisor to the President of the United States, Lt. Gen. H. R. McMaster, provides a thoughtful conclusion to this fascinating volume. Alexander's timeless campaigns remain as germane to this age as any other and demonstrate the critical importance of dynamic leadership and historical studies in an era increasingly dominated by the culture of technology.

The Military Legacy of Alexander the Great is expertly written for students and scholars in a variety of disciplines, including Classics, Ancient History, Modern History, Peace Studies, and Military Studies. It is also of great interest to senior defence leaders, military academies, leadership- and management-focused academic programmes, intelligence organizations, and senior service colleges. The volume is also suitable for the general reader interested in warfare, military history, and history more broadly.

Michael P. Ferguson (M.S.) is a U.S. Army Officer and Ph.D. student at the University of North Carolina at Chapel Hill. His decades of military experience include combat tours to Iraq and Afghanistan and postings throughout Europe and Africa. He has authored dozens of journal articles and is an opinion contributor at *The Hill*.

Ian Worthington (FSA, FRHistS) is Professor of Ancient History at Macquarie University, Australia. He has written numerous books, including *The Last Kings of Macedonia and the Triumph of Rome*; *Athens after Empire: A History from Alexander the Great to the Emperor Hadrian*; and *By the Spear: Philip II, Alexander the Great, and the Rise and Fall of the Macedonian Empire*.

Contents

Preface	*ix*
Acronyms	*xii*
List of Illustrations	*xiii*
Portrait of Alexander the Great	*xiv*
Map of Alexander's Empire	*xv*

Introduction: Why Alexander the Great? Then and Now — 1

PART I
The Environment — 17

1 Alexander's Macedonian Background and Influences — 19
2 A Brave New World? — 34

PART II
Military Organization and Structure — 55

3 The Macedonian Army and Greek Warfare — 57
4 Organizing, Innovating, and Prioritizing Modernization — 72

PART III
Choosing Battles – And Winning Wars? — 101

5 Alexander's First Campaigns — 103
6 Alexander in Persia 1: King of Asia — 115

| 7 | Alexander in Persia 2: Mission Accomplished? | 136 |
| 8 | The Art of Control and the Enduring Fog of War | 157 |

PART IV
Eastern Exposure — 179

9	Alexander in Central Asia	181
10	Alexander in India and His Final Years	197
11	West Meets East: Command *and* Control?	218
12	The Trials and Tolls of Expeditionary Warfare	231

PART V
The Human Domain — 261

| 13 | Alexander's Generalship | 263 |
| 14 | Alexander's Grand Strategy: Model or Model Failure? | 276 |

Conclusion — 308
LT. GENERAL H. R. McMASTER

Bibliography — *310*
Index — *345*

Preface

Alexander the Great was one of antiquity's greatest military strategists and conquerors and is still revered today in military and professional business circles for his accomplishments. In a campaign of less than a decade, he marched thousands of miles to topple the vast Persian Empire and for a time extend the Macedonian Empire as far as India. He was a pivotal and polarizing figure in and for his own historical period and remained so throughout the ages. Despite technological advances, especially in the field of AI, Alexander remains remarkably relevant to modern leaders, students, theorists, planners, and practitioners of the profession of arms far more than initial takes might tell.

We set the successes and failures of Alexander's leadership, command skills, and grand strategy amidst the backdrop of twenty-first century challenges, specifically, the human aspect versus the mechanical. Disruptive emerging technologies are more likely to make effective combat leadership more challenging rather than relieving the burden of ambiguity and decision-making from tomorrow's leaders. Studying Alexander's persona amidst his successes and tragic failures is therefore more important than ever as it stresses the need to refocus on the human talents that drive sound generalship, statesmanship, and grand strategy in our present digital era.

The authors have different backgrounds, training, and certainly different professions and therefore views of Alexander's personality. Ferguson is a decorated U.S. Army officer and combat veteran with expertise in modern warfare and defense analysis, and Worthington is an academic specializing in Greek history, especially Alexander the Great and his era, who writes about battles and strategy from the safety of his armchair. Both have different areas of knowledge and expertise, not to mention writing styles, which will be obvious to readers. Joining forces as we did for this book may well be unconventional, yet it exemplifies one of the most crucial lessons Alexander offers the modern world: the need for broader collaboration between defense and academia. As one of the referees of an earlier draft of our book said, our combined effort and approach turned out to be a unique concept that worked. Modesty prevents us from agreeing.

We have a number of people to thank for their help and support throughout the writing of this book, beginning with Amy Davis-Poynter, Marcia Adams, and all the staff at Routledge, who were always generous with their time and advice and patience.

We are indebted to Lt. Gen. H. R. McMaster, U.S. Army (retired) and former U.S. National Security Adviser, for writing the conclusion to the book.

We are very grateful to Ben Hodges, Frank Hoffman, David Lonsdale, and Joseph Roisman for generously giving their time to read a draft of the book: their sharp comments benefited our work greatly. Likewise, we thank the referees of the book for many valuable suggestions. Any remaining errors are of course our own.

In addition, Michael P. Ferguson would like to thank his wife Christine for her tireless support and patience, and to his young children, Emma and Luke, for their boundless curiosity throughout the process. This project would not have been possible without the wisdom of his coauthor, from whom Michael surely learned more than he had to offer. The idea for this book emerged after Michael published a 2018 article in *Joint Force Quarterly* comparing the premonitions of Demosthenes and Winston Churchill. A simple e-mail thanking Ian for his research led to a multi-year project that evolved into this book.

Over the last two decades, many educators and military leaders have shaped Michael's philosophy on leadership and the nature of war. Among them are Lt. Gen. H. R. McMaster, Lt. Gen. Ronald Clark, Maj. Gen. Carl Alex, Col. David Maxwell, Maj. Phil Gioia, Dr. Williamson Murray, and Dr. Antulio Echevarria II. Ferguson would be remiss if he failed to mention the impact of those who encouraged his writing over the years, including the late Maj. Gen. Gary Johnston, Secretary of Defense Gen. James Mattis, Col. James Greer, Col. Candice Frost, and Congressional aides who found the time to send a note. Such relatively small gestures personify the type of leadership we describe in this book as aspirational. Finally, Dr. Frank Hoffman of the National Defense University has been an exceptionally generous mentor who, despite his competing demands, was never too busy to live up to his service's creed by remaining *semper fidelis*.

Ian Worthington is hugely indebted to Michael P. Ferguson, who started off as a collaborator and became a friend. Worthington learned so much from him; his encyclopedic knowledge and incisive comments saved Worthington from numerous errors that he hopes he never divulges, and his enthusiasm was infectious. That Worthington and others *can* write freely from the safety of an armchair is also due to him and all who served in the armed forces for our protection, for which no words can adequately express gratitude.

Worthington is also obliged to Macquarie University for granting him OSP (research) leave in second semester 2020, allowing him to make substantial progress on this book.

Finally, he thanks again his family, Tracy, Oliver, and Rosie, for putting up with him while writing another book he knows they won't read.

Michael P. Ferguson
Fort Bragg, NC

Ian Worthington
Macquarie University, Sydney
March 2023

Acronyms

ACE	Air Combat Evolution
AI	Artificial Intelligence
ATLAS	Advanced Targeting & Lethality Automated System
BCAP	Battalion Commander Assessment Program
C2	Command and Control
CCP	Chinese Communist Party
CENTCOM	U.S. Central Command
DARPA	Defense Advanced Research Projects Agency
DIE	Diplomacy, Information, Economic
DIME	Diplomacy, Information, Military, and Economic
GLONASS	Globalnaya Navigazionnaya Sputnikovaya Sistema
IO	Information Operations
JAIC	Joint Artificial Intelligence Center
LAWS	Lethal Autonomous Weapons Systems
LSCO	Large-scale Combat Operations
MARS	Machine-Assisted Analytic Rapid-Repository System
ML	Machine Learning
OEF	Operation Enduring Freedom
OIF	Operation Iraqi Freedom
OODA	Observe, Orient, Decide, Act
PGM	Precision Guided Munitions
PME	Professional Military Education
PRC	People's Republic of China
RMA	Revolutions in Military Affairs
SOF	Special Operations Forces
TAILOR	Teaching AI to Leverage Overlooked Residuals
UAV/S	Unmanned Aerial Vehicle/System

List of Illustrations

Maps

0.1 Map of Alexander's Empire. Credit: Historicair via Wikimedia Commons.   xv

Figures

0.1 Portrait of a sculpture of Alexander the Great. Credit: Ann Ronan Picture Library/Heritage-Images/Alamy Stock Photo.   xiv
3.1 Macedonian Phalanx Formation carrying sarissas. Credit: Erin Babnik/Alamy Stock Photo.   62
4.1 Airmen conduct maintenance checks on a U.S. drone. U.S. Air Force Photo/Airman 1st Class Kristan Campbell.   91
6.1 Battle of the Granicus River. Credit: Andrei Nacu via Wikimedia Commons.   118
6.2 Battle of Issus. Credit: Frank Martini, Department of History, United States Military Academy.   128
7.1 Battle of Gaugamela. Credit: Department of History, United States Military Academy.   144
8.1 White House officials watching the killing of Osama bin Laden. Credit: Pete Souza.   158
8.2 Map of Afghanistan. Credit: Perry-Castañeda Library Map Collection, 2017.   162
8.3 Map of Iraq. Credit: ADuran via Wikimedia Commons.   165
10.1 Battle of the Hydaspes River. Credit: Frank Martini, Department of History, United States Military Academy.   203
12.1 Image of Ramadi's urban landscape. Credit: Michael P. Ferguson.   245
12.2 Image of Afghan mountains near Kabul. Credit: DoD Staff Sgt. Michael L. Casteel, U.S. Army.   249

Portrait of Alexander the Great

Figure 0.1 Portrait of a sculpture of Alexander the Great. Credit: Ann Ronan Picture Library/Heritage-Images/Alamy Stock Photo.

Map of Alexander's Empire

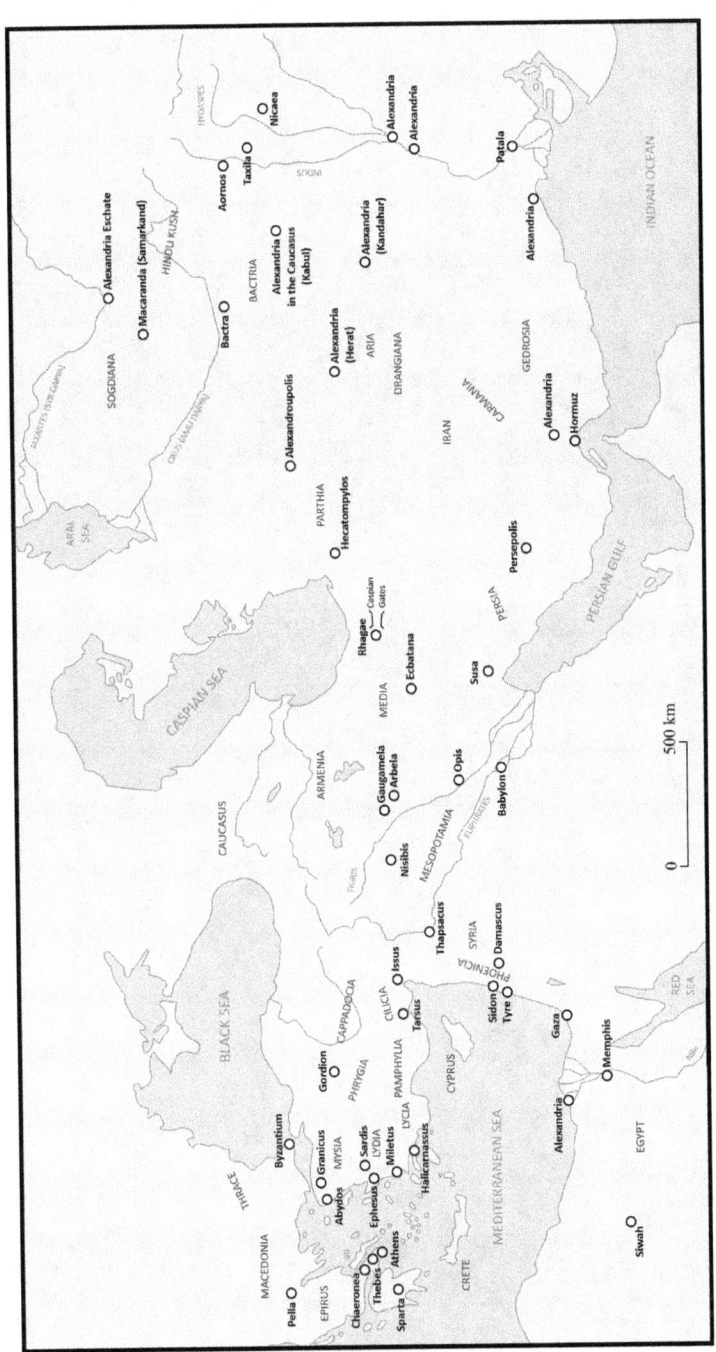

Map 0.1 Map of Alexander's Empire. Credit: Historicair via Wikimedia Commons.

Introduction

Why Alexander the Great? Then and Now

> All dates for Alexander and the ancient world are BC.
> The publisher has allowed British English and American English spellings, for which the authors are grateful.

Alexander the Great was one of the ancient world's most skilled military strategists and conquerors; arguably, he was *the* greatest and a true warrior king. As king of Macedonia from 336 to his death in Babylon in 323, his very name evokes images of hard-fought battles and sieges against superior enemy forces. He traversed thousands of miles, consistently ensuring he had adequate modes of transportation, manpower, and resources, to establish an empire from Greece in the west to what the Greeks called India (present-day Pakistan) in the east – remarkably within a decade from first setting foot on Asian soil in 334.

Alexander is relevant to today's leaders and students of the profession of arms far more than typically imagined. This book is not meant to be a biography or a strictly military treatment of Alexander as there are plenty of those already.[1] Instead, it is an account of his campaigns as well as a discussion of his background, influences, and personality to understand him in his own time and to see why and how the lessons from his reign, especially his leadership and art of war, inform us today, for better or worse.

Modern military campaigns are anchored as much in the planning as in the combat. They demand, among other things, that logistics have been worked out in advance; lines of communication established; topography researched; satellite reconnaissance scrutinized; contacts with locals established; maps prepared; troop numbers decided considering enemy forces and locations; and, ideally, clear exit plans made.[2] Though Alexander had some intelligence on Persia from Persians visiting his father's court and from his readings, he had almost none of the aforementioned information and knowledge when he sailed for Asia in spring 334. He may have had an insight into Persian numbers from the advance force that Philip had sent to Asia Minor in 336, but that was two years ago: in 334, he could not have known precisely how many men the Persians could field or even where he would fight them.

Nor was Alexander targeting a small number of capitals or bases in one country as the Persian Empire stretched from Turkey to Pakistan and included Egypt and Syria. By today's roads, the distance from the most westerly capital, Sardis (Sart in Turkey), to the most easterly, Persepolis (northeast of Shiraz in Iran), is roughly 2,000 miles and from Persepolis to the most northernly palace at Ecbatana (probably Hamadan, Iran) is 556 miles. In addition, in Central Asia to the Hyphasis (Beas) River, Alexander marched a further 1,865 miles. Yet for all his battles and distances navigated, even in his time, he was able to combine the three fundamentals of modern combat operations: attacking, moving, and communicating with his staff throughout his empire.

When we take into account that Alexander was not on an exploratory mission but an invasion (though exploration became a part of it), that everywhere he went was in enemy territory, that he had to battle large armies and deal with guerilla warfare in Bactria and war elephants in India, that he kept his men motivated, and that he had none of the tools of warfare available today, the empire he created was an astonishing achievement. His invasion from the outset was also a testament to how a foreign army can survive in distant, hostile, and unknown lands, proving that the need for sound planning and inspiring leadership was as important to Alexander as they are crucial to modern practitioners of national security and defence.

It was not just his battles that proved his strategic genius and quick thinking, but also his sieges, which can inform the study of megacity warfare and conflict in dense urban environments even today.[3] His sieges were against enemy cities in different terrains and with varying defence systems, such as thick walls, high ramparts, catapults, archers, and even cauldrons of boiling oil and sand emptied onto besiegers, as well as the defenders' determination to fight to the death if need be. These techniques presented myriad challenges that offer lessons for modern theorists, planners, and practitioners, not least how to attack and isolate an enemy force within a city, cut off supply lines, cope with firepower, disable communications, and force surrender. Although different in scale, Alexander still had to ensure that the enemy city was isolated and denied supplies and reinforcements, and he did so effectively by maintaining a persistent physical presence to oversee operations.

Despite his leadership, when Alexander reached the River Hyphasis (Beas) in 326, the second to last river of the Punjab, his men mutinied, refusing to cross the river into the territory of the warlike Nanda dynasty. They held out for three days before Alexander was forced to turn back. A mere two years later, in 324, Alexander faced another mutiny, this time at Opis, a city on the River Tigris not far from modern Baghdad. For another three days, his men defied him until he ended the mutiny and could focus on his next campaign to Arabia. These mutinies we will consider further in Chapter 10.

At the same time, there was never any attempt to replace Alexander as general or king, and ultimately the men's loyalty to him carried the day. He had identified with them throughout the Asian campaign, suffering as they had suffered, fighting as they had fought, drinking as they had drunk. He was king, yet he also made himself one of them. That was why they followed him into battle against armies that outnumbered their own and into alien regions inhabited by dissimilar cultures.

It might seem odd to begin a book on military leadership by touting Alexander's strengths and relevance but then describing not one but two mutinies faced by the commander of interest. But when that commander was Alexander the Great, who had a propensity for turning any adversity he faced into success, there is much to uncover when evaluating his authority and its lessons for modern leaders. Alexander's personal style of leadership, the loyalty he enjoyed (as even the mutinies show, for his army never overturned his power), his flaws, and above all, how he approached the challenges of dealing with culturally dissimilar people in different parts of the world can be studied with profit even in our technocratic age.

Alexander Today: Principles and Pitfalls

Major General J.F.C. Fuller's classic book on Alexander's generalship remains the consummate study of his command, but it was published more than sixty years ago. Since then, the world experienced dramatic changes that perhaps even Fuller could not have imagined. He did, however, recognize that one of the greatest lessons passed from Philip II of Macedonia to his son Alexander was that military force is not the most cutting weapon in a strategist's arsenal.[4] Alexander surely benefitted from this advice, and such wisdom is as germane today as it was then.

In this book, we not only revisit aspects of the history of Alexander, but also propose that many buzzwords consuming national security communities have been little more than fleeting distractions from the most consequential human aspects of war and warfare. As the reader will see, the timeless crafts of strategy and leadership also happen to be the challenges with which modern western armies most frequently struggle. Many of the technological advances since Alexander's time have made warfare more complicated, not less so. We therefore focused on the broader and more human art of leadership in these pages, as opposed to the purely military profession of generalship emphasized by Fuller. In the parlance of military historians, we aim to explore the cultural and social history of Alexander as much as the operational.[5]

Without question, much has been written on Alexander and his campaigns, and the fascination surrounding his tenure as king does not appear to be waning.[6] None of the available literature, however, views Alexander's story through a modern lens by highlighting the principles that defined his reign, for better or worse, and exploring their legacy in contemporary operations. The similarities reveal striking if not troubling continuities in the human nature of war and organizational leadership.[7] Alexander's influence on current military and political thought is hard to overstate despite the provocative interpretations of his character, as Chapters 11 and 13 discuss. In this way, he has become somewhat of a Protean historical figure as he is cast in the image of each observer's choosing. We do not aim to reinvent Alexander, only to reintroduce him to a world consumed by the future and somewhat ambivalent about the past.[8] With this in mind, we have identified three principles and three pitfalls that contributed most directly to his successes and failures, respectively. The significance of each, we argue, has not changed over time.

Regarding principles, the professionalization of his army, a relentless speed of action on campaign, and an inspirational physical presence characterized Alexander's success. His core pitfalls consisted of a deepening sense of strategic ambiguity, hubris that encouraged operational overreach not linked to a clear grand strategy, and a centralization of power that turned Alexander himself into Macedonia's center of gravity (COG) to use a Clausewitzian term.[9] Despite advances in public administration, weaponry (attacking), transportation (moving), and communications (communicating) since Alexander's time, these principles and pitfalls remain remarkably unaltered. A stubborn reliance on digital technologies to solve what are ultimately human problems has the potential to overshadow more urgent challenges associated with the conditions that spark and ultimately prolong war, which we address in these pages.

Ultimately, Alexander was a flawed man and leader, as discussed in Chapters 11 and 13, whose meteoric rise changed the course of human events. Barry Strauss put this aptly when he observed: 'Rarely has there been a leader whose virtues match his vices so closely'.[10] Perhaps this is what makes Alexander great. As flawed individuals ourselves, we may see familiar traits in him, thereby drawing inspiration that we, too, are capable of uncommon feats and exceptional aspirations despite our common nature. Even in failure, there is much to learn, not only from *how* Alexander went about trying to arrange something so monumental, but also from understanding *why* such an imperfect man is remembered even 2,400 years later as truly great.

On the Value of History

Beyond the need to consider Alexander's value in the twenty-first century, the premise of this book rests on two assumptions. The first is that the study of military history and the ancient world will remain vital to modern practitioners and theorists of national security, diplomacy, and leadership no matter how technologically advanced civilizations become. The second hypothesis, which we will address below, is that inspirational, transformative leadership is becoming scarcer when it is most needed, and poor leadership dictates long-term organizational culture.[11]

Regarding the first assumption, Aristotle's proverb on beginnings seems particularly appropriate in this context, considering the Greek philosopher had a profound influence on Alexander's thinking: 'In this, as in other fields, we shall be able to study our subject best if we begin at the beginning and consider things in the process of their growth'.[12] Alexander provides much of the historical basis from which springs modern knowledge of strategy and statecraft, teaching us not how to wage war and conduct diplomacy, but rather how to think about such important ideas to deter war. Much as the British strategic theorist Colin S. Gray saw the writings of Prussian officer Carl von Clausewitz as permanently relevant, Alexander's place in strategic and operational thought is cemented.[13] He is thus the indispensable leader.

This brings us to the question of the practical utility of studying history in an era when machines are rapidly surpassing their organic progenitors in both institutional knowledge and predictive thinking. Skeptics of applied history might suggest that the conditions under which Alexander waged his campaign were so vastly dissimilar to modern warfare that they are of little value to contemporary leaders. We disagree. The human condition remains stubbornly unchanged despite great leaps in technological prowess since the Macedonians charged their Persian enemy across the River Granicus in 334 (see Chapter 6). History's most instructive tales are not of things but rather of people. The decisions made by leaders today are as driven by human emotion and rationale as they were in ancient Greece. In his examination of wartime leadership, Andrew Roberts made this clear: 'If you want to know what will move the hearts and command multitudes today and in the future, there is only one thing to do: Study the past'.[14] Social scientists, historians, and strategists continue to make persuasive arguments cautioning against the tendency to marginalize history as a tool for leading in the information age.[15]

In 1997, halfway between the United States' two very different wars against Iraq, military historian Williamson Murray described what he considered a disturbing trend in the U.S. Department of Defense. He believed a declining interest in strategic studies in professional military education and a newfound obsession with data, systems, and technological Revolutions in Military Affairs (RMA) were obscuring the very human and quite messy political nature of war. He argued instead for the importance of historical continuity:[16]

> At its heart is the presumption that the future revolution in military affairs will be largely technological in nature. History suggests, however, that the three most important elements in virtually all past revolutions in military affairs were not technological in nature, but rather conceptual, doctrinal, and intellectual. Those military institutions in the 1920s and 1930s ... that attempted to leap into the future without reference to what had happened in the past ended up making mistakes that killed thousands of young men to no purpose. The success of new gadgets notwithstanding, successful innovation in the past worked when it was tied into a realistic appreciation of what was humanly possible.

Murray went on to suggest that these trends could lead to failures even more disastrous than the Vietnam War in the twenty-first century if America's leaders did not learn from past mistakes. Four years after he wrote these words, in response to the 2001 terrorist attacks on New York City and the Pentagon, a coalition of western military and intelligence teams entered Afghanistan to eradicate al-Qaeda, find Osama bin Laden, and expel the Taliban who harbored him. Army General Tommy Franks, then commander of U.S. Central Command, contributed to the invasion plans and surmised that the 2001 operation to remove the Taliban from Afghanistan represented a 'revolution in warfare' that would be prosecuted with weapons considered science fiction ten years prior.[17]

Observers marveled at the orchestra of synchronized destruction brought forth by a skilled combination of small, specialized teams, precision munitions, and close air support against a numerically and technologically inferior enemy in Afghanistan. Yet the 2009 U.S. Senate Foreign Relations Committee report on the failure to capture or kill bin Laden placed blame on flawed assumptions regarding the utility of such weapons in the labyrinthine mountain ranges of Afghanistan.[18] More than two decades after this incursion, in the shadow of myriad policy changes and thousands of lives lost, the western coalition withdrew all forces from Afghanistan, and the Taliban once again took control of the country.

Admittedly, political calculations played as much if not more of a role in the outcomes of recent conflicts than military decisions, so we cannot place the blame squarely on military officers.[19] Murray, however, was prophetic about the propensity for technological superiority to instill hubris and a subsequent lack of respect for historical trends in those who wield it. Similarly, British strategist B. H. Liddell Hart wrote in the mid-twentieth century that the lack of attention paid by universities to military history churned out poor products in the form of officers and elected officials ill-prepared to think deeply and broadly about strategic affairs.[20] There are modern exceptions to this rule, as we will explore in later chapters, but RMA thinking and an obsession with emerging technologies are as pervasive in 2023 as they were in 1992.[21]

Nations such as the United States have placed RMA thought into frames of reference focused on three strategic offsets, technological revolutions, and generational technologies (see Chapter 4). While such concepts promote understanding, they exaggerate the impact of technology in each generation because in history books and elsewhere, epochs come to be defined by the tools mankind used to reconcile its differences (Bronze Age, Industrial Age, Digital Age, etc.). Even for some of the sharpest minds in the field of military thought, the urge to view impressive new platforms or capabilities as a means of changing war's nature is tempting.[22] Technology becomes equated with power and power with strategic potential, thereby sidelining old lessons, and particularly ancient ones, that emphasize the role of human agency and culture in conflict.

Military historian Martin Van Creveld saw this trend of technophilia gaining steam in the last decade of the twentieth century. His conclusions lend to a deeper understanding of a human–machine paradox in which the integration of increasingly complex and powerful machines into military operations demands more, not less, intellectual rigor from their human operators. With the technological power now at a soldier's fingertips, combat leadership has become a much more consequential enterprise. Creveld explains the counterproductive pitfalls of this trade off:[23]

> The key is that efficiency, far from being simply conducive to effectiveness, can act as its opposite. Hence – and this is a point which cannot be overemphasized – the successful use of technology in war very often means that there is a price to be paid in terms of deliberately *diminishing* efficiency.

Chapters 2 and 8 address this topic in detail, demonstrating how various technological means, while useful in theory, have at times stifled human creativity, impeded momentum, and discouraged battlefield initiative. Comparing Alexander's campaigns to current challenges underscores the need for modern militaries to strike a balance between remaining technologically competitive and promoting a culture that holds the past in high regard.

U.S. Army Gen. George C. Marshall believed that one must read Thucydides to understand current events 'with full wisdom and with deep convictions', while U.S. Marine Corps general and former Secretary of Defense Jim Mattis saw nothing in Iraq or Afghanistan that he believes would have surprised Alexander.[24] In the age of impressive technologies such as artificial intelligence (AI), lethal autonomous weapon systems (LAWS), and hypersonic missiles, it is tempting to discount the past as separate from the present and therefore of little consequence to the future. While this perspective is certainly not fresh, as we will see in Chapter 2, new theories have emboldened technocratic thinking, which begs the need to revisit Alexander's story and seek a broader understanding of the factors that continue to govern war's conduct even as the world views conflict through an increasingly impersonal lens.

On the Nature of Leadership

The second underlying premise of this book emerges from an interpretation of the word 'leadership' and its role in international affairs. At first glance, the term appears simple – one knows it when one sees it. But the Oxford dictionary dedicates more than an entire column to the concept of what it means to lead and to be led, thus demonstrating the need to distinguish between leading and leadership.[25]

To lead is to occupy a physical space or prominent status, such as the front of a formation or a managerial role that involves directing actions, but we must not mistake leadership for a job title. One might assume the physical lead or be appointed to a prominent position without possessing any leadership qualities. John Gardner put this colorfully in 1990 by pointing out that many top officials in his country could not lead 'seven-year-olds to the ice cream counter'.[26] For many centuries this was the norm, as imperial armies developed a penchant for nepotism in their officer ranks. But when referencing leadership, we begin to see words like 'guidance', 'control', 'management', and 'supervision' appear in the dictionary, which denotes that a leader is a position, but leadership is a process. Gardner drew similar conclusions on the nature of leadership by defining it as a 'process of persuasion or example' that induces others to pursue shared objectives.²⁷ The bridge that connects leading to leadership therefore represents a transformation from the individual to the collective in both thought and deed, when the leader understands that the actions of the many, far away from his watchful eye, will determine success or failure as much as his own designs. To influence others in such a way requires a culture that transcends the leader's physical presence, and this takes something truly unique to cultivate.

In his historical analysis of how militaries adapt and learn, Frank Hoffman assessed that institutional learning driven by organizational culture is directly linked to a military's ability to innovate and win while at war.²⁸ Yet both the process of learning and an organization's culture are extensions of the priorities established by leaders. This begs the question: are we getting it right today? Gardner observed that the Founding Fathers of the United States were students of the classics who read Plutarch and Thucydides and were 'incomparably more interested than American leaders today' in matters of leadership.²⁹ Nearly thirty years after Gardner made this sobering observation, former CIA Director and U.S. Secretary of Defense Robert Gates admitted that, still, his country is desperate for leaders.³⁰ He went further by attributing failures in American bureaucracies almost entirely to short-term, unimaginative thinking among their leaders.³¹

Great leadership is not common, nor is it a minor contribution to a campaign's success as some have concluded; it is *the* factor upon which all others are hinged, and rank or position is immaterial to its benefits.³² With proper guidance, training, and supervision, the most junior soldier can exhibit leadership to turn the tides of battle, but there must first exist a culture that ushers into being such initiative.³³ Despite its many definitions and various forms, the purpose of leadership in war as much as in peace is to foster a *culture* that promotes collective success through individual excellence – this has not changed with time. There is no doubt that Alexander possessed exceptional traits that, like those great leaders before and since, were unmistakable to those in his presence. Yet despite the amount of literature dedicated to examining Alexander's exploits, most of it does not study seriously his role as a leader of other human beings. They are operational vice cultural histories.

The United States, United Kingdom, Australia, and France have each emphasized the importance of people and culture in their future-oriented strategies, which gives weight to the maxim attributed to Peter Drucker that 'culture eats strategy for breakfast'.³⁴ In 2019, however, U.S. Army Human Resources Command released a troubling report in which eighty-four percent of the elite Green Berets polled did not believe their regiment retained the highest quality leaders. By 2020, the U.S. First Special Forces

Command acknowledged it was suffering from an identity crisis.[35] Potentially 'unsustainable' military retention shortages in the United Kingdom prove that these problems are not isolated to specific units or countries, and are in some ways tied to the antiquated manner in which the Ministry of Defence selects and promotes its leaders.[36] Like those of many organizations, the cause of and therefore solution to these challenges are rooted in leadership and the interpersonal relationships that comprise an organization's culture.

Drucker's adage reflects a perception shared among war's participants that can remain elusive to its outside observers – increasingly so in an age of awe-inspiring gadgets. Advanced technologies will, in time, change the way governments conduct business. But culture defines an organization's ability to employ those tools coherently and achieve desirable strategic effects, particularly in the chaos of war. Numerous scholars and senior government officials have reached this conclusion, but abstract concepts such as culture and leadership fail to capture the imagination – or the purse strings of governments for that matter – as completely as shiny things.[37] Part of this distraction from studying leadership and organizational culture stems from the reality that, in the current age, the 'things' are shinier than ever.[38]

Concepts ranging from biotechnology to machine learning and directed energy weapons are framed as the key to the future of strategic deterrence and conflict resolution. Billions of dollars have been spent on defense contracts, countless articles and books on the revolutionary potential of military technology have been written, and national strategies are filled with mandates to gain and maintain a technological edge. One might say that the culture of technology is unavoidable in the twenty-first century, even as governments scramble to find and retain leaders capable of wrangling its complexity. Thomas Ricks, Anthony King, and Jim Storr have gone so far as arguing that the western world, and specifically its military vein, suffers from a leadership crisis.[39] The practice of leading is founded in personal interactions and relationships, which means a culture of technology increases the risk of losing sight of what inspires the people who bring teams together and make them thrive. Alexander's failures and victories placed in historical context – timeless as they are – can help bring us back to reality.

Leadership, of course, means different things to different people under different circumstances. Leading a Fortune 500 company requires a certain type of leadership that may not be as effective in political office or a military command position. Because of its largely esoteric qualities, many have attempted to capture the essence of leadership and package it for future generations, from ancient writers like Plutarch in his *Precepts of Statecraft* (who bade those seeking political office to get their own house in order before they sought to rearrange citizens' affairs) to historians and psychologists such as Ralph Stogdill and Thomas Carlyle.[40] While the contributions of the latter scholars are valuable, this work addresses leadership as a practice, specifically the kind that guides large organizations comprised of statespersons and warriors. We thus lean heavily on those who have put their leadership theories to practice at war where they are measured most arduously.

Napoleon interpreted wartime leadership as more of an inborn vision that could never be diluted into a 'real science', while more modern leaders, such as Gen. Stanley McChrystal, have argued that leadership is primarily a game of luck related to whom and what the leader is entrusted to lead.[41] Samuel Huntington and Williamson Murray profess that the modern military profession emerged in the post-Napoleonic era out of the apparent need to cultivate the natural genius of Napoleon through formal study.[42] These outlooks speak to the nature-versus-nurture dialectic surrounding leadership studies. Certainly Alexander, who benefitted from a brilliant mind and a well-trained army inherited from his father, would identify with both.

Although interpretations of leadership and its impact remain diverse, there is no debate over the deleterious effects of poor leaders. If this is true, then there must be common traits in history's most influential leaders worth examining, such as the ability to think creatively or even controversially, a willingness to challenge the status quo, and an insatiable hunger for knowledge. They nearly all had a knack for inspiring a productive organizational culture through leadership by example and a physical presence that encouraged trust. This has been and will continue to be a mounting challenge in an age when digital relationships have largely supplanted personal ones.[43]

A Legacy in Context

When examining accomplishments as renowned as Alexander's, it is easy to forget that he was but one man. Despite his military genius, his success was based equally on the individual actions of countless hoplites, subordinate commanders, and cavalrymen under his command, all making decisions based on a shared understanding of Alexander's goals and a faith in his ability to make sound decisions. These elements comprised a culture of excellence nurtured by Alexander so powerful that when pushed to their human limits against intractable foes, his men mutinied in frustration yet never imagined they could be led by a different king. Alexander's story reinforces Xenophon's depiction of leadership as a matter of trust and persuasion, which is equally relevant to leaders today.[44] In an age of remarkable weapons and rising political instability, it is incumbent upon twenty-first century leaders to understand the power of leadership and, as Andrew Roberts wrote, direct that power towards doing good.[45]

Murray has said that 'useful history is also difficult history, and learning from it takes serious work'.[46] This book contributes to that work and describes how Alexander built and led a culturally diverse army that nearly conquered the world in the face of a seemingly insurmountable opponent. We capture these lessons in a thematic presentation that places Alexander's story within the context of modern challenges that appear new but bear striking resemblance to those of the past. Part I addresses environmental and conceptual factors of Alexander's world and our own, before moving onto Part II and looking at technological and organizational considerations, such as innovation and training. Part III examines tactical and operational warfighting by juxtaposing principles of Alexander's Persian campaign to recent conflicts in Iraq and Afghanistan. As the Macedonian army moves further east into India, Part IV explores the social and cultural challenges of expeditionary warfare, before concluding with an analysis of the human domains of generalship and grand strategy in Part V. To present Alexander's period as a historical bookend to the present, modern chapters deal primarily with noteworthy figures, events, and assumptions surrounding major military operations since the mid-twentieth century in the regions through which Alexander marched his army. At its core, this book is a treatise on the enduring nature of war and the way leaders have navigated and might continue to navigate its contours.

Alexander's story is not prescriptive for twenty-first century challenges. If it were, the strategic conundrums of our time would not be so perplexing. Intellectual canyons exist between recognizing historical relevance and developing sound strategy – more so about making sound tactical decisions in battle.[47] But, we hope readers will see that the first step in achieving a clearer vision of the future is recognizing not only the type of logic that has worked but also the root causes of flawed logic. Making sense of an increasingly interconnected world demands an ever deeper and broader understanding of the events that brought us to this point and the social mechanisms that continue to shape the present. Thus, we argue that the impact of material developments on war will continue to be exaggerated in the coming years. Conversely, the study of personalities, intangible qualities, and war's nature will increase. As Eisenhower wrote in 1942, the real job of a commander – and by extension any leader charged with building teams – is finding the right people.[48]

We may be entering a brave new world in many ways, but it will still be a world governed by old minds and their similarly dated imperfections. Humankind may attempt to fix its future mistakes in new, interesting, or even more efficient ways, but it will still be making those mistakes the old-fashioned way. Here we turn to Alexander's story and the environment within which he emerged as king in the tumultuous wake of his father's assassination in 336.

Notes

1 See, for example, Lane Fox 1973; Green 1974; Bosworth 1988a; Hammond 1989a, Hammond 1997a; Bosworth 1996a; Cartledge 2003; Grainger 2007; Heckel 2008; Briant 2010; Worthington 2014a; cf. Keegan 1987, pp. 13–91. Focused studies on Alexander's generalship and strategy: Fuller 1960; Lonsdale 2007.
2 A clear exit plan was one of the shortcomings identified in U.S. planning for the 2003 invasion of Iraq: Ricks 2012, pp. 78–81.
3 Operating in megacities, which are defined as urban areas with a population of one million or more, is a key concern for the world's militaries. Many features of megacity warfare, such as isolation and denial of supplies to the besieged inhabitants, echo those encountered during sieges of antiquity, only on a much larger scale: see National Intelligence Council 2012; Kaune 2016, pp. 1–37; Konaev 2019, pp. 1–58.
4 Fuller 1960, pp. 264–265.
5 For more on cultural military history, see Lynn 2003; Lee 2017, pp. 1116–1142.
6 Green 1974; Kolenda 2001; Briant 2015.
7 This contradicts Clausewitz's theory that the nature of war is 'complex and changeable': Clausewitz 1976, 2.1 (p. 102); other military theorists, such as Col. Ardant du Picq, see war's nature as fundamentally moral. Ardant du Picq 2017, pp. 51–60.
8 For a look at the U.S. military's obsession with futurism, see Nelson and Montgomery 2022.
9 Clausewitz 1976, 8.4 (pp. 720–721).
10 Strauss 2012, p. 237.
11 For additional reading on this topic, see Ricks 2012; King 2019; Mazarr 2019; Storr 2022.
12 Aristotle, *Politics* 1.2.1252a24.
13 Murray and Sinnreich 2006, p. 121; Gray 2014, p. 7, Gray 2015, pp. 20–21.
14 Roberts, A. 2020, p. 221.
15 As a percentage, American undergraduate history majors decreased by 73 percent since the 1970s, dropping from 11 percent to 3 percent by 2021. The formal study of academic military history has become at best niche in top universities even as the western world continues to be shaped by its wars and struggles to overcome both domestic and foreign military challenges: Allison and Ferguson 2016; Greenfield 2021.
16 This article appeared first in *The National Interest*: Murray 1997a; see also Murray's essay in *Joint Force Quarterly* the same year: Murray 1997b, pp. 69–76.

17 Franks 2004, pp. 258, 379.
18 Committee on Foreign Relations in the United States Senate 2009.
19 Bolger 2014; Mattis and West 2019; Mazarr 2019; Stoker 2019; Whitlock 2021.
20 Liddell Hart 2019.
21 Karlin 2022, pp. 191–195.
22 Predictions include AI changing the nature of war and removing uncertainty from combat: Giles 2019; Sayler 2020, pp. 37–38; similar predictions accompanied the introduction of nuclear technology in the mid-twentieth century and stealth technology in the Gulf War of 1990. Most strategic theorists challenge this notion, however: Creveld 1991, p. 264; Luttwak 2001, pp. 178–184; Lonsdale 2004; Gray 2005, pp. 98–128, 165–167; Freedman 2013, p. 3.
23 Creveld 1991, p. 319.
24 Marshall made this comment while speaking at Princeton University in 1947. For Mattis' thoughts on Alexander's relevance today, see Mattis and West 2019, pp. 118, 257.
25 *Oxford New Desk Dictionary and Thesaurus* 2009, pp. 469–470.
26 Gardner 1990, p. 2.
27 Gardner 1990, p. 1.
28 Hoffman 2021, pp. 26–37.
29 Gardner 1990, p. 165.
30 Gates 2017, p. 220.
31 Gates 2017, pp. 9–19.
32 Strauss suggests that leadership is rather insignificant, and Alexander as one man was the same: Strauss 2012. Gen. Stanley McChrystal makes a similar argument in McChrystal 2018; great leaders should not be conflated with divine leaders, a mistake that Alexander made and a trap into which even great theorists of leadership such as Thomas Carlyle fell.
33 For more on cultural history, see Lynn 2003.
34 Burkhard 2020, pp. 1–20; Reynolds 2020, pp. 3–5, 26–27; Beaudette 2021, p. 5; Carleton-Smith 2021, pp. 7–11.
35 Brennan 2020; Schneider 2022.
36 In 2019, some British regiments suffered from near 40 percent personnel shortages. Sir Nick Carter recognized the need to adapt personnel management practices to the twenty-first century, and initiatives such as Project CASTLE aim to rectify these issues: Anon 2019; Freddie 2019.
37 Both comment on the importance of culture and leadership over things: Hanson 2001; Gates 2014, pp. 115–148, 591–592.
38 New war literature is abundant this century, most of which involves speculation surrounding the irrelevance of humans and conventional warfare or at least an increase in the role of machines: Coker 2002; Boot 2006; Singer 2009; Scharre 2018; McFate, S. 2019.
39 Ricks 2012; King 2019; Storr 2022.
40 Plutarch frames humility as one of a leader's most critical traits – in 2020, the U.S. Army made the characteristic an official value.
41 Chandler 1966, p. 144; Duggan 2002; McChrystal 2018, pp. 7–9, 372.
42 Clausewitz's mentor, Scharnhorst, is credited with launching this formal professionalization of military thought in the early nineteenth century: Huntington 1957, p. 14; Murray 2009, p. 138.

43 For more on this, see Spencer 2022.
44 Xenophon 3.18, 21.4. Xenophon highlights other leadership traits germane to Alexander in his *Anabasis*, such as those of Syracusan general Hermocrates who was admired for his ability to mix with his men and ask them to sometimes express their opinions: 1.1.30.
45 Roberts, A. 2020, p. xii.
46 Murray and Sinnreich 2006, p. 83. For a broader discussion on the challenge of history for the professional officer, see pp. 81–87.
47 Neustadt and May 1986, pp. 232–246; MacMillan 2008, pp. 150–164.
48 Eisenhower 1981, p. 84.

Part I
The Environment

This part describes Alexander's background and influences and what made Macedonia a regional military power. We then summarize for the reader what is supposedly 'new' in the twenty-first century security environment by assessing its similarities and differences with Alexander's world. Key to this chapter is framing the argument that the most consequential aspects of war remain largely unchanged. We use America's unipolar moment at the end of the Cold War as a starting point, before exploring faddish defense trends that have come and gone since that time to include the debate over whether RMA would create a transparent battlefield this century.

1 Alexander's Macedonian Background and Influences

Alexander the Great lived in the second half of the fourth century BC. It goes without saying that the world of two millennia ago was different from our own, yet it had the same constant as we do: warfare. For much of their history, the ancient Greeks were at war, which they settled with battles and sieges face-to-face unlike today when a drone can be flown thousands of miles to an enemy camp on either a reconnaissance or bombing mission.

Yet there was technology – Alexander's father Philip II of Macedonia founded an engineering corps, which developed the torsion catapult, and in 189 when Rome besieged the fortress of Ambracia (Arta) in Epirus, the defenders used poison gas in tunnels to block their enemy, filling jars with feathers, burning charcoal at the rims, and using bellows to blow out choking smoke.[1] For that period, the shock of these types of innovations was arguably on a par with the development of unmanned weaponry, artificial intelligence, and chemical munitions in our time.

Today's technology, however, theoretically brings with it a decreasing dependence on the enduring human element of war, which coincidentally is the sphere in which powerful western armies most struggle. This is an area of concern where we can learn from Alexander. As a strategist and a king, he was concerned not only with defeating his foes and protecting his people but also with post-battle diplomacy and administration, especially in his dealings with a multi-cultural subject population. As Major General J.F.C. Fuller rightly pointed out, 'the art of war – certainly in its essentials – was the same in Alexander's day as it is now'.[2] In other words, the nature of war may not have changed between then and now, but the character has, as the following chapter argues. With that in mind, Alexander's reign and especially its lessons present an opportunity for modern makers of policy and strategy, especially in culturally dissimilar parts of the world, to appreciate that the human element is becoming both more complex and essential even as the automation of conflict appears terminal. This is the thesis of the book.

DOI: 10.4324/9781003052951-3

Alexander was a product of his own times.[3] To try to understand his nature, his propensity for fighting, his goals and especially influences – in other words, what made him tick – we need to understand the background from which he came and his influences.

Macedonia and Macedonians

Alexander's spectacular military successes in battles and sieges, often against an enemy numerically superior to his own army, not only established him as one of history's greatest conquerors but also proved his genius on the battlefield and became the stuff of legend. He invaded Asia in 334, and in less than a decade carved out an empire stretching thousands of miles from Greece to present-day Pakistan (what the Greeks called India); when he died in Babylon in June 323, he had laid plans to invade Arabia and might even have targeted the western Mediterranean after that. Perhaps we ought not to be surprised: he was a product of the tough Macedonian society, and he always strove to outdo his predecessors, especially his father Philip II – no mean feat, when we consider Philip's record as we shall see.

Macedonia in antiquity was the area north of Mount Olympus, Greece's tallest mountain.[4] Natural features like mountains and rivers were often geographical barriers because of the lack of proper roads, tunnels through mountains, and the like. In the ancient world, if people had to travel from one place to another they usually walked, and only wealthier people who could afford a horse rode anywhere. Travel was limited; often, traders and envoys on diplomatic missions from one city to another were the largest group of travellers.

The people living north of Mount Olympus are usually referred to as Macedonians and those to its south as Greeks. The latter called the Macedonians 'barbarians', which had nothing to do with culture but was what they called anyone who did not speak Greek, which has led to a belief that the Macedonians were not Greek. The ethnicity of the Macedonians is a contentious issue, but they were surely Greek and Greek speaking but probably had their own dialect (which the Greeks could not understand).[5] Among other things, ancient writers accept that they were Greek: archaeological evidence (such as inscriptions and coins) is all in Greek; Macedonian proper names are Greek; and Macedonian religion is similar to Greek, with Zeus and Dionysus especially revered and Macedonian kings tracing their lineage to Heracles.

For the sake of convenience, when we refer in our book to 'Macedonians', we mean the people living north of Olympus, and when we refer to 'Greeks', we mean those living to its south as well as in Asia Minor.

Because of Olympus, the Greeks and Macedonians developed different political and social customs. Macedonia was a kingdom whose king was responsible for all domestic and foreign policy, had the right to make treaties and declare war, was commander-in-chief of the army (and led it personally into battle), chief priest in the state, and in treason cases his decision was not likely to be challenged.[6] He also identified with his people by being addressed simply by his name, eating the same basic meals, and dressing in similar manner apart from a purple cloak and the distinctive, wide-brimmed felt hat known as the *kausia*.[7] Here, the utilitarian nature of Macedonia's warrior culture, a likely contributing factor to Alexander's penchant for sharing the burden in battle, becomes evident.

It is not known whether Macedonia had a 'constitution', for want of a better word, with the king being one half and an Assembly of male citizens (which formally acclaimed a new king) the other, but he was under no obligation to heed its views or advice if it did exist.[8] For the purposes of this book, we do not need to engage with this controversy but stress that the king could and did act autocratically, even though there were checks on his power.[9] By contrast, Alexander, as we shall see, put himself above the law.

The Greeks lived in autonomous city-states (*poleis*), each with their own constitution, laws, coinage, weights and measures, and social customs; the vast majority were democratic with numerous elected officials and the people sovereign in the state. Yet their *polis* system was riddled with weaknesses, not least frequent outbreaks of violent civil strife (*stasis*) and an inability to unite effectively, even against a common enemy, because of their distrust of each other. Moreover, they recognized their weaknesses, which were even criticized by Aristotle, yet they never did anything about them – which played into the hands of kings like Philip and Alexander.[10]

Socially, the Macedonians (or at least their king) were polygamists. Kings often contracted marriages for political and military reasons; Alexander's father, Philip II, married no fewer than seven times without ever divorcing a wife (only his final marriage was apparently for love) – as one ancient writer says, he 'made war by marriage'.[11] Yet several wives could cause dissension in the palace, where they all lived, and, worse, multiple heirs to the throne from different mothers could cause succession issues on the death of a king.

Another social difference was that Macedonians drank their wine neat (*akratos*) rather than watering it down as did Greeks. A Greek symposium, for example, would begin with some intellectual discussion and perhaps talk of current affairs, with most attendees reasonably sober thanks to the lighter wine. Only after some time as the wine flowed and the courtesans arrived would the tempo change. Macedonian symposia were different.[12]

While wives and citizen women still could not attend, the men drank more heavily than their Greek counterparts, hence their symposia were rowdier, the men more drunk, and Alexander, it was said, 'would sleep without waking up for two days and two nights' after some of his drinking parties.[13] The presence of the king himself was no impediment – Demosthenes (a hostile source) spoke of Philip II being interested only in 'a life of drunkenness, debauchery and indecent dancing'.[14]

The Macedonians were warriors: when it comes to warrior culture over time, which still involves conditioning human beings to kill others at close range, nothing much has changed. Even at today's military formals or balls, the order of the day frequently involves partying as hard as a unit might fight; excess drinking, drunken boasting and jeering, and even physical altercations might also occur, just as they did at ancient Macedonian symposia. And yet, and in common with ancient Macedonians, the same men who might have recently been at someone's throat in a social setting will without hesitation stand shoulder to shoulder with their comrades against the enemy. Hence, Alexander and his army could just as easily be modern warriors.

It is not a surprise that Macedonian society was a rough and brutal one, akin to the Homeric or Spartan. From an early age, all boys (including those in the royal family) were taught to fight, ride, and hunt wild boar, foxes, birds, and even lions in the kingdom's rugged mountains. Just as the Spartans had customs linked to bravery (only Spartan males killed in battle and women who died in childbirth were allowed epitaphs for example), so too did the Macedonians – no male could recline to eat at a symposium until he had killed a ferocious wild boar without a net, and a Macedonian soldier had to wear a rope around his waist until he had killed his first enemy in battle.

Having to stand at a symposium or be seen in public with a rope belt encouraged men to strive all the harder to prove their mettle. A parallel with the latter could be made with such things as combat patches worn on the right arm of a soldier's uniform or ribbons for valour after serving in combat. These are meant to recognize the soldiers' service and bravery and inspire others to strive for the same, but they are not a social requirement, even though the lack of a combat patch can be stigmatized in U.S. military social circles after its long wars in Iraq and Afghanistan. In Macedonia, the stigma of wearing a rope in public was also a social one, for society was anchored in bravery, self-service, and honour. Alexander combined all these attributes.

Yet the hard-drinking and hard-living lifestyle had also a cultural side. Macedonian craftsmen produced beautiful gold, silver, and bronze art works and jewelry, and especially stunning tomb paintings and mosaics.[15] Their kings were well educated and indeed intellectuals, deeply into Greek philosophy and literature. Archelaus (r. 413–399), for example, invited Socrates and the Athenian tragic playwrights Agathon and Euripides to move to Pella (Socrates declined); Perdiccas III (r. 368–359) was a patron of Plato's Academy; and Philip II (r. 359–336) was a keen correspondent of the Athenian orator Isocrates and Speusippus (Plato's successor at the Academy). Philip also hired the foremost philosopher of the day, Aristotle, to tutor Alexander from the age of fourteen to sixteen. Alexander was a precocious boy and took a retinue of philosophers, artists, and scientists (botanists, biologists, surveyors) with him to Asia.[16] There is a story that before he invaded Asia he had met the Cynic philosopher Diogenes, famous for his ascetic lifestyle, and supposedly remarked that if he were not Alexander, he would want to be like Diogenes.[17] And beyond our period, Antigonus II Gonatas (r. 277–239) attended the lectures in Athens of Zeno, the founder of Stoicism.

But Macedonia was on the periphery of the Greek world. It was surrounded by aggressive Illyrian peoples to the northwest, Paeonians to the north, and Thracians to the east, and it had an uneasy relationship with the independent kingdom of Epirus to its southwest. In addition, Greek cities such as Athens and Thebes interfered in its domestic life, and the Athenians coveted its timber for their fleet.[18] Worse was that Macedonia's army was ill-equipped to deal with the marauding tribes; although the cavalry was strong, the infantry was largely comprised of conscript farmers, poorly trained and inadequately armed.

Then in 359, invading Illyrians under a chieftain named Bardylis killed King Perdiccas III and 4,000 troops in battle. At the same time, the Paeonians massed to invade the kingdom, and the Athenians and the king of Western Thrace (on Macedonia's eastern border) separately supported pretenders to the throne. To make matters worse, there was no strong successor, for Perdiccas' son, Amyntas, was only a minor. It thus appeared that the kingdom was doomed to oblivion, but then the Assembly did something that forever changed not just Macedonia's history but even that of Greece and the east: it acclaimed Philip, the dead king's brother, king.[19]

Philip II

Philip attended to the four threats facing his kingdom immediately, fashioning a strategy that would secure Macedonia's borders for the future and overcome his enemies. To this end, he resorted to a cunning union of deceit, diplomacy, and military force, which over a twenty-three-year reign turned

Macedonia into an imperial power.[20] For now, he needed to buy time and develop a strong army. He concluded an alliance with the Illyrians, which included his marrying Bardylis' granddaughter, bribed the Paeonians and the Thracian king to abandon their plans, and to neutralize the Athenian threat he withdrew a Macedonian garrison from the former Athenian colony of Amphipolis, close to his eastern border, which the Athenians had long wanted to win back, making it seem like he was willing to return it to them.[21]

He now put into effect a series of military reforms, creating in effect a new army, one that was both defensive *and* offensive, unlike most modern armies today, and which we discuss in Chapter 3. The very next year, 358, he led his army against the Paeonians and defeated them in battle. The Illyrians under Bardylis were next, with the octogenarian chieftain and his army routed by Philip and his men.[22] His victories secured his northwest and northern borders. Even more importantly, he united Macedonia for the first time in its history. Before then, the Pindus mountains had effectively split the kingdom into two parts: Lower Macedonia (the eastern part), in which the capital Pella was located (about twenty-two miles northwest of the Thermaic Gulf) and Upper Macedonia (the western part), whose transhumant peoples were ruled by tribal chieftains and showed no loyalty to the king.[23] Now there would be unity and the centralization of Pella.

These successes allowed Philip to introduce an economic policy that continued throughout his reign. Macedonia was rich in natural resources (silver, gold, copper, iron, and lead) and timber (oak, pine, fir, and cedar), but they had never been fully drawn on before. Philip also vigorously exploited the mines, so they yielded substantial annual incomes, drained swampy ground and installed irrigation systems to produce more landholdings, and built roads and towns to aid travel and communications. He also slowly expanded in Greece. In that same year (358), he came to an agreement with the powerful city of Larissa in Thessaly, which shored up his southern border, and, the following year 357, he made an alliance with Epirus on his southwestern border. Under its terms, he married Olympias (his fourth wife), who bore him a son, Alexander, one year later.

But 357 was also the year that the Athenians, realizing they had been tricked and were not going to get Amphipolis back, declared war on him. This war would last until 346 although it was more one of words than actual fighting, and it ended thanks to diplomatic negotiations by both sides. By that time, Philip had extended his influence deeply into Greece through political cunning. In doing so, he showed off a speed, decisiveness, and talent for deception that Alexander inherited. The *poleis* of Greece with their lumbering democracies could not compete.

The Athenians proved to be Philip's most resilient opponents, with their famous statesman and Greece's foremost orator, Demosthenes, his most rampant vocal opponent.[24] It was Demosthenes who fashioned an anti-Macedonian policy in the later 340s anchored in the city rallying the other Greeks against Philip and for its citizens to serve personally in the army rather than relying on mercenaries. In 340, Athens and Philip went to war again, culminating at the battle of Chaeronea (in Boeotia). There, on the two-mile wide plain, a coalition of Greek states led by Athens and Thebes faced Philip.[25] The king fielded 30,000 infantry and 2,000 cavalry and the allied side around 30,000 infantry and 3,800 cavalry, including the elite 300-strong Theban infantry *corps* known as the Sacred Band.

Philip, on the right flank, lulled the Greeks into thinking that he had decided to retreat to disrupt their line. As he had anticipated, the Athenians on the left, overcome with zeal, set off in pursuit, opening gaps in the Greek line, which the Boeotians in the centre moved to plug. However, the right flank, especially the extreme right where the Sacred Band was posted, held firm, as per orders. Philip had appointed his son Alexander, now aged eighteen, to command his left flank. Alexander charged with his cavalry through the gap to encircle the Greek right, annihilating the Sacred Band.[26] In the meantime, Philip suddenly stopped his feigned retreat, turned, and attacked the Athenians, cutting them to pieces. The Greeks were overwhelmingly defeated. The Athenians alone lost 1,000 men and had 2,000 taken prisoner; they condemned their general Lysicles to death.

Victory at Chaeronea gave Philip mastery of Greece. He may have always intended this, given he had forged an army that was designed not merely to defend his kingdom but, because of its offensive manoeuvre capabilities, extend it. He intended to establish Macedonia's prowess, and clearly Alexander felt the same. After Chaeronea, Philip moved to the strategically important city of Corinth on the isthmus and summoned representatives to him from all Greek states (only the Spartans refused him). There, he announced a Common Peace – an agreement by which every Greek city swore a separate oath of allegiance to the other cities and to Macedonia, promising to have the same friends and enemies and not to engage in anything subversive.[27] Each city was to send representatives to a council of the Greek states, which in theory oversaw affairs relating to Greece, but in reality was impotent – even though Macedonia was not a member, Philip was elected its leader (*hegemon*)! This constitutional body is better known by its modern name of the League of Corinth.

At a meeting of the league the following year (337), Philip announced his next grand plan: a panhellenic invasion of Persia, ostensibly to liberate the Greek cities of Asia Minor and to punish the Persians for their invasion of Greece in the early fifth century.[28] He was likely using these reasons to mask a possible shortage of liquid capital, given that the Macedonians practiced a rolling economy. He sent an advance force to Asia Minor in 336 to prepare the way for the main army he would lead that summer. But on the eve of his expedition, the day after celebrating his daughter's marriage to the king of Epirus, a personal bodyguard (and jilted lover), Pausanias, assassinated the forty-six-year-old king.[29]

Why Pausanias acted as he did is harder to fathom. The 'official' reason, which Alexander had Aristotle circulate, was that Philip and Pausanias had been involved in a homoerotic relationship which the king ended to take up with another man. Pausanias, unable to handle the upset and shame, killed Philip in a fit of jealous rage. On the other hand, Plutarch and Justin suggest a conspiracy to kill the king, involving Olympias (and/or Alexander), who may have used the unfortunate Pausanias as a pawn. The truth will never be known as Pausanias was killed as he tried to flee, but we should not reject the notion of a conspiracy involving Alexander or Olympias as some ancient writers suggest.[30]

Philip had more than doubled the size of Macedonia to encompass all of Greece and as far east as the Hellespont, increasing its population to as many as 500,000. His economic policy turned the kingdom into a prosperous state with a strong coinage, and he had created a formidable and unstoppable army, which we detail further in Chapter 3.[31] Moreover, he had laid the plans for the invasion of the Persian Empire, which Alexander inherited. The son thus achieved what his father had envisaged, and he did so in spectacular fashion, building a vast empire and being dubbed 'the great'. Now it is time to turn to Alexander.

The Young Alexander

Alexander was born in 356, the second son of King Philip II (r. 359–336) and his fourth wife Olympias, a princess of the royal house of Epirus. He had one elder brother, Arrhidaeus, the son of Philip and his third wife Philinna of Larissa (in Thessaly), who was born in 357, but at some point, and for reasons unknown, Alexander became the preferred heir. The image we have of him today is a clean-shaven man with his eyes famously turned upward as if looking to heaven (see frontispiece).

There were various stories about Alexander's divine conception, such as Olympias' dream that during a thunderstorm, a thunderbolt fell from the sky into her womb and impregnated her; another that Philip caught her having sex with a huge snake in their bed, and not long after she became pregnant with Alexander.[32] Likewise, the manner of Alexander's birth, for the day he was born the temple of Artemis at Ephesus burned down because, it was said, the goddess was at Pella, helping to deliver him into the world. The Magi at Ephesus believed the temple's destruction was symbolic: 'they ran around slapping their faces and lamenting aloud that on this day had been born only sorrow and great calamity for Asia'.[33] These stories we can put down to later propaganda, perhaps even circulated by the king himself to show he was destined for greatness after his visit to the Oracle of Zeus Ammon in Egypt and apparent confirmation of his divinity (see Chapter 7).

What we all know is that Alexander toppled the Persian Empire and brought the Achaemenid dynasty to an end in 330. He was only twenty-six years old, but by then he had been leading troops for a decade. In 340, Philip had appointed him regent of Macedonia while the king campaigned against Perinthus and Byzantium on the Hellespont. Despite being only sixteen, when he heard that the Maedians of the upper Strymon valley had revolted, he immediately led an army against them.[34] We have no details of his campaign, other than that he ended the revolt in battle. But then, and a sign of his later policy of founding cities in conquered lands, he established a settlement (probably a military outpost), naming it Alexandropolis after himself, to which he transplanted people from Macedonia, Greece, and Thrace to keep the Maedians in check.[35]

What Philip thought of his son's exploits in Thrace, not to mention his audacity in founding Alexandropolis, is unknown. However, he cannot have been too aggrieved as two years later, he made him commander of the left flank of the army at Chaeronea, and Alexander distinguished himself in the fighting. Philip's next goal of invading Asia was never realized as he was assassinated in 336. There was obvious chaos when he was cut down and even concern for Alexander's safety.[36] However, one of Philip's trusted generals Antipater immediately acclaimed Alexander as king, and Parmenion, another senior general (currently with the vanguard in Asia Minor), sent his support. At an Assembly held soon after, Alexander swore to rule according to the laws and adhere to his father's policies, and his people pledged their oath of allegiance to him.[37]

On Philip's death in 336, the Greek cities had revolted from the League of Corinth. After attending to the burial of his father at the former capital of Aegae (modern Vergina), in keeping with the tradition that a king buried his predecessor, the young king turned to Greece.[38] Little is known about this campaign. He won over 'some cities by diplomacy, others by striking fear into them, and others by the actual use of force'.[39] He overcame a Thessalian army to establish a position at Thermopylae, home to the famous pass that controlled the main route from northern into central Greece, at which time several Greek cities surrendered. At Thebes, which had expelled a garrison installed by Philip after Chaeronea, he resorted to a more military style of diplomacy: he ordered his men to wear full armour before the city's gates, as if ready to besiege it. Duly intimidated, the Thebans capitulated, but to be on the safe side, Alexander installed an oligarchy and garrison in the city.

From there, it was an easy march to Corinth, where he formally reestablished the League of Corinth and received the cities' oaths of allegiance. He also announced that the invasion of Asia would still go ahead for the same reasons as Philip had stated the previous year.[40] The Greeks had no choice but to approve him as the commander-in-chief, for their liberty had ended at Chaeronea. Satisfied with this reaction, Alexander returned to Pella, continuing a purge to eliminate opposition and even any suspect rivals to the throne, which continued into the following year – he 'did not want any reason for unrest festering in Macedonia while he was involved in campaigns far away'.[41]

Alexander's Influences: A Leader's Flaws?

The militaristic nature of Macedonian society had a profound influence on Alexander, as did his father's exploits, which he heard about and later experienced firsthand. But it was the latter's influence that contributed to a series of character flaws in Alexander as king, general, and man, which arguably impact his greatness most of all.

Philip was frequently absent on campaign, which is perhaps why their relationship does not seem to have been especially close, more like king and heir than father and son. Philip also seems to have disliked Olympias intensely, not least because she was forever criticizing him to his son. That is perhaps why in 342 Philip arranged for Aristotle to tutor him at Mieza, on the eastern slopes of Mount Vermion, so away from the court and especially his mother. Philip brought Alexander back to Pella in 340, when he was preparing a campaign in Thrace, and appointed his son regent, during which time Alexander overcame the Maedians (see above).

Yet Alexander admired his warrior father as he grew up, and the young boy who allegedly pestered foreign envoys about communications and military matters in the Persian Empire likely listened eagerly to Philip's stories after he returned from his many campaigns. But that admiration turned to resentment in the last years of Philip's life, mainly because of Alexander's misguided emotions and a belief that his father was intentionally marginalizing him from his inner circle. It is important to trace this estrangement for the light it shines on Alexander's character and paranoia, which manifested itself during his campaign in Asia.

In 337, Philip married his seventh (and final) wife, a young Macedonian girl named Cleopatra, this time marrying for love rather than for political or military reasons.[42] At the wedding banquet, a nobleman named Attalus (Cleopatra's former guardian) toasted the couple but then prayed that Macedonia might finally have a legitimate heir. This slur was especially directed at Olympias, who was from Epirus.[43] Everyone had been drinking heavily, as was to be expected among the Macedonians, and Alexander got into a furious argument with Attalus. When he turned to his father for support, the king took Attalus' side, ordered his son apologize, and even rushed him with sword drawn. He fell drunkenly over a table, prompting Alexander to remark contemptuously: 'Here is the man who was making ready to cross from Europe to Asia, and who cannot even cross from one table to another without losing his balance'.[44] Alexander and Olympias then left Pella for Epirus; although Philip recalled him shortly after, a rift was growing.

In the same year the so-called Pixodarus affair took place.[45] Pixodarus was the rebellious satrap of Caria casting around for allies against the Persian King. Offering his daughter in marriage, he approached Philip, who agreed to an alliance as Caria would be an excellent base for his army when he invaded Asia. He offered his eldest son Arrhidaeus as husband to the daughter, but for some reason Alexander was affronted and sent Pixodarus a message that he wished to marry his daughter. Philip along with Philotas, son of Parmenion, sought out Alexander and both men publicly rebuked him; Philip even exiled some of his son's friends in retaliation. Any potential alliance with Pixodarus was abandoned.

The first episode involving Attalus' toast understandably must have detached Alexander from his father: it reveals a son and heir aggrieved enough to withdraw from Pella and to go, first, to Epirus with Olympias, but then by himself to Macedonia's traditional enemy, the Illyrians. Perhaps Philip was so quick to recall him because he might have been trying to encourage them to attack Macedonia. Yet Attalus was never punished and was even sent as a commander of the advance force to Asia Minor.

The second episode to do with Pixodarus reveals a growing feeling of marginalization and even paranoia. It was the right of a Macedonian king to arrange marriages, so Alexander was committing an act of treachery by going against Philip's wishes. It seems that the king and his generals had formed something of a closed circle to decide on policy that did not involve the heir to the throne, and being on the periphery did not sit well with the young heir.[46] Throughout his reign Alexander took pains to be at the centre of everything, always claiming credit for victories, viewing anyone who criticised any aspect of his military or personal life with suspicion, and dealing ruthlessly with any opposition – from friend and foe alike. Even at the start of his reign he embarked on a purge of rivals to the throne, but he included Attalus among the victims, finally taking his revenge for the latter's insult to Olympias at Philip's wedding in 337. And Alexander had a long memory. In 330, seven years after the Pixodarus affair, he implicated Philotas in a questionable conspiracy and had him and his father Parmenion executed (see Chapter 9).

But what arguably turned Alexander against his father was the realization that he was not going to accompany Philip to Asia but would remain behind as regent and deputy hegemon of the League of Corinth. He had already experienced battle against the Maedians in 340 and at Chaeronea in 338 and was eager for greater military glory. Philip was now denying him that. Against this background, we can postulate a conspiracy on the part of Alexander and/or Olympias to kill Philip, as mentioned above. If this seems far-fetched, we should remember that Attalus' taunt carried the clear implication that were Philip and Cleopatra to have a son, he might be preferred over Alexander as the next king, and Attalus probably led a powerful faction at court that might well defy Alexander.

Thus, we have in Alexander a paradox. He was obsessed with honour and bravery, proved himself to be a great leader and inspirer of his men, and was a loyal friend and protector – promoting, for example, his friends exiled in the Pixodarus affair to senior posts, and keeping his older half-brother Arrhidaeus safe, perhaps because they had grown up together.

Yet despite Alexander's prowess, he was obsessed with outdoing his predecessors, especially Philip. That was why in Asia he wanted to keep marching forever eastward and his end goals seemed to be the reach the supposed ends of the earth.[47] Aristobulus, who accompanied him and wrote about him, remarked that he 'was insatiably ambitious of ever acquiring fresh territory'; Plutarch claimed that Alexander once reflected that he had no idea what to do for the rest of his life, and in Curtius' opinion Alexander could cope better with warfare than peace and leisure and that 'to seek and chase down peoples removed who were almost at the ends of human habitation was a challenging goal, yet his yearning for glory and his unquenchable desire for renown meant that he saw nothing as too inaccessible or remote'.[48]

Alexander's love of adventure and of a good fight is not a surprise, given his upbringing, not to mention that he was raised on the Homeric epics and emulated Achilles. But here lies the paradox in Alexander. He strove to be honourable, like a Homeric hero, yet in wanting to carve his own niche in history his character flaws led to him putting his men's lives in danger, never having a clearly defined strategic end state other than the pursuit of personal glory once he moved into Central Asia, disregarding the customs of the peoples he conquered as well as his own subjects, and eventually facing mutiny and revolt.

Today, the PME offered by most western nations includes a psychological evaluation for senior military leaders to prevent character flaws and personal self-aggrandizement before they take up major commands. There was no such thing in Alexander's time of course, hence when as next-in-line he assumed the throne in 336, he became *ex officio* general of the large and formidable killing machine that was the Macedonian army. Whether he would have passed the modern tests is another matter, but his paranoia, megalomania, ambition, and obsession with personal reputation would all too often endanger the lives of his men and compromise the leadership skills that we extoll throughout this book.

For all these reasons, modern soldiers, strategists, and even policymakers can draw valuable lessons, good and bad, from Alexander's life and reign.

Notes

1 Polybius 21.28 – the procedure is described at 21.28.12–18, and see Worthington 2023, pp. 158–159, on the siege.
2 Fuller 1960, p. 7.
3 On this, see Keegan 1987, pp. 13–91.
4 Geography: Hammond 1972, pp. 3–211; Hatzopoulos 1996, vol. 1, pp. 167–216, Hatzopoulos 2011a, Hatzopoulos 2020, pp. 4–48; Thomas 2010. On ancient Macedonia, history, and people, see the essays in Roisman and Worthington 2010; Lane Fox 2011; with Cloché 1960; Daskalakis 1965; Hammond 1972, Hammond 1992a; Hammond and Griffith 1979; Hammond and Walbank 1988; Kalléris 1988; Hatzopoulos 1996, Hatzopoulos 2020.
5 See Daskalakis 1965; Engels 2010; Hatzopoulos 1996, vol. 1, pp. 167–209, Hatzopoulos 2011b, Hatzopoulos 2011c, Hatzopoulos 2020, pp. 49–124, citing previous bibliography.
6 Hatzopoulos 1996, vol. 1, pp. 219–260; King 2010; Roisman 2012.
7 Hammond 1992a, pp. 64–70.
8 Hatzopoulos 1996, vol. 1, pp. 260–322.
9 Hammond 1992a, pp. 391–395; King 2010; against the constitutionalist view, see Anson 1985a, Anson 1991; see too Roisman 2012. There were also powerful factions at the court, but these too depended on the king's goodwill: Heckel 2003a, especially pp. 200–205; cf. Weber 2009.
10 Cf. Worthington 2014a, pp. 11–13.
11 Athenaeus 13.557b-e, 13.560c; see too Greenwalt 1989.
12 See Sawada 2010; Carney 2015, both citing further bibliography.
13 *Ephemerides*, *BNJ* 117 F 2b = Athenaeus 10.434b. See also *Ephemerides*, *BNJ* 117 F 2c = Plutarch, *Moralia* 623e, that Alexander could sleep for days at a time after drinking.
14 Demosthenes 2.18–19.

15 Hardiman 2010; Paspalas 2011; cf. Paliadeli-Saatsoglou 2011; Hatzopoulos 1994 (pp. 116–219) has many lavish illustrations.
16 Tutoring: Worthington 2014a, pp. 95–97. Retinue: Badian 1991; Tritle 2009.
17 Plutarch, *Alexander* 14.1–3; cf. Plutarch, *Moralia* 331f, 605d, 782a, Diogenes Laertius 6.32, with Worthington 2014a, p. 127.
18 On its weaknesses before Philip, see Hammond 1992a, pp. 71–99.
19 Background: Worthington 2008, pp. 20–22.
20 Philip's reign: Ellis 1976; Cawkwell 1978; Hammond and Griffith 1979, pp. 203–698; Hammond 1994; Worthington 2008, Worthington 2014a (comparing and contrasting him to Alexander); King 2018, pp. 70–106; see too Müller 2010; Hammond 1992a, pp. 100–119, 137–187; Lane Fox 2011a. Focusing on Philip as a general and his military accomplishments: Ashley 1998, pp. 111–162; Gabriel 2010.
21 Worthington 2008, pp. 23–25, Worthington 2014a, pp. 29–30.
22 Worthington 2008, pp. 33–35, Worthington 2014a, pp. 38–39. Battle against Bardylis: Hammond 1989c.
23 See further Xydopoulos 2012.
24 On Demosthenes, see Worthington 2013.
25 Diodorus 16.85–87, Plutarch, *Alexander* 9.2–3, Justin 9.3.8–11, Polyaenus 4.2.2, 7, with Hammond and Griffith 1979, pp. 596–603; Ashley 1998, pp. 153–158; Worthington 2008, pp. 147–151, Worthington 2014a, pp. 85–90; Gabriel 2010, pp. 214–216.
26 Alexander's action: Sears and Willekes 2016.
27 Worthington 2008, pp. 158–171, Worthington 2014a, pp. 99–101, citing bibliography.
28 Worthington 2008, pp. 166–169, Worthington 2014a, pp. 103–105.
29 Diodorus 16.93–94, 17.2.3–6, Plutarch, *Alexander* 10.4–7, Plutarch, *Moralia* 327c, Justin 9.6.4–7.14; cf. Arrian, *BNJ* 156 FF 9 and 22.
30 Justin 9.7.1 ('it was also believed that Pausanias had been suborned by Olympias, mother of Alexander, and that Alexander was not unaware of the plot to murder his father') and Plutarch, *Alexander* 10.6 ('it was Olympias who was chiefly blamed for the assassination, because she was believed to have encouraged the young man [Pausanias] and incited him to take his revenge, but a certain amount of accusation was also attached to Alexander'), with Worthington 2008, pp. 181–186, Worthington 2014a, pp. 112–115, citing bibliography, to which add Heckel, Howe, and Müller 2017.
31 Comments on Philip's legacy: Worthington 2008, pp. 194–208, Worthington 2014a, pp. 115–119.
32 Plutarch, *Alexander* 2–3, for the various stories, with Worthington 2014a, pp. 90–92.
33 Hegesias, *BNJ* 142 F 3 = Plutarch, *Alexander* 3.5–9.
34 Plutarch, *Alexander* 9.1, with Hammond and Griffith 1979, pp. 557–559; Worthington 2008, pp. 230–231.
35 Plutarch, *Alexander* 9.1.
36 Arrian 1.25.1–2, Curtius 6.9.17, 10.24, Plutarch, *Moralia* 327c; cf. Justin 11.1.1–2, with Worthington 2008, pp. 187–188.
37 Diodorus 17.2.2; Justin 11.1.7–10.

38 Philip's tomb was famously excavated by the Greek archaeologist Manolis Andronikos in 1977 and found unplundered: see Worthington 2008, pp. 234–241, citing bibliography.
39 Diodorus 17.3.6–4.9 (quote), Arrian 1.1.2–3, with Fuller 1960, pp. 81–83; Bosworth 1988a, pp. 188–192; Ashley 1998, pp. 165–167; Worthington 2014a, pp. 126–127.
40 Brunt 1965 argues that Alexander's invasion was merely his inheritance from Philip, but see Fredricksmeyer 2000; Heckel 2003b.
41 Quote: Justin 11.5.2. On the purge, see Bosworth 1988a, pp. 25–27; Ellis 1982.
42 Athenaeus 13.557b-e; cf. 13.560c, with Worthington 2008, pp. 172–174.
43 Worthington 2008, pp. 176–178, Worthington 2014a, pp. 109–110.
44 Plutarch, *Alexander* 9.10; Justin 9.7.4.
45 Plutarch, *Alexander* 10, with Worthington 2014a, pp. 110–111.
46 Cf. Plutarch, *Alexander* 10.1–3, with Worthington 2008, pp. 177–180, 182–186; Fredricksmeyer 1990.
47 Cf. Arrian 5.26.2.
48 Aristobulus, *BNJ* 139 F 55 (= Arrian 7.19.6); Curtius 9.2.8; Plutarch, *Moralia* 207d8.

2 A Brave New World?

Before attempting to place Alexander into any sort of historical context, one must first acknowledge certain realities of the present. One of which concerns distinguishing between past and present perceptions of war's character, and how human beings tend to package supposed trends in modern conflict for the purposes of planning, forecasting, and general understanding of the world around them. The intent is to offer the reader a deeper appreciation for, and perhaps connection to, the ancient world by showcasing flawed assumptions surrounding divergent trajectories of modern conflict. To that end, the tactics employed by Alexander were as timeless as they are effective. For example, so as not to compromise the security of his rear while his armies were far forward in Asia, he realized the need to first subdue parts of Thrace and Illyria. During this campaign in 335, discussed in Chapter 5, he was confronted by Thracians occupying the high ground of Mount Haemus bordering the narrow path upon which the Macedonian phalanx stood. Through an innovative tactic thwarting the initial assault, Alexander maneuvered on his opponent; he ordered archers on his right to move forward and engage targets, spoiling any hopes of a Thracian frontal assault, while he led a contingent of troops on a bold flanking maneuver to his left. This aggressive flanking element threw the barbarian army into disarray, and the Macedonians cut down some 1,500 of the enemy on the mountainside.

The concept of a stationary element used to restrict an opponent's freedom of movement while a mobile detachment attacks a weaker or unguarded position unexpectedly remains as prevalent in twenty-first century military doctrine as it was in Alexander's thinking. Humankind continues to change warfare and not the other way around, even when we think of our own era with its tanks, air strikes, and unmanned weapons. Nonetheless, the dynamics of armed conflict in the twenty-first century have swayed military thinking drastically despite such longstanding continuities. Experts have predicted for decades that cyber-attacks would soon be the decisive element in war, yet in February 2022, it was not malware that razed Ukrainian cities to the ground and triggered a refugee crisis in eastern Europe, but rather tanks, bombs, and forty-mile-long convoys of Russian armour.[1]

The inclination to favor recent history as a guide for strategic thought is due in part to the immense investment the western world has placed in the theories of Prussian officer Carl Von Clausewitz who, as a veteran of the Napoleonic age, saw little value in the ancient texts despite his affinity for historical study.[2] Modern history, he believed, should guide the conduct of war, and his thoughts reflected lessons learned through the total mobilization of society brought to life in Napoleonic France with its *levée en masse*. The problem with this, of course, is that in the twenty-first century and particularly in liberal democracies, such a massive war effort is not only unfeasible but also ill-advised. Clausewitz's *On War* deservedly remains the bar by which all other strategic theses are measured, but if one were to follow his logic concerning the study of ancient history to its inevitable conclusion, it would make his own assessments of battlefield manoeuvre and defense ill-fitted to deal with modern challenges.

There exists as much disparity between modern armies wielding laser-equipped helicopters and those of Clausewitz's time as there is between the armies of Clausewitz and Alexander. In this light, we might view Clausewitz's masterwork as ancient, and therefore by his own assertion 'useless'.[3] One could assume this is not the value Clausewitz intended his work to offer posterity, especially considering his respect for history in general. Indeed, later in *On War*, Clausewitz highlighted the indispensable value of studying the human element in war: 'History provides the strongest proof of the importance of moral factors and their often-incredible effect: this is the noblest and most solid nourishment that the mind of a general may draw from a study of the past'.[4]

None of this is to 'trash' Clausewitz, only to suggest that, during periods of revolutionary change, theories become inextricably tied to current events. From this we can conclude that Clausewitz wrestled with finding a balance between mastering the modern science of warfare that France had revolutionized, and the ancient art of war driven by unchanging moral factors. Those who deal with these issues might empathize with Clausewitz's struggle, as the same intellectual battle rages between political and military leaders today. Western officials, for example, aimed to avoid making twentieth-century Soviet mistakes in Afghanistan but ended up repeating nineteenth-century British ones, which were perhaps more germane.[5] If modern leaders are to have any hope of understanding the brave new world in which they live, they must nurture a healthier respect for the old one.

Enter the Modern Chimera

In the spring of 1989, British military historian Sir Michael Howard stood behind a podium at Oxford University to give the valedictory lecture. No stranger to apologia for the study of history, he sought in this instance to offer something more concrete; what students should expect to acquire from history, and a consideration of its role in the education of civilised society. Perhaps most relevant to this chapter, Howard emphasised that the study of history is not a soothing venture. Entertaining the idea that history holds kernels of truth for mankind's future is a practice that many approach with understandable timidity. It is for this reason that new political bodies, economic systems, or technological advances are lauded as pathways to a novel future in which the brutal trials of the past might be altogether avoided, or at least encountered with less frequency or intensity. If, as Howard proposed, history served as a 'manual for statecraft' and a 'guide for conduct', then some might prefer to view the study of history as a means of understanding methods of statecraft and conduct in a world long since expired.[6] In his reading of the classics such as Plutarch and Thucydides, Howard saw something worth holding onto:

> What was exemplified were the challenges which all generations had in turn to confront in conducting their affairs; and the qualities required to meet those challenges – courage, equanimity, moderation, loyalty, magnanimity, foresight, all the prudent skills of the statesman and the warrior – were considered to be as 'relevant' for the moderns as they had been for the ancients.[7]

In this way, Howard saw immovable consistencies in the human heart, the lessons of which retained their value long after the social and political realities of each epoch faded away. These constants meant that Howard had no words of comfort for his audience. There is no 'assurance of a happy ending', he said, and despite valiant efforts to unlock any truth that the past might offer, 'all may disintegrate into ruin and chaos on a scale never before seen'. His words are a sobering reminder that whether such a future unfolds is entirely dependent upon every individual's use of 'reason and judgment both educated and *created* by historical experience'.[8] Howard charged his audience to do better in this regard, making it clear that doing so must begin with an understanding of what is considered worse, which can only be gauged through the historical study of other's experiences with their own reason and judgment.

Less than two years after this speech, the world breathed a sigh of relief as the flag of the Union of Soviet Socialist Republics was lowered for the final time in front of the Kremlin. With the Cold War at an end, the western world appeared to enter a new era of freedom, prosperity, and technological innovation that would connect the world in new and exciting ways.

As the Soviet Union disintegrated, the United States led a vast international coalition to oust Iraqi President Saddam Hussein's army from Kuwait. *Operation Desert Storm's* deployment of new military platforms and technologies put on display for the entire world an expeditionary capability nothing short of revolutionary. Stealth aircraft that confounded radar systems, surgically accurate precision guided munitions (PGMs), and highly manoeuvrable rotary wing airframes decimated the Iraqi Army in what came to be known as the 100-hour war.[9] As success so often bequeaths to its benefactors, in short time defense analysts, military leaders, and public officials became captivated by the potential long-term implications of this victory. Some became wed to the belief that the operation foreshadowed a new type of warfare and a brighter future in which American military power, augmented with the latest technologies, was on the brink of creating uncontested battlefields in which no adversary could hide.[10] The last decade of the twentieth century appeared to validate Kant's theory of Universal History, a worldview further popularized by Francis Fukuyama's speech and article turned book, *The End of History*, in which mankind had reached its final frontier by vanquishing the last great ideological giant in the form of Soviet Communism.[11]

But less than two years into the twenty-first century, terrorists adhering to a feudal ideology waged a calamitous attack on the United States, and subsequently brought the past into focus with vicious clarity.[12] In the following years, Russian imperialism made its return after Vladimir Putin launched numerous incursions into Georgia and Ukraine between 2008 and 2022, nuclear war crept back into the security debate regarding the ambitions of North Korea and Iran, the permanence of small wars became doubtful, and the U.S. Department of Defense announced a new strategy focused on deterring and preparing for great power competition and large-scale combat operations (LSCO) – concepts that were long since cast into the dustbin of history by defense theorists.[13] The world soon found truth in a seemingly antiquated proverb: the past is not dead – it is not even past.

Revolutions in Military Affairs (RMA)

Experts scrambled to conceptualize this new environment, and while there emerged as many theories, concepts, and buzzwords as there were observers, the most accepted term used to describe changes in warfare during this period was Revolutions in Military Affairs or RMA.[14] Although references to the essence of RMA theory date back to the seventeenth century, the modern concept was derived from Soviet military thinking during the Cold War before gaining traction within the Pentagon and international think tanks during the last decade of the twentieth century.[15] The term describes a period in which technological, organizational, cultural, or political developments so fundamentally change the character of war that its impacts are irreversible.[16] Prominent technological examples include the invention of the flintlock rifle, combustion engine, nuclear weapons, and now the prospects of militarized artificial intelligence (AI). Organizational, conceptual, or political examples include Napoleon's *levée en masse* after the French Revolution (c. 1789–1799) and Germany's *blitzkrieg* tactics employed during the Second World War (WWII) (which were influenced by Alexander's use of cavalry to penetrate frontal defenses, as we know German officers confided in Liddell Hart's Alexandrian theory of the indirect approach).[17] Revolutions are not modern, though. As we know, Alexander and his father Philip II revolutionized the Macedonian army, introduced an engineering corps that used catapults in manoeuvres as well as siege operations, and made a shift from conscript to professional soldiers.

It is important here to clarify the distinction between the *nature* of war and the *character* of warfare. War's nature, rooted in the passions and often unpredictable decisions of human beings, governed by the application of military force to influence the will of an opponent, is considered by many to be rather static throughout history.[18] In Clausewitzian terms, war's nature encompasses ultimately the political *ends* for which all wars are waged – it is the use of force to convince an opponent to submit to one's will.[19] Warfare, or the *ways* and *means* through which nations go about achieving that end, defines the character of war – the tools, techniques, and resources underlying war's nature that coalesce to achieve a desired political end. Despite critiques of the ends–way–means trinity, the challenge today is the same as it was for Alexander: feasibly aligning the available ways and means of warfare in a manner consistent with the desired political ends of war.[20] These fundamental truths remain central to the success or failure of not only military affairs but also all affairs. The conflation of these concepts and the associated belief that changes in the character of warfare might radically alter war's nature – thereby making the achievement of war's ends more efficient or less costly – are recurrent themes in every generation's RMA.[21]

It is widely held that RMA are driven by numerous physical and metaphysical factors, such as disciplined formations, morale, and military doctrine that integrates new concepts and weapons effectively.[22] Yet the development of new technologies began to consume RMA thought, particularly after the success of stealth aircraft and advanced precision munitions against Saddam Hussein's army in Kuwait (c. 1991). As Murray observed, the technological aspect of RMA has played only one part in these revolutions, and frequently a less significant part.[23] In his study of strategic developments during the late sixteenth century, Gunther Rothenberg found that gunpowder was not the most important contribution to military revolution. In line with the positions of Max Weber and Machiavelli, it was the disciplined regimentation of gunpowder's application, Rothenberg argued, that proved decisive in war.[24]

Nevertheless, emerging technologies in the twenty-first century have pulled some 'future war' thinkers to posit the opposite – that it is indisputable that technology-driven RMA do shape history.[25] Lawrence Freedman found that the strategic environment of the 1990s gave birth to theories that technology would ultimately lift the 'fog of war', thereby making armed conflict more predictable and less protracted.[26] The more impressive the technology, the more potently it coats the imagination of RMA theorists, and the further the present becomes seemingly dislodged from the past. Robert D. Kaplan cautioned against such thinking in 2002 when he wrote that 'the more respect we have for the truths of the past, the more certain our journey away from it'.[27] Conversations surrounding machine learning, artificial intelligence, hypersonic missiles, and directed energy weapons have now ignited the imaginations of many in the defense industry, leading to calls for new RMA.[28] Some have taken this a step further by exploring the potential of human-less war or flirting with ideas that border on technological determinism – the belief that, in the future, all progress and understanding will flow from a reservoir of societal mechanization that severely devalues human beings.[29] While each of the above systems could play a significant role in future military operations, the overwhelming public fascination with them could be problematic, as we shall explore later.

First, RMA cannot be forced, and they probably should not be. Proclaiming an era of RMA without a major conflict to validate the technology associated with it assumes a great deal. Included in these assumptions are the availability of space-based and space-reliant technologies, the presence of telecommunications infrastructure capable of supporting networked systems, and the utility of high-maintenance platforms requiring sophisticated services in hostile environments. Each of these conditions would be in doubt depending on the ecological, geographical, and operational realities of the next major war.

While some reports suggest that AI could render battlefields safer for human soldiers or perhaps even change the nature of war, other studies have discovered that autonomous combat systems could lead to 'inadvertent escalation', decreased deterrence capabilities, and the perception of dwindling support from allies and partners who do not possess the same technology.³⁰ As evidenced by the 2022 Russo-Ukrainian War, despite overwhelming materiel support to Ukraine from the western world, Ukrainians were still forced to dig trenches and place thousands of lives at risk in defense of their national interest. Evident here is the paradoxical character of militarized AI, in which it is framed as both the cause of and solution to mankind's wars. In any case, the assumption that emergent, unproven technologies hold the key to the future not only encourages narrow thinking about the grim possibilities in war, but also it discourages the study of history because the nature of such thinking proposes a fundamental and irreversible detour from past experiences – what is often referred to as a historical *discontinuity*.³¹ Sending armies to fight the type of war that they had been led to believe no longer exists – that is, a costly large-scale ground war – is therefore an increasingly plausible scenario this century.³²

Questions remain pertaining to how one might quantify whether RMA has occurred, and many still debate the legitimacy of the term. Most agree that evidence of RMA can only exist during or after a war, at a time when the revolutionary effects of new technology or concepts outweigh their revolutionary potential.³³ The conditions for successful implementation of new systems are set during the interwar period, but throughout that period, RMA thinking is driven by potential only.

Precision munitions and nuclear weapons, for instance, were hailed as the tools to end ground wars in the mid-twentieth century. In 1949, four years after America's demonstration of the bomb, defense intellectuals told U.S. Army Col. Ralph Puckett (then a second lieutenant) that he was irrelevant because future wars would be fought with missiles.³⁴ This was presented to Puckett as a matter of fact. How could it not be? Even though Robert Oppenheimer himself insisted that the bomb was a weapon which had no military significance, atomic weaponry was new and shocking.³⁵ In keeping with the RMA trend, nuclear terror became the wellspring from which all strategic forecasting flowed as many assumed that all other forms of military power would fade into disuse.³⁶ Within a year, Puckett was fighting North Korean and Chinese troops in muddy trenches on the Korean peninsula. But this war was not enough to dash all hopes of a similarly decisive remote military capability.

Theorists who assessed the broadening suite of surveillance capabilities and networked communications at the Pentagon's disposal envisioned an imminent transparent battlefield in the last decade of the twentieth century.³⁷ And yet, despite incredible advances in space-based systems, synthetic aperture radar, and signals intelligence, insurgents in Iraq circa 2004 to 2011 used old-world tradecraft such as dead drops (the surreptitious placement of handwritten notes or devices for future retrieval) and rendezvous (face-to-face meetings that leave no digital signature) to confound these sensors. Consequently, human intelligence collected through hard-earned trust and at great risk to individual operators was responsible for many of the western world's biggest national security 'wins' of the early twenty-first century.[38]

Soldiers and marines had to clear house-to-house in places like Fallujah, Ramadi, and Aleppo, where air raids were either too catastrophic or targets too opaque to warrant the release of laser- or global positioning system (GPS)-guided munitions. Moreover, the expansion of communications technology during this period at times fed into what John Keegan refers to as 'châteaux generalship' or a '3,000 mile screwdriver' where senior leaders far removed from the realities of the battlefield meddled in day-to-day military decision-making.[39] As a result, miscommunication between political headquarters and ground force commanders was made possible by instantaneous communication systems that were ironically designed to reduce such confusion.[40] We see here the all too common disconnect between the assumed and actual effects of supposedly revolutionary systems in the chaos of war.

The stubborn belief that new inventions can alter war's brutal nature, however well intentioned, is behind many strategic blunders of the post-industrial age. In many cases, decision-makers had been led to believe that technology transcended mankind's proclivity for poor judgment and the enemy's will to resist and adapt in creative ways. Even the inception of nuclear weapons, often presented as the most significant RMA, provided little comfort to U.S. Marines in the Chosin Reservoir circa 1950, paratroopers in Vietnam circa 1967, or the author Mike Ferguson in Ramadi, Iraq during the 2006 battle there. The political will to deploy the weapon, the prudence of such deployment, and the associated moral considerations are of greater consequence to its revolutionary potential than the existence of the weapon itself. American diplomat Raymond Garthoff assessed that 'the most profound effect of the [RMA]' was a mandate to avoid war between major powers, which consequently shifted the focus of military aggression to the periphery of those nations' spheres of influence.[41] In turn, this produced an increased frequency of comparatively lower-cost, lower-risk proxy wars between powers.

Even if a major war were to break out between nuclear-armed states, few envision an immediate volley of nuclear weapons between them. Mutually assured destruction still applies, and so any potential onset of hostilities is likely to unfold in ways that veterans of the previously mentioned wars would not find wildly unfamiliar: establishing air, ground, and sea lines of communication, deploying advisor teams on the margins, inserting some sort of special operations task force, building combat power in contiguous partner nations, suppressing and sabotaging enemy air defenses and key command and control (C2) and communications nodes, and taking and retaking physical terrain with ground forces.[42]

A prominent shortcoming associated with RMA is that, apart from nuclear weapons, the tools driving its theories are inherently tactical in nature, yet they are often interpreted within an intellectual framework that influences strategic planning. Military campaigns throughout history were often lost after major combat operations ceased during what is now referred to as stability operations or the consolidation of gains phase in which the momentum achieved through tactical military victories is transformed into strategic success.[43] Key differences are expected to emerge this century in how the conditions for war are set – through cyber-attacks, coordinated information operations, proxy or paramilitary forces, and the probing of lines with various unmanned systems – but these measures will not win the war. Revolutionary weapons are a small piece of this large puzzle, and arguably the simpler piece.

Take hypersonic missile technology as an example. Capable of traveling between five to fifteen times the speed of sound before penetrating air defenses and striking numerous targets around the globe, hypersonic missiles are a leading system in the new RMA framework.[44] But as impressive as they are, the premise of their use is often presented in a one-dimensional scenario that assumes the destruction of military targets alone is decisive. If these missiles were used against an expeditionary opponent in a forward military posture, the destruction of deep targets must bring political conciliation from national leaders back home, which is not guaranteed. Even so, land forces must then seize and hold any lost terrain and likely contend with a resulting insurgency.

On the other hand, if hypersonic weapons were deployed against targets inside of an adversarial state's borders, assuming the strike was decisive or decapitating against the government, the nation deploying the weapons must account for the fallout.[45] With a weakened executive and gutted military, societal degradation, widespread lawlessness, humanitarian or refugee crises, and ultimately regime change via *coup d'etat* could ensue in the targeted state. Under such circumstances, the 'victorious' nation would wield little influence without a land force capable of establishing control and providing security for a requisite diplomatic mission. In other words, the hasty achievement of military objectives in this way could preclude the realization of political ones without sufficient prepositioning of human infrastructure prior to a strike. Influenced by Clausewitz's work, Liddell Hart characterized this fallacy as mistaking the military aim for the national object.⁴⁶ The revolutionary potential of these weapons is based also on the assumption that an opponent will lack countermeasures and that the targeting network for the missiles will remain uncompromised, neither of which is guaranteed.

When Alexander innovated, it was the result of a specific problem for which no solution existed, such as the creation of siege weapons, laying prone his forces to allow Thracian carts to pass over them, or adapting to guerilla warfare in Bactria. But today, innovation and exploration in the competitive space between states are driven by a dreadful fear of 'falling behind' between wars.⁴⁷ In this way, one nation is often pulled along by the other with its public statements and ongoing research pertaining to projected future war conditions. Soviet and U.S. officials made such declarations throughout the last century, which in many cases shaped the western RMA debate.⁴⁸ Now, Russian President Vladimir Putin and others do the same with AI.⁴⁹ The risks of RMA sensationalism are evident when considering the type of war a nation might fight in the future, and which specific capabilities might be required win it, is entirely unknowable. Treating future probabilities as scientifically measurable by using narrow data sets or exaggerating the permanence of recent trends is one of the fallacies associated with expert forecasting.⁵⁰

Nassim Nicholas Taleb encapsulated these phenomena best with his 'black swan' thesis examining the nature of human error and the 'depth and consequences' of highly improbable events. This presents unique and troubling challenges to defense planners as they run the risk of ushering into existence an RMA driven by billion-dollar technologies that are of little use in the next war. A lack of armoured regiment deployments to Afghanistan since 2001, landlocked states that are not vulnerable to maritime power projection, and the highly regulated application of airpower in dense urban areas throughout Iraq, Syria, and Africa come to mind as examples of such restrictions.⁵¹

A key symptom of RMA fervor is the need to cast each new conflict or military capability as a sort of operational crystal ball into the future, what is sometimes characterized as presentism or neophilia.⁵² Taleb describes these crystal balls as 'anchor events' in probabilistic theory and suggests they are relied upon far too heavily in probability analysis. Russia's 2022 invasion of Ukraine became an anchor event almost immediately, yet in the early 1990s, most defense experts agreed that the Gulf War portended a new RMA and may 'have provided a glimpse of a major transition to a different type of warfare heavily based on information processing and stealthy long-range precision strike weapons'.⁵³ Such thinking persisted into the war on terror and drove the invasion plans for Iraq and Afghanistan, as we later discuss. This crystal ball through which nations choose to view complex strategic problems is built from recent experiences and placed onto a supposedly linear timeline of warfare's progression.[54] But war is anything but linear.

Rorschach in Ramadi

When Hermann Rorschach created his now famous test in 1921, it consisted of five black-and-white and five color inkblots spattered onto cards in symmetrical shapes. They represented nothing and everything at the same time, a difference to be determined only by the mind of the patient. Despite Rorschach's passing the following year, his test became wildly popular in the mid-twentieth century but remained controversial due to its lack of standardized evaluation metrics.[55] The fundamental premise of the Rorschach Test is this: each inkblot serves as a projective psychological tool that reflects more about the subject than the contours of the blot. Each patient draws varied interpretations from the amorphous shapes based on his or her personal experiences, past traumas, and current interests. In other words, the patient sees what he or she wants to see. Interestingly, Rorschach's experience with schizophrenic patients who responded to blot tests in fascinating ways because of their inner identity crises is what sparked his research. In response to evolving threat environments, nations often enter a sort of schizophrenic flux as they wrestle with their military's operational and strategic identity. If there is a way to convey the complexity of modern security challenges and the way the western world reacts to them, Rorschach's inkblots are a good place to start.

The twenty-first century wars in Iraq and Afghanistan, and the security situation in the broader Middle East for that matter, emerged as inkblots in the offices of decision-makers the world over. Rather than seeing military operations there as a nonlinear response to the 'black swan' event of the 9/11 attacks, many interpreted them as profound indicators of the future. Circumstances gave birth to a maelstrom of semantic debates, evolving strategies, and proposed changes as diverse as the dozens of allied nations involved in operations there. Prior to the 2001 terrorist attacks on the United States, much of the western world was still sifting through the dust of its Cold War policies, and thus large-scale combat operations (LSCO) and interstate competition remained at the forefront of defense planning – particularly in the Pacific theater.[56] The first decade of the century turned this understanding on its head as nations discovered yet again how ill-prepared they were to fight an expeditionary counterinsurgency.[57] An urgent need to rectify this deficiency gave shape to the Middle East inkblot.

In 2005, the fight to secure Ramadi – the capital of Iraq's majorly Sunni Anbar Province, west of Fallujah and Baghdad – raged on. It was not until coalition forces began to harness their relationships in the city by empowering local sheiks to deputize their most trusted associates that the coalition saw progress. What transpired from 2006 to 2007 was arguably the greatest success story of Operation Iraqi Freedom (OIF), and perhaps the entire Global War on Terrorism. Through carefully nurtured relationships and the relentless targeting of insurgent forces, the city once considered lost to al-Qaeda became a beacon of prosperity for the region.[58] The story of the Anbar Awakening, as it came to be known, in which the Anbar Province 'awoke' to its need for self-governance, was interpreted as a case study for future joint operations and a road map for defense strategy.[59]

Many saw the convoluted wars in the Middle East and subsequent expansion of global terrorism as signposts of the future. In the process, the United States and many of its allies broadened their counterinsurgency abilities, special operations forces, and investments in technological augmentation of relatively small units in line with this thinking. Framing security needs within the context of 'today's wars' – in apparent juxtaposition to yesterday's wars – was commonplace.[60] The 2006 U.S. Quadrennial Defense Review laid bare such predictions, as did similar documents in the UK and Australia. The western world saw fit to discard existing military paradigms as antiquated by interpreting trends in Iraq and Afghanistan as windows into a future of 'asymmetric' challenges that demanded sweeping reformation.[61] Proposals included the reorganization of military command structures, divestment from large platforms such as aircraft carriers and tanks, and the restructuring of personnel to fight what amounted to a perpetual war on terror. The success with and heavy reliance upon special operations forces (SOF) in counterinsurgency and counterterrorism operations contributed to the prophetic interpretation of the Rorschach in Ramadi.[62] Some viewed it as symptomatic of a new strategic norm, while others saw it as indicative of an operational capability worth retaining but not necessarily critical to enduring strategic interests.[63]

The destruction of al-Qaeda in Iraq (AQI) and its leader, Ayman al-Zarqawi – who ran operations in Ramadi – eventually gave rise to the so-called Islamic State in 2011 after the United States ceased major combat operations in Iraq. AQI's spiritual transition from regional actor to international threat network with global reach and hyper-violent tendencies gave weight to the belief that the world was entering a new era of conflict that required smaller, more flexible expeditionary forces. As U.S. military commitment to overseas wars dwindled between presidential administrations in the years following Ramadi's awakening, Russia's 2014 annexation of

Crimea and its military occupation of eastern Ukraine eroded the legitimacy of small war theories. An increasing number of military leaders and theorists became less convinced that small teams of specialized soldiers, however well-integrated into a human–machine agenda, could be decisive against, for instance, a Chinese naval attack on Taiwan.[64]

Gen. Jim Mattis witnessed this intellectual revolution first-hand as a commander during the initial 2001 invasion of Afghanistan and the strategically ambivalent clearance of Fallujah, Iraq, in 2003 and 2004 (which we will address in later chapters). He remained particularly circumspect about the focus on counterinsurgency and the potential to develop strategic tunnel vision in relation to conventional state threats.[65] By the time President Donald Trump nominated him Secretary of Defense in 2017, Mattis' team began drafting the first National Defense Strategy (NDS) in nearly a decade, which published the following year. The document upended reigning defense theories by returning the Pentagon's focus on great power competition and LSCO against a peer threat, while still recognizing the need to pursue AI, autonomous capabilities, and cultivate top human talent.[66] For a world that had come to scoff at the concept of interstate conflict as Cold War thinking, the 2018 NDS sparked lively debate and served as a stark reminder that the free world had interests under assault outside of the Middle East, and from actors other than non-state extremists.[67]

A Reluctant Return to the Old Ways

This shift in strategy was based to a degree on what Michael O'Hanlon refers to as the Senkaku paradox, which describes how tensions over local geopolitical disputes with larger geopolitical undercurrents could trigger a global war.[68] Named after the Senkaku Islands off the Northeast coast of Taiwan, this paradox represents the potential for competition to escalate into military conflict between Japan and China over their shared interests in the region. More broadly, O'Hanlon's paradox also plays to the possibilities of a Russian incursion into the Baltics or Caucasus aimed at reestablishing its pre-1991 Warsaw Pact buffer zones, or an Iranian attack on Israel, each of which would likely trigger western military involvement, as evidenced by the avalanche of NATO aid to Ukraine triggered by Russia's 2022 invasion.[69] In any instance, by 2018, the western world began to officially shift its gaze away from the small wars of the Middle East and back onto presumably antiquated threats, such as Russia or China annexing territories they have coveted for decades.[70]

After a long and laborious exodus of western combat troops from their posts in Iraq and Afghanistan, in early 2020, armour units in Texas loaded tanks and artillery equipment onto railways and seafaring vessels to participate in one of the largest NATO exercises on mainland Europe since the Cold War. Known as DEFENDER-Europe 2020, the exercise was reminiscent of NATO's massive REFORGER exercises designed to deter Soviet aggression in West Germany decades prior.[71] The difference between then and now is found in a lack of clarity regarding the characteristics of the opponent. Rather than entering Europe with a mission to defend Germany against a known threat with rather transparent capabilities, NATO must now explore the complexities of cross-border mobility in major joint operations waged throughout the continent against multiple and varied threats, from kamikaze satellites that remove NATO's technological advantage to megacity warfare against irregular proxy forces that would strain its most capable platforms. In such instances, NATO could find itself fighting in an environment that has more in common with Alexander's campaigns than current future war prognosticators foretell. Precisely such a situation arose after Russia massed combat power and invaded Ukraine on 24 February 2022, which led to western sanctions on Moscow officials and NATO weapons' shipments to Kyiv that brought the world closer to nuclear war than at any point this century.[72]

The world is in an exceptionally fragile place, it seems, and the arc of military history is long and non-linear. Willful personalities rooted in deeply entrenched cultural and sociopolitical divides are converging in ways that are hard to predict and harder even to prepare for. Challenges to global security have rarely appeared in the form that nations envision, and triumphing over those challenges has been primarily a conceptual and intellectual endeavor driven by human personalities.[73] Yet for all the progress since the time of Alexander, human beings today remain as subject to compromise and confirmation bias as any king of antiquity.

In an information environment where war is broadcast in near real time and disinformation sometimes outweighs truth, algorithmic reporting systems aim to drudge through massive troves of data and make them sensible to the human mind. By 2025, the world is expected to be home to more than 50 billion devices capable of connecting to a wireless signal.[74] Everything from refrigerators to watches can not only collect, store, and transmit information but also communicate with other wireless devices for various purposes. Each of these sensors is ripe for exploitation in a war footing, which contributes to the understanding that future battlefields will be increasingly difficult to control not because of a lack of information, but because of a surplus. Hardening space assets that provide command and control infrastructure to the world's militaries will be a key priority in the search for greater control. Though critical, these initiatives still address war's character only;

the tools, techniques, and resources required to find and destroy targets more remotely and more completely, to manoeuvre forces more rapidly and more safely, and to acquire, protect, and distribute critical information and intelligence to key decision-makers. But the political nature of war and its causal factors remain as challenging as they are unchanging.

Militaries now possess weapons that can be launched from thousands of feet in the sky and strike a single human target without collateral damage; they are developing unmanned tanks, aerial vehicles, and even submarines; they are experimenting with cybernetic and genetic performance-enhancing projects; they are investing aggressively in artificially intelligent programs; and they are doing this with a sense of breathless urgency.[75] If leaders become captivated by the potential of these tools to solve their problems, then the likelihood increases that they will favor such systems as the most viable solutions to every emerging threat. Subsequently, the employment of or investment in additional instruments of national power could be sidelined in favor of quick wins promised by exquisite military capabilities.[76]

New Weapons, Same Leadership Challenges

The above developments place most militaries in a precarious position that is as rich with potential as it is risky. Armed forces must engage in rapid 'transformational change' while at the same time prioritizing the human element to attract, train, and retain the highest quality leaders. Such leaders must be capable of harnessing these technologies in the rigors of combat while making decisions that support human interests.[77] Amid all this change, there are those qualities identified earlier by Michael Howard that permeate the nature of any struggle: moral courage, foresight, loyalty, and an ever-present range of personality traits and emotions that orbit human faction and define the relationships therein. This was as true in Ramadi and Afghanistan with drones and laser-guided bombs as it was for Alexander who fought with sword and shield. In the words of French war hero Lt. Col. Ralph Monclar, it is 'almost impossible for a unit with high morale and cohesion to perform poorly in combat'.[78] Inversely, it is quite easy for a well-equipped and well-trained unit shackled by toxic leaders to perform poorly. These are the currents of history that have most often shaped the political and military landscape, but mankind has displayed a remarkable penchant for zeroing in on paradigm-shattering technological or organizational revolutions in its efforts to place history in context. If nations lose sight of the importance of the human relationships behind their machinery, and those relationships become the price paid for increased mechanical efficiency, they risk disaster.

New ways of warfare have not equaled new realities at war – it is still a brutal and often personal affair defined by state-sanctioned violence between humans. There is no guarantee that faddish concepts or weapons will survive the next decade, much less the next generation. This is not reassuring, considering the cruel nature of war's history. Continuity, however, does have redeeming qualities. If the future is likely to preserve remnants of the past, then the study of the latter – and especially the values and principles of leadership – may help illuminate a more appropriate path to the former. Learning from the triumphs and misfortunes of those who came before us, each fraught with human emotion and reason, can serve as a window into modern decision-making as well as a humbling framework that helps us recognize how little we have changed as a species.

Strong arguments do not exist for the irrelevance of technological revolutions. Yet if there is any credence to the understanding that war is the ultimate auditor of strategic assumptions, then the last several decades are particularly problematic for technocratic visions that see algorithms and airframes as the main rudders in the great stream of time.[79] There are promising indicators that leading thinkers in the military and technology fields are keen to avoid the RMA fanaticism of the past.[80] But awareness does not eliminate the risk of a runaway tech binge induced by the promises of efficiency that accompany advanced technologies. Balancing this array of new capabilities with the human skill and strategic wisdom necessary to synthesize them in an interconnected world will be the metric by which war and peace are measured in the coming century.

Every military leader has dealt with change, new weapons, and novel tactics. Alexander was certainly no exception. The question then becomes, what kind of leadership does the modern world demand, and is it so different from demands of the past? John W. Gardner wrote that motivation, values, and social cohesion are the bedrock issues behind most leadership challenges.[81] If true, when the systems and tools of any organization come to define its culture, humans will suffer, and the quality of leadership follows suit.[82] Some military leaders have recently criticized Thomas Carlyle's 'Great Man Theory', but it is not without merit.[83] Alexander's army was often inferior in numbers to his enemy, but his presence on the battlefield and his relationship with his soldiers spurred on his men like no other commander. Numerical superiority was therefore indecisive in battle against him. His soldiers believed they were led by the best, and their herculean efforts reflected this collective faith. Is this still true today?

President Volodymyr Zelensky of Ukraine seemed to occupy this space after Russia's 2022 invasion. His courage and tenacious physical presence in the face of a larger and more capable nuclear power made him a legend in his own right.⁸⁴ Many have since attributed Ukraine's shocking rout of the Russian Army that year at least in part to Zelensky's leadership. That said, some of the most profound lessons we can extract from Alexander's story may be those of a cautionary nature concerning human flaws that we should seek not to emulate, but rather to avoid. In a brave new world of machine wars, châteaux leadership, and endemic risk aversion, what can we glean from a king who met the eyes of his enemies in battle and always placed himself at the decisive point of friction, thereby assuming the greatest risk? The following chapters explore these questions and contribute to the unavoidable conclusion that our new world might not be so new, and as with any generation, great reward often demands the assumption of great personal and professional risk from its leaders. In ancient Macedonia, this was a way of life.

Notes

1. RAND scientist John Arquilla declared in 1993 that 'Cyberwar is Coming!', but thirty years later it is still a supporting function of war's ugliest continuities. The two sides of this argument are represented well here: in favor of cyberwar is Stiennon 2015; against it is Rid 2013, who was not alone in his skepticism; see also Lonsdale 2004.
2. Clausewitz 1976, 2.6 (pp. 203–204).
3. U.S. defense contractor Raytheon, for instance, has mounted directed energy weapons known as HEL (high energy lasers) on AH-64 Apache gunships; Clausewitz refers to the history of antiquity as 'the most useless and the barest of all [histories]', and though he admits this ruling is not 'absolute', he believed allusions to such history must 'be looked upon as sheer decoration, designed to cover gaps and blemishes' (Clausewitz 1976, 2.6 [p. 204]).
4. Clausewitz 1976, 3.3 (p. 217).
5. Rice 2011, pp. 90–91; for more on this see Chapters 8 and 12.
6. Howard 1991, p. 189.
7. Howard 1991, p. 189.
8. Howard 1991, pp. 199–200.
9. Holmes 2016.
10. O'Hanlon 1998.
11. Fukuyama's article-turned book is cited far more often than it is understood, considering he left open the possibility for the world to descend into chaos. Nevertheless, *The End of History* is generally viewed as an optimistic thesis that assumed world leaders and their societies would inevitably liberalize after the fall of the Soviet Union. Fukuyama 1992.
12. Wright 2006 for perhaps the most comprehensive history of how these attacks came to be; see also Coll 2004. For a deeper look into the roots of al-Qaeda's ideology, see Qutb 2002; Calvert 2010; Kennedy 2016; Maher 2016.
13. Mattis 2018.
14. Murray 1997b; Freedman 2013, pp. 215–220; For a take on Canada's RMA, see Sloan 2002.

15 Particularly regarding Michael Roberts' analysis of Swedish officer Gustavus Adolphus in Knox and Murray 2001, pp. 1–3.
16 Further reading on RMA can be found in professional western military journals, such as *Joint Force Quarterly*, *Parameters*, *Military Review*, and the U.S. Naval Institute's *Proceedings*, but also in Congressional Research Service reports and Congressional hearings in the 1990s.
17 For *levée en masse* and *blitzkrieg*, see Chandler 1966; Horne 1969; Frieser 2005; Liddell Hart 1954, pp. 5–6, follows Alexander to create an 'indirect approach'; *Blitzkrieg* was essentially the modern adaptation of Alexander's tactics with the companion cavalry, as was Napoleon's strategical penetration. See Guderian 1996, pp. 20, 295.
18 Colin Gray, Hew Strachan, Michael Howard, H. R. McMaster, and Williamson Murray each views strategy and war through such a human lens. French theorist and military officer Col. Ardant du Picq crystallizes the nature of war as depicted in these pages: moral and unchanging. Ardant du Picq 2017, p. 33, 57–58.
19 Clausewitz 1976, 1.1.1–2, 1.1.11–12, 1.1.26–28, 1.2.
20 Meiser 2016, pp. 81–89; Cavanaugh 2017.
21 Examples of such claims include how the invention of gunpowder, the Maxim machine gun, ballistic missiles, or nuclear weapons could eliminate war, or how the rise of precision munitions would make war more rapid and decisive. Now, some see AI and the international order making war less costly, less likely, or even post-human: Coker 2002; McMaster 2015, pp. 12–15, identified 'four fallacies of future war' in 2015, each of which remains prevalent in futurist literature.
22 Murray and Millett 1996, pp. 372–376, assessed that RMA take at least a decade if not two, and are dependent upon numerous factors, from sound doctrine that guides tactical integration to cabinet-level advocacy.
23 Murray 1997b, p. 70.
24 Rothenberg 1986, pp. 32–63.
25 Singer 2009, p. 182; Freedman 2013, p. 215, surmised in 2013 that on the surface, RMA appear to be technologically driven.
26 As explained in Chapter 8, quite the opposite occurred: Freedman 2013, pp. 216–217; Murray 1997a.
27 Kaplan 2002, p. 155.
28 Brose 2019.
29 See, for instance, Harari 2017, pp. 309–355; Scharre 2018. Harari argues that technological advancements will create a 'useless' class of 'superfluous' humans, which, on its face, has frightening implications. Harari's take on data religion as a means of passing the torch from the outdated human to his better version is a rather cold humanist perspective. But humans might not go so quietly into the night. Simply because machines exist that can 'do things better' does not mean the leaders of civilization will or should favor them. The mutinies against Alexander in 326 and 324 are particularly relevant in this context.
30 Wong, et al. 2020, pp. x–xiii, 69–83.
31 McMaster 2015, pp. 6–19.
32 Military leaders in the United States and United Kingdom, as well as several NATO studies, have highlighted the risk of fighting wars without access to critical technology. Such studies resulted in recommendations that armies

train to work in technologically degraded environments. Probably the most sobering modern account of a military unprepared to fight a brutal ground war is Fehrenbach 1963 (the Korean War).
33 Schneaubelt 2007, pp. 95–107.
34 Puckett 2007, p. 33.
35 Bird and Sherwin 2005, p. 292.
36 Freedman 1986, pp. 735–778; Carver 1986, p. 779.
37 O'Hanlon describes how this transparent battlefield never came to pass, and 'the laws of physics continued to limit what sensors could accomplish' in complex terrain: O'Hanlon 2015, p. 19; see also Freedman 2013, pp. 214–236.
38 The operations that targeted Osama bin Laden and Abu Bakr al Baghdadi were both products of intricate and carefully woven human intelligence networks: Warrick, Nakashina, and Lamonthe 2019. McChrystal, who led the shadow war against AQI from 2004 to 2007, admitted that organizational, conceptual, and creative developments were as critical to fighting AQI as any technological advantage: McChrystal 2015, p. 18.
39 The term is a nod to the World War I generals who established their headquarters in a châteaux and issued their orders far from the fields of battle: Keegan 1987, p. 316.
40 Gen. Franks, Gen. Mattis, and even Secretary of Defense Robert Gates all described challenges with evolving and convoluted guidance from Washington. Though he had immense respect for both presidents under which he served, Gates expressed deep frustration with the 3,000-mile screwdriver. In his memoirs he wrote that by 2010, the Obama White House and National Security Staff 'took micromanagement and operational meddling to a new level', becoming an 'operational body with its own policy agenda': Gates 2014, pp. 482, 587.
41 Garthoff 1996, p. 108.
42 It is worth noting that in 1954, Liddell Hart warned of an overreliance on nuclear power leading to a divestment in other instruments of power (Liddell Hart 1954, pp. xviii–xix). While there will certainly be battles in air and at sea, no government's helm of power rests in those domains, nor do their constituencies live there.
43 Burke and Wright 2022.
44 The U.S. Navy announced that its Virginia class submarines would test these missiles by 2028, while both Russia and China have introduced hypersonic missiles of varying capability and integrity: Sanger and Broad 2021.
45 In May 2022, testimony from a senior U.S. defense official suggested that Russia's most advanced missile systems are not operating effectively in Ukraine: Grady 2022.
46 Liddell Hart 1954, pp. 338–352.
47 This is not new: see Freedman 1986, p. 738. NSC-68, the 2017 U.S. National Security Strategy, and 2018 National Defense Strategy frame an urgent need to keep up with the arms race involving weaponized technologies and AI. David Johnson found that civilian intervention and service culture are some of the most prominent factors driving military change, neither of which are optimal. Johnson, D. E. 1998, pp. 12–15, p. 92.
48 U.S. officials repeatedly justified further nuclear weapons' research and development under the auspices of a need to stay ahead of Russia's programs: see Bird and Sherwin 2005, pp. 293–295.

49 Associated Press 2017. A lengthy 2022 report from the Special Competitive Studies Project also underscores the nature of challenges the United States must win, one being AI: Schmidt, et al. 2022.
50 Taleb 2010, pp. 332, 341–343; see also Barnes 2022.
51 The first U.S. tanks arrived in Afghanistan in 2010, nearly a decade after the war started. It was a mere company of sixteen tanks in the southwest: Chandrasekaran 2010; Byman 2016.
52 Barnes 2022.
53 Fitzsimonds and Van Tol 1994, p. 27. Allison 2012, p. 158, credits Andrew Bacevich with describing a sort of technological utopianism that emerged after the Gulf War's rapid military successes.
54 One study examines trends in applied history and the philosophy of history, in one part, analysing how George W. Bush believed 'liberty is the direction of history', and it was incumbent upon the United States to use military force to move that history forward: Ehrhardt 2022, pp. 11–32.
55 Searls 2017.
56 Prior to the September 2001 attacks, the George W. Bush Administration focused on issues such as the Kyoto Protocol and Hainan Island crisis in the far east. In the Middle East, tensions between Palestine and Israel dominated the security agenda. Counter-terrorism adviser to the National Security Council Dick Clarke later mentioned how hard it was to get the council's attention regarding the threat posed by al-Qaeda: see Wright 2006, pp. 334–335; Rice 2011, pp. 41–50.
57 For more on expeditionary warfare and counterinsurgency, see Chapter 12. For reading on how poorly prepared nations have been to go abroad and fight such wars, see Birtle 2007; Oren 2007; McFate, M. 2018.
58 Smith and MacFarland 2008, pp. 41–52; Kagan 2009.
59 Phillips 2009, pp. 27–46; Kolenda 2021, pp. 111–113, 215–217.
60 Commentary regarding what is needed in today's wars fills countless reports and professional journals, mostly referring to a heightened focus on competition or the 'gray zone': see Hybrid Conflict Project 2022.
61 The 2006 Quadrennial Defense Review emphasized a shift in focus from major conventional combat operations to multiple irregular, asymmetrical operations: Quadrennial Defense Review 2006.
62 See for instance, Burgos 2018, pp. 109–128; Haynes 2019.
63 Pentagon advisor John Arquilla considered large, conventional weapons systems wrong for modern battle in 2006: Pontin 2006.
64 Despite Russia's abysmal performance in Ukraine circa 2022, the Neptune missiles that sunk the Russian Moskva ship on 14 April 2022 were not tools built for counterinsurgency, which suggests that the ability of standing armies to employ large weapons is still a critical factor in war.
65 Mattis was wary of the overwhelming focus on counterinsurgency, or COIN, in U.S. doctrine and training methodology at the time: Mattis and West 2019, pp. 155–157.
66 Mattis 2018, Section 7.
67 President Barrack Obama and former Secretary of State John Kerry, for instance, both mocked the claim that Russia was a major geopolitical threat in 2012, a mere two years before Vladimir Putin annexed Crimea: Calvan 2012.
68 O'Hanlon 2019.

54 *The Environment*

69 Gronholt-Pedersen 2022.
70 Some Russian leaders still doubt the sovereignty of the Baltics and Caucasus, just as Beijing has never recognized Taiwan as an independent country (Baptista and Kasolowsky 2022; Kolodyazhnyy, Balmforth, and Trevelyan 2022).
71 The outbreak of a novel coronavirus forced NATO to modify the exercise, but it was still the third largest military exercise in Europe since the Cold War: Williams, T. 2020.
72 In response to Russia's veiled nuclear threats, France's foreign minister reminded Putin that NATO, too, is a nuclear power. A mere five days into Russia's invasion, Putin put his nuclear forces on alert: Roth, et al. 2022.
73 Robert Gates famously wrote that the United States' record of predicting where and how it will fight next is perfect because it 'has never once gotten it right': Gates 2014, p. 590; What would the Marshall Plan be without George Kennan, and what could be said of French counterinsurgency without the minds of Charles de Gaulle and David Galula?
74 Johnson, R. 2019.
75 The U.S. Navy invested $2.7 billion in ten large, unmanned surface vessels over the five-year period from 2019 to 2025 as part of a larger plan to purchase various unmanned vehicles for numerous domains: Eckstein 2019.
76 National Intelligence Council of the United States 2021, pp. 1–12.
77 U.K. Secretary of State for Defence Ben Wallace described the complexity and potential of emerging technologies in his country's Defence Artificial Intelligence Strategy: Wallace 2022, p. 1. See also the U.S. and Australian defence strategies: Burr 2020, pp. 17–18, 22; Austin 2022.
78 One of France's most decorated war heroes of the twentieth century, Lt. Gen. Ralph Monclar, reduced himself in rank to Lt. Col. to lead a French battalion in the Korean War. His full name was Raoul Charles Magrin-Vernerey. Hamburger 2003, p. 70.
79 Gray 2015; Gaddis 2018.
80 Western military leaders, strategists, military historians, as well as futurists such as Peter Singer, August Cole, and Paul Scharre, have all commented on the importance of avoiding RMA fanaticism that relies too heavily on new technologies.
81 Gardner 1990, p. xiii.
82 Creative and innovative companies struggle with this challenge and go to great lengths to find ways to prioritize the employee rather than the software: see, for instance, Catmull 2014.
83 The thesis of Gen. Stanley McChrystal's book *'Leaders'*, for instance, is a counternarrative to Carlyle's theory.
84 When offered options for extraction by the United States, Zelensky supposedly replied, 'I need ammunition, not a ride': Wall Street Journal Editorial Board 2022.

Part II
Military Organization and Structure

Here, we describe the organization, structure, and innovation of Alexander's army and juxtapose that history with the way modern governments have gone and are going about technological, organizational, and structural changes within their defense and security institutions. Part of this analysis focuses on PME and what military educators might learn from Alexander. We then highlight Alexander's gift for prioritizing engagements and fighting on his terms by exploiting his existing strengths, rather than trying to meet those of his opponents. We contend that this targeted approach might be a better model for governments to emulate, as opposed to attempting to master every domain, weapon, or operational concept, especially considering the breadth of options available today.

3 The Macedonian Army and Greek Warfare

The Macedonian army that Philip II brought into being became the most successful of antiquity before it was finally overcome by the Roman legions at the battle of Cynoscephalae in Thessaly in 197.[1] Given its woeful condition before Philip's reforms, few could have predicted the army's longevity and success, especially under Alexander. He fought epic battles and sieges from modern Turkey to Pakistan, always victorious over higher enemy numbers, and, if we believe our sources, he suffered fewer casualties than his foes.[2] Technological innovation and different types of training proved more than a match for Greek, Persian, and Indian armies. Yet the army had a fatal flaw, which kings either did not recognize or disregarded, and which enabled the Romans to bring its enviable history to an end. That serves as a salutary warning today against blind trust or complacency in any military system considered 'state of the art'.

The Earlier Army

Information on the Macedonian army prior to Philip's reforms is sparse, but it appears that it was only the cavalry that mattered and that infantry was inferior.[3] Thucydides, for example, relates that the cavalry was its only arm and infantry was not needed against invaders, perhaps explaining why in the era of the Persian Wars Alexander I (r. 498–454) sent only cavalry to support the Persians at the battle of Plataea in 479.[4] Yet according to Thucydides, Archelaus (r. 413–399), a particularly energetic ruler, provided new arms and armour for the cavalry and introduced some reforms for the hoplites.[5]

Possibly Macedonian kings thought it was better to hire mercenaries – we are told that during the reign of Perdiccas II (448–413), the infantry consisted of some Greeks but mostly 'barbarians', who were most probably mercenaries.[6] But mercenaries were not the 'dogs of war' operating covertly or at least on the periphery of conflict as today. In ancient Greece, mercenary service was respected work; the men were highly trained, and they were not cheap to hire. How, then, could Macedonian kings pay them? Macedonia was rich in natural resources, but these were not properly exploited until Philip's reign, hence kings had little liquid capital and practiced a 'rolling economy', funding their next campaigns from the proceeds of the previous one.

More plausible is that infantry in the earlier army were conscripts, probably ordinary farmers called up from their fields as needed, probably with next to no advance warning, and with little in the way of training and arms; hence they received little attention in the sources. The existence of infantry is supported by a unit that may have existed prior to Philip II's reforms called the *pezhetairoi* or foot companions. The historian and orator Anaximenes attributes their introduction to an 'Alexander', but it is unknown to which Alexander he refers as his account is fragmented.[7] It is surely not Alexander the Great, given that Arrian implies they had been part of the army for a while, which leaves either Alexander I or II.[8] Alexander II had a very short a reign (370–368), which leaves Alexander I. Later, some *pezhetairoi* became a form of 'special forces' known as the hypaspists (see later), but, by Alexander's time, *pezhetairoi* referred to the infantry overall.

When Thucydides says that only the cavalry was needed against invaders, he could mean that they were trained and did a better job than the infantry. The cavalrymen were from the noble and wealthy strata of society as they had to pay for their own horses and may also have had to pay for their own armour – helmet, greaves, a sword, spear, and a cloak (*chlamys*) – at least before Archelaus' reforms.[9] Their high social status is confirmed by them being known simply as *hetairoi* or companions of the king as they socialized with him at symposia and when hunting.[10] Presumably these wealthy men had leisure time to undertake some formal training, unlike farmers who were levied on an *ad hoc* basis, which perhaps explains why someone like Archelaus may not have wished to spend money on arms and armour for them.

It was this motley collection of troops that Philip II found himself commanding when he became king in 359. His challenge was not simply to replenish the 4,000 men who had just died fighting the Illyrians but also to protect his kingdom's borders more effectively than before by fashioning an army that was both defensive and offensive, and thereby as skilled in attrition as manoeuvre. Unlike today, where nations tend to have one type or another – thus Russia, with its vast, porous borders and history of being invaded, has built a primarily defensive army, whereas the United States or Australia, surrounded by at least an ocean, has developed largely offensive forces – Macedonia needed both types. In other words, for border security

Philip needed to defeat enemy peoples like the Illyrians and Paeonians: his first campaigns achieved that. It was only later, perhaps upon realizing the potential of a defensive and offensive army, that his ambition turned to expanding Macedonia's influence in the Greek world by a combination of force and diplomacy.

A New Army

At age thirteen, Philip was sent as a hostage to the city of Thebes in Boeotia under the terms of a pact between it and his brother Alexander II. He spent two years there, which likely influenced him more than we might think when it came to military innovation.[11] Among other things, he saw firsthand that any city with the right combination of military power and leadership could dominate affairs – and from 371 to 362, Thebes exercised hegemony over Greece. He met in Thebes two of the most influential generals of the time, Epaminondas and Pelopidas, and he watched the daily training of the famed 300-strong Sacred Band, the crack infantry corps of 150 pairs of lovers, selected so that each man fought all the more ferociously to protect his mate. Philip and Alexander held bravery in the highest esteem. Thus, when Philip walked the battlefield of Chaeronea in 338 and came across the corpses of the Sacred Band, who fought to the last man, he burst into tears and ordered the Thebans to build a lion monument to honour their bravery.[12] This war memorial, albeit restored, still stands on the battlefield.

As soon as Philip became king in 359, Diodorus claims that he enacted his military reforms.[13] They would continue throughout his reign.[14] He was not a supporter of the standard Greek hoplite style of fighting, where the infantry of both sides marched neatly against each other at a brisk pace and on a prearranged signal broke into a charge. As one line smashed into the other, any neat formation was abandoned as the soldiers likely pushed and shoved (known as the *othismos* or 'push') and engaged in brutal hand to hand fighting, while the cavalry bore down on the flanks to trap the enemy between two offensive lines.[15]

Instead, Philip wanted something that would demoralize and trap an enemy from the outset and lead to a total rout with minimal casualties on his side. To this end, and in a reversal of Greek hoplite tactics, he trained his cavalry to attack an enemy in a powerful opening salvo, followed by the infantry, a shock and awe tactic that was devastating. The cavalry thus penetrated an enemy line with its own *othismos* (the crowd control exercised by today's mounted police is a less aggressive form), wheeling around it before the mass infantry came into play, thereby trapping the enemy between two offensive lines. Bold and novel, Greek armies never caught on to it, relying on their traditional style of fighting with disastrous consequences.

Philip arranged his cavalry in squadrons (*ilai*) of about 200 men, trained to charge the enemy line in a new, wedge-shaped formation (like the Thracians and Scythians), with the riders slashing and stabbing with their spears and short swords from on high before the onslaught of the infantry phalanx. He may also have created the fast, mounted cavalry scouts (*prodromoi*) that Alexander relied on so heavily in Asia.[16] A separate unit was the *sarissophoroi* or sarissa-bearers, the sarissa being a long infantry weapon twenty-four-feet (7.4 metres) long, which needed both hands to wield it, which is discussed below.[17] It is difficult to accept that horse riders carried this long weapon so there may well have been a shorter cavalry sarissa requiring only one hand, though under Alexander the main cavalry weapon was the lance (*xyston*).[18]

Backing up the Macedonian cavalry was that of the Thessalians, which time and again proved vital in Philip's and Alexander's victories; although they were organized like the Macedonian cavalry into regional *ilai*, their commander was always a Macedonian. New armour was introduced, with the 'heavy' cavalrymen wearing a metal helmet, cuirass, and greaves, and carrying a round shield, spear, and sword, while the 'light' cavalrymen had lighter armour and fought in a more open formation. They threw javelins or fired arrows before engaging the enemy at close quarters with their swords like their 'heavy' comrades.[19]

Philip knew that conscript infantry, especially if they were untrained farmers, would be the weak link in his army as well as detrimentally impacting the economy. When the farmers were away on campaign, likely taking their plough oxen and wagons with them, their farms and crops must have suffered greatly, and if some of these men were killed on campaign, who would farm their lands then? The king needed to keep these men on the land while still deploying at a moment's notice a fully trained infantry corps to complement his cavalry. That was why with the infantry he likely started afresh, in the process creating a skilled, full-time army. The contrast to Greek cities like Athens, which could not afford the upkeep of a permanent army and whose citizens had an apparent apathy to personal service, was as marked as that of today's professional volunteer armies in relation to an enemy's conscripted forces.[20]

Philip organized his infantry into a phalanx line of varying depth, anything from eight to thirty-two men deep, though sixteen was often the norm, composed of different units often with specific functions.[21] These were divided into six *taxeis* (battalions), each of 1,500 men, under a complex command structure.[22] There was also a unit called the *pezhetairoi* or 'foot companions', who were lighter-armed and marched at faster speeds, and at times the term is used of the entire phalanx line. Another unit was the hypaspists or 'shield bearers', perhaps introduced towards the end of Philip's reign from the best of the *pezhetairoi*, who were akin to 'special forces'.[23] The hypaspists were always seen as especially important and their numbers were never allowed to decline, even if that meant taking men from other parts of the phalanx. They also formed a 1,000-strong royal bodyguard (*agema*) flanking the king when he fought on foot (just as the royal cavalry squadron protected him when he fought on horseback).[24] From them he personally chose his seven *somatophylakes* (bodyguards), who became part of the senior staff. They always attended the king and were armed, even at symposia when other attendees surrendered their weapons.

The phalanx infantrymen were called phalangites and were recruited from the different regions of Macedonia.[25] They were supported by lighter-armed troops or peltasts, who carried a crescent-shaped shied or *pelte* (hence their name) and had the vital role of preventing enemy cavalry and infantry attacking the phalanx's flanks or rear. Included among them would be specialist light troops from outside Macedonia, such as Agrianian and Thracian javelin men, Paeonian scouts, and Scythian and Cretan archers; of these, Alexander relied on the Agrianians the most in both battles and enforced marches, and he had roughly 1,000 of them.[26] All of these different units came together as the Macedonian infantry corps, just as today most infantry forces are divided into light, mechanized, heavy, and airborne categories, each with different capabilities but ultimately all part of the infantry branch.

Philip had noted that the regular Greek hoplite was encumbered by his panoply of a bronze cuirass, greaves, a bronze helmet with narrow visor (allowing only limited vision), and a round, heavy shield (*hoplon*). He therefore gave his 'heavy' infantry lighter armour than their foes – a cuirass, greaves, a small shield carried over one shoulder, a short sword, and a more lightweight iron open-faced hoplite-style helmet, which provided better all-round vision than the Greek hoplite one.[27]

Perhaps most fearsome was a new weapon, the *sarissa* (a Macedonian dialect word meaning 'hafted weapon'), which was likely made of cornel wood. At one end was a narrow razor-sharp blade and at the other a sharpened spike. The second-century Greek historian Polybius tells us that it was originally sixteen cubits (twenty-four feet or 7.4 metres) long, but by his time it was fourteen cubits (twenty-one feet or 6.45 metres).[28] Its length and weight (roughly fourteen pounds) meant that both hands were required to wield it (hence why the shield was carried on the shoulder) and it was carried in two parts and joined in the middle for action.

The infantrymen approached an enemy line carrying these weapons upright (in 'close order' or *pyknosis*) so as not to impede any turning manoeuvres; the first three ranks of the phalanx then lowered their weapons to charge, their comrades in the fourth and fifth lines brought their sarissas down but not straight, and the remaining men kept theirs upright until needed and to deflect missiles (Figure 3.1).[29] Since the sarissa projected about ten cubits (eighteen feet or 5.6 metres) in front of each soldier, enemy combatants could not reach the Macedonian soldiers before being impaled by the deadly blade. Faced with this new and intimidating sight, the psychological effect on enemy combatants must have been tremendous.

Training was essential on a regular, fulltime basis, something that farmers could not commit to doing, so Philip made his army a career and a home for his troops, providing pay, a promotion pathway, and arms and armour (although the wealthy cavalrymen still had to pay for their own horses).[30] All rates of pay are unknown, although a hypaspist was paid one drachma a day by the end of Philip's reign, which was higher than a Greek hoplite soldier who was paid five obols daily (a drachma was the equivalent of six obols) and a cavalryman was paid three drachmas.[31] In addition, Philip awarded cash bonuses and grants of land in conquered territories for feats of exceptional valour or other types of service including longevity in position.[32] Suddenly, here was a chance for men to enter into a guaranteed fulltime job, to work their way up through the ranks, and to be paid appropriately.

The men earned their pay though. Philip expected his cavalry and infantry to work seamlessly together. He was demanding in his expectations and quick to punish those who lacked discipline or were derelict in their duty by making them remain on guard in full armour or flogging and even

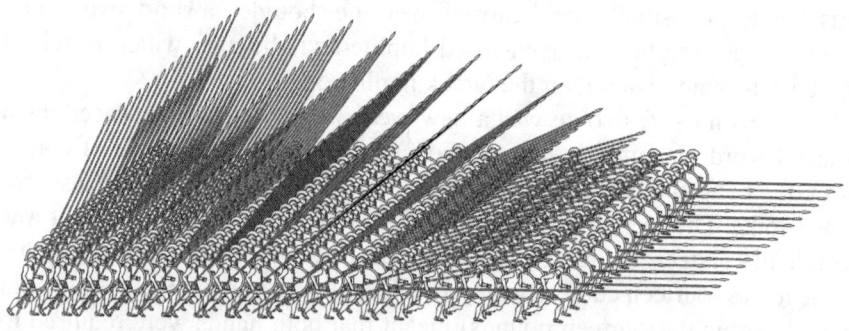

Figure 3.1 Macedonian Phalanx Formation carrying sarissas. Credit: Erin Babnik/Alamy Stock Photo.

executing them.³³ The training was arduous to say the least.³⁴ Philip took his men on forced marches of 300 stades (roughly thirty miles) over all manner of terrain, from plains to high mountain passes, carrying all their equipment and rations so they learned to be self-sufficient.³⁵ He also taught his men to forage for provisions and trained them to fight in any season, in contrast to Greek armies which tended not to operate in winter and preferred engagements in spring since the bulk of hoplite soldiers were farmers.³⁶ The Macedonian army thus became an all-weather outfit trained to operate in any condition – perfect for waging war in uncharted lands far from one's borders

We learn about aspects of training from a campaign that Alexander waged in Illyria in 335, the year after he became king. When he was trapped between two enemy Illyrian tribes, he decided a distraction was needed so he could surprise them. Accordingly, he ordered his men to perform a series of military drills.³⁷ First, he arranged his phalanx into a single block 120 ranks deep with cavalry squadrons of 200 or so on either side of it. Then he ordered his men to march back and forth with their sarissas up, lowered as if readying for an assault, and then pointing to the right and left before forming into a standard wedge formation. Everything was done in silence apart from directional commands. The Illyrians crept forward, arguably fascinated by the Macedonians' disciplined drills, but suddenly Alexander gave a prearranged signal. His men immediately turned to face the enemy, clashed their swords against their armour, and at the tops of their voices roared out their battle cry *Alalalalai*! The enemy turned tail and fled.

To make the army even more self-sufficient the 'hangers-on' that normally accompanied Greek and Persian armies, from wives and families to various attendants and prostitutes, were banned from travelling with the troops. Instead (and in contrast to a modern army that must operate at times without sophisticated infrastructure and even maintenance support) Philip had his army accompanied by a plethora of logistical and supply personnel, including surveyors, road builders, rivercraft builders, doctors, siegecraft designers and builders, and repairers of arms and armour.³⁸ All of these would be the equivalent of a modern army traveling with, and in command of, Amazon distribution services, the Raytheon Corporation, and leading architects.

But there was a weakness. For the phalanx to operate with maximum efficiency and deadly effect, its long line needed space and especially level ground. As Polybius remarked, it was difficult to find a large flat battlefield, free of ditches, ravines, depressions, ridges, and river beds in Greece.³⁹ Once the line was disrupted by uneven ground, movement became limited because of the long forward-pointing sarissas and unity was lost while a side-on attack was most dangerous. Although the phalanx line was disrupted at Alexander's battles at Issus and Gaugamela, it was not overcome. However, the Roman legionaries who attacked Philip V's phalanx from the side at Cynoscephalae in 179 and Perseus' phalanx at Pydna in 168 decimated it in hand-to-hand fighting. Their long swords and tall oblong shields were far superior to the phalangites' small daggers and light shields.[40]

Philip II presumably recognized the danger to his phalanx's sides as his peltasts were meant to protect them. But as the Macedonian army appeared unstoppable, later kings seem to have grown complacent about its successful track record or felt they did not need to keep pace with Rome's revolutions in warfare. Philip V and Perseus realized the error of this too late.

Philip's military reforms continued throughout his reign, perhaps influenced by the conflicts he found himself in at various times and a need to counter future threats. Thus in about 350, he formed an engineering *corps*, headed by Polyidus of Thessaly, who was designing new siege machinery.[41] Among this technology was the torsion catapult, which was akin to a spring-loaded crossbow that fired arrows further and faster than the traditional mechanically drawn catapult.[42] Philip first used the torsion catapult at his siege of Byzantium in 340, and the weapon enabled Alexander to take many walled cities and force others into capitulation. In fact, two of Polyidus' students, Diades and Charias, accompanied Alexander on his campaigns.

Also ongoing was Philip's integration of specialist troops from the areas he conquered. For example, after his campaigns in Illyria in 358, Agrianian javelin men (who lived in the Upper Strymon region, south of Sofia) joined his ranks, providing a unit that Alexander used often when facing tough challenges. Also joining the army were Thracian javelin men and Scythian archers after his conquest of Thrace in 342–341, along with infantry units called the *asthetairoi*, perhaps from Upper Macedonia, although Alexander may have formed them in 334 or 333.[43]

Maintaining the loyalty of men from different tribes and peoples, especially as no one likes to be conquered, was something Philip took seriously. To this end, he deliberately kept previous foes in their own territorial divisions, encouraged fierce competition between the units, and promoted outstanding commanders to his senior staff.[44] Possibly another means of ensuring passivity was the school of Royal Pages (*basilikoi paides*), which Philip may have created based on Persian practice.[45] The pages were young boys (possibly as many as 200) from prominent families who lived at court from fourteen to eighteen years of age and received a military training. In effect, they were being trained as the next generation of military leaders, and in their final year, they accompanied the king on campaign as his personal attendants. But this system was hardly a Classical forerunner of enrolling at Sandhurst or West Point: it was also a form of hostage taking as the boys' well-being depended on their fathers' allegiance to the king.

Philip's army proved its mettle almost immediately. In 359, he had been forced to make some sort of armistice with the invading Illyrians and bribed the Paeonians to stay at home. All of this was to buy him time. One year later, in spring 358, he led 10,000 infantry and 500 cavalry (presumably this early on in his reign, he had hired some mercenaries to boost his numbers) against the Paeonians and defeated them in pitched battle. His victory gave the kingdom access to the trade route along the Axius valley to Dardania in the north. Then, Philip turned to the Illyrians. Alerted to Philip's movement, Bardylis had massed his troops into a hollow rectangle to fight their enemy on all sides. Undaunted, Philip's cavalry opened gaps in the sides, allowing his cavalry and infantry to pour through into the hollow middle and fight the Illyrians front and behind; 7,000 Illyrians were killed before Bardylis surrendered.[46]

This stunning victory allowed Philip to unite Upper and Lower Macedonia for the first time in its history and to introduce much-needed economic reforms, including the exploitation of the rich gold and silver mines of the region and later others in Thrace, which brought him abundant revenues.[47] His manpower reserves immediately increased, and it was the success of his army and the need to keep it on campaign (and winning) that eventually led to his more imperialistic ventures.[48] But there was more. The Macedonian army was more than a defensive and offensive force: it was an integral part of the state, even its backbone.[49] In this way, it was more akin to the armies of China and certain modern African nations in which the military enjoys an oversized role in politics and governance.[50]

By the end of his reign, Philip had increased manpower from about 10,000 infantry and 600 cavalry in 359 to 24,000 infantry and 3,000 cavalry on his death in 336.[51] He had a disciplined, standing army that could march quickly and effortlessly regardless of terrain or weather conditions and overcome an enemy with dreadful precision and ruthlessness. What had started out as an army to secure his borders and introduce economic reform had enabled him to expand Macedonia's reach in every direction and conquer the Illyrians, Thracians, and Greeks south of Olympus. By the time of his death, his empire on the mainland was about to become international with an invasion of the Persian Empire.

The impression we have so far is that Philip was constantly leading his men into battle and deciding any issue by way of conflict. That is not so. He was also a diplomat and he understood – in a way that Alexander did not – that defeated in battle does not mean conquered or necessarily allow a transition to a new regime, or even that war was a primary means to an end. In fact, he preferred diplomacy, for which he had an uncanny ability, over military action.[52] In doing so, he set a pattern for the importance of personal diplomacy as both a first resort in dealing with potential enemies and as a necessity in the aftermath of military conflict. These are lessons that need to be applied today, particularly in the realm of grand strategy addressed in Chapter 14, though Philip's particular brand of diplomacy, including shameless deceit and political marriages, might be looked at askance.

Alexander's Army

When Alexander invaded Asia in 334, our sources put his army anywhere between 30,000 infantry and 5,000 cavalry to 43,000 infantry and 5,500 cavalry, which included 12,000 Macedonian infantry and 1,800 Macedonian cavalry.[53] This was his father's army.[54] Diodorus hyperbolically stated that Philip left so vast and powerful an army that Alexander never needed to ask for allies, but the latter often needed large numbers of reinforcements in Asia, which put pressure on Antipater on the mainland (who he left behind to control Macedonia and Greece) to supply him with troops. For example, in 330 alone, 3,000 infantry and 500 cavalry joined him at Gordium and a short while later another 5,000 infantry and 800 cavalry joined as he marched to meet Darius at Issus.[55] Before Gaugamela in 331, 6,000 Macedonian infantry and 500 cavalry in a force of 15,000 had joined him.[56] At that point, presumably Antipater could not afford to dispatch any more Macedonians, for all reinforcements after 331 were non-Macedonians, even when Alexander asked specifically for his own people in 327 and 324.[57] It is not surprising that Alexander had to turn to his subject peoples to boost his numbers, which created problems with his men as we trace below.[58]

Alexander had no need to resort to the sorts of reforms as his father had done; his principal fighting units and specialist troop detachments were well established, and he employed the same shock and awe tactics, varying the depth of his phalanx and its position depending on the enemy line he faced. Likewise, the army had a complex organizational and command structure going back to the time of Philip.[59] Nevertheless, Alexander made changes to it, especially in Central Asia, often due to specific circumstances of battle, topography, or even the integration of locals.[60]

For example, after he moved into Bactria in 330, he rearranged the eight squadrons (*ilai*) of the companion cavalry, each under the command of an individual officer (*ilarches*), into two companies (*lochoi*) commanded by a single *lochagos* (captain), perhaps because he faced no pitched battles as in Persia but guerilla warfare.[61] Perhaps, though, he wanted to make a break with the army he had inherited from Philip and bring in more of his friends as commanders – as Bosworth sagely notes, 'technical terms, especially traditional ones, are not changed simply for novelty's sake'.[62] As we shall see, in 330, Alexander split the single command of the elite companion cavalry into two, with one being his boyhood friend Hephaestion.[63]

By 329, the organization of *ilai* had all but disappeared in favour of eight *hipparchiai* (cavalry regiments), under individual hipparchs, with two or more *ilai* in each one only as sub-units.[64] Further, the royal squadron of cavalry (*ile basilike*), which defended the king in cavalry engagements, experienced a name change to the *agema*, the same as the infantry *agema* or bodyguard, and possibly in our period numbered 300.[65] The specialist *prodromoi* also seem to have been disbanded after the Great King Darius' death in 330. In 334, Alexander had taken six of the twelve *taxeis* of the *pezhetairoi* with him (leaving the other six with Antipater), but by the time he moved into India in 327, he apparently had added a seventh.[66] Perhaps also there, he rewarded outstanding hypaspists with a special shield with silver engravings, from which they acquired a new name, *argyraspides* ('silver shields').[67] It is interesting that for the entire infantry, Alexander introduced only a new battalion and a name change compared to the various innovations to the cavalry outlined above.

Other innovations were made to meet specific needs. Most notable occurred in the siege of the island city of Tyre in 333–332 (on which, see Chapter 7). The Tyrian defenders had boldly set fire to a wooden mole that Alexander was building from the mainland, along with siege engines he had mounted on it. Alexander immediately grasped that rebuilding the mole with its fixed towers would invite the same response from the Tyrians, so he had to think creatively: as he rebuilt the mole he mounted his siege engines on boats, which sailed safely up and down protecting the workmen. His creativity and quick-thinking were shown again when he later tried to breach the thick walls of Tyre: he fixed battering rams to the ships, the first known instance of this floating weapon in the history of siegecraft. The novelty of its employment only further secured its effectiveness.

Arguably the greatest change to the army was one that led to dissent among the ranks: the integration of foreigners.[68] Philip absorbed foreign troops into his army, keeping them in their own ethnic or specialist units, and, for much of his reign, Alexander followed suit. Towards the end of his reign, however, he started to put foreign and Macedonian and Greek troops together. For example, he placed Arachotians, Bactrians, and Sogdianians into the companion cavalry, and nine Persians into the royal *agema* (bodyguard).[69] Today we think nothing of company divisions comprised of men and women from different ethnic and racial backgrounds, which is a strength of liberal democratic armies. But Alexander's was a different time. Since his first campaigns in 334, he had been ordering local youths to be trained in Macedonian fighting style. In 324, 30,000 youths from Lydia, Lycia, Syria, Egypt, and the north-east satrapies joined the army at Susa, with Alexander naming them the *epigonoi* – successors – even calling them a 'counter unit' (*antitagma*) to the Macedonian phalanx.[70]

Alexander's actions were a failure in leadership and a major factor in the mutiny at Opis in 324 (see Chapter 10). The decreasing Greco-Macedonian element, with troops not tied to a native Greece but viewing the army camp as home, brought about another 'new' army.[71] This one was not destined for longevity. After Alexander's death, his senior staff, given the name Successors, divided his empire among themselves, with each man taking a portion of the troops to serve under him. In the ensuing Wars of the Successors that broke out soon after, men who had stood next to each other while fighting Persians, Bactrians, and Indians under Alexander now faced their former comrades under rival commanders. The army of Philip and Alexander was no more.

Lessons to be Learned?

An army from antiquity (no matter how good) is obviously not equipped to deal with current and future security challenges of our era, but there are interesting parallels to be made and, by extension, lessons to be learned today from the Macedonian army.

Philip's military reforms did not merely refashion an existing army but created one from anew, in the process revolutionizing on a wider scale Greek warfare and weaponry. As Russia, China, and the United States pursue dramatic military reforms, what impact might they have not just on their own armies but on the wider scale of warfare? Philip saw the downsides of conscription and worked to build an enormously successful and feared regular army. What might Sweden take from this as its government reintroduces conscription? Are several traditionally conscript militaries – the Russian Federation for example – prudent in reassessing the value of conscript forces in their large-scale operations? Moreover, even if the United States *should* maintain its all-volunteer force, *could* it do so amid deepening recruitment challenges?

In his battles Alexander was always faced by far greater enemy numbers, yet his use of psychological warfare, audacity, leadership skills, and surely luck, always carried the day for him. He employed the same elements, backed up by his formidable siegecraft (the result of his father's technological innovations), in his sieges. Should modern militaries therefore lean more heavily on numbers or on technological offsets, and just how vital is the role of human leadership in digitized warfare and in face-to-face diplomacy? But what happens when leadership fails for all the wrong reasons, as the final years of Alexander attest? Finally, Philip and Alexander were autocratic kings, making policy, waging wars, conducting business as and when they saw fit. Today we need checks on power, but when we assess their speed of reform and achievements, we must ask whether liberal democracies are stifling much needed and perhaps rapid changes in defense reformation.

The following chapter addresses these issues.

Notes

1 Polybius 18.21–27; Livy 33.6–10; Plutarch, *Flamininus* 8, with Hammond and Walbank 1988, pp. 432–443.
2 On casualty rates with discussion of the sources, see Hammond 1989b.
3 See especially Kalléris 1987; Nogueira Borel 2007; cf. Sekunda 2010, pp. 446–449; King 2018, pp. 107–110. On the Macedonian army before Philip and through to the Antigonid era, see Sekunda 2010; King 2018, pp. 107–130; Taylor 2020.
4 Thucydides 2.100.5–6.
5 Thucydides 2.102.2.
6 Thucydides 4.124.1, 4.1251.
7 Anaximenes, *BNJ* 74 F 4.
8 Arrian 1.28.3 and 7.2.1; cf. Demosthenes 2.17 (of 349) also referring to them. Alexander II had a very short a reign (370–368), so perhaps Alexander I (498–454) is the likely candidate. See further Milns 1976, pp. 89–101; English, 2009a, pp. 3–6. Summary of scholarship on the attribution: King 2018, p. 126 n. 19.
9 Cavalrymen's outfits: Karunanithy 2013, pp. 81–99.
10 English 2009a, pp. 36–59 (pp. 43–44 on the Companions); cf. Heckel 2003a; Sekunda 2013, pp. 67–77.
11 Aymard 1954; Hammond 1997b; cf. Hatzopoulos 1996, vol. 1 p. 178; Worthington 2014a, pp. 27–29.
12 Plutarch, *Pelopidas* 18.5.
13 Diodorus 16.3.1–2.
14 Philip's military reforms: Fuller 1960 pp. 39–54; Hammond and Griffith 1979, pp. 405–449; Keegan 1987, pp. 33–40; Hammond 1992a, pp. 100–106; Lloyd 1996; Lonsdale 2007, pp. 37–42; Worthington 2008, pp. 26–32; Gabriel 2010, pp. 62–92; Sekunda 2010, pp. 449–452; Worthington 2014a, pp. 32–38; King 2018, pp. 107–114.
15 Greek warfare, see for example: Hanson 1989; Van Wees 2000, Van Wees 2004; Rawlings 2007; cf. Lonsdale 2007, pp. 22–44. On hoplites, see Hanson 1991; cf. Wiseman 1989.
16 English 2009a, pp. 41–43.
17 Arrian 1.14.1; Curtius 4.5.13.
18 Arrian 1.15.5, with English 2009a, pp. 55–59.

19 Hammond and Walbank 1988, p. 541 with n. 1, citing references for the functions of the light cavalry; see further Hatzopoulos 2001, pp. 32–54; Matthews 2008, pp. 59–73; Sekunda 2013, pp. 67–77.
20 In his first *Philippic*, dated to 351, Demosthenes demanded the establishment of a citizen army on standby and of a strike force to operate in the north against Philip, but was unsuccessful: Worthington 2013, pp. 116–122.
21 Organization: English 2009a, pp. 10–16, 110–120; Sekunda 2010, pp. 456–458; Taylor 2020 (from Philip to the Roman era); cf. Bosworth 1988a, pp. 266–271.
22 Wrightson 2010.
23 Milns 1967; Hammond and Griffith 1979, pp. 705–709; Anson 1985b; English 2009a, pp. 28–35; Sekunda 2010, pp. 454–456; cf. Hatzopoulos 2001, pp. 56–66; Matthews 2008, pp. 28–58.
24 English 2009a, pp. 115–117, cf. Bosworth 1988a, pp. 274–275; Hatzopoulos 2001, pp. 66–73; Sekunda 2013, pp. 52–56.
25 Hammond and Walbank 1988, p. 477; cf. Hatzopoulos 2001, pp. 73–84, 133–140.
26 Arrian 4.25.6.
27 On infantry equipment, see English 2009a, pp. 16–25; cf. Hatzopoulos 2001, pp. 61–66, 80–84; Karunanithy 2013, pp. 100–115; Sekunda 2013, pp. 78–87.
28 Polybius 18.29.1–5. On the sarissa, see Sekunda 2001; with Hammond 1980a; Anson 2010, and especially Noguera Borel 1999.
29 Cf. Polybius 18.29.2–30.4.
30 On promotion, see Karunanithy 2013, pp. 154–157.
31 Pay rates are better documented under Alexander: Sekunda 2010, pp. 465–466.
32 For example, the division of the land of Methone in 354: Diodorus 16.34.5; Alexander also gave out land: Plutarch, *Alexander* 15.4–6.
33 Aelian, *Varia Historia* 14.48.
34 Karunanithy 2013, pp. 19–39 and 174–175 (marching with weapons); cf. Hatzopoulos 1996, vol. 1, pp. 451–452. Demosthenes 18.157 says Philip ordered his troops to carry forty days' worth of food, so these training exercises may have lasted that long.
35 Polyaenus 4.2.10.
36 Hanson 1998.
37 Arrian 1.6.1–4.
38 Karunanithy 2013, pp. 164–170, 209–223.
39 Polybius 18.28–32.
40 Disruption in those battles: Arrian 2.10.5, 3.14.4–5.
41 Garlan 1974, pp. 202–244; Marsden 1977, p. 212 for the date. On siegecraft, see English 2009b, pp. 17–32.
42 Marsden 1977; Keyser 1994; English 2009a, pp. 100–109; Gabriel 2010, pp. 88–92.
43 Milns 1976, pp. 97–101; Hammond and Griffith 1979, pp. 709–713; Hammond 1992a, pp. 148–150; English 2009a, pp. 25–27.
44 Sekunda 2010, p. 454, citing bibliography in n. 28.
45 Arrian 4.13.1 (who explicitly says the institution was Philip's creation), Curtius 8.6.2 (who talks of them as 'customary'), with Hammond 1990; Carney 2008.
46 Hammond 1989c; Gabriel 2010, pp. 105–109.
47 Economic reforms: Hammond and Griffith 1979, pp. 657–671; Worthington 2008, citing bibliography; cf. Millett 2010.

48 Worthington 2003a.
49 Errington 1990, pp. 229–249; Hatzopoulos 1996, vol. 1, pp. 443–460; cf. Errington 1978.
50 See Sullivan 2021.
51 Diodorus 16.4.3, 17.7.5.
52 Ryder 1994; Cawkwell 1996.
53 Numbers: Diodorus 17.17.3–5; Arrian 1.11.3; Plutarch, *Alexander* 15.1, with Fuller 1960, p. 88; Bosworth 1988a, pp. 259–260; Heckel 2008, p. 158 – see also his Appendix 2 (pp. 158–163); Worthington 2014a, pp. 139–140; King 2018, p. 115. Fuller 1960, Appendix 2 (pp. 153–157), lists Alexander's officers and their commands.
54 See Fuller 1960, pp. 39–54, 292–301; Burn 1965, pp. 140–146; Milns 1976; Sekunda and McBride 1984; Bosworth 1988a, pp. 259–277; Devine 1989a; Lloyd 1996; Ashley 1998; Sekunda and Warry 1998; English 2009a, English 2009b, English 2011; Karunanithy 2013; King 2018, pp. 114–125; cf. Hatzopoulos 1996, vol. 1, pp. 443–460; Matthews 2008, pp. 28–84.
55 Arrian 1.29.4 (Gordium); Polybius 12.19.2 (Cilicia); cf. Curtius 3.1.24 for other troops arriving before the battle of Issus.
56 Diodorus 17.65.1; Curtius 5.1.40–42.
57 Arrian 4.18.3 (327); Arrian 7.12.4 (324); Diodorus 18.12.2 (Antipater); see Bosworth 1988a, pp. 266–268, citing references.
58 Diodorus 16.1.5.
59 Bosworth 1988a, pp. 273–277; Wrightson 2010, for example.
60 See Olbrycht 2007; cf. Milns 1976, pp. 106–129; Lloyd 1996; English 2009a, pp. 10–16, 110–120.
61 Arrian 3.16.11; cf. Brunt 1963, pp. 28–32; Bosworth 1988a, p. 268; Hammond 1992a, pp. 123–126. Command structure: Bosworth 1988a, pp. 273–277.
62 Bosworth 1988a, p. 269.
63 Arrian 3.27.4.
64 Arrian 3.29.7 (name and dating of hipparchies); Arrian 6.21.3–4 (*ilai* as parts of them).
65 Arrian 4.24.1, 6.14.4. The number 300 is attested only after Alexander's death but might be a carryover from his reign: Diodorus 19.28.3.
66 Arrian 4.22.7.
67 Arrian 7.11.3; Justin 12.7.5; cf. Karunanithy 2013, pp. 147–149.
68 Bosworth 1980, pp. 13–20; cf. Bosworth 1988a, pp. 271–273.
69 Arrian 7.6.4–5.
70 Diodorus 17.108.3.
71 Bosworth 1980, pp. 13–20.

4 Organizing, Innovating, and Prioritizing Modernization

During a Pentagon press briefing in February 2020, U.S. Air Force Lt. Gen. Jack Shanahan, then director of the recently commissioned Joint Artificial Intelligence Center (JAIC), brought to light the department's newly minted five principles of AI. These principles were designed to guide the department's development and implementation strategy. In his brief, Shanahan underscored the 'stark contrast' between liberal democracies and competitors such as Russia and China in their approach to researching and developing militarized AI. Shanahan expressed concern about the implications of AI-enabled weapons vis-à-vis 'human rights, ethics and international norms' if they are not restricted by international law.[1] His apprehensions were rooted in the understanding that, historically, the United States rarely fought enemies who honored international law or any kind of regulation governing the conduct of war, which presents unique challenges to leaders responsible for shaping the arms race in which the great powers of the world remain locked.[2] If the true power of autonomous weapons is held back only by western notions of morality and legality, then who will be the first to cast these ideas aside, and what does this mean for the future?

The fulcrum of contemporary modernization efforts is that they will be meaningless if governments cannot attract, recruit, and retain the human talent necessary to harness their benefits and craft purposeful integration strategies. This will become increasingly problematic as the defense enterprise begins to compete more aggressively with the lucrative private sector for human talent.[3] Million-dollar missiles and unmanned aircraft have no trouble capturing the attention of the public and its elected officials, but the efficacy of these systems still depends entirely on the skill of each operator and how leaders decide to employ them. These competing yet complimentary mandates are evident in the 2018 U.S. National Defense Strategy. A single page directs simultaneous investment in the military application of autonomy, AI, and machine learning, in addition to recruiting, developing, and retaining a high-quality military and civilian

DOI: 10.4324/9781003052951-7

workforce.⁴ This balance will be challenging for several reasons. The sort of sophisticated technical talent required to apply the former is rare, which complicates the latter. Further, polling data displays a rather poor reflection of the U.S. military's ability to prepare service members for civilian life, with forty-five percent of them expressing a negative view of their preparedness to transition out of service, which could scare away top technical talent.⁵ Financial compensation cannot be a significant lure in attracting such talent, which leaves historical, cultural, and social factors as the primary appeals of public service to a tech-savvy generation. If the armed services cannot retain leaders capable of giving that next generation the type of military experience that fulfills those ideals, modernization visions are irrelevant.

Leader development therefore remains by far the most critical and underrepresented modernization initiative, despite recent efforts to improve upon talent management in the American, Australian, British, and Russian militaries.⁶ This is a byproduct of the 'curse of success' in which a military's track record of noteworthy accomplishments lends to an assumption that it will always attract and produce leaders capable of such success, even in the midst of a rapidly evolving technological and strategic landscape.⁷ The greatest shortcomings in western military leadership over the last ten years, however, had little to do with tactical decision-making or combat performance, and everything to do with civil–military dynamics and the relationship between leaders and those entrusted into their care.⁸

On future battlefields littered with AI and weapons with seemingly infinite range, toxic leadership could be even more fatal. The technology described in this chapter, when placed into the hands of less capable leaders, could be unimaginably destructive and counterproductive to the national interest in all phases of competition and conflict. More concerning, the breadth of ongoing modernization pursuits runs the risk of drowning leaders in a mélange of jargon, equipment, and concepts that distract from their core duties, sap the energy of their staffs, and ultimately result in decision paralysis through information fatigue.⁹ The progression of service member from recruit to senior leader takes place over a lifetime, but as advanced technologies reduce end strength, leaders will likely be called upon to do more at earlier points in their careers and with fewer human resources at their disposal.¹⁰ This chapter therefore gives considerable attention to some of the more underemphasized elements of modernization, such as education, organization, and talent management, while also addressing the more popular material topics of AI and the increasing reliance on space-based systems. This unconventional focus also happens to be where we might learn the most from Alexander.

A Historical Mind

Professional Military Education, or PME, resides at the center of the modernization process. Placed at specific points along a military leader's career, PME consists of various levels of formalized education meant to prepare service members for their next phase of leadership. The concept has existed in formal and informal systems since Philip commissioned his Court of Royal Pages and sent Alexander away to study with Aristotle.[11] Even today, conversations continue regarding what should be expected of a military leader intellectually and academically.

Formalized PME remains wed to a military's potential to modernize effectively. It stokes the intellectual curiosity of military leaders and expands their familiarity with emerging technologies and operational concepts. Even so, it is not without flaw. David E. Johnson found that PME can also serve as a means of confirming existing biases rather than challenging them, as he wrote of the service branches in his history of U.S. Army innovation between 1917 and 1945:

> They proved largely incapable of critical self-analysis, consistently interpreting reports from the Spanish civil war, the invasion of Poland, the fall of France, and the Battle of Britain in ways that supported their predilections. . . . Thus, innovation in the interwar Army was constrained by unquestioned faith in ruling paradigms – paradigms that shaped perceptions of external experiences.[12]

Due in no small part to RMA and changes in a nation's cultural or political affairs, PME is in a perpetual state of revision. In 1996, for instance, military historians in the United States called for a 'fundamental' rethinking of PME based on their research of suboptimal relationships between the education sector and the world of operations in the era between the two world wars.[13] In 2012, Thomas E. Ricks produced one of the most stinging critiques of officer development and the American military tradition with his history of commanders from World War II to NATO's war on terrorism.[14] He cited careerism and risk aversion in the senior ranks, not battlefield capability or lethality, as the harbingers of America's recent military failures. Such observations are reminiscent of Alexander's generals in Sogdiana refusing to charge Satibarzanes' army for the risk it involved. Comments from senior military leaders as recently as 2021 prove that the process of rethinking the way militaries educate their best and brightest is still underway.[15] The same holds true for the far east. Since Chairman Xi Jinping rose to power in 2012, the PRC has invested heavily in reforms designed to offer PLA officers a superior education, which Jinping considers essential to realizing China's strategic goals.[16]

Eliot Cohen and Francis Gavin have called on educators to find ways of developing a 'historical mind' in their PME courses, similar to the type of thinking to which former U.S. Secretary of Defense Gen. Jim Mattis subscribes.[17] But others argue that history is a dying academic field in a technology-drenched world – military history in particular – which bodes poorly for the future of PME.[18] Alexander certainly benefitted from a historical mind, taking the throne with a rich understanding of Macedonia's capabilities, its past, and its relationships with bordering states, the Persian King, and his satraps. Still, education and strategic awareness are but two pillars in the foundation of a historical mind. Research has continually shown that the gap between good and great leaders is bridged with interpersonal skills that are becoming harder to nurture in a fast-paced digital world.[19] Results from the U.S. Army's first Battalion Commander Assessment Program (BCAP) in 2019 are a testament to the lasting importance of intangible leadership qualities.

Prior to this program, centralized boards selected future battalion commanders after briefly reviewing each candidate's file. The old board identified commanders using quantitative metrics almost exclusively, such as trends in evaluation reports, which sidelined qualitative metrics such as empathy, cognitive agility, and analytical thinking. According to the Chief of Staff of the Army at the time, Gen. James McConville, those days are over.[20] Included in the BCAP is a psychological examination of each candidate, a topic about which Alexander has much to offer the modern world, as we will see in later chapters. At the pilot BCAP's conclusion, most of the candidates selected at the top of the centralized list were replaced with officers lower on the list because of a lack of physical preparedness or toxic personality attributes that became evident only in person.[21]

The contradiction is glaring, for even as government agencies and militaries increase their reliance on digital systems, they find need to reinvest in old practices like face-to-face evaluation and qualitative metrics to locate, attract, and retain people capable of effectively managing and employing those systems. The recently commissioned U.S. Army Talent Management Task Force is quickly finding that its quantitative systems of record for personnel management are an inadequate means of meeting the leadership challenges of the twenty-first century.[22]

While the BCAP is new to the U.S. military, it was the type of assessment Alexander favored when hand picking his commanders based on personally observed performance and potential. For example, in 331, on his way from Babylon to Susa, he was said to have reviewed his ranks to 'promote some of his officers and to strengthen his army by the number and the ability of his commanders'. Diodorus, who provides this information, claims that the king's motive was to bind his newly promoted officers closer to him.[23] Arrian, who places the promotions at Susa, speaks of the king creating two cavalry companies and giving the commands to particularly brave companions.[24] We can therefore see that Alexander selected his leaders through personal observations of his own choice, even at times organizing contests of military valour and giving the bravest competitors significant commands, as Curtius explained.[25] A higher regard for the historical mind in PME might reveal additional best practices that have stood the test of time.

Selective Innovation

Much of what modern armies aim to achieve in the selection of their leaders may appear new, but it is in fact a return to the principles of leadership that generations of evolution in military operations and administration have obscured. Among these principles are a conservative eye for when, where, and how conflict should be pursued, and the ability to challenge consensus even when it appears overwhelming, all of which feed into prioritizing modernization efforts. Alexander encountered just such a challenge while he camped on the outskirts of Miletus in 334, not long after he routed a large Persian army at the Granicus River (see Chapter 6).

Persia's naval supremacy remained at the forefront of his mind, particularly the adept Cypriot and Phoenician navies loyal to Darius. Parmenion, one of his senior generals, urged Alexander to meet roughly 400 Persian ships with his comparatively small Macedonian navy in a battle that would prove crippling to Persian military power and prestige if successful.[26] After all, the Macedonians had just defeated a Persian army at the Granicus River and liberated many Greek cities of Asia Minor from Persian control, so it is understandable that a commander of Parmenion's experience saw value in a maritime engagement exploiting that momentum and delivering a *coup de grâce*. Parmenion outlined how a victorious sea campaign could deal a crushing blow to Darius whereas a loss would be less crippling to Macedonia. The balance of power would remain unchanged, so the risk was worth the reward. Further supporting Parmenion's analysis was the fact that the Persians were still processing their disastrous performance at Granicus and could therefore be caught off guard, if not materially and in relation to the disposition of their forces, then at least psychologically.

Alexander disagreed, seeing no value in throwing his small navy into a sea battle that, even if successful, would amount to little more than a pyrrhic victory within the context of his broader strategy. Arrian describes what he believed to be Alexander's decision-making process:

> It made no sense to engage a much larger force with a small number of ships, or to set their own unpractised fleet against the trained Cypriot and Phoenician navies; he was not prepared to expose Macedonian expertise and daring to the barbarians on an element where there could be no guarantee of success; if they were defeated in the engagement it would do serious damage to their initial reputation in the war, not least because news of a naval defeat would encourage revolt in Greece.[27]

Here emerges the mind of Alexander the strategist, in which the perception of Greek citizens was as important as the operational demands imposed upon him by the current military situation. While the authenticity of Parmenion's protest is still debated among historians, the king's course of action is not. Instead of meeting the Persian ships in their own domain, Alexander decided to attack their naval ports by land, thus neutering their sea power from a domain of his own choosing. The Macedonian king knew his strengths and played to them, molding his capabilities around operational realities in unique ways that allowed him to avoid wasting precious time and resources competing directly with Persian naval power.

So sure of his vision, soon after his discussion with Parmenion Alexander disbanded the Macedonian navy, dedicating all resources to land dominance and assuming immense strategic risk. The decision to cut investment in sea power came easily as it was not theoretically or doctrinally tied to any military capability as many services are today, but it would be a decision the king soon had to reverse to combat renewed Persian naval aggression (see Chapter 6).[28]

Alexander's decision against engaging the Persian navy as Parmenion wanted came from his life of study as much as raw intuition. It was an example of his prudent ability to prioritize how, where, and why he chose to fight. Other commanders since his time have likewise exercised restraint despite urgings from senior staff, from Napoleon Bonaparte to Gen. George S. Patton, but Alexander was one of the first.

Military innovation is often seen as obligatory amid the backdrop of any new technology or operational concept, but one of Alexander's gifts was the ability to innovate selectively, which maximized his return on investment in new tactics and methods. Philip's engineering corps, for instance, invented the torsion catapult from which Alexander benefitted, and yet his Macedonian phalanx remained as terrifying in the eyes of enemies 200 years later, as evidenced by the remark of the Roman commander Lucius Aemilius Paullus after the battle at Pydna in 168.[29] In stark contrast, there is a growing sense that current modernization programs have become self-fulfilling prophecies that demand revolutionary change across the entire defense enterprise whether or not they are tied to specific mission requirements and strategies.[30] In other words, they are a solution in search of a problem because the question they aim to answer exists only in a hypothetical future battlefield.

Evolutions and revolutions in warfare since Alexander's time often fail to account for his wisdom and instead see military competition as a struggle of parity between weapons and operational constructs. Conventional military wisdom assumes that if an opponent has something, one must have it also, and if an opponent does something, one must do it better. This pattern is no less prevalent with the introduction of new weapons, organizations, and domains of warfare, such as air, space, and cyberspace. As various states pursue new technologies and capabilities, others become further convinced that they too must possess these things, or they run the risk of 'falling behind' in their modernization and innovation efforts.[31] Large militaries are often tempted to pursue every capability to remain competitive in all manners of warfare. In the present century, those requirements are nearly infinite. The urge to innovate and modernize in response to emerging technologies has consumed the defense enterprise, with the potential surrounding AI, autonomous weapons, and robotics leading the way.

While promising technologies have largely stolen the show, Shanahan's observation at the opening of this chapter concerning personalities highlights an essential point in the modernization debate: the tools matter less than the character of the operators. Michael Howard's conclusion regarding German naval modernization prior to the First World War applies:

> The naval race was the result of a rivalry that eventually culminated in war, but it was the rivalry itself that caused the war rather than the weapons that expressed it. It was not the German fleet itself that alarmed the British but the intentions that lay behind it.[32]

Personalities, relationships, and cultures are likely to control war's inception and termination in the future, but what does that future look like?

Racing to Arms

The number of policies or national strategies concerning the development and application of AI in modern military operations has risen sharply in recent years. So much so, in fact, that the race to harness AI has been compared to the space programs of the 1960s that competed to put a man on the moon.[33] Russian Federation Chief of the General Staff Valery Gerasimov raised eyebrows in the west not only with his purported 'doctrine' of hybrid war, coined regrettably by Mark Galeotti, but also with his interest in automated warfare.[34] In a 2013 article, he predicted that in the near future, a fully robotized unit will be created, capable of independently conducting military operations.[35] Even the most advanced defense research is nowhere near realizing this vision, but its implications filled the minds of world leaders all the same. By 2017, Vladimir Putin proclaimed during his State of the Nation address that the country to lead in AI would rule the world, and the Russian tech industry took notice.[36] Not to be outdone by the Russian Federation, in July 2017, the Chinese government released its New Generation Artificial Intelligence Development Plan, which laid out a vision to lead the world in the technology by 2030.[37] The 2018 U.S. National Defense Strategy also made clear the need to pursue these technologies in an effort to remain competitive with other major powers, such as China and Russia: 'The department will invest broadly in military application of autonomy, artificial intelligence, and machine learning, including rapid application of commercial breakthroughs, to gain competitive military advantage'.[38] Most nations have drafted similar mandates, from the UK to Australia.[39]

This modernization movement has given birth to countless working groups, committees, and teams dedicated to identifying capability gaps and discovering creative ways of filling them with new technologies. Within the last several years in the United States alone, there emerged a robust architecture of modernization bureaucracies, three of which are dedicated to AI research at echelons from the National Security Council to the Department of the Army.[40] In addition, the U.S. Army built eight cross-functional teams to tie key private industry stakeholders into the army's modernization initiatives concerning everything from long-range precision fires to synthetic training environments.[41] Truth be told, many of these efforts are designed to simply gain a clearer understanding of what AI can do in the realm of military operations, and it is the unknowns that drive much of the trepidation surrounding the technology.

Modernizing for the Unknown

The question of planning to meet the requirements generated by future threats plagues leaders of every generation, but there is arguably a more strained debate taking place over this inquiry in the twenty-first century. Personal and professional interests influence the debate (such as rivalry between military branches), as do financial concerns. Even stripped of these considerations, the most genuine argument for modernization of any military is bound to be riddled with hyperbole, misunderstandings, and exaggerations.[42] Compounding these problems is the fact that many of the technologies driving the conversation are theoretical. Chief among these nonexistent capabilities are two of the three forms of AI referred to respectively as artificial general intelligence (AGI) and artificial super intelligence (ASI), neither of which would govern the potential use of lethal autonomous weapon systems (LAWS) anytime soon.[43] Even theoretically, the implications associated with these weapons have already led to heated debates surrounding their potential development.

At the 71st session of the United Nations (UN) General Assembly in 2016, the director of the U.N. Interregional Crime and Justice Research Institute (UNICRI) announced a new initiative to establish a Centre on Artificial Intelligence and Robotics at The Hague, the Netherlands.[44] Three years later in October 2019, the annual NATO Information Assurance Symposium brought industry leaders together in Mons, Belgium, to discuss these issues, as various institutions explored the legal ramifications and restrictions associated with the implementation of LAWS and AI in war. By 2023, the U.S. State Department's undersecretary for arms control and international security, Bonnie Jenkins, declared at The Hague a 'focal point for international cooperation' on militarized AI consisting of twelve points.[45] Among them were the demands that military AI applications abide by international law, and nuclear weapons' employment remain detached from autonomous decision-making systems. While mostly exploratory in nature, these developments reflect the sense of urgency driving militarized AI and robotics research. Leaders assert the need to be morally right in the process as emphatically as the need to be the first to develop the technology for fear of missing out on its benefits. But modernization is about much more than smart machines and better weapons. Questions regarding how militaries should be organized, whether conscripts should play a role in war, and in what way the defense industry might better compete with the private sector for human talent also consume the debate.

The challenge of modernization is the same challenge that has beset strategic forecasting for millennia: the struggle to predict the future.[46] Especially when considering the sluggishness of most defense acquisitions programs, militaries must develop these plans years or even decades before a projected adversarial capability might emerge. Gripes associated with the need for dramatic acquisition reform have filled Pentagon hallways since it was built, and it recently stood up its Defense Innovation Unit in response to this slothful process.[47] All the while, threats evolve, and the geopolitical competitive space takes on new shapes. Trends are subject to Nassim Taleb's improbable 'black swans' and treaties and agreements can be broken by dishonest actors or ones whose interests have changed.[48]

It is important to frame these challenges within the context of Thucydides' oft misinterpreted human catalysts to war. Usually diluted into the causalities of fear, honor, and interest, a more complete translation of the Athenian historian's philosophy is that of 'fear, the desire for respect, and gain'.[49] Even some 2,200 years later, Gen. Antoine Henri de Jomini added little to these causal factors with his objects of war, thus proving their value.[50] The fear Thucydides spoke of in his time was likely related to an opponent's power. But fear is now more dynamic. Modern nations are not motivated simply by the threat of physical harm, but also by a fear of irrelevance or national impotence, which are both tied to the other catalysts. As many nations have discovered throughout history, it is much easier to become a superpower than it is to stay one, which means this type of fear can be paralyzing to great powers unaccustomed to such emotions.[51] It is for this reason that the fear of failing to modernize, and thereby becoming irrelevant on the world stage and incapable of competing militarily, can lead to convoluted thinking about warfare.

In their struggle to harness every capability, governments run the risk of striving to prepare for everything while in actuality being prepared for nothing – the strategic implications of which we will address with greater detail in later chapters.[52] It was Thucydides, after all, who first wrote that a jack of all trades was a master of none.[53] If each technological development is sold as groundbreaking and every modernization effort promises to be decisive, leaders must practice restraint as demonstrated by Alexander in keeping his ships at harbor when even experienced leaders like Parmenion believed victory was at hand.

Intentional Organization

With the limited means available to world leaders, military modernization strategies are typically designed around specific capabilities seen as requirements to support the national interest. Chapter 2 described how these interests and requirements can change rapidly, as many western nations shifted from a focus on counterinsurgency and special operations missions to conventional warfare after the first two decades of the twenty-first century. Purpose is therefore the lifeblood of organizational theory. How that purpose manifests itself in organizational reforms reflects each nation's forecasting methodologies or, in other words, how it sees the future. Despite the fascination with remote warfare and emerging technologies in the public domain, nations such as the United States, China, and Russia are increasingly training for and shaping their force structure around large-scale ground wars fought with armour, mechanized infantry, artillery barrages, and aerial bombardments.[54] These longstanding concepts are supported by robotics and militarized AI, they do not support them. As of 2015, roughly three-quarters of the world's twenty million active military members were ground forces trained and equipped to take and hold physical terrain.[55] Far from dwindling, that number could expand as global insecurities rise. Russia's 2022 invasion of Ukraine compelled Polish officials to announce that they would nearly double defence spending and triple the strength of their land army from 114,000 to 300,000, making it the largest in Europe next to Russia. To protect these troops Warsaw requested thousands of additional tanks from the United States and South Korea in February 2023.[56] In this way, it appears the characteristics of today's wars that resemble those of the past are as likely to shape the future as the aspects that make wars different.

The army Alexander inherited from Philip changed the world. Similarly, tomorrow's leaders will fight with the army built today, which requires balancing modernization efforts by projecting not only the character of future threats but also the size, structure, and purpose of a military designed to meet them. In terms of the four instruments of national power or DIME (diplomatic, information, military, and economic), since the end of the Cold War and rise of the United States as a unitary superpower, the western world has relied heavily on the 'M' while the far east – China specifically – invested in its 'DIE' construct.[57] The last decade of the twentieth century elicited deep contemplation from countries seen as competing with western powers. China's infamous *Unrestricted Warfare* thesis, written by two People's Liberation Army colonels in 1999, proposed a framework for challenging American military might by focusing on the DIE as opposed to Cold War-style increases in troop numbers and armaments.[58] Despite some western analysis that waved the document off as of little consequence, its authors were promoted and praised in PRC military and media circles for their efforts. This approach has since been manifest, either through correlation or causation, by China's co-option of western academia, theft of intellectual property, coupling of economic interests, and information operations surrounding Taiwan's independence and more recently the origins of the 2019 novel coronavirus.[59] But Chinese officials have also instituted some sweeping changes to military strategy, including efforts designed to achieve overmatch with artillery fires, increases in their capacity to wage cyber and information war, and improved proficiency in the realm of combined arms manoeuvre.[60]

Russia similarly learned many lessons in that fateful decade, particularly during its ugly wars with neighboring Chechnya that inspired several policies aimed at mastering the information domain and waging irregular warfare.[61] The discussion culminated in what some analysts refer to as 'new generation warfare', and Gen. Gerasimov has since underscored the value of 'political, economic, informational, and other nonmilitary measures' when competing with the United States specifically.[62] That said, Russia is also paying close attention to conventional ground war.

Despite premonitions of computerized conflicts in many defense circles, mass development of Russia's next-generation main battle tank, the T-14 Armata, coupled with its increased anti-access and area denial (A2/AD) capability, proposes conventional military problems to Eastern European militaries and NATO in general.[63] These concerns metastasized in November 2021 as Russia massed forces on Ukraine's border and placed units in Belarus, culminating in a ground invasion and Moscow's recognition of independent republics in Ukraine's eastern Donbas region.[64] Perhaps not surprisingly, the fight that transpired there in 2022 had more in common with wars of the last century than any spectacular vision proposed by military futurists. Armoured convoys became bogged down in the mud, small Ukrainian foot teams hit Russian tank patrols with anti-armour weapons, and major cities were subjected to encirclement and isolation.[65] Mercenaries and irregulars played a role in the fighting as well. More tragically, they participated in the slaughter at places such as Bucha and Izyum, but considering how prevalent hired swords were in Alexander's day, this is more of a return to normal than a revelation.[66]

Despite its abysmal early performance in Ukraine, Moscow continues to professionalize its forces by offering contracts to enlisted soldiers in the spirit of the U.S. noncommissioned officer (NCO) corps and other western nations.[67] A driving force behind this shift was the increased technical skill and experience required to operate modern systems for which inexperienced conscripts were poorly suited. Ukrainian forces put the efficacy of such troops to the test, and they were found wanting.[68] One of the core tenets of U.S. military might is its empowered NCO corps – an element lacking in most militaries throughout history that relied heavily on commissioned officers to plan and execute operations. Russian officials toyed with the notion of abolishing conscription entirely, even though compulsive service accounted for roughly half of its forces as recently as 2016, and by 2020 it still conscripted 120,000 soldiers into its army.[69]

The end of the Cold War led understandably to significant drawdowns in military end strength in both the United States and Russia. Since then, new NATO member Sweden has reinstated conscription – in Norway even for females – and the United States is reassessing its selective service obligation after allowing women into combat arms roles in 2015.[70] This question has vexed leaders since at least December 1945 when Gen. Eisenhower argued against keeping selective service in play for more than a year after World War II.[71] The transition to an all-volunteer force after the Vietnam War influenced strategic thought for the remainder of the century, at which time planners sought to do more with fewer personnel by augmenting formations with advanced technologies such as unmanned aerial systems (UAS), precision guided munitions (PGM), and robust packages of air support assets. The strategic offset concept pioneered by the United States stems from the numerical force imbalance between it and the Soviet Union during the Cold War – an effort to achieve operational equanimity through technological innovation without drafting additional forces into service.[72] This concept may have deterred the Soviets, but military failures this century have brought its utility into question.

There can be no doubt that the world's militaries are in a period of extreme reforms that will challenge longstanding assumptions about organizational norms. Most of these changes aim to counter the existing or projected capabilities of a potential threat, and the urgency of such changes is usually tied to the perceived interests of the threat's leadership. Like the United States and the Soviet Union during the Cold War, Alexander had a singular antagonist to plan against in the form of Darius, which allowed him to prioritize resources and focus efforts on a specific threat. This binary relationship has now expired, and the United States is a superpower with numerous challengers. Reforms in the Chinese and Russian militaries are inspired primarily by known and assumed capabilities and interests of the United States. On the other hand, reforms in the U.S. military must account for potential scenarios around the world against various state and non-state actors. In other words, the net of defense considerations cast by the United States is much wider than that of its competitors. Herein lies the fundamental leadership challenge of military organization: specificity and prioritization.

Williamson Murray and MacGregor Knox found that productive innovators 'have always thought in terms of fighting wars against *actual* rather than *hypothetical* opponents, with *actual* capabilities, in pursuit of *actual* strategic and political objectives'.[73] A military must be shaped to meet a physical threat and not a vague conceptual theory, such as competition, deterrence, or domains of warfare, each of which mean different things and require special means of support depending on the opponent with which one is competing and the capacity in which one competes. Specificity and prioritization are not simply important aspects of modernization and innovation, they are the only aspects. Although there are hundreds of weapons, technologies, and platforms in development, modernization initiatives today are driven primarily by three factors: the implications of AI, space-based warfare, and perhaps the most critical, human talent.

AI in Theory and Practice

Artificial narrow intelligence, or ANI, already shapes much of what we know through algorithmic catering in online services such as Google and Amazon, as well as their associated home smart devices, like Alexa. What we buy, read, and peruse online is customized to our preferences through machine-learning programs tailored by every click we make and image we view. While AI's prospects have captured the world's attention since the mid-twentieth century, the conversation remained rather benign in the public sphere until it became likely that AI could be used in war. The potential for an autonomous weapon to adjudicate lethal force is chief among these concerns, leading to various directives aimed at either forbidding the development of LAWS or at least severely restricting their level of autonomy.[74]

AI as a concept is direct – it refers to any learning machine that adjusts its behavior based on given information. The more common process of machine learning (ML) or deep learning is an example of ANI. AI pioneer Kai-Fu Lee describes this as 'intelligence that takes data from one specific domain and applies it to optimizing one specific outcome', which explains the technology behind everything from market predictions to driverless cars.[75] As Lee implies, the challenge of operationalizing AI for military application would be the same in any other venue: feeding the AI enough data to make its conclusions reliable. The more data the better.

For most commercial applications, the risk associated with the data question can be limited by continuously exposing the AI to new scenarios, images, and information. In war, though, verifiable data can be harder to come by, even without enemy AI systems attempting to thwart your own. It is here that the utility of predictive and analytical AI in large-scale combat is called into question. In an environment where the unknowns outweigh the knowns, a system that relies on massive dumps of accurate information to perform accurately is bound to run into challenges related to data of questionable fidelity.

These challenges became apparent during the short-lived Pentagon–Google partnership venture known as Project Maven, which experimented with fusing AI and military sensors, such as drones, to sift through vast troves of battlefield information and identify targets. Early versions of the program achieved a roughly fifty percent success rate, prompting the JAIC's then director to compare the process of finding data fit for the AI's consumption to mining for mineral ore.[76] Ambiguities regarding enemy capabilities, composition, strength, and disposition are enduring battlefield realities. For this reason, the most valuable AI applications are appearing in the fields of predictive maintenance and knowledge management, such as the Defense Intelligence Agency's Machine-Assisted Analytic Rapid-Repository System (MARS) program, but even in these areas there emerges a logical paradox.[77]

If the purpose of AI is to ultimately assist humans in processing information and making decisions, then the digital neural pathways that lead to actionable AI-derived information remain masked to the human operator, thus making human decisions more consequential. Several Harvard-based economists examined these AI characteristics and determined that the most significant implication of prediction machines is that they increase the value of judgement.[78] Others in the technology sector have argued that no AI can be truly autonomous because 'the social context established by other human beings' is what gives it purpose.[79] In an AI-driven war, the value of human judgment translates into further-reaching second- and third-order effects with fatal implications.

The U.S.-based Defense Advanced Research Projects Agency (DARPA) is already working to build explainable AI that can rationalize its conclusions in a way that is comprehensible to the human mind.[80] This is essential. If the human leaders who are ultimately responsible for a machine's actions cannot describe how or why decisions were made, they can hardly claim to be in control of outcomes. Future research may force militaries to choose between the fastest, smartest AI and the AI that is easiest to understand – demanding blind trust in the former and explainable thought patterns in the latter.

In such a scenario, leaders who are willing to assume the greatest risk, and those who are not bound by obligations to explain their wartime decisions, such as those of the authoritarian persuasion, could hold a key competitive military advantage over liberal democracies. The Chinese government is already experimenting with the fusion of mass surveillance technology, facial recognition, and AI with its Integrated Joint Operational Platform currently deployed against the Uighur population in Xinjiang. Supposedly, this program scans faces and mobile devices in the city before aggregating all data, including facial recognition patterns, text messages, and even body language, to 'pre-emptively' identify threats and make arrests.[81]

Post-doctoral researchers at the Massachusetts Institute of Technology track issues related to the integrity of AI discretion by examining what are called 'adversarial examples'. Once thought to be flaws in the AI's programming that caused it to misidentify objects, later studies revealed that these mistakes may instead be the result of an AI picking up subtle variances in an image that are imperceptible to the human eye.[82] These discrepancies can be significant, along the lines of an AI mistaking an oil tanker for an aircraft carrier, or worse.

One could imagine the confusion such uncertainty might nurture, not to mention the implications for countermeasures in which an adversary is able to develop an AI that uses these subtleties to deceive or corrupt its opponent's identification and targeting algorithms.[83] Such corruption could occur during the development and coding phase or while the system is deployed in a theatre of operations. These revelations come at a relatively early point in military AI research when the sophistication of the current technology is rudimentary compared to potentially 'world altering' capabilities that might be available twenty years from now.[84] The 'human in the loop' or 'on the loop' is often presented as a failsafe for AI decision-making, inasmuch the AI is restricted from making certain decisions or a human can intervene when the AI is about to make a mistake.[85] But if human judgment cannot be trusted or is slow enough to be irrelevant, a human in the loop would hardly be capable of improving the accuracy of the AI, which reinforces the paradox of AI decision-making at war.

While the risks are many, the existence of this technology has created a seemingly endless array of potential defense applications that will be pursued and ultimately used because they exist.[86] J. Robert Oppenheimer articulated as much in his 2 November 1945 farewell speech regarding his research into the atomic bomb:

> If you are a scientist you cannot stop such a thing . . . it is good to turn over to mankind at large the greatest possible power to control the world and to deal with it according to its lights and its values.[87]

Gen. John Murray of U.S. Army Futures Command stated clearly that 'AI is coming to the battlefield, it's not a question of if, it's when and who'.[88] To a degree it is already here.

The U.S. Navy's Aegis gun and the army's Advanced Targeting & Lethality Automated System (ATLAS) already use predictive algorithms to auto correct and detect targets. Still, trust in these weapons will require years of performance, and the human operator remains in the loop. Dozens of unmanned ground, sea, and aerial vehicles of different types are under development, primarily in the United States, China, and regarding aerial platforms, Israel.[89] DARPA is even developing autonomous aerial vehicles that could potentially assist in air-to-air dogfights with its Air Combat Evolution (ACE) program, and in 2023, the United States fielded an AI that flew an F-16-type aircraft for seventeen hours.[90] This fascination with AI extends beyond the microchip and into human biology and cognitive science.

DARPA's Teaching AI to Leverage Overlooked Residuals (TAILOR) program is a human performance optimization initiative designed to employ AI to make soldiers fitter, happier, and more productive, which is ironic because it uses inorganic means to improve the organic functions of the human body.[91] In the far east, the Central Military Committee in China's Science and Technology Commission funded research into the military application of cognitive neuroscience and biotechnology through what it calls 'hybrid intelligence'.[92] The PRC's research makes sense, as the cognitive demands placed on leaders in future wars are almost certain to increase.

AI applications appear interminable, but tying them together coherently during military operations requires network interconnectivity, spatial awareness, and extreme levels of coordination, all of which rely upon space-based assets that are as vulnerable as they are prevalent.

The Final Frontier?

Every facet of modern warfare is administered by support from space. Militaries rely on commercial satellites for positional data, geospatial visualization, and situational awareness, which feeds everything from maritime navigation aids to the targeting systems on guided bombs. But space is growing congested. According to some estimates, in 2020 the number of requested commercial satellite deployments from private organizations such as Space X and Boeing exceeded 15,000.[93] Even in the absence of malicious activity, the risk of inadvertent satellite collisions or interference is higher than ever.

In 2015, a Russian satellite nearly collided with a commercial one 22,000 miles above earth's surface while travelling at 6,800 miles-per-hour. As of 2019, there have been at least three collisions since 2005.[94] The European Union launched its Galileo satellite system in 2016 as an alternative to the U.S. Air Force-owned global positioning system (GPS), which gives European NATO members an additional layer of security between them and Russia's Global Navigation Satellite System (GLONASS) or China's Bei-Dou satellite constellations. Luckily, when Galileo suffered a week-long outage in July 2019, its systems were able to fall back on GPS.[95]

To better harmonize the number of deployed satellites, the United States commissioned an information-sharing program in 2009 that invited nations to report the positions of their satellites so others could better coordinate their own space programs. Most nations except Russia and China have opted in, both of which are in various stages of building systems that collide with targets in space rather than inspect them. Some of these weaponized satellites even tout a grappling arm to manipulate others, potentially while in geostationary orbit where satellites controlling the most sensitive services are stationed, such as those responsible for early warning of nuclear weapons' deployment and national surveillance assets.[96] These threats are far from theoretical. In November 2021, Russia conducted a counter satellite weapon test that sent 1,500 pieces of debris into orbit, prompting an emergency alert to the International Space Station.[97] Making matters worse was another mysterious Russian satellite that disintegrated in orbit in February 2023, scattering space debris that could remain for a century and endangering other space-based systems that support modern civilization.[98]

In addition to NATO recognizing space as an operational domain in late 2019, nations such as the United States and Australia have taken drastic measures to remain competitive there, even creating an entirely new branch in the U.S. military known as the Space Force.[99] Modern militaries rely on space-based assets to function, but controlling space is costly, time consuming, and requires a volume of human talent that governments will likely struggle to gain and maintain. Nevertheless, it is clear what a catastrophic attack in space would do to the future battlefield. According to retired Gen. William Shelton, former commander of U.S. Air Force Space Command, in the event of such an attack, 'we'd go back to the way we fought back in World War II'.[100] Suddenly, the distant past does not seem so distant.

Other Considerations

The above is by no means a comprehensive review of military modernization initiatives. Such a review would fill multiple books, and this alone is evidence of the vastness of modernization's scope in the twenty-first century. Offensive cyber capabilities, hypersonic missiles, quantum computing, and directed energy weapons are all in various and vacillating phases of funding or defunding, and many nations have established a center, commission, or command to address them. Some of these will be discussed in later chapters, but they encompass an effort that no nation – with limited time, expertise, and resources – could truly master. It is also important to remember that some of the most promising ventures in these realms of innovation are driven by AI or space support, such as the United Kingdom's Darktrace Antigena system that fends off cyber-attacks autonomously.[101] Raytheon also has a 'smart' laser that detects and tracks manned and unmanned aerial platforms as well as missiles and boats, supposedly as a counter to the drone-swarming problem.[102]

The art of innovation, though, is a layered process that involves building proficiency in new skillsets without losing proficiency in enduring ones. One study found that 'what is lost in an innovation process may be as important as what is created' because the process often leads to 'cannibalizing traditional capabilities before beliefs about the effectiveness of the new ones are justified'.[103] A leading pioneer in the modernization movement put this aptly in 2018 when speaking about AI to an audience at Arizona State University: 'We can't lose sight of the fact that there are many dimensions of national security. We have to add a new one without losing any others'.[104] Considering the number of programs on the table, this is a tall order for any military. It will force leaders to prioritize and assume risk in ways far beyond their traditional comfort zones.

Risks

Grand predictions associated with past RMA and modernization efforts have rarely materialized. The dawn of nuclear weapons, as Allan R. Millett observed, produced neither nuclear Armageddon nor world peace as many suggested it would. Instead, nuclear proliferation led to further military innovation that ultimately caused twenty million war-related deaths in conflicts carried out below the threshold of nuclear war.[105] Martin Van Creveld assessed as much when he wrote that although 'the power of modern weapons may cause some forms of war to become extinct, others will take their place'.[106] The spirit of innovation in military thought is one of the paths of least resistance, and this will be no less true in the age of AI and LAWS. Thus, one should expect similar dynamics to appear regarding 'game-changing' technologies now touted as capable of altering the nature of war.[107] Many such claims might be more a product of human financial interests or the desire to be right than a sincere concern for combat effectiveness. These innovations will exchange one operational reality for another, just as information operations have done for many weaker states and coordinated digital propaganda has done for violent extremist groups.[108] When that new reality emerges, it will be the junior leaders of today who are called upon to negotiate the challenge, and they will be armed only with the tactical knowledge, historical wisdom, and capabilities at their disposal to make decisions.

A flood of grand theories and impressive technologies encourage an almost dismissiveness toward historical consistencies in war and warfare. Modernization advocates demand more money and faster acquisition processes to solve military quandaries.[109] The belief that autonomous weapon systems 'are cheaper to field and cheaper to lose' is not uncommon, despite the fact that such systems have not yet been vetted significantly on any battlefield, and western militaries lack sufficient data from a modern interstate war upon which it could base such assumptions.[110] Prior to Russia's 2022 invasion of Ukraine, the costly Iran–Iraq War (1980–1988) is perhaps the most germane and historically proximate example, which makes its obscurity in defense studies somewhat puzzling. Though scarce, histories of that war surmise that Saddam Hussein's tactical reforms and the comparatively superior discipline of his troops were essential to Iraq's offensives, despite Iran's massive numbers.[111] Emerging data from the Russo-Ukrainian War of 2022 exposed similar trends in Russia's tactical and operational shortcomings.[112]

Researching, developing, acquiring, fielding, training, maintaining, updating, and codifying into doctrine tactical autonomous systems are generational endeavors that some theorists tend to underestimate, resulting in the perception that the process involves little more than a credit card swipe. Those skeptical enough to challenge the coherence of autonomous all-domain warfare are branded Luddites who derive power from their mastery of the current system.[113] But who will derive power from the next system? Power is not a zero-sum game.

Figure 4.1 Airmen conduct maintenance checks on a U.S. drone. U.S. Air Force Photo/Airman 1st Class Kristan Campbell.

To claim that the present military industrial complex is driven by blind self-interest while assuming that the next generation will be motivated by pragmatic altruists would be quite the leap of faith. Militarized AI is an emerging multi-billion-dollar industry, and, not wrongly, many will benefit from brokering the technology into defense contracts. But as Lt. Gen. Shanahan highlighted in numerous statements before the U.S. Congress, AI is not a panacea for defense problems, nor is it applicable to every military situation.[114] Certainly there is risk on both sides of the advocacy spectrum, and each endeavor is as likely to be rooted in human ambition as the operational needs of an uncertain future.

Balancing the need to integrate modern technologies into military formations with the reality that those formations could be forced to fight without them is a growing concern. Col. Robert Dixon, who served as a strategic planner on the Pentagon's joint staff, coined the relationship between technological progression and adversary-induced technological regression as 'trading queens' because certain armies might benefit from fighting in degraded technological environments.[115] Defence institutions have taken note of this vulnerability and implemented measures to mitigate risk. Yet the future remains as esoteric today as it was in any other age. Dixon put this bluntly: 'U.S. forces largely cannot move, shoot, or communicate without satellite-enabled technology. An adversary who figures out how to neutralize those systems, even briefly, and who is prepared to operate without high-tech tools, will have an insurmountable advantage'.[116] Some senior officers even maintain that these vulnerabilities are 'perhaps most prominent in the U.S. military'.[117] Armed forces must still train to fight in the past even as their existence is consumed by the possibilities of the future.

As Alexander understood long ago, the desire to master all domains of warfare is alluring – particularly to a wealthy nation with the winds of victory in its sails. But due to the sheer vastness of competitive options this century, leaders must be willing to specialize their formations through a strict regimen of strategic calculus that drives modernization priorities. The U.S. Marine Corps appears to have started this process with its bold ten-year plan published in early 2020. In addition to reducing its number of infantry battalions and removing certain capabilities entirely, such as river bridging and tank units, the plan also triples its missile defense elements and doubles its number of UAS units.[118] This somewhat extreme shift rattled many, while the Marine Corps commandant, Gen. David H. Berger, described the move as leaning toward a necessary specialization that would return the Corps to its maritime roots and orient long-range planning on the designated pacing challenge of China.[119]

The ramifications of these pursuits are entirely dependent upon whether they are used the right way, which makes talent management and leader development the modernization initiatives upon which all others are hinged.[120] The future of military innovation may ask leaders to sacrifice efficiency for effectiveness, or even vice versa, if the employment of certain weapons becomes unaffordable, immoral, or uncontrollable. How militaries choose to select, educate, and advance their leaders will govern this process and in turn be as consequential as any technology.

Modernizing Military Thought

After the tragic end of America's long jaunt into Afghanistan in 2021, one cannot help but ask: are free nations putting the cart before the horse by prioritizing systems over people? Fostering a coherent AI integration strategy, as well as a more complete understanding of how, when, and where military force should be applied, will overshadow the utility of any technology discussed in this chapter. This process takes time, and must therefore begin early in a professional's career, much as it did in Alexander's childhood. This formulaic sequence of professional development ultimately created a leader who thought clearly and creatively about innovative solutions to challenging problems.

Clausewitz compared the physical aspects of war to the hilt of a sword and moral factors to the 'precious metal, the real weapon, the finely-honed blade'.[121] If there is any truth to Clausewitz's analogy, then modern armies might be dedicating the preponderance of their time, budget, and effort to the hilt, and whatever remains to the blade. Western nations with strong economies have operated for some time under the privileged assumption that, with enough money and manpower, they can compete in and ultimately dominate every domain of warfare. Realities pertaining to the operational cost of developing, fielding, and maintaining new technologies, such as hypersonic missiles and AI-driven aircraft, have challenged this assumption for even the wealthiest powers – much more so for militaries accustomed to operating under significant budgetary constraints.[122]

These challenges are compounded by military–civil fusion initiatives spearheaded by China, which obligate non-government entities and even individual citizens to contribute to its military and intelligence programs. In contrast, the United States has already run into several contractual hang-ups with the private industry during its modernization push.[123] Western states might be forced to take a page out of Alexander's asymmetric playbook to devise creative, cost-effective, and potentially unconventional ways of challenging the strength of their peer competitors.

Modern militaries face a crisis of modernization not in the form of too little activity, but rather too much. Countless high-level working groups, command headquarters, and research centers erected to explore opportunities have inundated the military mind, but, in the process, left gaps in the connective human framework that transforms opportunities into effects. In this frenzy of activity, it is often the most novel devices that receive the most attention and funding, which exposes nations to the vulnerability of overlooking smaller or more subtle changes that could prove decisive, such as modernizing human optimization programs and education systems, or simply getting computers to work.[124] Failing to do so might result in nations dedicating time and money to capabilities that wind up irrelevant, marginalized, or degraded in war through indirect or creative means. This was precisely the type of thinking that led to Darius' overwhelming confidence in his naval supremacy before Alexander captured his main ports by land.

Despite Parmenion's urgings to the contrary, Alexander understood that combat power is not an equalitarian concept, and fire does not always need to be met with fire – nor should it be. On the Greek peninsula, this landlocked manner of thinking appeared almost counterintuitive, and yet it was astonishingly effective, perhaps because the Persians relied too heavily on their naval fleet. Like the dependence modern nations have on network-centric warfare and space connectivity, Darius assumed that his navy would bridge the competitive gap between Persian land forces and the Macedonian army. Alexander's approach to the Persian naval problem was one of ruthless prioritization and creative thinking that recognized operational limitations and played to his strengths. It should serve leaders well in the twenty-first century who have come to view competition as simply a matter of doing what an opponent does, only better. Alexander therefore shaped the competitive space around his abilities, forcing his enemies to fight when and where he chose. Although it was these principles that enabled Alexander to innovate and organize for victory in his campaigns across Asia to which we now turn, it was his own personal flaws that proved most crippling to his legacy and, ultimately, his empire.

Notes

1 Strout 2020.
2 Russia certainly showed no regard for international law during its 2022 invasion of Ukraine, as numerous reports describe the Russian military's widespread use of torture, targeting of civilians, and mass graves. U.S. Army Field Manual 27-10, 'The Law of Land Warfare', imposes strict limitations on everything from handling prisoners of war to protecting populations against certain consequences of war. The first edition ran in 1940.

3 For shifting recruiting and retention dynamics in the U.S. Armed Forces, see Ferguson 2021b; Linn 2023. For a conversation on the war for talent, see Kania and Moore 2019.
4 Mattis 2018, p. 7.
5 Parker, et al. 2019.
6 The U.S. Army's pamphlet for Multi-Domain Operations explains the following: 'The army builds and sustains multi-domain formations through the selection, training, and education of the leaders, Soldiers, and teams in them'. The document also mentions that improving 'resilience of leaders and Soldiers' is the 'Army's most valuable capacity . . .'. Townsend 2018, p. x. Other examples include Russia's 2008 'New Look' reforms that aimed to restructure the country's approach to military service contracts and developmental timelines: Grau and Bartles 2016, pp. 3–5.
7 Chapter 14 explores how the curse of success contributed to Alexander's flawed grand strategy and to that of the United States much later in Afghanistan and Iraq.
8 For instance, the perception of political bias in the armed forces as more retired officers become politically active in public, the ongoing military housing debacle in the United States, drug rings on military bases, sexual predators occupying senior leadership positions, and the British military's ambivalence toward its strategic future and force strength. Each of these alone is a problem but taken together they create an image that sours the idea of service.
9 On information fatigue, see Chapters 8 and 12 as well.
10 Some educators believe that the first step to solving this conundrum is a more robust liberal education that helps military leaders understand better how to think about complex problems (Silverstone 2019, pp. 65–76).
11 Arrian 4.13.1; Curtius 8.6.2.
12 Johnson, D. E. 1998, p. 223.
13 Murray 1996, p. 327.
14 Ricks gave a lecture at University of California Berkeley on 15 March 2011 covering his thesis on the shortcomings of general officer management. He published a book based on his research the following year, entitled *The Generals*.
15 See the Joint Chiefs of Staff visions for officer and enlisted leader PME: Milley 2020; Colón-López 2021.
16 See Kamphausen 2021, pp. 125–164, 167–205.
17 See Gavin 2019.
18 Brands and Gavin 2018; Wall Street Journal Editorial Board 2019; Economist Editorial Board 2019; Alterman 2019; Wexler 2020; granted, some drew attention to this trend nearly half a century ago: Ravitch 1985.
19 Gates 2017, pp. 98–130; McChrystal 2018, pp. 398–399.
20 McConville and McGee 2019.
21 In the pilot BCAP, one officer at the bottom of the centrally selected list rose to the top after a series of interviews and physical and mental tests: McConville and McGee 2019.
22 Daly 2022; see also Enriquez 2020.
23 Diodorus 17.65.2–3.
24 Arrian 3.16.11; cf. Curtius 5.2.6.
25 Curtius 5.2.2–6.
26 Arrian 1.18.6–8.

27 Arrian 1.18.6–9.
28 Arrian 1.20.1; this is reminiscent of modern service biases and favoritism. In planning for a response to the 9/11 attacks, the various U.S. service chiefs each wanted to shape the fight to their specialty: navy wanted a sea battle, air force wanted an air campaign, and army wanted to slug it out on the ground: Franks 2004, p. 275.
29 Plutarch, *Paullus* 19.2.
30 One example is the multi-year, multi-billion-dollar Future Combat Systems (FCS) program adopted and eventually phased out by the U.S. Army: Feickert and Lucas 2009. The spiritual successor to FCS is known as Joint All Domain Command and Control (JADC2), which some senior military officials claim has a higher chance of success as of 2021: Freedberg 2021.
31 The British Army's 2021 Integrated Review resulted in the 'Future Soldier' plan for an army that is 'more lethal, agile and expeditionary' to be 'ready for the future, not the past': Carleton-Smith 2021, p. 3. Australia's 2020 Defence Strategic Update reached similar conclusions: Morrison and Reynolds 2020, pp. 3–4.
32 Howard 1991, p. 96.
33 Allen and Husain 2017.
34 Gerasimov 'Doctrine' is neither a doctrine nor was it created by Valery Gerasimov, though many western analysts use the term in such a way. Mark Galeotti coined the phrase, but Gerasimov's philosophy on hybrid war echoes that of China's unrestricted warfare. Gerasimov confirmed that such strategies are underway in a March 2019 address at the Academy of Military Science: Galeotti 2018; cf. Liang and Xiangsui 1999.
35 Gerasimov 2016, p. 26.
36 During the speech, Putin also called on Russia's tech industry to act accordingly: Putin 2017; Associated Press 2017.
37 Webster, et al. 2017; Dahm 2020; Roberts, et al. 2021, pp. 59–77.
38 Mattis 2018.
39 Noonan 2020; Wallace 2022.
40 Examples of such entities include the National Security Commission on Artificial Intelligence, the National AI Advisory Committee, the Joint Artificial Intelligence Center (JAIC), the Defense Innovation Board, and the U.S. Army's AI Task Force.
41 For more on U.S. Army Futures Command's initiatives, see Kern, et al. 2022.
42 Branch rivalries have been highlighted as a point of friction by everyone from strategic theorists to combat generals: Franks 2004, p. 275; Knox and Murray 2001.
43 Artificial narrow intelligence, or ANI, consists of the learning algorithms behind functions like Apple's Siri, Amazon's Alexa, and other programs that search the digital space for answers and learn from human inputs.
44 UN Interregional Crime and Justice Research Institute: www.unicri.it/in_focus/on/unicri_centre_artificial_robotics
45 Corder 2023.
46 Gray 2005, pp. 37–45, 2014.
47 For acquisition reform issues, see Bracken and Alcala 1994.
48 Strategy before 2001 was uprooted by a single terrorist attack, and the strategies after 2001 were altered drastically by Putin's decision to invade Crimea in 2014: Taleb 2010.

49 Thucydides 1.76.
50 Jomini, c.1, pp. 1–2.
51 Graham Allison characterized this phenomenon as the 'Thucydides Trap', in which two competing great powers are ushered into an inevitable military confrontation (Allison 2017).
52 Hoffman 2020a.
53 Thucydides 3.82.
54 For instance, the United Kingdom's Integrated Operating Concept 2025 stated that the 'willingness to commit decisively hard capability . . . is an essential part of the ability to operate and therefore of deterrence' (Carter 2021, p. 12).
55 O'Hanlon 2015, p. 27.
56 Roberts, I. 2023.
57 More recent interpretations have added a 'C' for cyber to this concept. But cyber is not an instrument of national power any more than the sea. Cyber is a domain where the instruments of DIME can achieve influence, not an instrument itself: see Lonsdale and Kane 2020, p. 17.
58 Diplomatic, information, and economic warfare as opposed to simply competing militarily: Liang and Xiangsui 1999.
59 For more reading on the CCP's long game, see: Tobin 2020; Schuman 2020, pp. 295–318; Doshi 2021, pp. 68–100, 261–296; Economy 2022.
60 Saunders et al. 2019.
61 Post Russo-Chechen War policies emanating from Moscow focused increasingly on the information environment, many of which proved valuable as the Russian Federation began competing openly with NATO in 2014 and meddling in western elections two years later.
62 Gerasimov 2019, p. 4.
63 A2/AD consists of various integrated missile defense, air defense, and electronic warfare capabilities that deny an opponent access to a given area: Flannigan 2019.
64 Ferguson 2022a; Kagan et al. 2022, pp. 1–37.
65 Ferguson 2022e.
66 McFate, S. 2022a, McFate, S. 2022b.
67 Russia's 2008 'New Look' reforms under Defence Minister Anatoliy Serdyukov aimed at increasing the number of contracted soldiers while also establishing a professional corps of contracted enlisted soldiers: Grau and Bartles 2016, pp. 3–4; Radin et al. 2019, pp. 41–44.
68 Cohen 2022; Polyakova and Herbst 2022.
69 As of 2019, the Russian military consisted of 260,000 draftees and 370,000 contracted soldiers but added 120,000 draftees in 2020. Russia's Spring 2022 conscription was a failure, yielding only 89,000 draftees of its 134,500 goal. Russia Monitor 2019; see also Grau and Bartles 2016, p. 5; Luzin 2022.
70 Sweden reinstated conscription in 2017 shortly after Norway became the first NATO member to make service compulsory for women in 2016. As more American women enter combat roles, female enrollment in the U.S. selective service program has been called into question.
71 Eisenhower 1981, p. 136.
72 The three offsets consist of nuclearization, stealth technology and PGMs, and now AI and its utilizations. The Third Offset came to fruition under the guidance of Deputy Secretary of Defense Robert Work during the end of President

Obama's administration and just after Russia's invasion of Crimea in 2014: see Eliason 2017, pp. 6–11; Hasik 2018, pp. 14–21.
73 Knox and Murray 2001, pp. 192–193.
74 For example, the U.S. Department of Defense Directive Number 3000.09, Autonomy in Weapon Systems, which bans the production of LAWS for set periods.
75 Kai-Fu Lee 2018, p. 10.
76 Freedberg 2019.
77 Defense Intelligence Agency of the United States 2019.
78 Agrawal, Gans, and Goldfarb 2018.
79 Weyl and Lanier 2020.
80 DARPA calls this technology XAI: see Turek 2022.
81 Barnwell and Mohammad 2020.
82 Matsakis 2019.
83 Ferguson 2019, pp. 132–142.
84 The U.S. National Security Commission on AI emphasized this potential early in its massive 756-page report: National Security Council of the United States 2021.
85 A human in the loop means human operators still make the decision to act, while machines remain responsible for all decisions up to the point of action. A human on the loop means the machine will continue to cycle through its OODA loop unless a human interferes, up to firing on targets and re-acquiring and adjusting firing data.
86 This echoes Robert Oppenheimer's comments on atomic weapons' research. He believed that scientific progression made such research inevitable, and it was not a scientist's place to consider the potential political use of scientific breakthroughs. In other words, mankind will and must continue to conduct such research because it is possible. The same is true for AI: Bird and Sherwin 2005, pp. 287–289.
87 Oppenheimer 2022.
88 South 2019.
89 The U.S. Navy, for instance, is pouring $2.7 billion in researching ten different unmanned sea vehicles (USVs) over the five-year period between 2019 and 2025 as part of a plan to purchase 232 unmanned platforms for various domains. It is even decommissioning an aircraft carrier to compensate (Eckstein 2019).
90 Defense Advanced Research Projects Agency 2020; Applied Physics Laboratory 2021; Gans 2023.
91 Atherton 2019. The U.S. Army is also looking into human/machine fusion with its Cyber Soldier 2050 research: Combat Capabilities Development Command Chemical Biological Center 2019.
92 China even developed a microchip known as the 'Brain Talker' – a brain–computer interface chip that decodes brain information: Kania 2020, pp. 83–94.
93 Hallex and Cottom 2020, pp. 20–28.
94 McClintock 2019.
95 Newman 2019.
96 This generally refers to satellites more than 12,000 miles above the earth's surface: Sciutto 2019. In January 2022, a Chinese satellite physically pulled another out of orbit: Tingley 2022.

97 Roulette 2021.
98 Newcomb 2023.
99 For an assessment and overview of the U.S. Space Force, see Venable 2022. The Australian Defence Force established its Defence Space Command in March 2022: Kerr 2022; De Silva 2022.
100 As quoted in: Sciutto 2019.
101 Wired Magazine 2019.
102 The Raytheon-developed Multi-Spectral Targeting System is already employed in training scenarios using high-energy lasers, or HEL, in conjunction with U.S. Special Operations Command while attached to an AH-64 Apache attack helicopter.
103 Kuo 2022, pp. 48–50.
104 These are the words of former U.S. Undersecretary of Defense for Research and Engineering, Dr. Michael Griffin: Broadway 2018.
105 Millett 1996, p. 331. Liddell Hart anticipated this strategic evolution decades prior in his preface to *Strategy*. Liddell Hart 1954, pp. xviii–xix.
106 Creveld 2001, p. 310.
107 McDevitt et al. 2004. Nearly twenty years later, after the United States lost a two-decade war against tribal fighters with rudimentary weapons, similar discussions on the supposed changing nature of war continue.
108 Atwan 2015; Ostrovsky 2015; Ferguson 2020.
109 For instance, established in 2003, the Future Combat Systems intended to make the U.S. Army lighter and faster, but it was eventually scrapped. A 2010 GAO report highlighted acquisition as a key problem: Government Accountability Office 2010.
110 Brose 2019; Collins and Morgan 2020. In fact, the most recent data from the Russo-Ukrainian War shows that poor leadership, training, and morale were most detrimental to Russia's military operations there, not its equipment: Ackerman 2022.
111 Murray and Woods 2014, pp. 286–289, 296–297.
112 Dickinson 2022; O'Brien 2022.
113 Brose 2019, Brose 2020.
114 Shanahan 2019a, Shanahan 2019b.
115 Dixon 2017.
116 Dixon 2017.
117 Silva 2017, p. 3.
118 Berger 2020.
119 Berger and Evans 2020.
120 Scharre 2018, p. 8; Singer maintains that how militaries select leaders is their most important innovation: Singer 2009.
121 Clausewitz 1976, 3.3 (p. 217).
122 Despite all the attention on AI, the JAIC's 2019 budget was only $93 million, but Lt. Gen. Shanahan requested a budget of $268 million for 2020: Shanahan 2019b.
123 McMaster 2020b. For instance, the Pentagon's JEDI Cloud contract triggered a Microsoft and Amazon rivalry.
124 Nations should look to the strength and conditioning programs available in their SOF ranks for ideas on how to elevate the performance of their forces in general. The 'fix our computers' movement began with a viral LinkedIn post from U.S. Air Force officer Michael Kanaan: Waterman and Hadley 2022.

Part III
Choosing Battles – And Winning Wars?

Part III provides a history of Alexander's early campaigns, his triumph over the Persian Empire, and his eventual decision to press further east. We then look at modern wars through a tactical and operational lens, primarily the invasions of Afghanistan in 2001 and of Iraq in 2003. The thesis of Part III revolves around the complexity of mission command in a sensor- and information-saturated battlefield – challenges with which Alexander was unfamiliar. We assess that achieving speed and maintaining operational momentum have increased in complexity with the advent of RMA technologies, which contradict the purpose of systems designed to bring clarity to the battlefield. Based on lessons from Alexander's campaigns, and the findings in Chapters 2 and 4, we conclude that simplifying military operations to the extent possible could increase the likelihood of their tactical success in the twenty-first century.

5 Alexander's First Campaigns

Alexander had moved quickly after his accession to stamp out the revolt of the Greek states. After resurrecting the League of Corinth, he returned to the capital Pella for the winter, continuing a purge of opponents. Instead of making plans to invade Persia as soon as he could, he decided to delay for one year as he needed to pay some attention to his borders and, perhaps more importantly, give the army the experience of serving under its new king. Although in 340 he had launched a successful offensive against the Maedians, who had revolted from Macedonian rule, he had been only regent then. Likewise, in 338, he had distinguished himself in action at Chaeronea when Philip had given him command of the companion cavalry.[1] But he was still heir at that time. It therefore made sense before the uncertainty and challenges arising from invading Persia to win the confidence of his troops as general and king. Accordingly, he prepared for a campaign in Thrace and Illyria the following spring.

The following chapters treat Alexander's reign in some detail so that readers can appreciate his military greatness, his generalship and leadership skills, and his achievements as a king, and to balance those against his character flaws and other shortcomings. In doing so we recognize the lessons to be learned today not only from his successes and failures but also from his approaches to problems and issues, especially the further east he marched. Parallels between then and now become obvious, making Alexander as relevant today as in his own time.

The Early Battles

Demosthenes had spoken of Philip's speed and decisiveness, and Alexander soon showed that he had inherited both of those traits.[2] With probably 15,000 infantry and 5,000 cavalry, he left for Thrace the following spring of 335.[3] He marched without issue for about one week via Amphipolis and Neapolis (Kavala) to Philippopolis (Plovdiv), but then some unknown

DOI: 10.4324/9781003052951-9

Thracian tribes blocked any further advance at a narrow pass over Mount Haemus (the modern Shipka Pass?). They intended to let fly a row of wagons (probably only carts), which they had set up on the heights, at Alexander's men as they entered the pass, disrupting his line and in the chaos, attack him in force.[4]

Alexander was ready for them. As the wagons tumbled down the slopes gaining momentum, he bade the men in the wider part of the defile to move to one side, opening gaps in their line through which the wagons passed causing minimal damage.[5] At the same time, he shouted to the soldiers in the narrower parts of the pass, where movement was more restricted, to kneel or lie down, locking their shields over their heads so that the wagons rolled loudly but harmlessly over them. Next, he regrouped his entire line and, leading from the front, charged the enemy, killing 1,500 of them before the rest fled home. Their wives and children (who had travelled with them) were captured and sent back to Macedonia as slaves.[6]

Alexander's counter tactic was a stroke of genius and a tribute to his quick thinking. It was also testimony to the training and loyalty of the soldiers to follow his orders without hesitation. We shall see him using a similar tactic against Persian scythed chariots at the battle of Gaugamela in 331 (Chapter 7).

From there, Alexander marched to the Danube to engage the Triballi, a collection of fierce Thracian tribes.[7] Here, his motive was revenge. In 339, his father had been returning from a campaign in Scythia laden with booty when he was confronted by the Triballi, who demanded some of it. Philip refused and engaged them. In the fighting he was badly wounded when it seems a sarissa caught him in his upper leg or thigh and killed his horse under him. He had to be carried off the field to safety, allowing the Triballi to seize all the booty. Philip recovered, but he was lame for the rest of his life.[8]

Alexander knew he could not deal with the Triballi in all their different locations, so he tricked them into thinking that they were being attacked by only a small force of archers and slingers. The Triballi came together against this force but suddenly found themselves facing Alexander at the head of his entire army. In a pitched battle, he killed 3,000 of them, losing apparently only eleven cavalry and 41 infantry.[9] These figures seem oddly unbalanced. That is because ancient writers tended to exaggerate Alexander's victories by increasing the numbers of his opponents and of those killed in action while decreasing his army's size and his casualty rates.[10] We will discuss the sources at the end of this chapter.

Alexander had avenged his father, but his dealings with the remaining Triballi were not over. A number of them had fled after the battle to an island on the Danube called Peuce, where other Thracians came to support them.¹¹ The fast-flowing water prevented Alexander crossing with ease, so rather than keep making attempts to cross the river and being sitting ducks to enemy missiles from the opposite bank, he decided to starve his foes into surrender. His plan, however, came unstuck when 4,000 cavalry and 8,000 infantry belonging to the Getae tribe (of the northern Danube plain) arrived to relieve those trapped on the island.¹²

Ordinarily, Alexander might have been expected to engage the Getae as soon as they arrived. But doing so might allow those on Peuce to take advantage of the distraction to escape or even join with the Getae against him. He therefore decided on a tactic to demoralize both groups of his enemies.¹³ One dark night, he had his men put together rafts of tent covers stuffed with hay and then, with 1,500 cavalry and 4,000 infantry, he crossed the Danube and in a campaign of coercion ravaged the crops and lands of the Getae. Despite the enemy's high numbers, they were taken by surprise and surrendered at once. When those on the island found out and realized they were now isolated, they followed suit. Alexander's cunning and rapid execution had carried the day, thanks to having all power concentrated into his hands as king and being always physically present. He thus demonstrated once again his tactical patience, and that despite his lust for glory in battle, he fought with his mind as much as his sword.

Two months had gone by since leaving Pella, so Alexander took his troops south to the land of his ally, Langarus the Agrianian, for some much-needed rest and recreation. It was not to be. While there, news reached him that a certain Cleitus, king of the Illyrian tribe of the Dardani (around Kosovo), and probably the son of the Bardylis whom Philip II had resoundingly defeated in 358, had joined with Glaucias of the Taulantii tribe (around Tirana) and the Autariatae tribe (in modern Bosnia) to threaten Macedonia.¹⁴ This was a threat to his northwest frontier that Alexander had to neutralize immediately.

The Campaign in Illyria

Alexander worked in tandem with Langarus for what ended up being a major operation in Illyria.¹⁵ He ordered Langarus against the Autariatae while the king moved at speed across the Axius river to Stobi and then south to the plain of modern Florina to besiege Cleitus in Pellium, on the western border of Macedonia, before the Taulantii could rendezvous with him.¹⁶ But his plan to assault Cleitus' position had to be checked when Glaucias arrived and positioned his men behind Alexander's camp in the heights opposite Pellium.¹⁷ That gave him control of the high ground and put Alexander in an inferior position.

In the meantime, Glaucias attacked a foraging party under Philotas, forcing Alexander to mobilize his Agrianians, along with some archers, hypaspists, and cavalry, to rescue Philotas and the men before they suffered any harm. Alexander, hemmed in, needed to gain the upper hand, and so turned to psychological pressure, something for which he would become famous. He ordered his army to put on a series of military drills, which we described in Chapter 3 for the light they shed on the phalanx's training.[18]

The spectacle of a phalanx line moving forwards, backwards, and sideways with sarissas at the ready and in total silence must have been thrilling, and it is no surprise that Glaucias and his force drew closer for a better view. This was what Alexander had anticipated. On a prearranged signal, the Macedonians deafeningly clashed their swords against their amour while yelling out their battle cry *Alalalalai!* so that it bounced off the surrounding hills. Panicking, Glaucias' soldiers fled, allowing Alexander to extricate himself with some difficulty from the heights and across the river.[19] Despite the impressive weaponry in Alexander's army, it was their remarkable discipline that made the difference here, further demonstrating the critical role of moral factors in RMA discussed in Chapter 2. But the danger for the king was still not over as Glaucias rallied his men and kept Alexander trapped between them and Cleitus' troops.

When Alexander was told that the Taulantii had relaxed the guard around their camp and not erected a palisade or dug a trench around it he pounced that night. His speed again shows that he realized he was in a perilous position. Catching the enemy by surprise, he killed a number of them before the rest fled, thus robbing Cleitus of reinforcements.[20] The latter was now forced to escape by setting fire to Pellium and using the smoke as cover. Alexander was not prepared to let his adversary go, but then news reached him that Thebes in Boeotia had again revolted and was calling the Greeks take up arms against him.[21]

Alexander now had two choices: pursue Cleitus or deal with Thebes. His heart perhaps told him to go after Cleitus since he had not completely defeated him. But the Theban situation was more dangerous to the Macedonian hegemony of Greece, bringing sharply into focus that in any transference of power a leader cannot afford to be complacent, so he headed to Thebes. Fortunately, Cleitus did not bother him again.

Despite some worrying moments in Illyria, Alexander's first campaigns as king had been successful, even if Cleitus had escaped. It also provides us, albeit on a smaller scale, with an illustration of Alexander the king and general: his speed, his quick thinking, his leadership qualities, and his willingness to take risks along with his men, not to mention the training and responsiveness of his troops. Those qualities would also carry them through the hard fighting they faced in Asia – until he lost touch with the rank and file of his army to show that no matter the charisma and success, a commander needed his men's loyalty and trust as much as they needed his.

The Revolt of Thebes

After Philip II defeated the Greeks at Chaeronea in 338, he had installed a pro-Macedonian oligarchy and garrison in Thebes, forcing several democrats to flee into exile.[22] On Philip's death in 336, there had been a revolt of the Greeks states, including Thebes, which Alexander quickly ended. Now, in 335, the rumour reached the exiled democrats that Alexander had been killed in Illyria, which they exploited to persuade their fellow citizens to besiege the Macedonian garrison on the Theban Cadmea (Acropolis).[23]

This was no ordinary revolt, for the Thebans were actively calling on the other Greeks to join them against 'the tyrant of Greece'.[24] The Thebans may also have been supporting Amyntas, who had been next in line to the throne in 359, and who was perhaps in Thebes planning a coup.[25] Apparently the Persian King, evidently worried about Philip's – now Alexander's – plan to invade his empire, sent the enormous sum of 300 talents to Athens to encourage the city to support Thebes, though we should be sceptical about this episode.[26]

Alexander's death was fake news as the Thebans would soon discover. He marched south with 30,000 infantry and 300 cavalry, covering 250 miles of flat and rugged terrain (including the Pindus range) in only thirteen days (with only one day off at Pelinna in Thessaly to give his men a break). He had averaged eighteen to twenty miles a day, an astonishing achievement of endurance and leadership, and was already in Boeotia at Onchestus when the Thebans first learned of his approach.[27] It is not surprising they did not believe it was him but thought it was Antipater or even a different Alexander (son of Aeropus), who had marched south from Macedonia.[28]

But it was Alexander, and he wasted little time in besieging the city. The Thebans were outnumbered, even though they had added to their numbers with slaves and metics (resident aliens), but they were not going to give in without a fight. They also expected support from the other Greeks, but it never came. Their strategy was to blockade the Macedonian garrison on the Cadmea so it could not open the city gates to Alexander's men while making daring sallies to disrupt his siege preparations. To ensure that Alexander could not rescue the garrison, the defenders built a double palisade to reinforce the southern section of their wall, which formed part of the Cadmea.

The siege was a challenging one for Alexander, but inconsistency in our ancient writers does not allow us to paint a complete picture of it (on sources see below). Arrian, following Ptolemy, states that Alexander was thinking of charging the palisade when one of the commanders, Perdiccas, jumped the gun and rushed it.[29] His action prompted Amyntas, another general, to follow suit, leaving Alexander with no choice but to follow with all his men. The Macedonians breached the first palisade but became trapped between it and the second one and were attacked by a contingent of Theban infantry. Seventy of Alexander's Cretan archers were killed (including their commander Eurybotas), and many others were wounded, including Perdiccas, in bitter fighting.[30] Fortunately for Alexander, the Theban formation lost its unity; the king rallied his men to counterattack the Thebans and push them back to the city gates, saving themselves from further casualties.

In their rush to retreat for safety, the Thebans jammed the city gates open, allowing Alexander and his men to force their way through them. Brutal hand-to-hand fighting in the streets followed, though our sources contradict themselves by saying that the Thebans fought bravely or were in disarray. The Theban cavalry was able to escape, leaving the infantry to fall victim to the hardened Macedonian troops. Massacre followed, with the Macedonians even ignoring religious convention to drag suppliants, including women and the elderly, from sanctuaries and slaughter them. Six thousand Thebans were killed, 30,000 taken prisoner and sold into slavery to the loss on Alexander's side of about 500 men.[31] Those Thebans who managed to escape were cursed.

Worse was to come. Alexander called together the Phocians, Plataeans, and the other Boeotians who were with him and held an *ad hoc* meeting of the League of Corinth to decide Thebes' fate. Despite there being so few members of the league present, thus calling into doubt the legitimacy of the meeting, they decided that Thebes should be burned to the ground, ostensibly because the Thebans had medized (turned pro-Persian) during the Persian Wars. Alexander left standing only the temples as well as houses belonging to the poet Pindar (who had written an encomium to a former king of Macedonia, Alexander I) and his descendants.[32] Thebes would not be rebuilt until 316.

The razing of Thebes was likened by the late fourth-century rhetorician Hegesias of Magnesia to removing one of the 'eyes' of Greece.[33] There is no question that it was a dark episode in Alexander's reign, which in many respects set a pattern to the rest of his tenure as king: once Alexander felt crossed, there was no chance of redemption. As he marched further eastwards, his dealings with the local people grew increasingly bloody if they resisted him. Likewise, at Thebes, the Macedonians had sacrilegiously murdered civilians who had taken refuge in temples, where they were supposedly protected. Alexander often showed a similar disregard for the civilians in the cities he besieged in Asia, where also rape and murder of women and children with impunity were part of taking a city.[34] Today, such abuse is rightly condemned and outlawed, though it still exists as we see in the Taliban's retaking of Afghanistan, Russia's war on Ukraine, or in Ethiopia's civil war with its Tigray population.

The siege of Thebes also demonstrates the paradox of Alexander's nobility and admiration of courage and dignity in his enemies as well as in himself and his men.[35] A Thracian soldier in the Macedonian army was said to have raped a Theban noblewoman, Timocleia. In retaliation, she told him she had thrown all her treasure down a well, and after he climbed down, she pelted him with stones and killed him. Brought before Alexander she showed no remorse but only defiance, proudly telling him that she was prepared to die now than suffer the same experiences as before.[36] Impressed by her brave demeanour, Alexander spared her life.

We can understand Alexander's personal frustration with Thebes, but there are strategic reasons for making an example of the city. He needed to emphasize, as our ancient writers claim, that while he was away in Asia, resistance to Macedonian rule was futile. His punishment, then, was one of deterrence. It 'presented possible rebels among the Greeks with a terrible warning', according to Diodorus, while Plutarch stated that:

> Alexander's principal object in permitting the sack of Thebes was to frighten the rest of the Greeks into submission by making a terrible example. But he also put forward the excuse that he was redressing the wrongs done to his allies.[37]

Certainly, the Greeks remained passive from now on, apart from an abortive attempt by Sparta in 331 to incite war against Macedonia, until Alexander died in 323 when many states again revolted.

After the fall of Thebes, Alexander returned to Pella via Dium, the Macedonian religious centre in the foothills of Mount Olympus, where he sacrificed to the Macedonians' principal deity Zeus Olympios.[38] At Pella, he fine-tuned plans for the invasion of Persia. He was anxious to put his father's grand plan into effect after the delays on campaign and at Thebes and hence he ignored the advice of his senior generals Antipater and Parmenion to have an heir first.[39] He appointed Antipater as regent (*epitropos*) of Greece and deputy *hegemon* of the League of Corinth in his absence, entrusting him with a force of 12,000 infantry and 1,500 cavalry.[40] Then in the spring of 334, a little shy of twenty-two years old, he set off to march the 300 miles from Pella to Sestus on the Hellespont (Dardanelles), from where he set sail for Asia.

What he had not done before he left – a significant failing on the part of any ruler – was to marry so he could have an heir, although who the lucky lady might have been is debatable.[41] When he did finally marry, to Roxane of Bactria (Afghanistan) in 327, it was too little too late: she was still pregnant (with the future Alexander IV) when Alexander died in Babylon in June 323. The uncertainty over their heir to the throne contributed the most to the Macedonian empire's dismemberment on Alexander's death (see Chapter 13).

For now, Alexander had proved himself as a general and king, displaying the leadership skills and bold, quick thinking that would become his legendary trademarks. If that meant punishing enemies and even treating them inhumanely, so be it: he was in military conflict and needed both to win and protect his own troops. He could not allow himself (even if it were in his character) to have a 'squeaky clean' image when it came to dealing with his foes or leading his men or indeed protecting his kingdom. He expected a lot from his soldiers, and he placed them in jeopardy, but he rewarded them for their valour and the risks he demanded they take. For Alexander and the Greeks, war was never anaesthetized: commanders at times had to send troops into life-threatening situations for the greater good.

At the same time, Alexander's early forays reveal a darker side to his character, one that came to the fore often in his invasion of Asia. This was to punish anyone who crossed him, including high-level generals. We should therefore ask whether a commander's successes in warfare outweighed flaws in his character – both in antiquity and down to the present day. How might Alexander's 'greatness' (or the reputation of any feted leader) be impacted by the tendency to put personal reasons over strategic, especially when this meant putting the lives of his soldiers at risk and not serving his kingdom?

The Literary Sources on Alexander

We have already commented on some aspects of the sources' presentation of Alexander, but more needs to be said before we move to Persia to act as a warning when we consider all his actions, and indeed whether we are dealing with the historical king or a legendary figure.

Surviving narrative accounts of Alexander's reign date from centuries after he lived and died.[42] The first is by Diodorus Siculus (of Sicily), who in the late republican era wrote a *Universal History* from mythical times to Julius Caesar's campaigns in Gaul of 54 (of which only fifteen of the forty books survive intact); then we have Arrian (Lucius Flavius Arrianus), who in the second century AD wrote a history of Alexander; Quintus Curtius

Rufus, whose history of Alexander was written in the mid to later first century AD (only eight of the ten books survive); and Justin (Marcus Junianus Justinus), who sometime in the second to fourth centuries AD wrote an epitome (précis) of a first century BC work by Gnaeus Pompeius Trogus.

To these we can add other writers, such as the biographer Plutarch, who in the first to second century AD composed a series of lives of prominent Greeks and Romans (including Alexander) to the end of the Roman Republic. Then we have the geographers Strabo (first century BC to first century AD) and Pausanias (second century AD), who provide descriptions of many areas and cities, together with historical events, and scattered mentions of our period by, for example, Polybius (second century BC) and Livy (first century BC).

These later ancient writers used a number of earlier works contemporaneous with Alexander's life. We call these latter works 'primary' sources and the much later ones 'secondary' sources. The problem, however, is that none of the primary sources has survived intact for us to consult. We know there were at least forty such 'primary' writers, of which the more important were Ptolemy, Aristobulus of Cassandreia; Duris of Samos; Callisthenes of Olynthus; and Cleitarchus of Alexandria. In addition, there was the *Ephemerides*, or royal journal, which supposedly recorded Alexander's actions in his final days and his death. All these primary works today exist only as fragments (over 400 of them, some short and others lengthy), which were quoted or paraphrased by the secondary writers. To make matters worse, when earlier works are cited, they often show differences between the various accounts of Alexander's life and reign.[43]

The source problem now comes into focus, and by extension the historical Alexander for we have no way of knowing how accurately our later writers (the secondary sources) used the earlier ones, whether they quoted them correctly or whether they cherry-picked to fit their own presentation of the king, especially because of the Roman background and attitude to kingship against which they were writing.

Of our later writers, Arrian is generally viewed as the most reliable. Among other things, he used the accounts of Alexander's bodyguard Ptolemy (who later was king of Egypt and founded the Ptolemaic dynasty) and Aristobulus (an engineer or architect since he is never mentioned in any of the fighting), who accompanied him on campaign.[44] Arrian even tells us this in the *Preface* to his work:[45]

> Wherever Ptolemy son of Lagus and Aristobulus son of Aristobulus have both given the same accounts of Alexander son of Philip, it is my practice to record what they say as completely true, but where they

differ, to select the version I regard as more trustworthy and also better worth telling. In fact other writers have given a variety of accounts of Alexander, nor is there any other figure of whom there are more historians who are more contradictory of each other, but in my view Ptolemy and Aristobulus are more trustworthy in their narrative, since Aristobulus took part in king Alexander's expedition, and Ptolemy not only did the same, but as he himself was a king, mendacity would have been more dishonourable for him than for anyone else.

Yet while there is value to using writers who had marched with Alexander, Arrian's explanation that Ptolemy's account is more trustworthy because he was a king, and therefore less likely to falsify facts, immediately triggers a warning bell – do kings really not lie? Yes, they do, and Ptolemy was no different. His *History* of Alexander is problematic because he had his own agenda, to make himself out to be greater than he was and a close confidant of Alexander, which even ancient writers noticed – thus Curtius' statement that Ptolemy was 'truly no detractor from his own glory'.[46] Worse, though, is that he shows animosity toward individuals, especially Perdiccas (who in 320 had invaded Egypt to topple Ptolemy from power but had been killed in the attempt).[47]

When Ptolemy began to write his *History* towards the end of his life, in the 280s, he skewed his presentation of Perdiccas.[48] This explains the confusion in our sources, mentioned above, about how the attack on Thebes in 335 began. It is only Ptolemy who accuses Perdiccas of recklessness, an account that Arrian followed.[49] Diodorus, following a different source, states that he followed Alexander's orders loyally, and Curtius does not even mention it.[50] Since Ptolemy was an Alexander apologist, always out to portray the king in the best light, he likely strove to shift the blame away from him for the Macedonians' sudden disadvantage and losses by blaming Perdiccas.

Getting to the real or historical Alexander is fraught with difficulty thanks to the nature of our sources. We need to bear this in mind, especially when it comes to his battles and sieges in the Persian Empire.

Notes

1 Sears and Willekes 2016.
2 Demosthenes 1.12–13, contrasting Philip's speed and decisiveness with the slowness of the Athenian Assembly (at which all male citizens over eighteen debated and voted on domestic and foreign policy).
3 Campaign: Diodorus 17.8.1–2, Arrian 1.1.6–13, Plutarch, *Alexander* 11.5, Justin 11.2.8, with Fuller 1960, pp. 219–226; Keegan 1987, pp. 66–71; Bosworth 1988a, pp. 28–32; Hammond and Walbank 1988, pp. 32–55; Ashley 1998,

pp. 167–175; Lonsdale 2007, pp. 111–114; English 2011, pp. 19–32; Worthington 2014a, pp. 128–130.
4   Arrian 1.1.7.
5   Arrian 1.1.8–10.
6   Arrian 1.1.13–2.1.
7   Arrian 1.2.1–7. On the Triballi, see Papazoglou 1978, pp. 9–86.
8   Plutarch, *Moralia* 331b, with Worthington 2008, p. 140, Worthington 2014a, p. 80.
9   Arrian 1.2.7 from Ptolemy.
10 Hammond 1989b; cf. Hammond 1992a, pp. 129–136.
11 Arrian 1.2.2–3.
12 Arrian 1.3.1–2.
13 Arrian 1.3.3–4.8.
14 Arrian 1.5.1, with Papazoglou 1978, pp. 87–130.
15 Arrian 1.5–6, with Hammond 1974, Hammond 1977; Bosworth 1982; Hammond and Walbank 1988, pp. 39–48; English 2009b, pp. 25–34; King 2018, pp. 138–141.
16 Arrian 1.5.5.
17 Arrian 1.5.8–9, 12.
18 Arrian 1.6.1–4.
19 Arrian 1.6.6–8.
20 Arrian 1.6.9–11.
21 Arrian 1.7.1–4.
22 Diodorus 16.87.3, 17.13.5, Justin 9.4.7–8, with Worthington 2008, pp. 154–155, Worthington 2014a, pp. 97–98.
23 Diodorus 17.8.2–14, Arrian 1.7–9, Plutarch, *Alexander* 11.7–13, Plutarch, *Demosthenes* 23.1–3, Justin 11.3.6–4.8, with Fuller 1960, pp. 85–88; Bosworth 1988a, pp. 32–33, 194–196; Hammond and Walbank 1988, pp. 56–66; Ashley 1998, pp. 175–181; Worthington 2003b, English 2009b, pp. 34–40; Worthington 2014a, pp. 131–135; King 2018, pp. 142–146.
24 Diodorus 17.9.5; cf. Arrian 1.7.1–2, Justin 11.2.
25 Worthington 2003b.
26 Aeschines 3.239–240; cf. 133, 155–156, Dinarchus 1.10, 18–20, 24–26, with Worthington 2010a.
27 Arrian 1.7.5; cf. Diodorus 17.9.1. for appearing 'suddenly'.
28 Arrian 1.7.6.
29 Ptolemy, *BNJ* 138 F 3 = Arrian 1.8.1.
30 Diodorus 17.11.3–12.1; Arrian 1.8.3–7.
31 Diodorus 17.14.1; Plutarch, *Alexander* 11.12.
32 Arrian 1.9.9–10; Plutarch, *Alexander* 11.11–12; cf. Diodorus 17.14.2–4.
33 Hegesias, *BNJ* 142 T 3. The sacking of Thebes became a topos in contemporary Greek oratory and in later written accounts of the period.
34 See Rawlings 2007, pp. 218–220.
35 See Roisman 2003.
36 Aristobulus, *BNJ* 139 F 2b (= Plutarch, *Moralia* 259d–260d); Plutarch, *Alexander* 11.12, with Worthington 2014a, p. 134, on the episode.
37 Diodorus 17.14.4, Plutarch, *Alexander* 11.11.
38 Arran 1.11.1; cf. Diodorus 17.16.3.

39 Diodorus 17.16.1–3.
40 Diodorus 17.17.4–5.
41 See Baynham 1997.
42 For a discussion of the ancient sources, including epigraphic and numismatic, see Worthington 2014a, pp. 311–319, citing bibliography, especially Hammond 1983, Bosworth 1988b; Hammond 1993a; Bosworth 1996a, Baynham 1998.
43 *BNJ* nos. 117–153. Roughly one-quarter are translated in Worthington 2011, which also contains a selection of modern scholars' works on various aspects of Alexander's reign.
44 Bosworth 1988a, pp. 40, 61–64, 79–83.
45 Arrian, *Preface* 1–2; trans. Brunt 1976, *ad loc*.
46 Curtius 9.5.21.
47 Ptolemy's *History*: Worthington 2016, pp. 231–219, citing bibliography; animus towards Ptolemy: Worthington 2016, pp. 215–216. On Arrian's *Preface* and why he used Ptolemy, see now Worthington 2022.
48 Dating: Worthington 2016, pp. 216–219.
49 Ptolemy, *BNJ* 138 F 3 = Arrian 1.8.1.
50 Diodorus 17.12.3; but note that we do not have the first two books of Curtius' work (see Baynham 1998).

6 Alexander in Persia 1: King of Asia

The Persian Empire stretched from Turkey to Pakistan and included Egypt and Syria.¹ To help administer it, in 513 Darius I divided it into twenty satrapies (regions) each under a satrap subservient only to the Great King (the capitalized K is a modern practice to refer to Persian Kings rather than other kings like Alexander). The King had several palace centres dotted throughout his empire, which were far apart. As noted in the Introduction, by today's roads the distance from the most westerly capital, Sardis (Sart in Turkey), to the most easterly, Persepolis (northeast of Shiraz in Iran), was roughly 2,000 miles while the distance from Persepolis to the most northernly palace at Ecbatana (probably Hamadan, Iran) was 556 miles. Hence the King could move to any satrapy or palace as he saw fit, covering hundreds of miles in the process, to challenge Alexander's communication and supply lines and keep him on the back foot.

Much of Persia's history and customs were already known to the Greeks from the *Histories* of Herodotus, the *Persica* of Ctesias of Cnidus (a doctor to Artaxerxes II), and Xenophon's *Anabasis* or *March of the Ten Thousand* (the account of the Greek mercenaries who had joined the army of Cyrus in 403 only to have to march by themselves to Greek towns in the Black Sea area). In addition, Alexander was said to have questioned Persian envoys closely at his father's court about the kingdom's resources and communications.²

But as Alexander marched further east in Central Asia and what the Greeks called 'India' (present-day Pakistan after partition), lands unknown to them, he was forced to depend on local guides while ensuring proper communication and supply lines. Equally, he relied on locals as interpreters, especially in India, though we are told that in Sogdiana he appointed a civilian named Pharnuches of Lycia to help with a threat to Maracanda because he knew the local language.³

If pitched battle was indeed the 'true test of leadership', then Alexander more than passed the test. He marched thousands of miles and defeated large enemy forces without modern navigational and information-collecting aids or weapons systems; he mobilized his army effortlessly, at times leading it on demanding forced marches, and he unfailingly maintained contacts with commanders throughout his empire, all showing that, even in his time, he combined the three fundamentals of modern combat operations: attacking, moving, and communicating.[4] Unlike modern combat, in which the general or senior military staff do not lead an army into battle but delegate that to other officers, Alexander as king personally led from the front – he was 'both the thinking and fighting head of his army'.[5] His campaign was therefore also a testament to his strategic and leaderships skills, the value of psychological warfare, and to how a foreign army can survive in distant, hostile, and unknown lands, all of which are lessons for today's military operations.

For reasons of time and space, the following accounts of Alexander's battles and sieges cannot give all their details but only their main sequences of events.[6]

The Battle of the Granicus River

Alexander's army of Macedonian and allied troops numbered at least 30,000 infantry and 5,000 cavalry, perhaps even as high as 43,000 infantry and 5,500 cavalry.[7] It also had with it non-military personnel, researchers to record information about the topography, flora, and fauna of the areas through which they marched, and even a retinue of intellectuals to keep the king company.[8] From Sestus it crossed the mile-wide Hellespont, separating Europe from Asia as it does today. Before landing in the satrapy of Hellespontine Phrygia, Alexander threw a spear into Asian soil, making it plain that he was out to conquer the entire empire – it would be his 'spear won' territory.[9] His successors, who broke up his empire on his death, claimed the same right as the basis for their rule: constitutional legitimacy thus gave way to military might.

Rather than immediately linking up with the vanguard force sent shortly before Philip II was assassinated, Alexander detoured to Troy (Hisarlik) to sacrifice at the tomb of his hero and ancestor on his mother's side, Achilles.[10] His rationale was threefold: to proclaim his piety to a family ancestor; to underscore his Homeric nature and intention to be a second Achilles; and to cause consternation among the Persians that another mainland warrior had arrived intending to bring destruction. The last was part of a continuing psychological strategy.[11]

King Darius III, then at Susa, did not initially see Alexander as a threat and ordered his satrap of Hellespontine Phrygia, Arsites, to defeat the invader.[12] Arsites called a meeting of his commanders to decide strategy at Zelea at which the mercenary commander Memnon of Rhodes proposed a scorched earth plan to rob Alexander's army of much-needed provisions.[13] Alexander had taken with him only ten days' worth of supplies and intended to forage as he went along, like most armies throughout antiquity. Memnon knew about the disadvantages a foraging army faced, hence his plan had merit and the potential to force Alexander to retreat.[14] His proposal was unpopular because of its effect on the land, not to mention it would rob Arsites of the personal glory of defeating the Macedonian king. Therefore, the satrap opted for a pitched battle and chose the Granicus (Biga) River as it was a natural barrier obstructing Alexander from continuing his march east. His mistake, however, would prove that, at times, the most unpopular plan might also be the most effective.

In May, the Persian army took up a defensive position on the east bank of the river, above the plain of Adrasteia.[15] In Chapter 5, we discussed issues with the ancient sources, especially how they present troop and casualty figures. With this battle, we have embellishment of numbers, with Arrian claiming the Persians had 20,000 cavalry and the same number of Greek mercenaries under Memnon as well as infantry, but 10,000 is more likely, including 5,000 rather than 20,000 mercenaries.[16] Alexander's army, which arrived at the river's western bank early one evening, matched or even outnumbered the enemy one for once.

The details of the battle and the deployment of the Persian line are uncertain because of inconsistencies in our two major sources, Arrian and Diodorus. Arrian places the Persian cavalry on the riverbank with the infantry behind it on the slopes or at least atop the the river bank, so they could launch arrows and spears down onto the Macedonians.[17] But that would leave the front cavalry ranks open to Macedonian missiles as Alexander crossed the river, not to mention the infantrymen's difficulty of having to run down the steep bank – if like today, about twelve feet (3.6 metres) high and covered in woodland – and into the river in any formation. Diodorus is preferable, who tells us that the cavalry along with the infantry was set back from the riverbank to charge the invading force with fewer losses or even intimidate Alexander from trying to cross to their side.[18]

The Macedonians at the top of their equally high and wooded bank were at a disadvantage, which is why the general Parmenion advised Alexander to wait and find another way to cross the river.[19] The king famously retorted that after crossing the Hellespont, it would be embarrassing to pause at a stream like the Granicus.[20] Regardless of the veracity of Alexander's reply, we should follow Arrian's account that he ordered a sudden attack the same evening to catch the enemy off guard as one of his favourite stratagems was the element of surprise.[21] Crossing the river bed, which was about eighty feet wide and no more than a small channel about three feet deep (as is the case today in summer), was less of a challenge than moving his men. They needed to make their way down the steep western bank, across the river, engage the enemy, and then push up the opposite bank without heavy losses.

For these reasons, Alexander ruled out a frontal assault with his phalanx in its regular formation. Thanks to being able to make informed on-the-spot decisions, he moved his men to a bend of the river where there were lower banks on both sides, and to distract the Persians he decided to send his line across the river diagonally. The flank closest to the Persian line would thus draw enemy fire while the rest of the line crossed with, he hoped, minimal casualties before regrouping. Since his line was over a mile long, the execution of this manoeuvre was going to be a major challenge to his tactical skills and the men's training and courage.

The infantry was arranged into six battalions at the centre at eight men deep, flanked on both ends by the cavalry at ten horses deep (Figure 6.1). Parmenion, on the left flank, was in command of the Thracian, Thessalian, and other Greek cavalry, but Alexander split the cavalry on the right flank into two groups: the one closest to the centre was composed of one squadron

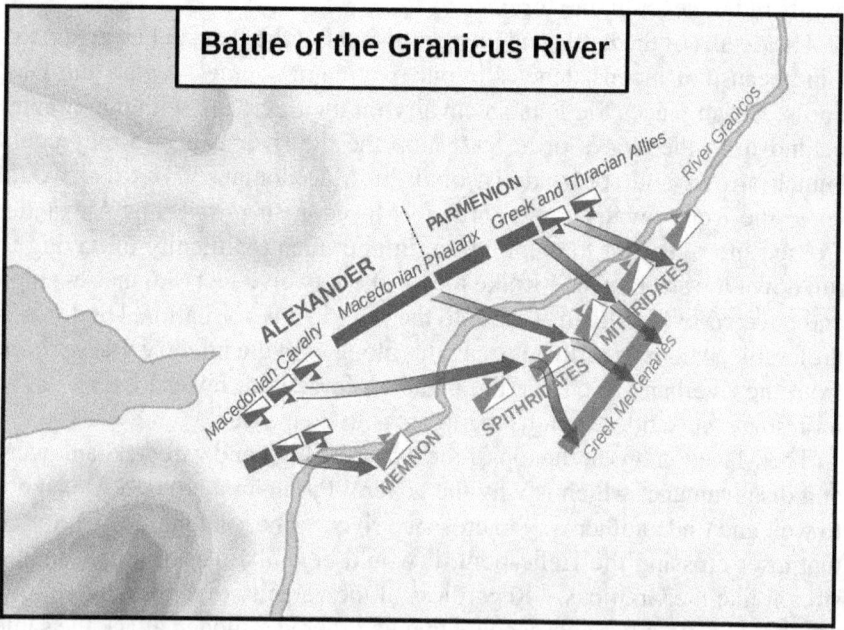

Figure 6.1 Battle of the Granicus River. Credit: Andrei Nacu via Wikimedia Commons.

of companion cavalry and the *prodromoi*, commanded by Amyntas, and the one on the extreme right of mostly Companions, Agrianians, and archers under Philotas.[22] Alexander stood by Amyntas. When the Persians saw that Alexander had massed more cavalry on his right flank than his left under Parmenion, they naturally suspected he was going to charge their left and reinforced it. But this was not the king's plan as became clear once he gave the command to advance.

Alexander had noted that enemy cavalry's position was a weakness as it could not charge at full speed because of the river bed and could not fall back without running into the slopes. He decided to focus on the Persian centre, intending to open a gap in it through which he would lead some of his cavalry and two battalions of the phalanx to encircle the enemy line. To this end, instead of crossing the river in a straight line, as the enemy may have expected, he ordered Amyntas and a small strike force of fast cavalry (*prodromoi*) to set off first and cross in a diagonal line towards the Persian left – a 'pawn sacrifice' as the manoeuvre has been dubbed.[23] Thinking that this was the prelude to a full-scale onslaught on their left, the Persians moved even more troops to there, and in doing so created what Alexander wanted – a gap between the left and the centre of the line.[24]

We can only imagine Amyntas' reaction to this seemingly suicidal plan, but he obeyed the king's orders without question, a tribute to his training, loyalty, and the king's leadership. As his men approached the opposite shore, javelins rained down on them followed by a cavalry charge, which they were able to absorb and so protect Philotas on the extreme right and the line to their left. The fighting was brutal, especially at the outset according to Arrian, as the Macedonians had to fight from the river, and their footing was at times unsteady.[25] The fatal flaw of the phalanx was of course that it needed stable, level terrain to operate with maximum deadly efficiency. But the men succeeded in distracting the Persians enough for Alexander to send out a prearranged trumpet blast alerting his men that he and his right wing were on the move and focused on the opening in the Persian line.

The Persian cavalry attempted to regroup and plug the gap, but Alexander's men were too quick. While they engaged the enemy cavalry, Parmenion led his left flank across the river without challenge. Once the Thessalian cavalry under him joined in the fight, the Persian horsemen fled. That left only the Greek mercenaries under Memnon, who had not taken part in the fighting. Nevertheless, Alexander declared them traitors as he thought that Greeks, even if they were mercenaries, should not fight other Greeks.[26] He killed most of them and sent the 2,000 survivors back to Macedonia to work in the mines. Memnon and Arsites survived, but the latter, who had made the costly mistake of favouring a pitched battle, committed suicide.[27]

During the battle Alexander was almost killed in hand-to-hand combat, although the fight was probably exaggerated to make him more of a hero.[28] Before the Persian cavalry fled, the white plume on his helmet was spotted by Darius' son-in-law Mithridates, who immediately recognized it as belonging to the king and threw a javelin at him, piecing his breastplate. Alexander grabbed a sword (his was broken) from one of his men, and killed Mithridates, but then a Persian named Rhoesaces came up from behind and sheared off his helmet to expose his bare head. As Alexander dispatched Rhoesaces the Persian Spithridates raised his sword to decapitate the king, but Cleitus the Black, commander of the companion cavalry, slashed off the latter's arm in the nick of time. Embellishment or not, Alexander's willingness to be in the thick of fighting made his men feel he was one of them, and, as Diodorus tells us, they always recognized his bravery.[29] Yet he was also a king and needed to balance his generalship and love of a fight with the duties of a ruler. Had he died in battle, and with no one to lead his army and no heir to succeed him, the future of Macedonia would have been in jeopardy. His risk-taking nature was therefore not always for the greater good, something we will see even more as his campaign progresses.

Our sources distort the number of casualties for rhetorical effect: 'of the Barbarians, we are told, 20,000 infantry fell and 2,500 hundred cavalry. But on Alexander's side, Aristobulus says there were 34 dead in all, of whom nine were infantry'.[30] We have said before that the sources tend to downplay Alexander's numbers while exaggerating those of his foes for propaganda reasons.[31]

Alexander's first victory on foreign soil illustrated the fighting prowess of the army and his personal ability to lead and devise and implement strategy at a moment's notice. But his leadership qualities did not end when the fighting did.[32] He solemnly buried the dead with their arms and armour by the battlefield, as was the Macedonian custom. But then he visited all those wounded in the battle even as they were tended to by doctors and patiently listened to their versions of the fighting.[33]

Alexander followed up his victory with a speedy campaign to liberate the Greek cities of Asia Minor from Persian rule in keeping with the mandate of the League of Corinth.[34] He may also have had another, more pressing, reason for moving so swiftly and that was to secure supplies, money, and the cities' loyalty to protect his rear. Therefore, he sent Parmenion to secure Dascylium (Erkili in Turkey), the capital of Hellespontine Phrygia, while he himself marched the 200 miles to Sardis (Sart), capital of the satrapy of

Lydia, taking care to travel along known routes and supply lines to ensure his men had provisions.[35]

Sardis was one of the Great King's palace centres so was not only a seat of power but also a treasury. As Alexander was approaching the city, its garrison commander, Mithrenes, came out to meet him and surrendered the city to him. Alexander granted the Lydians their freedom, although 'freedom' meant paying taxes now to Alexander, living under Macedonian rule, and (ostensibly for security reasons) suffering garrisons, despite Alexander favoring democracies.[36] To try to distance himself from the Great King, he changed the name of the taxes from *phoros* ('tribute') to *syntaxeis* ('contributions'), but people, like today, must surely have recognized euphemisms when they came across them, and cynical disguises are never endearing.[37] His proclamation of the freedom of these cities was only for propaganda reasons.

From Sardis a march of more than eighty miles over four days to Ephesus followed, where Alexander ended the existing pro-Persian regime, restored democratic exiles, and stopped the people from wanting to stone to death those who had been sympathetic to Persian rule. Whether he was right to see pro-Persian rulers as oligarchic is arguable, but his ideological bent – like today – is not surprising, and in liberating cities from Persian control he felt the need to promote democracy in them. At the same time, in several cities (such as Halicarnassus, Ephesus, Aspendus, Priene, and Mytilene on Lesbos), he installed Macedonian garrisons to ensure their loyalty and the stability of the area rather than simply being there for protection. They may also have been intended to counter threats from the Persian fleet and to prevent civil strife (*stasis*) – by 331, all garrisons had been withdrawn except at Ephesus and Rhodes when that fleet was no longer a danger.[38] These cites may even have become members of the League of Corinth.[39]

The Siege of Miletus

In the meantime, Parmenion had taken over Magnesia and Tralles, and another Macedonian, Alcimachus, had secured the cities in Aeolia and Ionia to give Alexander control of the northern part of the Asia Minor coastline. But the record of success ended further south at Miletus (near Balat) in Caria thanks to the unexpected arrival of the Persian fleet. When Alexander first arrived at Miletus, its garrison commander, Hegesistratus, was preparing to surrender, but then a powerful Persian fleet of 400 ships (including superior Cypriot and Phoenician crews) sailed into view, giving him hope that resistance might not be futile.[40] Alexander had only about 160 vessels with him, and since Miletus was surrounded on three sides by the sea, it was very likely that it could hold out against the invaders not to mention enable the Persians to bring in supplies.

Alexander rightly considered the enemy fleet his most dangerous threat, so with the benefit of being on the ground he moved quickly to neutralize it. He had already stationed troops on the island of Lade, off the harbour mouth, and now he ordered his own ships there. The Persian vessels were thereby thwarted of putting into Miletus and chose not to engage him but to sail instead to Mount Mycale, ten miles away, for supplies. Parmenion was eager for the king to engage the enemy at sea as there was little to lose but everything to gain for the men's confidence. Apparently at some point, an eagle had landed on the shore behind Alexander's beached ships, which Parmenion interpreted as a sign that Zeus was on their side. But Alexander over-rode his general; he knew he was vulnerable in open combat at sea against the superior Phoenician and Cyprian contingents in the Persian navy, and instead claimed that the eagle was showing he would be triumphant on land not water. As has been aptly said, Parmenion 'had not grasped the overarching range of the young king's vision'.[41]

Hegesistratus nevertheless resolved to go it alone, pulling his troops from the main city and taking a stand in the citadel. Probably to hedge his bets he sent an embassy to Alexander offering to surrender if Miletus could be neutral and have an open harbour – in other words, allow access to the Macedonian and Persian fleets. But Alexander besieged the city and at the same time repositioned his vessels from Lade to blockade the harbour mouth by turning them to face forward in case of a Persian naval strike.

When his initial charge at the walls of Miletus failed, Alexander ordered his tall siege engines deployed with archers protected at their tops by reinforced low walls.[42] The archers rained down arrows on the defenders while battering rams pounded the walls, breaching them in places so that the Macedonians could scale them using ladders mounted on their boats. With no means of escape, dwindling provisions, and no Persian fleet able to sail to their rescue, the Milesians capitulated. Alexander ordered the execution of all military personnel but spared the civilian population, a dual message that resistance would not be tolerated but he would show mercy to noncombat personnel provided they did not unite against him.[43]

He also spared the lives of 300 Greek mercenaries who had swum on their shields to a small island, presumably knowing the fate of the Greek mercenaries at the Granicus River. This time, however, Alexander enlisted them in his army; he may have been swayed by their bravery as they were ready to fight to the death, but more likely is that he needed to boost his manpower. Things therefore were going well but then he committed a major blunder by sending his fleet home, keeping only a small Athenian contingent of twenty triremes and some transport vessels.[44] He did so because he had seen firsthand that once he had blocked the harbour at Miletus the Persian navy had no choice but to sail along a coastline looking to find somewhere to beach or anchor the ships so that the crews could forage for provisions. If he could do that to the enemy, they could do the same to him, so he decided his own fleet was a liability. There were protests, but he disregarded them.[45]

Alexander granted the Milesians their liberty though Miletus was hardly free: he imposed a tribute on the Milesians and installed a garrison there before marching to Halicarnassus (Bodrum) in southwest Caria. The city was the home of the 'father of history' Herodotus, and the Tomb of Mausolus (satrap of Caria in the mid fourth century), one of the seven wonders of the ancient world and which gives us the word 'Mausoleum'. Here, Alexander faced his adversary from the Granicus River, Memnon of Rhodes.

The Siege of Halicarnassus

It was Memnon rather than the satrap of Caria who was tasked with defending Halicarnassus and who clearly had military authority over the satrap.[46] This would be a challenging tactical siege for Alexander. The city was built into a hillside and had a six-foot thick defensive wall with fortified battlements running around it. In addition, Memnon had built a moat about forty feet wide in front of the walls to obstruct Alexander further. And even if Alexander breached the defensive wall, the defenders could retreat to two citadels in the city area and continue the fight. Halicarnassus' harbours were also protected and open to the Persian navy, which could deliver supplies and even harass the besiegers as Alexander no longer had a fleet.

Halicarnassus thus seemed impregnable. Undaunted, Alexander decided on a frontal assault as at Miletus. He focused on the northeast part of the wall, but it was too thick, and his men were suffering badly thanks to defenders on the ramparts, so he had his siege engines shipped from Miletus, which took about two days to reach him. This time he set up catapults along with archers atop them to launch a dual bombardment, with the archers shooting the defenders on the walls and the catapults bombarding them with stones to smash them open.[47] While all of that was going on, Alexander had his men fill in the moat so he could use his battering rams against the bottom of the thick wall.

Even so, Halicarnassus held out against this systematic offensive. When parts of the walls gave way, Memnon's men quickly filled them in with bricks, and some of the defenders even rushed the siege engines with torches to try to set them on fire – in one sally, 300 of Alexander's men were wounded. To make matters worse, one night two drunken members of Perdiccas' unit tried to climb the defensive wall and some of their comrades followed suit. The defenders easily repelled them with blazing arrows, which led to a major clash in which several of Alexander's men were killed or wounded. The king was forced to make a truce with Memnon so he could recover and bury the dead, something he saw as a personal weakness.[48]

Two more weeks passed as the defenders resisted to their utmost, but eventually the outer defensive wall fell. Undeterred, they fell back to a brick, semi-circular inside wall on which they had craftily positioned siege towers to fire arrows at the Macedonians from catapults. Around 2,000 of Memnon's forces attacked Alexander's men by the city's west gate, while a contingent of Persians led by the Athenian mercenary commanders Ephialtes and Thrasybulus stormed the siege towers by the defensive wall, burning some of them, and overwhelming the enemy in bitter fighting. It took some time before the Macedonians regrouped and in bloody fighting forced them back into the city; among the dead was Ephialtes.[49]

That night Memnon set fire to the arsenal and siege towers on the wall and, under cover of the smoke, retreated to the two inner citadels of the city. Shortly after, he fled to the island of Cos to join the Persian fleet. Alexander finally had an easy entry into the city. He ordered the fires to be put out, but rather than personally dealing with the remaining defenders in the citadels, he razed the city's walls and buildings, except for the Mausoleum. He also installed a garrison of 3,000 infantry and 200 cavalry under Ptolemy (not the future ruler of Egypt) to mop up the defenders, though it turned out to be too small to hold the Persians in check.[50]

Ultimately, Halicarnassus never completely fell to Alexander, for the Persians' continued control of its citadels meant they were also able to control its harbour. Alexander had already spent longer on the siege than he anticipated, and Memnon in any case had escaped, so he decided to cut his losses and leave Halicarnassus. Still, the siege is important for the light it shines on Alexander's tactical skills, such as stationing catapults on top of his siege equipment and especially his snap planning and adaptability in the field.

From Halicarnassus, Alexander moved southwards to Lycia and Pamphylia (southern coast of Turkey), though little is known of his operations there.[51] In Pamphylia, he was set on by the inhabitants of Pisidia, whose defiance of him was so great that one night 600 of them burned their families alive in their houses to escape the attackers. The towns of Aspendus and Sillyum surrendered to him, though at first the Aspendians baulked at his demand for horses, a sign perhaps that he needed to replace older or wounded ones. Termessus, a city built into the side of a mountain in the Taurus range, however, resisted him.[52] Its strong fortifications and his inability to use his siege equipment because of the difficult terrain got the better of him. Alexander abandoned the siege but made an alliance with the town of Selge, an enemy of Termessus, and gave permission for the former to attack the latter on his behalf. By the middle of spring 333, Alexander controlled all of Pisidia.

Refusing to stop and rest his men, Alexander pushed on with a ten days' march to Celaenae, capital of Greater Phrygia, and a strategically important city on the famous Royal Road, built by Darius I to link Sardis to his capital at Susa (Shush, Iran) over 1,600 miles away. Alexander was sensible to use the same supply and communications routes as the Persians, including the Royal Road. Celaenae defied him, so he ordered its siege; ten days later, it capitulated. Interestingly, he agreed to accept the people's surrender in two months' time if Darius did not send them any help, presumably anticipating that if the Great King did offer support, he would run out of time arranging it.[53] Alexander's approach here reflected his father's diplomatic acumen, as he aimed to strangulate Persian alliances and political access. He left behind his general Antigonus Monophthalmus ('one-eyed') with 1,500 mercenaries to oversee operations; this was the same Antigonus who played a major role in the Wars of the Successors after Alexander's death and who gave his name to the new dynasty of Macedonia, the Antigonid.

Alexander's eagerness to leave so quickly was perhaps because of his desire to make a deliberate detour to Gordium, which he reached in the summer of 333. Asia Minor might now be in his clutches, but Darius was mustering a huge army in Babylon, which would battle Alexander at Issus. It was therefore time to resort to a psychological tactic to rally his men and spread fear among the enemy by undoing the fabled Gordian knot.

Gordium was home to the wagon that, legend had it, in the eighth century Gordius (founder of the Phrygian dynasty) had brought with him from Macedonia; his son Midas had dedicated it to Zeus. It was said that whoever untied the famous knot on its yoke, made from cornel wood and tied in such an elaborate manner that its ends were hidden, was destined to be lord of Asia.[54] Alexander 'untied' it – either by slashing it with his sword or removing the pin of the yoke and detaching the whole thing.[55] It was enough for him to say that he had fulfilled the prophecy. His reason for going to Gordium, then, was part of a strategy in which he excelled – psychological warfare. He wanted to relay to all and sundry that he was the next ruler of Asia. Capitalizing on the legend of the Gordian knot was no different from allied forces dropping leaflets into enemy territory or broadcasting appeals to hostile forces for propaganda effect today. And even the exploitation of religion came into play, for that same night Gordium suffered a powerful thunderstorm, which Alexander seized on to declare that Zeus was welcoming the conqueror of Asia.

But now the issue of Persian naval power revealed Alexander's error in standing down his fleet, causing him to change his plans.[56]

Alexander Compromised

After Alexander had disbanded his fleet, the Persians had complete liberty to sail wherever they wanted. Once Memnon joined their navy after the siege of Halicarnassus, they struck. Memnon, in command of the fleet in the northern Aegean, went on the offensive.[57] In the early summer of 333 (while Alexander was still en route to Gordium), he recaptured Chios and several towns on Lesbos.[58] Alexander was sufficiently worried to send troops to the town of Mytilene (on Lesbos) when Memnon moved to besiege it, and as a result Mytilene held out against Memnon, who was killed during an attack on it.

Memnon's death removed one of Alexander's most significant opponents, but his nephew Pharnabazus immediately succeeded him. In the summer he took Mytilene, and with it the whole of Lesbos. At that point Miletus revolted, and in the Hellespont Pharnabazus established a Persian base at Callipolis before sailing off to Siphnus in the western Cyclades, from where he might potentially launch an offensive on Greece and Macedonia. This was precisely the time when the Spartan king Agis III was trying to rally the Greek cities to revolt from the Macedonian hegemony. It is no surprise that Agis met with Pharnabazus at Siphnus, who gave him ten triremes and thirty talents, which he sent to his brother Agesilaus in Crete (a base for the Persians as well as for mercenaries).

For once Alexander was on the back foot. His rear was endangered by the Persian activity off the coast and in the Hellespont, while on the mainland Agis stood a very real chance of defeating Antipater if he received support from the other Greek states and the Persians. Alexander had to move quickly to restore his lines of communication across the Aegean. Realizing his earlier error, he ordered a new fleet to be built.[59] Then in separate actions before and after the battle of Issus he sent Amphoterus to the Hellespont to keep the enemy navy at bay there, tasked Hegelochus with recapturing the islands that Pharnabazus had won over to his side, and dispatched Menes with 3,000 silver talents to Antipater to hire mercenaries if needed against Agis.

Fortunately for Alexander, his commanders did not let him down and were able to undo the various Persian successes. But luck played no small role in their actions, for as Darius mustered his huge army in Babylon, he ordered all mercenaries to join him. That meant the commanders of the Persian fleet lost much-needed manpower to the Great King's army. Had Darius not issued this directive, the Persian fleet would have been at full muster, and the war at sea might not have gone Alexander's way. The king learned the valuable lesson relevant to all ages of protecting a rear and maintaining a strong line of communication when operating away from home. In this respect a navy was as vital as a land army, to which resources nowadays we add an air force – or even a space force as explained in Chapter 4 As we will see later, however, the rear and forward areas of battle are converging in frightening ways.

The Battle of Issus

Even before Alexander fought the next battle, he had already shocked and intimidated his enemy because of his exploitation of the Gordian knot myth. As he marched to meet his adversary, Alexander dealt successfully with various peoples, but when he reached Tarsus in Cilicia (south-central Turkey) his impulsivity almost cost him his life.[60] Despite the warnings of locals, he swam in the freezing waters of the Cydnus River but had to be pulled out when he started shivering and succumbed to a tropical fever, from which he was 'saved with difficulty' a week later by his doctor.[61] Even so, he was weak and unable to move properly for several weeks.

Darius increased his speed to take advantage of his weakened foe. He had set off from Babylon at the head of a huge army.[62] Our sources give varying numbers for it: 600,000 with 30,000 Greek mercenaries (Arrian and Plutarch), 400,000 infantry and 1,000 cavalry (Diodorus and Justin), or 250,000 infantry and 62,200 cavalry (Curtius). It was probably 100,000 to 150,000, with at least 10,000 Greek mercenaries, and outnumbered the Macedonian army of about 40,000 including 5,800 cavalry. To put the scope in perspective, even when using these lowest possible numbers, Darius brought to a single battle more soldiers than were ever deployed at one time by the United States to the country of Afghanistan between 2001 and 2021.[63]

By marching east of the Amanus mountain range in the plains of northern Syria, Darius forced Alexander to abandon his intention of fighting the Persians on the narrow plain between the Amanus mountains and the sea, which would have caused problems for their infantry and cavalry. When Alexander recovered, he marched south along the coast to confront his adversary further east, but Darius cleverly outflanked him by marching one hundred miles via the Bahce Pass to Issus on a narrow plain by the Gulf of

Iskenderun (southern Turkey). There, the Great King came across the sick and stragglers the Macedonians had left behind for their own safety. He brutally cut off their hands, cauterized them with pitch to stop the bleeding, and sent the mutilated men to tell Alexander he had arrived. His callous act got Alexander's attention, who did not believe that Darius was at Issus and sent a ship along the coast to find out for sure.[64] The confirmation forced him to station troops to his rear in the southern passes (from where he had expected Darius to march) just in case the Great King had hidden troops there to ambush his rear, which may well have had a demoralizing effect on his men – as Major General Fuller states, 'there is nothing soldiers dread more than to feel that their line of retreat has been blocked'.[65]

Exactly where the battle took place is unknown, but the general opinion is that it was on the two-mile-wide plain between the Gulf of Issus and the Amanus range with the Pinarus (perhaps Payas) River running between the two sides (Figure 6.2).[66] Alexander was faced by superior numbers and a skilled opponent, even though Darius has received a bad press for fleeing the battlefield, a portrayal by hostile Greek and Roman writers intended

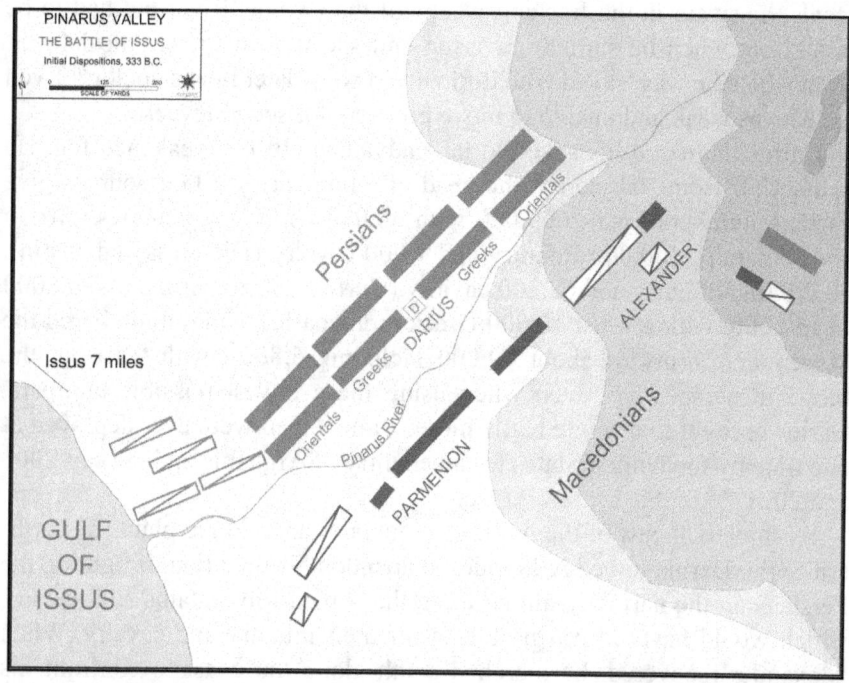

Figure 6.2 Battle of Issus. Credit: Frank Martini, Department of History, United States Military Academy.

to make him inferior to Alexander.[67] As Lonsdale remarks, Darius was an 'obvious centre of gravity in Persia'.[68] Darius drew up his line first, which stretched for over a mile. Its left flank was extended and angled like a dog's leg to go around the Macedonian right wing by the foothills of the mountains. On the Persian right flank, by the Gulf, was stationed the bulk of the cavalry; then came a contingent of Persian archers, the Greek mercenaries in the centre, another unit of Persian archers, and finally the Persian infantry merging into allied cavalry on the left flank. Darius, in full view in his high war chariot, along with his 3,000-strong Royal Bodyguard of infantry known as the Immortals and cavalry were stationed in the centre or even behind the front line as it was customary for Persian Kings to take up this position for safety and to help communicate with their lines.[69]

Alexander matched his line to the Persian. On his left flank, so by the Gulf, was the Thessalian and allied cavalry under Parmenion, then the various units of the phalanx (originally thirty-two men deep), and on the right flank by the mountains were Macedonian and allied cavalry, along with archers and mercenaries whose job was to keep the Persian 'dog leg' left flank at bay. Alexander at the head of the Macedonian cavalry together with a line of allied and mercenary infantry stood to the right flank but could still see Darius. Perhaps to mitigate any feelings of unease, he rode up and down his line exhorting his men and calling on the battalion commanders and other men he recognized by name. This combination of inspirational rhetoric and leadership had the troops yelling out 'to delay no longer but charge the enemy'.[70]

The Great King, who had also exhorted his troops with a speech, planned for his cavalry to break through the Macedonian left and encircle the phalanx, driving it to the mountains where the uneven terrain would make the long forward-pointing sarissas hard to wield and so hinder the phalanx's effectiveness. Alexander's strategy was a psychological one and a set aim in classical battles: to kill the enemy commander, in this case Darius, thereby spoiling the enemy's fighting spirit and giving his men victory.[71] To this end, he kept his line moving slowly forward until it came within bow shot of the enemy when it broke into a sudden run. Taken by surprise, the Persians could not stop Alexander and the cavalry detachment with him breaking through their centre and rushing Darius.

Until then the Macedonians had been in difficulty. Their line also had gaps in it because the infantry was struggling on the boggy plain and had not kept up with Alexanders' cavalry charge.[72] Dangerously for the Macedonians, Persian troops were able to pour through and attack the Macedonians side on, exposing the weakness of the phalanx, and on the left flank, Parmenion was being pushed by the Persian cavalry into the Gulf.[73]

Nevertheless, Alexander was determined to capture Darius so did not go to Parmenion's aid. The sources are at odds with each other as to when Darius fled.[74] Most likely it was not as soon as Alexander breached his line but when he saw more of his bodyguards fall in the bitter fighting and the sarissas of the enemy encircling his position. He jumped into a smaller chariot and fled the battlefield, which, as Alexander had anticipated, had the desired effect on his troops. They lost heart. First the infantry fled and then the cavalry, as did the Greek mercenaries, who probably had heard of the fate of the mercenaries after Granicus.

Now followed a massacre as the Macedonians chased down and killed many of the fleeing Persians, whose huge numbers over the rough and boggy terrain were slowing them down. Even worse was that because the cavalry had fled after the infantry the galloping horses mowed down many of the infantrymen in their rush to escape – Ptolemy, who fought in the battle, makes the sensational claim in his *History* that the Macedonians crossed over a ravine on a bridge of Persian corpses.[75] At the end of the day, the Persians, it was said, lost 100,000 infantry and over 10,000 cavalry to Alexander's 500.[76] Alexander made a point again of visiting each of his wounded men and listening to their stories, and as a reward for the valour of the Thessalian cavalry under Parmenion he allowed them to pillage Darius' main base at Damascus in Syria.

Several postscripts to the battle may be mentioned. The first is that it spawned an artistic tradition. Alexander and Darius never fought each other, even though for his heroic image, he sent a letter to Antipater in Greece describing how Darius had wounded his thigh with a sword.[77] But a contemporary painting perhaps by Philoxenus of Eretria showed Alexander on his horse Bucephalas charging at Darius, their eyes fastened on each other, as Macedonian soldiers surround the King's chariot. It is likely that this painting was propaganda and the 'model' for the famous 'Alexander mosaic', which was found in the House of the Faun at Pompeii in 1831 (see this book's cover).[78]

The second postscript concerns Alexander, who sent Parmenion to Damascus to seize the Persian baggage train – Alexander's financial pressures were now over. At Damascus, Parmenion came across Barsine, the daughter of Artabazus, a previous satrap of Hellespontine Phrygia who with his family had lived for some years at Pella in Philip's reign. Presumably, the young Barsine and Alexander got to know each other there. Now, in her thirties, Parmenion sent her to the king; the story goes that he 'did not have sex with any woman before he married apart from Barsine', and the two lived together in a de facto relationship even after he married Roxane of Bactria in 327 (Chapter 9).[79] Whether Alexander lost his virginity to her is unknown, though there is a story that his disinterest in the opposite sex while growing up concerned Philip and Olympias, who even hired a Thessalian prostitute named Callixeina to seduce him.[80] Of course, he went on to have numerous lovers, of whom the most famous were his boyhood friend Hephaestion, the eunuch Bagoas, and supposedly the Amazon Queen Thalestris.[81]

A final postscript is that Alexander built on the fulfillment of the prophecy of the Gordian Knot and his victory at Issus to start calling himself Ruler of Asia.[82] This should not come as a surprise, and it was intended to send out the message that a new ruler of Persia had emerged. He could not call himself Great King – and he never did – because he did not have the religious bond shared by the Achaemenids with Ahura Mazda, the God of Light, which gave them the right to rule. Not that that mattered as Alexander's rule would be anchored not in constitutionality, but military might – it was by the spear. A new era in the near east had now arrived.

Alexander's speed and relentlessness certainly contributed to his victory, but we should not overlook the element of luck on Alexander's side in the battle: what if Darius had not fled, had somehow rallied his men, and with his vast numbers turned the tables on the young invader? Every commander needs luck, and rarely did it leave the young Macedonian king. Darius did flee, and so Alexander's strategy worked. The Greek sources tend to depict Darius as a coward and a weak ruler, but as we noted above, he outfoxed Alexander by marching around his rear and forced him to change his battle plan. Darius left the battlefield to prevent his capture and so live to fight another day; in putting his kingdom first, he also made a personal sacrifice, for he left behind his family, which had accompanied him to the battle, to fall prey to Alexander.

Alexander was said to have heard crying the night after the battle, and was told it was Darius' sister-wife, mother, and two daughters, who thought he was dead.[83] When brought before him, Alexander treated them respectfully, telling them his war was not against them but Darius, and significantly ordered they were to learn Greek and receive a Greek education, as well as pledging to find husbands for the princesses.[84] The last stands out: since a king was responsible for arranging royal marriages, Alexander was assuming Darius' role, cementing his claim to be ruler of Asia. He thus put Darius, who had fled to Thapsacus (on the west bank of the Euphrates, perhaps now in Syria) under greater pressure to win the next battle, which would be at Gaugamela in 331.

The scare Alexander had earlier suffered from the activities of the Persian navy prompted him to let Darius escape after Issus so he could turn to securing the entire eastern Mediterranean seaboard. This was his main communication route to Greece and control of it would also deny the Persians safe harbours as he marched further eastwards. On the one hand, his decision made strategic sense. On the other, it allowed the Great King to regroup and add significantly to his army with first-class cavalry provided by Bessus, the satrap of Bactria and Sogdiana (between the Hindu Kush and the Oxus River in what is now parts of northern Afghanistan, Tajikistan, and Uzbekistan). At the same time, fighting a battle was Alexander's greatest strength, something on which he anchored his strategy to take Persia.

Notes

1 On the Persian Empire see, for example, Dandamaev 1989; Briant 2002; Allen 2005; Brosius 2020.
2 Plutarch, *Alexander* 5.1–2.
3 Arrian 4.3.7.
4 See Fuller 1960; Lonsdale 2007, especially pp. 79–144, on military operations. On logistics, see Engels 1978.
5 Fuller 1960, p. 301.
6 In addition to the studies cited in the following notes and in Chapter 7 (second part of the campaign in Persia), 10 (Central Asia), and 11 (India), see too Keegan 1987, pp. 74–87; Strauss 2003; Gilley and Worthington 2010; Yenne 2010; Worthington 2017; King 2018, pp. 151–177.
7 On numbers, see p. 66.
8 See Badian 1991; Tritle 2009.
9 Diodorus 17.17.2, with Degen 2019. Marching to the ends of the earth: Heckel 2003b; cf. Briant 2010, pp. 24–38. Keeping to Philip's original intention: Brunt 1965.
10 Diodorus 17.17.3; Arrian 1.12.1; Plutarch, *Alexander* 15.7–8; Justin 11.5.12. Lineage: Plutarch, *Alexander* 2.1.
11 On strategy, the lessons to be learned about it from analysis of Alexander's generalship, and a consideration of Alexander as strategist, see especially Lonsdale 2007.
12 Good comments on Persia's size and resources: Strauss 2003, pp. 147–149.
13 Diodorus 17.18.2; Arrian 1.12.9. On the need for provisions and Alexander's means of foraging for them, see the comments of Matthews 2008, pp. 141–143.
14 Cf. Strauss and Ober 1990, pp. 118–119; at pp. 124–131, they argue that Darius' strategy of battling Alexander was the wrong one, and he should have adopted a scorched earth policy throughout.
15 Diodorus 17.19–21; Arrian 1.12.8–16; Plutarch, *Alexander* 16; Justin 11.6.8–13; Polybius 12.19.1, with Fuller 1960, pp. 147–154; Bosworth 1988a, pp. 39–44; Devine 1989a, pp. 109–113; Ashley 1998, pp. 187–202, Lonsdale 2007, pp. 97–104; Heckel 2008, pp. 46–51; Worthington 2014a, pp. 144–149; Sekunda 2018; in-depth: Badian 1977; Hammond 1980b; Devine 1986a, Devine 1988; Thompson 2007 (with discussion of the Macedonian army and Persian Empire); English 2011, pp. 33–60.
16 Arrian 1.14.4; numbers: Fuller 1960, p. 147; on sources, see English 2011, pp. 36–49.

17 Arrian 1.14.4–5.
18 Diodorus 17.19.2.
19 Arrian 1.13.3–7.
20 Arrian 1.18.6–9; Plutarch, *Alexander* 16.3.
21 Diodorus 17.9.3 has Alexander following Parmenion's advice and waiting till dawn.
22 Arrian 1.14.1.
23 Devine 1988.
24 Diodorus 17.19.6 has Parmenion carrying out a similar move on the left, but this is doubtful.
25 Arrian 1.15.2–4.
26 Plutarch, *Alexander* 16.3, says they were expecting a truce and then to surrender.
27 Arrian 1.16.3.
28 Diodorus 17.20.1–7, Arrian 1.15.7–8, Curtius 8.1.20, Plutarch, *Alexander* 16.7–11. Embellished: Heckel 2008, p. 50.
29 Diodorus 17.21.4.
30 Aristobulus, *BNJ* 139 F 5 = Plutarch, *Alexander* 16.15.
31 Though see Hammond 1989b, with pp. 57–62, on casualty figures in Alexander's battles.
32 Arrian 1.16.5.
33 The army travelled with medical personnel including doctors: see Matthews 2008, pp. 217–218; Karunanithy 2013, pp. 166–170.
34 See in more detail Hammond and Walbank 1988, pp. 72–76; Worthington 2014a, pp. 150–152.
35 Arrian 1.17.3
36 Cf. Arrian 1.18.2.
37 Kholod 2013.
38 Kholod 2010. See further, Ehrenberg 1938; Badian 1966; Hammond and Walbank 1988, pp. 72–76; Bosworth 1988a, pp. 250–258; Faraguna 2003, pp. 109–115; Nawotka 2003.
39 *Contra* Bosworth 1988a, pp. 255–256, principally because of lack of evidence.
40 Diodorus 17.22, Arrian 1.18.4, 1.19.1–8, Plutarch, *Alexander* 17.2, with Bosworth 1988a, pp. 46–47; Ashley 1998, pp. 204–206; English 2009b, pp. 41–46; Worthington 2014a, pp. 152–153.
41 Keegan 1987, p. 42.
42 On siegecraft, see English 2009b, pp. 11–32.
43 Diodorus 17.22.4–22.5; Arrian 1.19.6.
44 Diodorus 17.22.5–23.3; Arrian 1.20.1.
45 Not all saw his action as rash: Diodorus 17.23.1 refers to some that said 'Alexander's strategic conception was sound when he dismissed his fleet', and cf. Lonsdale 2007, pp. 70–71, in support.
46 Diodorus 17.23.4–27, Arrian 1.20.2–23.8, Curtius 5.2.5, 8.1.36, Plutarch, *Alexander* 17.2, with Fuller 1960, pp. 200–206; Bosworth 1988a, pp. 47–49; Ashley 1998, pp. 206–210; English 2009b, pp. 47–55; Worthington 2014a, pp. 154–156.
47 Catapults: English 2009b, pp. 1–8.
48 Diodorus 17.25.5–6; Arrian 1.21.1–4.
49 Diodorus 17.26.7–27.3; Curtius 5.2.5. See Fuller 1960, p. 205, that Ephialtes' troops were young and inexperienced.

50 Diodorus 17.27.6; Arrian 1.23.6.
51 On the following, see Bosworth 1988a, pp. 49–52; Worthington 2014a, pp. 156–159.
52 Arrian 1.27.5–28.2.
53 Arrian 1.29.1–2; Curtius 3.1.6–8.
54 Arrian 2.3.6–7; Curtius 3.1.16; Plutarch *Alexander* 18.2–4; Justin 11.7.4–14 and see Fredricksmeyer 1961; Frei 1972; Roller 1984.
55 Aristobulus, *BNJ* 139 FF 7 and 7b (= Plutarch, *Alexander* 18.2–4); Arrian 2.3.7; Justin 11.7.16.
56 Discussion of Persian navy as a 'centre of gravity' in Persia, though in support of Alexander disbanding his own fleet, see Lonsdale 2007, pp. 65–66, 68–72.
57 Ruzicka 1988; cf. Worthington 2014a, pp. 160–161.
58 Diodorus 17.29.2; Arrian 2.1.1–2.
59 Arrian 2.2.3; Curtius 3.1.19–20.
60 Diodorus 17.31.4–6; Arrian 2.4.7–11; Curtius 3.5.1–6.20; Plutarch, *Alexander* 19.2–9; Justin 11.8.3–5.
61 Anonymous, *BNJ* 151 F 6.
62 Numbers and route: Diodorus 17.31–6, Arrian 2.6–11, Curtius 3.3–4, 7–11, Plutarch, *Alexander* 20, Justin 11.9; cf. Polybius 12.18.2, with Bosworth 1988a, pp. 58–60.
63 In 2011, U.S. troop presence in Afghanistan peaked at 100,000 and dropped precipitously until the end of the war in 2021: Peters 2021.
64 Arrian 2.7.2; Curtius 3.8.17.
65 Fuller 1960, p. 156.
66 Diodorus 17.31–6, Arrian 2.6–11, Curtius 3.3–4, 7–11, Plutarch, *Alexander* 20, Justin 11.9; cf. Polybius 12.18.2, with Fuller 1960, pp. 154–162; Bosworth 1988a, pp. 60–62; Devine 1989a, pp. 113–116; Ashley 1998, pp. 222–235; Lonsdale 2007, pp. 80–86; Heckel 2008, pp. 57–65; Worthington 2014a, pp. 165–171; in-depth: Murison 1972; Devine 1985a; Devine 1985b; Hammond 1992b; English 2011, pp. 71–109. Site: English 2011, pp. 75–77 and 83–84.
67 Nylander 1993; Badian 2000; Briant 2010, pp. 42–44, 48–52, especially Briant 2015. Less complimentary of Darius' strategic skills and command: Strauss and Ober 1990, pp. 103–131 ('Darius III of Persia: Why he Lost and Made Alexander Great'), especially pp. 124–131.
68 Lonsdale 2007, p. 65.
69 Xenophon, *Anabasis* 1.8.22.
70 Arrian 2.10.2; cf. Justin 11.9.3–6. See too Iglesias-Zoido 2010.
71 Cf. Fuller 1960, p. 148, noting a British mission to kill Rommel in WWII.
72 Arrian 2.10.4–7; Curtius 3.1.4–6.
73 Arrian 2.11.12; Curtius 3.11.1.
74 Start: Arrian 2.114; cf. Polybius 12.22.2 from Callisthenes. Later: Diodorus 17.34.2–7; Curtius 3.11.7–12; Justin 12.9.9.
75 Ptolemy, *BNJ* 138 F 6 = Arrian 2.11.8.
76 On the figures and especially Arrian's account of them see Hammond 1989b, pp. 57–62.
77 Chares, *BNJ* 125 F 6 = Plutarch, *Moralia* 341c.
78 Cohen 1997; Stewart 1993, pp. 130–157.
79 Aristobulus, *BNJ* 139 F 11 (= Plutarch, *Alexander* 21.7–9); Justin 11.10.2–3, 12.15.9, with Worthington 2014a, p. 172.

80 Athenaeus 435a. On the story: Ogden 2011, pp. 144–146 and 174–184.
81 Ogden 2011, pp. 124–154 on his wives and dalliances; cf. Ogden 2009.
82 Plutarch, *Alexander* 34.1.
83 Diodorus 17.67; Arrian 2.12.3–8 (from Ptolemy, *BNJ* 138 F 7); Justin 11.9.12–16.
84 Diodorus 17.67.1; Curtius 5.2.17; Justin 11.9.16.

7 Alexander in Persia 2: Mission Accomplished?

The League of Corinth had endorsed a plan, first put forward by Philip II in 337 and reintroduced by Alexander in 336, the year he became king, to inflict vengeance on the Persians for their invasion of Greece in the early fifth century and to liberate the Greek cities of Asia Minor. To achieve these goals, Alexander based his strategy on military engagements, disabling the enemy navy, and seizure of enemy capitals – the Persian centres of gravity. As we will see in this chapter, he achieved the objectives, toppling the Persian Empire and ending the Achaemenid ruling dynasty. But is this Mission Accomplished?

The question though is what was meant by revenge. Philip may well have wanted to operate only in Asia Minor largely for financial gain, but for Alexander, eager for his own glory, this was not enough.[1] In the previous chapter we noted that Alexander threw a spear into Asian soil before landing to show he was out to conquer the entire empire. Revenge was certainly a motive, then, but so was complete conquest: as we shall see below, his demolition of the palace at Persepolis in 330 broadcast the end of the Achaemenid dynasty and the new age of Macedonian rule.

Perhaps we should not be surprised at Alexander's intention, given his young age – he was only twenty-two when he invaded Asia – and thirst for battle and glory, not to mention he commanded a formidable and battle-tested army. Still, at the same time, in contrast to his father Philip, who favoured diplomacy over battle where he could and whose political wisdom increased with his years, Alexander's youth and zeal for fighting arguably were weaknesses when it came to dealing with his subject peoples and even his own men, as later chapters will reveal.

The Siege of Tyre

As Alexander marched from Cilicia into Phoenicia (now Lebanon), several cities including Byblos (as the Greeks called it, whereas to the Phoenicians it was Gebal) and Sidon surrendered to him. Then in late January 332, he arrived at Tyre, which in antiquity was an island city as well as a vital port city commercially and militarily between Cilicia and Egypt. It had two natural harbours, one to its north facing Sidon and the other to its south facing Egypt, and huge walls 200 feet high, coming down to the water's edge on the landward side. Its location, fortifications, and harbours meant that Alexander could not allow it to be independent and a base for the Persian fleet.

The king of Tyre, Azemilk, initially surrendered to him, but then Alexander wanted to sacrifice in the Temple to Melqart. He believed that the god was a local equivalent of Heracles, one of his ancestors with whom he identified.[2] The Tyrians refused, however, as his action would be blasphemous to them, and it coincided with a festival to the god about to take place when their temple was closed to all foreigners.[3] They professed their friendship to him but requested that he sacrifice at Old Tyre (Palaetyros), on the mainland opposite the island.

Alexander took their refusal as a personal insult and demanded their surrender. He did not even pretend to take the Tyrians' religious beliefs into account, a signal failing in his leadership. Yet not grasping the mix of religion, warfare, and politics remains prevalent among makers of modern strategy. For example, in 1998 the American and British missile strikes against Iraq during the holy month of Ramadan were denounced, with President Bill Clinton arguably contravening the 1973 War Powers Act. Perhaps even more disastrous, America's hasty 2021 withdrawal from Afghanistan was to some degree the product of a remarkably naïve outlook on the Taliban's Deobandi religious ideology, which forbade them from delivering any of the moderate political reforms they had promised.[4]

Alexander sent envoys to the Tyrians to convey his demands, but the Tyrians, expecting military support from their colony Carthage, murdered the envoys and threw them off the ramparts in full view of the Macedonians. A furious Alexander ordered the siege, rallying his troops by claiming that he dreamt Heracles was stretching out his hand to him from the ramparts and calling him forth.[5]

Since the straits were relatively shallow until closer to Tyre, where the water depth was about fifteen to twenty feet, Alexander hit on the plan of constructing a mole or causeway, perhaps as wide as 200 feet, from the mainland to the island. He had taken military engineers and specialist personnel with him, an advantage of an ancient army, and he now tasked Diades of Thessaly, a student of Polyidus who had founded Philip's engineering *corps*, with the building of the mole. For materials, he razed Old Tyre for its earth and stones and brought in wood from Lebanon. This operation reads easily enough, but when we step back and imagine its execution at the time, the scope of this logistical undertaking was enormous.

If the king intended to coerce the Tyrians into surrender, he was disappointed. As the mole began to stretch out towards Tyre, archers on the battlements shot and killed numerous workers, forcing Alexander to position two huge siege towers, each 160 feet high, on the farthest end of the causeway as protection. On top of them were archers firing their arrows at the defenders along with catapults that bombarded the walls with heavy stones. The defenders decided to target the siege towers, and, in a move worthy of Alexander, they made a floating fire-bomb. They packed a ship with wood and attached two long masts to its prow, hanging pitchers of bitumen and sulphur on each one. Then they loaded the stern with rocks so that the prow was angled above the water and rowed the ship towards the end of the causeway with the siege towers, setting fire to the wood and contents of the containers before jumping overboard and swimming to safety. A strong southwest wind did the rest. As the ship smashed into the mole at some speed the two protruding masts broke off, emptying their burning contents onto the mole, which along with the siege towers was destroyed in the conflagration.

Alexander stoically accepted the loss – he had no choice. He ordered Diades to build more siege engines and rebuild the mole, but this time he abandoned the idea of fixing his siege engines in one spot. Instead, he mounted the new ones along with stone-throwing catapults on ships, which sailed alongside the mole screening off the workers for their protection.[6] By midsummer, all was finished. In the meantime, eighty Phoenician ships that had deserted the Persian fleet and 120 ships from Cyprus, both places being enemies of the Tyrians, joined his ranks. The king used them to blockade Tyre's two harbours, rendering its own fleet ineffective.

The writing was on the wall for the Tyrians, who turned from offence to defence in anticipation of the Macedonians marching across the mole. They fixed skins stuffed with seaweed on their walls to strengthen them, installed revolving wheels on the battlements to deflect enemy arrows, fired burning arrows or flaming darts at any Macedonian ship, dropped rocks and stone slabs into the water at the foot of their walls to try to prevent any approach, and prepared boiling sand in cauldrons to drop from on high on the enemy.[7] The sand would find its way through any gaps, no matter how small, in the men's armour and clothing, and once trapped would severely burn skin. In addition, and a sign of their ingenuity, they built an inner defensive wall behind the area where the mole reached their outer one, filling the gap in between with rocks and soil to slow down Alexander's troops and allow their own archers to shoot and kill at least some of them.

Faced by likely unacceptable losses even if successful, Alexander switched to a southern section of the wall that had no inner wall behind it. The problem was how to get his battering rams to that part of the wall. To solve that, we see again Alexander's quick, innovative thinking thanks to his eye on the ground. He mounted the battering rams onto ships – the first time that ships were outfitted in this way – and using his fleet and the Cyprian vessels to take on any remaining Tyrian ones in the harbours as a distraction, he sailed his mobile battering rams towards the wall. His plan was working until strong winds (a feature of the region) blew up and forced him to pull back for two days.

The third day brought calm conditions. Alexander renewed his attack on the southern wall, and that time the battering rams began to break through. At the same time, he led a contingent of hypaspists and a division of Coenus' phalanx that had sailed on other boats up scaling ladders and across the mole. That was the beginning of the end for the Tyrians. As he and his troops battled their way into the city, the rest of his army smashed through the ruptured part of the wall. Perhaps as a release for their frustration of the past six months, for it was now July, they slaughtered the inhabitants indiscriminately. Arrian tells us that over 8,000 Tyrians were killed and 30,000 seized and sold into slavery, while the Macedonians allegedly lost only 400 men and had 3,000 wounded.[8] In addition, Alexander ordered the crucifixion of 2,000 Tyrians, displaying their bodies along the Syrian coast as a warning to any other city thinking of defying him. He then resettled Tyre with people from the surrounding areas and installed a garrison to ensure his control.

Despite his victory, Alexander still apparently refused to respect local religious beliefs, for he sacrificed to Melqart, cynically dedicating to the god the Tyrians' sacred ship along with the first battering ram that had breached their walls. The siege of Tyre gave Alexander control of the Levant, but it had cost him dearly in time, money, and manpower. Of course, he could have garrisoned Old Tyre and stationed a fleet there to keep Tyre in check and deny the Persian navy a base, but once he was personally defied, redemption was well-nigh impossible, a pattern starting with the revolt of Thebes in 335. Likewise, a Carthaginian delegation was captured in Tyre (Tyre being a colony of Carthage), which Alexander allowed to depart unharmed, but with a warning: he considered the Carthaginians his enemies now and would deal with them later.[9] At the end of his reign, he may well have been planning a campaign in the western Mediterranean, which perhaps explains the presence of a Carthaginian embassy at Babylon in 323 (see Chapter 10).

The Siege of Gaza

Alexander now marched south at speed towards Egypt. By September, he had reached Gaza, an important city on the route from Palestine into Egypt. There, his route was blocked by the garrison commander, an Iranian or Babylonian eunuch named Batis, who clearly thought that since Gaza was a fortified city that stood on a hill about 250 feet high, he could successfully withstand a siege or even force Alexander back.[10] He was wrong.[11]

Alexander knew that his men would be sitting ducks to the arrows and other missiles of the defenders on the ramparts if they moved against the walls. After taking stock of the soft ground, on which the thick defensive walls were built, he decided he would deploy soldiers to start digging away at the sand underneath what he perceived to be the weakest section of the wall while his siege engines bombarded it with stones. He was confident that this double-pronged action would collapse that section of the wall and his men would do the rest.

But to deploy his siege machinery, he needed to be on a level with Gaza itself. Accordingly, he gave orders to build a mound as high as Gaza's walls and set up his siege towers (which he built in view of the defenders) on top of it. But the siege towers he had built were not powerful enough, so he brought in the larger ones he had used against Tyre. Perhaps he hoped to intimidate the defenders by constructing in plain view the machines that would be used against them, much the same rationale as the mole at Tyre, and later at the Rock of Chorienes in Bactria (for details on which, see Chapter 9). When Batis refused to back down, however, the king was forced, despite the delay, to ship in those from Tyre.

The siege of Gaza lasted about two months. The defenders repelled three assaults by Macedonian solders and surprised their enemy with a sudden sally; in the first, Alexander was shot in the shoulder by a catapult bolt and lost a great deal of blood, and in the third he was wounded in the leg and forced to withdraw. When a section of the wall finally gave way, Alexander led his hypaspists on a fourth and final charge and poured into Gaza. As at Tyre, a massacre followed, with 10,000 men killed and the women and children sold into slavery.

Batis, captured alive, was executed in barbaric fashion. Curtius tells us that Alexander had Batis' heels pierced, a rope run through the holes and attached to the back of a chariot, and then he was dragged around the walls of Gaza until he died, with the Macedonians laughing at his squeals of agony.[12] Certainly, Batis had defied Alexander, causing him a further delay while Darius was regrouping, and the king had been badly wounded twice in the siege. But his treatment of Batis recalls Alexander's personal association with Achilles, for the latter had dragged the body of the defeated Hector around the walls of Troy – except that when he did, Hector was already dead. Whichever the reason, Batis' cruel death illustrates that an autocratic king who was also general of his army was answerable to no one when it came to making any decision, including the fate of an enemy. The need for a system of checks and balances, and accountability when those norms are violated, is obvious.

It was now November, and Alexander finally crossed into Egypt at Pelusium and made his way to the capital Memphis. Its Persian satrap, Mazaces, surrendered the country when Alexander reached the border – a wise move as the native Egyptians hated the Persians, who had controlled the country since 525 and would not have supported Mazaces.[13] The king was not formally crowned pharaoh, but he did receive all the attributes of that title, including identification with Horus and Osiris and as such was worshipped by the Egyptians as a god on earth – at the age of twenty-five.[14]

While in Egypt Alexander founded what would become Egypt's capital under Ptolemy I and the premier city of the Hellenistic era, Alexandria.[15] He also visited the Oracle of Zeus Ammon in the Oasis of Siwah (Libyan Desert), which would be a turning point in his pretensions to personal divinity.[16] He already had divine ancestors in the shape of Zeus and Heracles, and his father Philip was likely deified on death.[17] However, as Aristobulus claims, Alexander went to Siwah to find out 'his own origin more precisely or at least be in a position to say he had learned it'.[18] In other words, he wanted to be identified as a son of Zeus.[19] Since he met with the Priest of the Oracle in private, we have only Alexander's word for what took place, but, from then on, he openly claimed that Zeus was his real father and Philip only his 'mortal' one.[20]

On their journey to Siwah, the Macedonians became hopelessly lost on the 150-mile trek southwards from Paraetonium (Mersa Matruh) to the oasis because of flash sandstorms and torrential downpours in the desert that obliterated landmarks and tracks. The normal one-week journey took them a grueling fortnight, with their supplies running out after the first week.[21] Eventually, they followed two ravens flying to the oasis, though Ptolemy claimed that it was actually two snakes (sent by Zeus) who spoke to them and led them to the oasis.[22] If the soldiers with Alexander had their doubts about the return journey, they would have been relieved to know they had Zeus as guide. Yet Alexander's proclaimed divinity did not go down well with his men: at their mutiny in Opis in 324, they mockingly told him that if he wanted to invade Arabia, he could go with his father Zeus.[23]

In the late spring of 331, Alexander had left Egypt and returned to Tyre, where he held grandiose athletic contests and a drama festival to celebrate his successes and received a congratulatory embassy from the Athenians.[24] Probably also on this occasion he received a letter from Darius offering to pay a ransom of 30,000 talents for the return of his family, allowing Alexander to marry his daughter Stateira, recognizing him as his friend and ally, and ceding all lands west of the Euphrates to him.[25] His terms prompted the famous exchange (if it is historical) between Alexander and Parmenion, in which the latter said that if he were Alexander, he would accept it, to which Alexander replied that if he were Parmenion he would. The king therefore wrote to Darius grandly stating that these lands were already his, he was avenging the Greeks for their sufferings at Persian hands, he would marry whomever he wanted, and if Darius wanted to talk terms he should come to Alexander. Of course, Alexander was deliberately provocative as Darius was not going to put himself in the position of approaching Alexander cap in hand. Both sides consequently prepared for battle.

The Battle of Gaugamela

About seventy miles northwest of Irbil, the capital of Iraqi Kurdistan, on the way to Nineveh and north of Mosul is the small town of Tell Gomel, thought to be the location of the ancient Gaugamela.[26] Both Alexander's army and that of Darius had arrived there by late September 331, and the actual battle took place on either the last day of that month or the first day of October.[27]

Darius had reason to be optimistic. The Bactrian cavalry were on a par with the Macedonian, and he also had a *corps* of 200 deadly scythed chariots, each one with razor-sharp blades attached to the wheels, chassis, and yoke, and pulled by four horses. He knew he could not allow Alexander to penetrate his line as at Issus, so his strategy was to disrupt the Macedonian formation by having the chariots, which were stationed in four groups of fifty along his line, open gaps in the phalanx. Through these, his cavalry would gallop, thereby trapping his enemy between two offensive lines while the Persian infantry struck in the chaos. To ensure his chariots would not overturn, he smoothed out the ground in front of them and to hamper the Macedonian horses he buried spikes (caltrops) in the plain.

Alexander set up camp behind a small row of hills seven miles from the Persians on a wide plain between the Bumelus (Gomel) River and the Jabel Maqlub hills.[28] One night he and some of his companion cavalry scouted the battlefield to try to gain insight into how Darius was going to arrange his forces. They observed where the chariots would be positioned and even where the spikes were buried before the group was spotted. For them to be seen there must have been a moon, hence Alexander may have deliberately wanted to alert Darius to his presence as the Great King kept his troops in battle order for the rest of the night in case of attack.[29] By daybreak the Persians were tired and stressed and could only have felt worse as temperatures in the plain rose to over 100 degrees Fahrenheit.

Actual numbers on both sides are again unknown thanks to inconsistency in our sources. Arrian speaks of a Persian army of 1,000,000 infantry, 40,000 cavalry, 200 scythed chariots, and fifteen war elephants from Indians west of the Indus. Diodorus and Plutarch have a total of 1,000,000 (Diodorus specifies 200,000 cavalry, 800,000 infantry, and 200 chariots), while Curtius gives 45,000 cavalry, 200,000 infantry, and 200 chariots – we are on safe ground estimating 100,000–150,000 in total.[30] Alexander's army, according to Arrian, was about 40,000 infantry and 7,000 cavalry.[31] He was clearly outnumbered and outflanked as Darius' line was far longer than his (Figure 7.1). In addition, Darius' Bactrian cavalry posed a substantial threat, and perhaps intimidating the Macedonians were the war elephants, topped with wooden towers protecting riders who hurled down javelins and other missiles.

Some of Alexander's Companions had urged him to strike by night, which the Persians would not have anticipated, but Alexander was not persuaded, perhaps because the night was too dark and his men could stumble or his communications might go astray.[32] The next day he did lead his army onto the plain and set up his line, after which he rode up and down it urging his troops to fight courageously as he had done before Issus.[33] This time he appealed to the gods for help if he were really a son of Zeus as he had been referring to himself after visiting Egypt. Out of the blue, literally, an eagle swooped down and perched on the Persian line, which Alexander quickly interpreted as a sign of Zeus' support for him.[34] Eagles were useful. Three years earlier at the siege of Miletus, an eagle landed on his line, which he took to mean he would conquer the Milesians on land and not in any naval battle. That the same portent could be explained in two different ways might show that now, before Gaugamela, he needed to rouse his men's spirits that the king of the gods was on their side against Darius' massive army.

Arrian claimed that had Alexander ordered his right flank directly forward at the outset, it would have been almost level with the Persian centre, such was the extreme length of Darius' line.[35] The Persian right flank, commanded by Mazaeus, comprised troops from Syria, Mesopotamia, and the Persian Gulf region. In front of them were fifty scythed chariots and cavalry from Armenia and Cappadocia. Darius with the Immortals (a heavy infantry unit that was also a bodyguard), flanked on either side

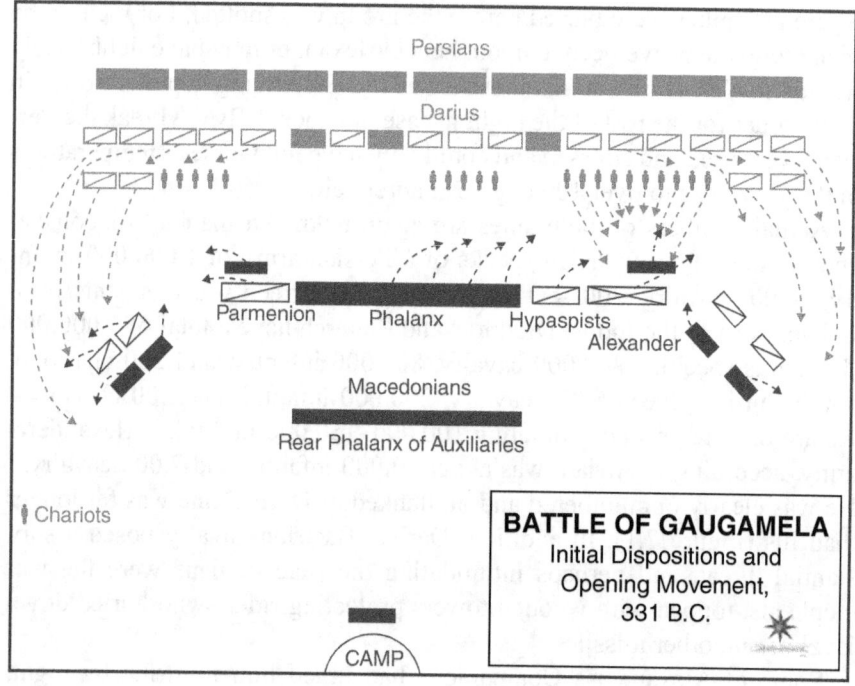
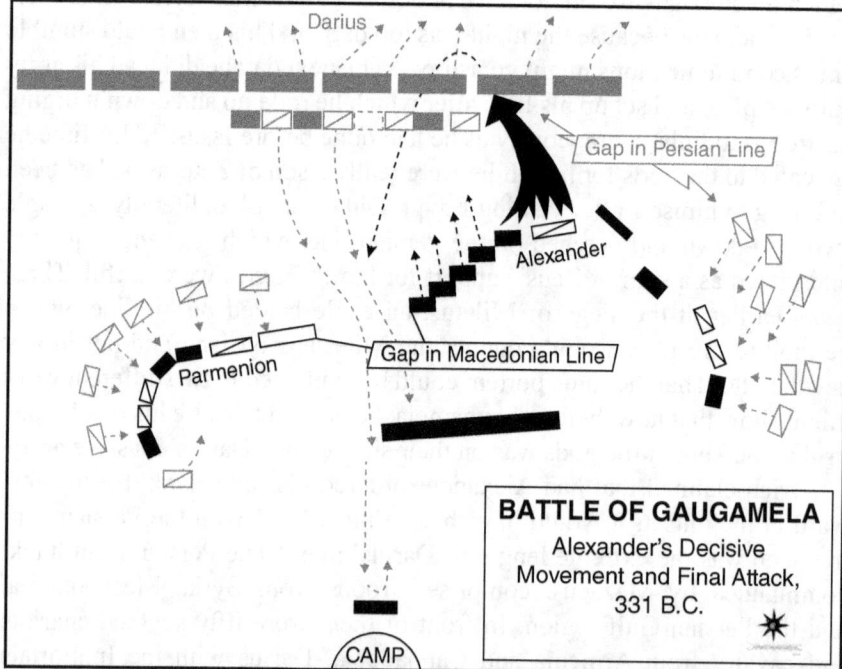

Figure 7.1 Battle of Gaugamela. Credit: Department of History, United States Military Academy.

by Greek mercenaries, was in the centre with the fifteen war elephants and fifty scythed chariots in front of them and most of his infantry behind him. On the left flank, commanded by Bessus, were the cavalry from eastern satrapies and subjects, including Bactria and Arachosia (Afghanistan) and the Sacae, Dahae, and Massagetae peoples (in Turkmenistan, Uzbekistan, and southern Kazakhstan), and in front of them were yet more cavalry and 100 scythed chariots.

On the Macedonian right flank, facing Bessus, stood the hypaspists under Hephaestion (experiencing his first significant command) and then the companion cavalry. In the centre, opposite Darius, were the infantry phalanx, with Alexander next to them to the right leading the Royal Squadron. The cavalry of the Greek allies, including the Thessalians, commanded by Parmenion, were positioned on the left flank facing Mazaeus. Alexander knew his right wing was going to be the most vulnerable as it faced Bessus' cavalry and 100 chariots and the Persian line outflanked it, but he also wanted to be ready for Darius striking at any point in his line.

Alexander's innovative nature now came into play. He set up a second line of infantry parallel to his front line comprising mostly mercenaries and other troops from the Balkans. Both flanks were further reinforced – on the right with infantry, archers, and the elite Agrianians, and on the left Thracian infantry and mercenary cavalry. Their job was to shield the gaps between the two lines, so the result was that Alexander's line mirrored a hollow rectangular formation.[36]

Alexander intended to use the same strategy as at Issus – to kill or capture Darius and dishearten the enemy – so he needed to protect his flanks while moving his centre forward at an oblique angle with the right leading the way to coax the Persians to mirror his movement as at Issus and open a gap. That meant executing more of a defensive than offensive measure at the start until he and his Companions could charge through the gap against Darius and then switch his line from defensive to offensive. Timing, like luck, was therefore essential for the king's trademark rapid and audacious attack to succeed.

The details of the actual engagement are not fully known primarily because of the dense, swirling dust clouds from the horses that obscured visibility.[37] Alexander moved first, leading his men to the right at a 45-degree angle to make his right flank face more of the Persian left in the hope of enticing Darius to follow him and so open his needed gap. But Darius was not going to be fooled twice. He moved some of the Bactrian and Sacae cavalry on his extreme left to check Alexander's diagonal movement but took care not to break his line too much as he knew Alexander would pounce on any opportunity. A setback for him though was that thanks to Alexander's reconnaissance of the plain, his direction took him away from the areas that the Persians had levelled for their chariots, forcing Darius to keep them on standby longer than he had intended.

Despite the enemy cavalry numbers Alexander ordered his mercenary cavalry under Menidas against the Bactrians and Sacae, supporting them with Paeonian cavalry and more mercenaries. Darius was forced to call on all the Bactrian cavalry to meet this threat and to try to stop Alexander's continued march away from the levelled ground so he could use his scythed chariots against his enemy. Menidas and his troops grittily stood their ground despite sustaining heavy losses, at which point Alexander ordered Aristion with his Paeonians and Greek mercenary cavalry against the Sacae. They were forcing them back when Bessus rushed to their rescue with the cavalry on his left wing, which led to a fierce cavalry clash.

Darius must have seen that despite his numbers the battle was getting away from him as he now deployed his chariots from his left flank against Alexander's right. Clear proof that the latter had anticipated this was the prearranged signal, presumably a shrill trumpet blast, that now rang out above the din of the battle and was an essential part of his combat operations. It communicated to the Agrianians and javelin men at the front to shoot the horses pulling the chariots, which went out of control. Some of them made it to the Macedonian line, where the troops jumped to their left and right with split-second precision, opening passages that the chariots had no choice but to race through – and as they did, their horses and riders were shot and killed.[38]

It was not long before Alexander had his chance with Darius. Bessus and his Bactrian troops moved too far to the left of their flank in their fight against the Macedonian cavalry, breaching the line and handing victory to Alexander. He immediately directed the companion cavalry and adjacent phalanx brigades into a wedge formation and charged through the gap towards Darius. As he got closer, the Great King again bolted, for which Arrian condemns him for cowardice.[39] Alexander set off at full gallop after Darius, who fled first to Arbela and then over the Zagros Mountains, by which time Alexander and his men gave up their chase and returned to the battlefield.

When Alexander took off after Darius there was still deadly fighting on the Macedonian right flank. On the left, Parmenion was struggling against Mazaeus' forces, especially as the scythed chariots there had managed to penetrate Parmenion's line, and he found himself encircled by some Parthian and Indian cavalry. He had been tasked with blocking the Persian right's advance to enable Alexander to rush Darius, but as the enemy troops began to get the better of him, he sent an urgent appeal to the king.

The sources are inconsistent about what happened to the message: the messengers either caught up to Alexander who turned around to help Parmenion (Arrian, Curtius, and Plutarch), or they saw the king too far away to catch him (Diodorus).[40] The latter is probably closest to the truth because of the speed of Alexander as he pursued Darius and poor visibility on the battlefield.[41] We will consider a more sinister explanation as part of the king's relations with his senior staff in Chapter 13.

Before long Bessus ordered his men to retreat, soon followed by the bulk of the Persian cavalry and the infantry on the left and centre. Their hasty departure allowed Parmenion the chance to rally his men and with the support of the Thessalian cavalry overcome Mazaeus, forcing him to flee. The battle was won but not all the fighting was over. As Alexander and his Companions returned to the battlefield they clashed with some fleeing Persian, Parthian, and Indian soldiers, which Arrian claims saw the bloodiest fighting of the day, with sixty Companions killed in it.[42]

Actual numbers of casualties in the battle differ dramatically in our sources, though there was not the carnage that the defeated enemy experienced at Issus. According to Arrian, 300,000 Persians were killed and 300,000 captured, whereas Curtius claims 40,000 were killed, and Diodorus 90,000. Alexander lost, according to Arrian, 100 men and 1,000 horses; Curtius speaks of less than 300, and Diodorus 500, but perhaps Curtius' figures are the closest to reality.[43] Alexander's victory against such a numerically superior army was so momentous that it hardly needed to be exaggerated in the first place. Darius had fled, presumably hoping to fight another day as after Issus, but this time it was not to be. In addition to losing at Gaugamela and earlier at Issus, Darius had shattered his subjects' belief in his omnipotence and had strained relations with his nobles, all of which also played a role in Alexander's ultimate victory.[44]

Alexander let Darius escape; more important was the seizure of the palaces at Babylon, Susa, and Persepolis not only to rob the Great King of resources but also to send out the clear signal that Alexander was now hegemon.[45] He marched 300 miles south along the Royal Road through Babylonia to Babylon, arriving there on October 24th or 25th. Its satrap Mazaeus – the commander of the Persian right at Gaugamela – surrendered the city and its enormous treasury to him. Alexander entered the city in grand style through the Ishtar Gate to a cheering throng and set up his headquarters in the palace of Nebuchadnezzar, overlooking the fabled Hanging Gardens.[46] Babylon yielded 40,000 talents of gold and silver bullion – along with what Alexander would go on to capture, and despite his huge expenditures, his eventual wealth was beyond measure.[47] He gave each of his soldiers a cash donative and one month of rest and relaxation.[48]

After making some important administrative arrangements, which we will discuss in Chapter 11, Alexander left Babylon and moved into what today is Iran. A twenty-day march of 230 miles followed to Susa (Shush), where the satrap of Susiana, Abulites, surrendered to him.[49] Alexander again came into possession of a vast reserve of gold and silver bullion.[50] In the palace the king discovered art works that the Persians had plundered from Athens during the Persian Wars (480–479), which he returned for symbolic as well as genuine reasons.[51] It was also said that when he sat on the throne of Darius and Xerxes under its golden canopy his feet dangled as he was obviously not as tall as Persian Kings.[52] To cover his embarrassment, not to mention diffuse the comic spectacle at Alexander's expense, a page slid one of the low tables from which Darius was said to have eaten under the king's feet as if they rested on a foot stool. At Susa, 15,000 troops (13,500 Macedonian, Thracian, and mercenary infantry and 1,500 Macedonian, Thracian, and Peloponnesian cavalry) arrived to take the army to about 50,000, back to the strength it had been at least at the time of Issus.[53]

There is a symbolism to the scene of the conqueror lounging with his feet on the Great King's table. At the same time, the episode reminds us that Alexander was far from being a big, muscle-bound 'action hero' and was not tall and imposing. Yet given his military cunning, remarkable victories, and impeccable leadership, his charisma and self-confidence clearly inspired everyone who met him. The same is true of Napoleon, who was 5'6" or 1.7 metres tall. A more recent equivalent might be Gen. Austin Scott Miller who, having commanded the elite Delta Force, U.S. Joint Special Operations Command, and the last U.S. mission in Afghanistan, exerts a captivating presence that belies his modest stature (he is roughly 1.7 metres tall).

It was now December, but Alexander was anxious to press on, fearful that if he waited out the winter at Susa Darius might have time to rally support. Leaving Abulites as satrap, Alexander set off into the satrapy of Persis, bound for Parsa – what the Greeks called Persepolis ('city of the Persians') – the symbolic heart of the Persian Empire. The crossing of the 15,000-feet-high Zagros Mountains in midwinter with the snow-blocking passes was an arduous one, but he also encountered resistance along his route including a surprising and challenging battle.

The Battle at the Persian Gates

While Alexander was marching through Uxiana, southeast of Susa, he was confronted on two occasions by the Uxians.[54] The first time was when a group of them from the lowland region refused to let him pass through their territory, which was not a wise move against the man who had just defeated huge numbers at Gaugamela. Alexander sent some Agrianians and mercenaries by a circuitous route that brought them out above his enemy. Once in position, they struck from the heights while Alexander and the men with him fought the Uxians head on, bringing them to terms.

Clearly, the Uxians of the upland area did not learn any lessons from this rout as they confidently demanded Alexander pay a toll (as was their practice) to allow safe passage through their pass. He had no intention of paying and called a meeting with them at the entrance to the pass. While they were on their way there, he devastated their lands, looting and burning nearby villages, and with 8,000 men marched at speed over a lightly used track to beat them to the pass. A little earlier he had sent Craterus to its heights to strike them from above, a similar strategy as that against their lowland counterparts. In the ensuing fighting, the Uxians lost many men before they surrendered and agreed to pay him an annual tribute of 100 horses, 500 oxen, and 30,000 sheep.[55]

These two engagements showed Alexander's quick thinking and his reliance on local advice when it came to topography. It is unlikely that he already knew of the path his men took against the lowland Uxians, and so had to make an on-the-spot decision about its value in helping overcome the sudden obstacle he faced. In addition, since the upland Uxians did not have a monetary economy but relied on barter, the tribute he demanded of them shows his constant attention to his supplies.

Close to modern Fahlian (Fars Province), Alexander decided to send the slower moving baggage train under Parmenion, supported by the Thessalian cavalry and other troops, to travel to Persepolis along an easy road (perhaps via Shiraz).[56] The king and 20,000 men including the companion cavalry took a more direct but dangerous route through the Persian (or Susian) Gates, a narrow gorge six miles long with sheer cliff faces on each side and passable only by foot. But when they arrived there five days later, Ariobarzanes, satrap of Persis, with as many as 40,000 infantry and 7,000 cavalry, blocked their path.[57] He had walled off the entrance to the pass and stationed Persian troops in the heights on either side to delay Alexander's progress and so give Darius time to reach Persepolis and rally support.[58]

Alexander was in a dilemma. There was every chance that Parmenion and the baggage train would reach Persepolis before him, even though it was moving slowly, and be overcome by the Persians, especially if Darius was there. Alexander therefore had to gamble, despite his inferior position, so the day after his arrival, he ordered an assault on Ariobarzanes' position. For once, he was lured into a trap. As Alexander's men marched into the defile, many were shot and killed by Persian archers or bombarded with missiles and boulders from the enemy above. When the Macedonians tried to turn and escape, they were blocked by their comrades who were still marching into the narrow pass. Alexander had no choice but to fall back. Even worse, he had to leave behind his dead, a major stigma for a general as Greeks believed that 'no military duty was as sacred as burying the dead'.[59]

Ariobarzanes held Alexander at bay for an entire month. The degree of frustration must have been great, especially after the Macedonians' successes in their shorter decisive battles against the Persians, and the worry of Parmenion and the baggage train must have been on the king's mind. Nonetheless, Alexander held steady rather than try to rush Ariobarzanes and suffering another costly defeat. Then his break came. He captured some locals, one of whom, a shepherd, told him of a narrow and overgrown twelve-mile path over the Boloru pass that came out behind Ariobarzanes' camp.

Alexander had no choice but to trust that the shepherd was not leading him into a trap. He decided on a method of attack like that used against the Uxians, namely a frontal strike at the walls, but instead of just one ambush from the heights of the pass there would be two, one from the side, roughly halfway down the track, and the other towards the rear of the pass. That night he left Craterus and Meleager with their infantry and 500 cavalry with orders to burn additional fires and make extra noise to create the illusion of an entire army still in camp. With his select troops, Alexander set off along the path, taking three days' worth of provisions and led by the shepherd. Along the way, he divided his men into two: perhaps half with Alexander were to attack from the rear of the pass and the rest under Philotas (Parmenion's son) from the side. Ptolemy, according to Arrian, was tasked with mopping up any survivors who fled through the pass.[60]

The path was so taxing and through thick forest that it took Alexander the whole of the following day (allowing his men a short rest period around midday) and night to reach the end. At dawn, he gave a trumpet signal loud enough for Craterus to hear, who on cue launched the frontal assault, while Philotas and Alexander rushed from their chosen positions. Caught off guard, the Persians were routed and massacred. Ariobarzenes' fate is controversial: some sources claim he died in the fighting, others that he escaped but surrendered, and even others claim that he fled and managed to reach Persepolis before Alexander caught up and killed him.[61]

The battle at the Persian Gates had again proved Alexander's brilliant problem-solving skills, perseverance, deft use of battlefield intelligence, and patience. It is hardly surprising that Fuller describes the campaign as 'one of the most hazardous, audacious, and certainly most profitable of mountain campaigns in the annals of history'.[62] At the same time, we wonder what Alexander would have done if the path had not been pointed out to him. He was lucky, then, but, as we have noted elsewhere, for any commander – then and now – luck was essential.

After his victory, Alexander quickly regrouped his army and marched at speed to Persepolis. Darius was not there, and its citadel commander, Tiridates, surrendered without resistance. It was now the end of January 330. Alexander established himself in the palace of Darius I and Xerxes outside the city walls (perhaps even at Istakhr) shortly before Parmenion and the baggage train arrived. Persepolis yielded an enormous haul of bullion and treasure for Alexander, some of which he kept with the army and the rest he sent to different parts of his empire.[63]

Alexander had travelled over 3,100 miles after leaving Achilles' tomb at Troy to where he now was deep in southwestern Iran in less than five years. His men had fought courageously and loyally and won some astonishing successes against great armies. He had exhibited the charisma and leadership skills that had brought his army thus far and would keep it going almost as far again. How different would the planning and execution of such a mission be today, how different the combat, and how different the outcome? Given what Alexander had available to him, or rather, the many things he did not that are part and parcel of a modern military, we cannot stress enough how astounding his achievements were and the speed with which he undertook them.

Mission Accomplished?

Persepolis was the traditional heart of the Persian Empire. It was here that the Persian King's subjects brought him gifts to show their subservience and his omnipotence. Even though Tiridates had surrendered, Alexander gave free rein to his men to kill and rape both military and civilian people and loot indiscriminately in revenge for what the Greeks had suffered during the Persian Wars.[64] Perhaps also the carnage was meant to be a release for the men's frustration at being held up at the Persian Gates and even for the thousands of miles they had marched, and battles and sieges waged.

The Macedonians spent four months in Persepolis and prepared to leave in May (of 330) to hunt down Darius. Before they did so, Xerxes' palace burned to the ground. Two explanations for the destruction are usual. The first is that at a drinking party, a fire was lit at the urging of the Athenian courtesan Thais, as revenge for the Persians' burning her city, which quickly spread to engulf the whole palace.[65] The second is that the palace was symbolically destroyed to recall the Persians' burning of the Athenian Acropolis in 480 and, especially, to show the Achaemenid Empire was no more.[66]

The accidental burning may be discounted. Among other things, Arrian recounts a conversation between Alexander and Parmenion with the latter warning of a native revolt if it were destroyed but Alexander wanting to exact retribution for the Persian sacking of Greece, while Diodorus speaks of Alexander's removing all treasures from Persepolis as an indication he was going to destroy the palace.[67] Alexander was said to have regretted his action, which also points to a deliberate burning.[68] The destruction was thus to send out a message: the Great King had been replaced by the Macedonian 'Ruler of Asia'. In this respect the destruction ties in with Alexander's motives in invading Persia: the young and ambitious king had always wanted more than what the members of the League of Corinth envisaged – his own empire.

The symbolism of demolition to show 'out with the old and in with the new' continues today. One obvious example is the toppling of Saddam Hussein's statue in Baghdad in 2003 at the beginning of Operation Iraqi Freedom. This was an image broadcast worldwide, no different from the 'broadcasting' by word of mouth of the palace's destruction, for equal effect.

Darius was still at large. News reached Alexander that he had originally stayed in his summer residence at Ecbatana (Hamadan, western Iran), the capital of Media, but when his attempt to raise an army failed, he fled into Bactria (now Afghanistan). Alexander resolved to capture him. He sent Parmenion and 6,000 soldiers with the huge bullion train to Ecbatana, and with 20,000 faster-moving troops set off on a series of forced marches through the harsh terrain and intense heat of the Dasht-e-Kavir or Great Salt Desert of Iran. Eventually, after more grueling forced marches and a couple of close encounters with Darius, Alexander caught up with him at Hecatompylus (Qumis), the capital of Parthia.

The Macedonian king never took the Great King alive. At some point earlier Bessus, Nabarzanes, a former cavalry commander, and Barsaentes, the satrap of Drangiana and Arachosia (southern Afghanistan), had deposed Darius. Bessus, who was related by blood to Darius, then declared himself Great King.[69] Now, as Alexander charged towards Hecatompylus, Satibarzanes, the satrap of Aria (western Afghanistan), and Barsaentes treacherously stabbed Darius to death.[70] The story that Darius sent Alexander a message of thanks for treating his family well and that Alexander gave the dying Darius water before he died in his arms, promising he would avenge him, is likely fiction to show Alexander's magnanimity to a fallen foe.[71]

It cannot be denied that Darius' death was fortunate for Alexander, for had he lived he would have become a martyr and even galvanized supporters. Still, Alexander ordered Darius' body to be buried with full honors at Persepolis, an indication of his respect for a worthy adversary and of his duty as a king to bury his predecessor.

The Macedonian invasion had thus achieved its strategic objective, and the men at Hecatompylus saw 'mission accomplished' and were ready to go home.[72] In fact, the troops provided by the League of Corinth were sent home although any wanting to remain with the king were hired as mercenaries.[73] The problem was that Bessus had declared himself Great King, taking the name Artaxerxes (V). For the security of the Macedonian Empire, Alexander had to take down Bessus: this would be the object of a new war, with therefore a new strategy. Yet as we shall see in Chapter 9, after the capture of Bessus, hence another mission accomplished, Alexander showed no signs of an exit policy. His thirst for reputation and conquest remained unquenched, and he seemed intent on marching as far east as possible, regardless of obstacles.

The removal of Bessus meant marching into Bactria, north of the Hindu Kush, something his men were far from enthused about and were querying. Despite Alexander's appeals in a passionate speech, they remained unmoved until he stressed that what was at stake was the future of the empire and, hyperbolically, that Bessus might undo everything the Macedonians had achieved or even invade Greece.[74] That appeal and the promise of a cash donative to continue with him changed their minds. He had given his troops bonuses before, usually as a reward for their valour; this time the sweetener was more of a bribe, which was significant. Arguably, the men's reaction at Hecatompylus was the genesis of the mutiny Alexander faced at the Hyphasis River in India in 326 (for the details on which, see Chapter 10).

In his battles and sieges in Persia across many thousands of miles, Alexander had brilliantly and single-handedly demonstrated his ability to wage war and his mastery of attacking, moving, communicating, and sustaining his army, which was even more astonishing in someone so young. He was only in his early twenties when he invaded Asia and twenty-six years old when he toppled the Persian Empire. In keeping with his maturity as a commander is his implementation of a psychological strategy to intimidate his enemy and his leading from the front under the deadliest circumstances.

At the same time, it was having his boots on the ground that allowed him to adjust his plans of attack when misfortune struck, just as today, the ability to adapt in rapidly evolving situations is a key to success. Despite the most careful planning and sophisticated twenty-first century technology, it is still the human commander on the ground whose thinking and skills are needed to turn battlefield adversity into advantage, as will be argued in the following chapter.

Notes

1. Philip's objectives: Worthington 2008, pp. 167–169.
2. Curtius 4.2.3; cf. Herodotus 2.44.4 on the identification.
3. Diodorus 17.40.2 (suggesting that their refusal was because of their loyalty to Darius); Arrian 2.15.7; Curtius 4.2.2–3. Festival: Curtius 4.2.10.
4. For a review of this grave misunderstanding, see Ferguson 2021g; Serhan 2021.
5. Diodorus 17.40.2–46.6, Arrian 2.18.3–24.6, Curtius 4.2.8–4.18, Plutarch, *Alexander* 24.4–25.3, Justin 11.10.10–14, with Fuller 1960, pp. 206–216; Keegan 1987, pp. 74–77; Romane 1987; Bosworth 1988a, pp. 65–67; Bloedow 1990; Ashley 1998, pp. 237–249; Lonsdale 2007, pp. 114–118; English 2009b, pp. 56–84; Worthington 2014a, pp. 173–178.
6. On his naval siege equipment, see English 2009b, pp. 18–21.
7. Diodorus 17.43.1–2, 17.43.9–44.5; Curtius 4.3.24–26.
8. Arrian 2.24.4.
9. Arrian 2.24.5; Curtius 4.4.18; cf. Justin 21.6.1–7.
10. Hegesias, *BNJ* 142 F 5; Arrian 2.25.4.
11. Siege: Diodorus 17.48.7, Arrian 2.25.4–27.7, Curtius 4.6.7–31, Plutarch, *Alexander* 25.4, with Fuller 1960, pp. 216–218; Bosworth 1988a, pp. 67–68; Romane 1988; Ashley 1998, pp. 249–251; English 2009b, pp. 85–101; Worthington 2014a, pp. 178–179.
12. Curtius 4.6.25–29; cf. Hegesias, *BNJ* 142 F 5.
13. Alexander in Egypt: Bosworth 1988a, pp. 68–74; Worthington 2014a, pp. 179–184.
14. Burstein 1991 on not being crowned pharaoh.
15. Worthington 2016, pp. 133–146.
16. Bosworth 1988a, pp. 278–290; Worthington 2014a, pp. 265–269, to which add Collins 2014.
17. Fredricksmeyer 2003; cf. Dreyer 2009. Philip: Worthington 2008, pp. 228–233.
18. Aristobulus, *BNJ* 139 FF 13 = Arrian 3.3.2.
19. Cf. Ptolemy, *BNJ* 138 F 9 = Arrian 3.4.5, that Alexander 'heard what he found agreeable to his wishes'.
20. Cf. Hamilton 1953.
21. Worthington 2014a, pp. 181–182.
22. Ptolemy, *BNJ* 138 F 8 = Arrian 3.3.5. Ravens: Arisotobulus, *BNJ* 129 F 14 = Arrian 3.3.5; cf. Plutarch, *Alexander* 27.3–4.
23. Diodorus 17.109.2; Arrian 7.8.3; Justin 12.11.6.
24. Arrian 3.6.2; Curtius 4.8.12.
25. Diodorus 17.39.1–2; Arrian 2.14; Curtius 4.1.7–14; cf. Diodorus 17.54.1–5; Curtius 4.5.1–8; Justin 11.12; Plutarch, *Alexander* 29.7–8; cf. Diodorus 17.48.6; Curtius 4.5.11 for the other Greeks honoring Alexander back home.
26. Routes of Alexander and Darius: Bosworth 1988a, pp. 79–80, citing bibliography.
27. Diodorus 17.56–61, Arrian 3.8–15, Curtius 4.9–10.12, 4.12–16.33, Plutarch, *Alexander* 31–33, Justin 11.13–14.7, with Fuller 1960, pp. 163–180; Bosworth

1988a, pp. 76–85; Devine 1989a, pp. 120–124; Ashley 1998, pp. 257–269; Lonsdale 2007, pp. 127–134; Heckel 2008, pp. 75–80; Worthington 2014a, pp. 188–193; in-depth: Griffith 1947; Marsden 1964; Devine 1975, Devine 1986a, Devine 1989b; English 2011, pp. 110–137.
28 Arrian 3.9.1–2.
29 Arrian 3.11.1; Curtius 4.13.11.
30 Arrian 3.8.6; Diodorus 17.53.3; Curtius 4.12.13; Plutarch, *Alexander* 31.1. Sources: cf. English 2011, pp. 110–115.
31 Arrian 3.12.5.
32 Arrian 3.10.2; cf. Plutarch, *Alexander* 31.10–14.
33 See Iglesias-Zoido 2010.
34 Callisthenes, *BNJ* 124 F 36 = Plutarch, *Alexander* 33.1–2.
35 Arrian 3.13.1. Order of lines: English 2011, pp. 121–129.
36 Cf. Arrian 3.12.1–5; Curtius 4.13.31–32, with Devine 1975, pp. 374–378.
37 Diodorus 17.61.1; Curtius 4.15.32.
38 Arrian 3.13.5; Curtius 4.15.4.
39 Arrian 3.15.1–3.
40 Diodorus 17.60.7; Arrian 3.15.1–2; Curtius 4.16.3; Plutarch, *Alexander* 33.9–10.
41 Cf. Bosworth 1988a, p. 84.
42 Arran 3.15.1–2.
43 See Hammond 1989b, pp. 57–62, on casualty figures.
44 Strauss and Ober 1990, pp. 103–131, though they are too critical of the Great King's military capabilities: see Nylander 1993; Badian 2000.
45 Lonsdale 2007, p. 156.
46 Arrian 3.16.3–5; Curtius 5.1.17–45.
47 See now Holt 2016; cf. Ashley 1998, pp. 377–382.
48 Diodorus 17.64.6; Curtius 5.1.45.
49 Diodorus 17.65.5–66.7; Arrian 3.16.6–11; Curtius 5.2.8–17. Time and distance of march: Arrian 3.16.7.
50 Diodorus 17.66.2; Arrian 3.16.7; Curtius 5.2.11; Plutarch, *Alexander* 36.1; Justin 11.14.9.
51 On his reasons for so doing, see Finn 2014.
52 Curtius 5.2.13–15; cf. Plutarch, *Alexander* 37.7.
53 Bosworth 1988a, p. 88, with references.
54 Diodorus 17.67.3–5; Arrian 3.17.1–6; Curtius 5.3.3–16, with Ashley 1998, pp. 271–274.
55 Arrian 3.17.6.
56 Arrian. 3.18.1; Curtius 5.3.16.
57 Numbers: Arrian 3.18.2–3. But Diodorus 17.68.1 has 25,000 infantry and 300 cavalry and Curtius 5.3.17 just has 25,000 infantry.
58 Diodorus 17.68.2–7, Arrian 3.18.1–9, Curtius 5.3.17–4.34, with Fuller 1960, pp. 228–234, Heckel 1980; Bosworth 1988a, 90–92; Ashley 1998, pp. 274–277; Speck 2002; Lonsdale 2007, pp. 105–107; Worthington 2014a, pp. 202–204.
59 Curtius 5.3.2. It is significant that Arrian, who usually lauds Alexander's generalship, says next to nothing about this episode: 3.18.2–3.
60 Arrian 3.18.9. In his *History*, echoed by Arrian, Ptolemy claims he led the second force, but this is a likely instance of his exaggeration as we noted in the sources (see pp. 111–112).
61 Curtius 5.4.33–34 but see Arrian 3.18.9 for him escaping.

62 Fuller 1960, p. 234.
63 Diodorus 17.71.1–2; Curtius 5.6.9–10; cf. Arrian 3.18.10.
64 Diodorus 17.70.1–6; Curtius 5.6.1–8 (who claims Alexander ordered his men not to violate the women); Plutarch, *Alexander* 37.3–5.
65 Cleitarchus, *BNJ* 137 F 11 (= Athenaeus 13.576d-e); Diodorus 17.72.1–6; Curtius 5.7.2–7; Plutarch, *Alexander* 38.1–8; cf. Arrian 3.18.10–12.
66 Borza 1972; Hammond 1992c; Sancisi-Weerdenburg 1993; Briant 2010, pp. 107–111.
67 Arrian 3.18.11–12; Diodorus 17.71.3.
68 Arrian 6.30.1; Curtius 5.8.11, Plutarch, *Alexander* 38.8.
69 Arrian 3.21.1, 4; Curtius 5.9.2–8. A fragmentary Aramaic inscription calls him 'Artaxerxes the king', see Briant 2010, pp. 178–179. Related to Darius: Arrian 3.21.5.
70 Diodorus 17.73.3; Arrian 3.21.10; Curtius 8.16–17; Justin 11.15.5, with Worthington 2014a, pp. 209–211.
71 Curtius 5.13.25; Plutarch, *Alexander* 43.3–4; Justin 11.15.7–14; cf. Diodorus 17.73.3–4.
72 Diodorus 17.74.3; Curtius 6.2.15–16; Plutarch, *Alexander* 47.1–3; Justin 12.3.2–3.
73 Arrian 3.19.5–7; Curtius 6.2.17; Plutarch, *Alexander* 42.5; Justin 12.1.1–3.
74 Curtius 6.3.1–4; on the donative, see Diodorus 17.44.4.

8 The Art of Control and the Enduring Fog of War

After his impressive victory over Darius at Gaugamela in 331, Alexander seized the Persian capitals of Babylon, Susa, and Persepolis. The last was especially important as it was the traditional heart of the Persian Empire; Alexander's capture of it would thus send out the clear message that the Achaemenid dynasty was no more. But, as covered in the previous chapter, his march to Persepolis was thwarted for a month by Ariobarzanes, satrap of Persis, at the Persian Gates. Since Alexander had to reach Persepolis before Parmenion and the baggage train arrived there via another route, time was of the essence.

Throughout the course of the campaign at the Persian Gates, as we saw, Alexander split his forces at least three and possibly four times (if Ptolemy was tasked with the mopping up operation), in each instance issuing specific orders to commanders like Craterus and Philotas with whom he would be out of contact for several days.[1] When he finally attacked, his three-pronged assault surprised the Persians, sending them into an uncoordinated response that resulted in their slaughter. Alexander's clearheaded planning and sagacious orders won the day – just as they had done a week or so earlier when he had split his forces and relied on Craterus to defeat the Uxians.

Alexander's operation at the Persian Gates, considering its complexity and scope, would be impressive even with today's technology. But it was accomplished without radios, maps, motorized vehicles, artificial lighting, or exhaustive mission rehearsals. The same can be said of his crossing of the Hydaspes River in India with tens of thousands of troops to wage battle against Porus (see Chapter 10). Such synchronization of geographically dispersed military activities, executed at speed to disrupt an opponent's decision cycle, is the envy of even modern armies. Splitting one's forces numerous times within the same operation complicates command and control (C2) systems, communications, and shared understanding across any organization. As the range of weapons, distance between armies, and number of moving pieces in battle increased since Alexander's time, so too have the quantity of systems employed to synchronize such activities. In the process, the interdependent trust that commanders such as Alexander relied upon to execute their missions eroded, if only because tools emerged to supplant them with other means of verification.

Satellite communicable aerial drones with full motion video (FMV) pods that overwatch ground forces and the Blue Force Tracking network that provides a graphic representation of friendly force locations have transformed a commander's ability to understand the battlefield.[2] One of the more iconic photographs of recent years showing the distances between an observer and its targets is that of White House officials watching the May 2011 killing of Osama bin Laden in Pakistan from the comfort of a White House office (Figure 8.1).

As discussed in Chapter 2, near the end of the twentieth century many theorists predicted that such emergent technologies would lift the 'fog of war', resulting in a transparent battlefield.[3] At the same time, however, these resources turned war into a spectator sport by offering a view of the battlefield to officials far removed both geographically and psychologically from the realities of ground warfare. Rather than thinning it, these factors have in many ways thickened the fog of war, a term used to describe the myriad complexities that blur truth and hinder control amid the chaos of armed conflict.

Figure 8.1 White House officials watching the killing of Osama bin Laden. Credit: Pete Souza.

Endless streams of battlefield data have led to expectations of clarity that are increasingly challenging to sustain even in peacetime while below the threshold of large-scale, conventional warfare.[4] Technological innovation is progressing at a rate that makes operational control more complicated, not less so, and such control is paramount to aligning the outcomes of individual battles with strategic objectives – what is often referred to as operational art.[5] New military technologies and concepts, once hailed as gateways to a hyper-efficient future that simplifies this process while allowing similar degrees of speed, control, and understanding have not delivered any such reality. This chapter builds on the skills Alexander displayed at the Persian Gates by examining the principles of unity of command, mutual trust, and information clarity in modern military operations.

New but Familiar Challenges

Alexander's unity of command was supreme. For better or worse, its effectiveness contributed to a long legacy of how commanders understand the art of war. When the French Directory asked Napoleon to share command with Gen. François-Christophe de Kellermann in 1796, he threatened to resign directly with a biting retort: 'Better one bad general than two good ones'.[6] Napoleon saw unity of command as the first necessity in war, but such centralized authority, when coupled with the tyranny of distance, later eroded his ability to control far-flung regions of his empire. Jomini would later observe the importance of Napoleon's use of the semaphore or optical telegraph, but the emperor's inability to translate that capability into a mobile system led to a breakdown in communication.[7]

In the mid-twentieth century, unity of command was so important to Gen. Dwight Eisenhower that he nearly resigned his position as supreme commander of allied expeditionary forces. He considered taking drastic action in March 1944 – a mere three months before the D-Day invasion – over disputes regarding the scope of his authority.[8] Subordinate commands, such as the Army Air Corps, were uncomfortable with an army officer leading their forces. But Eisenhower understood that such unity of command would prevent a loss of control in the fog of war; something senior officials debated nearly fifty-eight years later while planning the coalition invasion of Iraq.

During the initial phases of OIF, command authority was unified under the responsible geographic combatant command, U.S. Central Command (CENTCOM), which placed Joint Special Operations Command and clandestine activities' assets from the Central Intelligence Agency under the authority of U.S. Army Gen. Tommy Franks. At the time, Franks commanded CENTCOM. This decision was essential to the invasion's initial success. Yet three weeks after the fall of Baghdad in April 2003, that unity of command was dismembered and replaced with the Coalition Provisional Authority headed by CENTCOM's deputy for reconstruction, Paul Bremer III.[9] Attempts to fill the ensuing communication gaps between diplomatic and military channels often took the form of additional layers of bureaucracy, such as the Iraqi Stabilization Group established later that same year.[10] Despite ongoing efforts to build seamless communication networks and digital mapping capabilities that provide commanders with a clear picture of the battlefield, flaws in communication, control, and trust remain the bane of modern military operations – and the world is getting no less complex.

Like Alexander, former U.S. Secretary of Defense Gen. Jim Mattis seemed to always find himself at the point of friction during his tenure in the marine corps, if only because he made a point to put himself there. Leading a tank battalion to expel Saddam Hussein's forces from Kuwait in 1991, pulling together Task Force 58 to secure a foothold in southern Afghanistan in 2001, seizing Baghdad as a division commander in 2003, taking charge of the brutal 2004 Fallujah campaign, and commanding CENTCOM at a critical juncture are highlights of his command experience. There are few living professionals with a deeper personal understanding of modern warfare than Mattis. What makes his philosophy on the nature of war unique, though, is that despite his decades of experience in and around the digitized battlefield, he remains intellectually grounded in the experiences of those leaders who came before him, most notably those of antiquity, such as Alexander.[11]

Accounts of leaders like Mattis illustrate how some of the most pervasive challenges to twenty-first century leadership are the same with which Alexander struggled. These problems involve bridging the gap between the theory and practice of mission command, and negotiating floods of conflicting information to enable timely decision-making in ambiguous environments characterized by 'grey zone' activities and political warfare.[12] Notwithstanding the use of these terms to describe supposedly nascent forms of warfare involving the use of military and non-military means in the competitive space short of declared war, Plato described this blurring of the lines between peace and war long ago:

> ...there is always, for all of us, a lifelong and continuous state of war against all other cities...what the greater part of mankind calls peace is merely a name; the reality is that for cities the natural state of affairs is an undeclared war of all against all.[13]

Interestingly, the U.S. Department of Defense codified this wisdom in its joint doctrine note on strategic competition, signed 3 February 2023, which outlines the need to compete more aggressively in peacetime to deter war and to be better positioned strategically if war cannot be deterred. It is trite to say there is nothing new under the sun, but, in this instance, it is also true. Each of these terms, while useful in furthering the discussion on the character of modern warfare – such as Russia's purported new-generation warfare or China's unrestricted warfare – essentially describes the age-old concept of interstate competition escalated above diplomacy but remaining below the threshold of Napoleonic war – a concept which certainly is *not* new. These intellectual frameworks came to personify the strategic environment for much of the early twenty-first century, and they tie further into the elusive operational art that ultimately played a role in Alexander's descent into strategic incoherence.

Mission Command

While briefing his joint task force staff during the second year of OIF on 22 April 2004, Maj. Gen. Mattis was blunt: 'If you're not confused, then you don't know how confusing the situation is'.[14] He referred to the nebulous political calculations that frustrated progress during the clearance of Fallujah, made possible with communications networks that provided instantaneous links between his forward headquarters and Washington, D.C. This process, in which distant observers use modern technology to dictate tactical maneuvers far below their traditional scope of authority, is dubbed colloquially 'the 3,000-mile screwdriver'.[15] Mattis' comments paint a picture far removed from the world of absolute clarity that RMA and advanced C2 systems were supposed to usher into existence this century. His solution as described in his memoirs is the longstanding but increasingly popular philosophy referred to as mission command, which is now heavily codified into American, British, and Israeli military doctrine – though certainly not perfected.[16]

At its core, mission command describes a decentralized form of control that relies on issuing clear orders, with the shared understanding that subordinate leaders will assume risk and develop a bias for action instead of seeking constant guidance. Mission command is a counterbalance to the traditional centralized leadership design of hierarchal militaries that rely heavily on incremental adjustments from senior leaders to conduct operations. It is rooted in principles such as cohesion and mutual trust, disciplined initiative, the acceptance of risk, and clear commander's intent. Although the concept is often attributed to the style of command practiced within the Prussian military that ultimately toppled Napoleon (*Auftragstaktik*), for thousands of years, initiative taken within the confines of a commander's

162 *Choosing Battles – And Winning Wars?*

broad intent was common because it was obligatory. Lacking any manner of remote communication, such as radios, soldiers of antiquity could not seek constant guidance from their commanders in battle. Martin Van Creveld explains this relationship as it applied to ancient warfare: 'Unable to Command the army as a whole but unwilling to relinquish all tactical control, generals put themselves at the head of what they hoped would be the decisive wing, entrusting the other to some experienced subordinate'.[17] Long before Napoleon sacked Europe, Alexander mastered this concept, and the Persian Gates is only one example.

When a commander gave an order, it had to contain enough information to account for contingencies and allow the subordinate room to adjust.

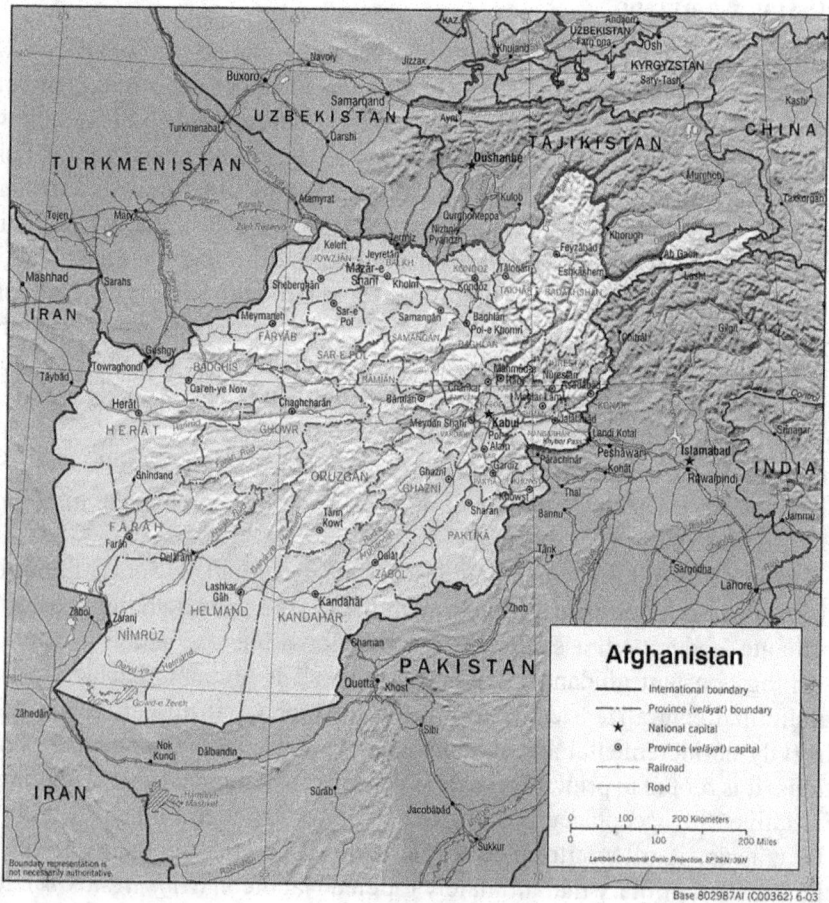

Figure 8.2 Map of Afghanistan. Credit: Perry-Castañeda Library Map Collection, 2017.

Arrian tells us that while preparing to fight Porus at the Hydaspes River, Alexander issued detailed guidance to Craterus that included contingency plans and *if-then* scenarios – what intelligence planners today might consider 'branches' – thus demonstrating Alexander's gift for predicting his opponent's moves.[18] This allowed Craterus to never be at a loss for guidance even when far removed from his king's physical presence. Trust was compulsory once the fighting began and winning was all that mattered.

Mission command is a core aspect of what some suggest makes free armies so effective, such as their liberty to innovate, improvise, and take prudent action without fear of reprisal both on and off the battlefield.[19] Granted, Macedonia was no democracy, but its military commanders were encouraged to fight fiercely and rewarded generously for overcoming adversities in battle. Authoritarian states lack such armies, for reasons Victor Davis Hanson explains:

> Every army possesses men of daring, but few encourage initiative throughout the ranks, and welcome rather than fear innovation, so apprehensive are they that an army of independent-thinking soldiers in war just might prove the same as citizens in peace.[20]

At first look, the philosophy might appear intuitive to western minds, but it is only as effective as the trust held between leaders and the clarity of their superior's mission orders.

Into the Fog

Gen. Tommy Franks was commander of CENTCOM in 2001, and therefore responsible for planning and overseeing the initial military invasions of Afghanistan and Iraq after the terrorist attacks on New York City and Washington, D.C. Secretary Donald Rumsfeld headed the Defense Department, and Mattis led a task force on the ground – first in Afghanistan but quickly transitioning to command the armoured cavalcade from Kuwait to Baghdad in 2003. Each of them had singular perspectives of the war's early progress and different priorities stemming from their respective levels of authority. Rumsfeld had to manage the public 'optics' of a heavily publicized ground war along with its associated political considerations, while Franks and Mattis focused on gaining and maintaining the tactical and operational initiative, which at times led to debilitating halts in momentum. This reached an apex in the opening phases of the Afghanistan and Iraq wars.

Mattis' task force established a foothold in southern Afghanistan via amphibious assault less than two months after the 9/11 attacks, where he awaited further orders to assist coalition efforts designed to expel the Taliban and locate the mastermind of the attacks, Osama bin Laden. Though Mattis' marines were eager to join the fight, that order never came.[21] Gen. Franks, mindful of the Soviet excesses in Afghanistan decades prior – of which President George W. Bush was also aware – refrained from playing a strong military hand.[22] Instead, the Pentagon and CIA relied upon small special operations units – fewer than 100 commandos – to root out Bin Laden in the mountainous reaches of Tora Bora east of Kabul, roughly 400 miles north of Mattis' position. Although the special operations mission to rally the Afghan Northern Alliance against the Taliban proved wildly successful, the refusal to deploy Mattis' task force to Tora Bora was depicted in a 2009 Senate Foreign Relations Committee report as contributing to the al-Qaeda leader's ability to escape into Pakistan.[23] Bin Laden's redoubt should have come as no surprise. A 1998 wargame held at an undisclosed location in Virginia identified Tora Bora as the most likely hiding place for al-Qaeda operatives in Afghanistan.[24]

The decision to withhold a larger force, however, was based on reasonable guidance from both Secretary Rumsfeld and President Bush that this operation would not be reminiscent of the Soviet invasion (1979–1989). National Security Advisor Condoleezza Rice recalled that everyone, including the vice president, secretary of state, and secretary of defense, agreed that the United States would not fight a large ground war in Afghanistan, but instead rely on small special operations teams and local fighters.[25] Administration officials expected surveillance platforms, airstrikes, and other technologies to compensate for a shortage of ground forces.[26] But there were too many gaps in the labyrinthine mountain passes of northern Afghanistan, and their prey eluded them. Bin Laden remained at large for another decade until he was killed by a joint special operations team in 2011 during a night raid in Abbottabad, Pakistan.[27]

A similar minimalist approach drove planning efforts for the invasion of Iraq a year later, and it was met with resistance. Most U.S. officials who huddled at Camp David in the days following the 9/11 attacks displayed little interest in Iraq, to include White House Chief of Staff Andy Card and President Bush himself.[28] Deputy Secretary of Defense Paul Wolfowitz was one of the first to present the Iraq option, and dubious circumstances over the following year, including reports from Iraqi exiles such as *Curve Ball* and Ahmed Chalabi, swayed U.S. policy to the Wolfowitz camp.[29] Secretary of State Colin Powell strongly opposed action in Iraq at this point, and, once the decision had been made to invade, he telephoned Gen. Franks on 5 September 2002 to discuss the numbers.[30] Powell believed that the 60,000 strong invasion force presented troubling tooth-to-tail problems that would require a much larger effort. Granted, this was an improvement from earlier proposals that called for invading Iraq with as little as 10,000 troops.[31] Powell promised to voice his concerns during the next National Security Council (NSC) meeting at Camp David. The nation's senior diplomat advocating for a stronger military approach might seem odd, but considering Powell had served as the nation's senior uniformed service member ten years prior during the Gulf War, his opinionated stance makes sense.

Ultimately, Powell's recommendations were sidelined by Franks' counter argument to the NSC, in which he declared that the world was moving into a 'new strategic and operational paradigm' characterized by long-range precision fires, uncontested air dominance, and small specialized ground

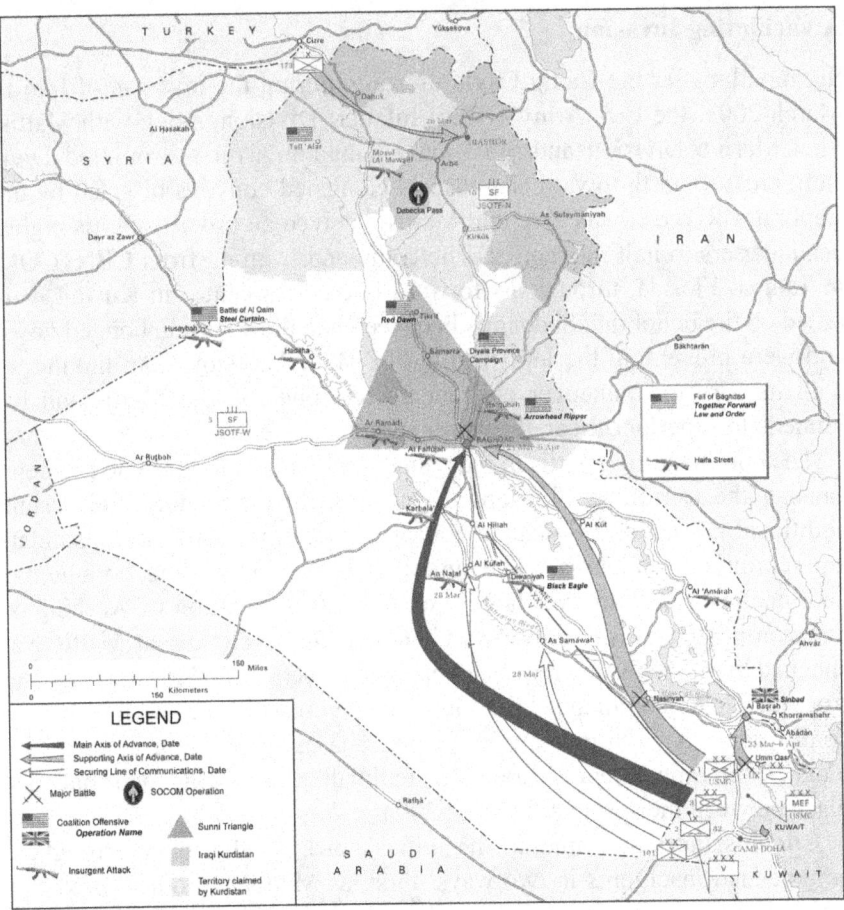

Figure 8.3 Map of Iraq. Credit: ADuran via Wikimedia Commons.

units.[32] His view, held by Rumsfeld and others at CENTCOM, was perhaps in the minority. Franks' predecessor, Gen. Anthony Zinni, recommended sending a force of 350,000 into Iraq, while a later report from CENTCOM's own Joint Task Force IV upped that estimate to 470,000.[33] To put this debate in perspective, the force that pushed Saddam Hussein's army out of Kuwait in 1991 was close to a million strong, despite President George H. W. Bush's suggestion that airpower might compensate for less mass.[34] New military capabilities encouraged similar suggestions in 2002. But by 2008, the United States had nearly tripled its number of troops in Iraq to roughly 160,000 – still less than a quarter of the force leveraged to expel Saddam from Kuwait during the Gulf War.[35] Conditions on the ground in Iraq would not be so easily controlled.

A Vacillating Invasion

Six months after the Camp David meeting, during the invasion of Iraq in March 2003, the U.S. Army's Third Infantry Division, along with Mattis' First Marine Division and the United Kingdom's First Armoured Division, pressed north toward Baghdad in elongated convoys bisected by the Euphrates River. It was here that Mattis received an order from his higher headquarters to halt movement. The command, coming from CENTCOM in Tampa, Florida, through its forward operations center in Kuwait, was based on the belief that Saddam's Fedayeen had the coalition bogged down and were preventing the logistical tail of Mattis' convoy from linking up with its forward maneuver elements. According to both Mattis and his immediate superior officer, this was simply not true.[36]

The command for Mattis to halt came at the most inopportune moment, causing the assaulting divisions to lose critical momentum and sustain additional casualties as Saddam's army gained three days to consolidate and reinforce its defenses.[37] The number of battlefield sensors, both human and machine, pushing ever larger volumes of information to Washington decision-makers was simply overwhelming. So much so that Mattis was shocked by the reporting requirements and expectation of constant updates from his higher command.[38] But these human errors in communication and control were not limited to the opening phases of the war, as they also plagued the ambivalent clearance of Fallujah west of Baghdad that took place between the spring and fall of 2004.

Circumstances surrounding the initial attack on the Sunni stronghold emboldened insurgents in two ways. First, as Mattis and others predicted by advising against the immediate clearance of Fallujah with U.S. forces, insurgents weaponized collateral damage to religious and cultural sites to bolster propaganda and recruiting efforts, which fueled resistance in the city.[39] Mattis had opted for an asymmetric approach that involved engaging the local populace and courting tribal leaders to build inroads into Fallujah before dismantling the insurgency there. Second, the vacillating decision to clear Fallujah gave hope to the budding insurgency in the form of an apparently indecisive enemy.[40] Any show of confusion or hesitancy in the early phase of the invasion was used as evidence that the U.S. military was not invincible, and perhaps not convinced of its purpose. The situation became so foggy that Bing West, who was on the ground with Mattis at the time, wondered who was providing the White House with information when on 23 April 2004 President Bush declared that most of Fallujah was returning to normal.[41] Convoluted command relationships, miscommunication, and sputtering momentum told insurgents that with enough civilian casualties and enough time, the coalition could be bested.[42] Al-Qaeda pursued this strategy for most of the war until direct combat operations ceased officially in December 2011, at which time ISIS, an outgrowth of al-Qaeda in Iraq, emerged.

The problem was not that leaders in Washington sent Mattis' marines into Fallujah against his advice, but rather that they sent them and then pulled them out numerous times, thus thickening the fog. It is still unclear whether a swift and violent clearance of Fallujah would have been more costly than an ambivalent one, but at a minimum it would have secured the city months earlier and prevented countless insurgents from arming and staging for a fight while coalition forces sat on the sidelines. Once committed, periodic assessments are important, but speed, mass, and surprise were as imperative to combat forces in Iraq as they were to Alexander in Persia.

The value of modern communications and C2 systems is not in question, but the extent to which they are abused certainly should be. Mattis frames the challenge as such: 'I'd always found first reports to be half wrong and half incorrect . . . the fog of war can actually thicken when misinformation is instantly amplified'.[43] This observation applies to all consumers of information. The convergence of global communications systems and a fickler information environment gave commanders greater awareness but perhaps less control, and therefore slowed momentum of major operations due to feelings of increased uncertainty. Unity of command and mutual trust became more vexing when leaders could *verify* more than they were required to *trust*. A nod to President Ronald Reagan's 'trust but verify' mantra, the modern world has turned the trust–verify matrix on its head with the influx of information systems in modern campaigns. Manipulating information to mislead human judgement remained a focal point of planning that bore fruit on both ends of the Iraq and Afghanistan wars, and further thickened the fog of war.

Information and Understanding

In the opening days of OIF, also known to CENTCOM planners and defense officials as OPLAN 1003V, disinformation and information operations (IO) played a key but understated role. A U.S. military officer code-named 'April Fool' convinced a contact in Iraq's *Mukhabarat* foreign intelligence service that an outdated version of OPLAN 1003 was in fact the current OPLAN.[44] The old plan depicted an airborne joint forcible entry operation in northern Iraq. Planners in Baghdad were persuaded of its authenticity when the U.S. Army's 173rd Airborne Brigade out of Vicenza, Italy, conducted an airborne assault into Bashur, Iraq, where Kurdish Peshmerga and U.S. Special Forces held ground. This feint proved valuable as it enabled Mattis' armoured units to sweep north in record time, covering 251 miles in just six days.[45] Key to this distraction was first knowing what the opponent wanted, and then giving it to him – otherwise known as confirmation bias. As we cover in Chapter 10, Alexander deployed a similar tactic against Porus in 326 when, night after night, he rode up and down the Hydaspes River being sure to attract plenty of attention.[46] Porus eventually grew tired of mobilizing his army in response, to include his war elephants and their riders, and in turn became complacent. When Alexander did cross, he kept fires burning on his side of the river to deceive Porus and feed into the Indian general's complacency.

Misinformation and deception, though, are very much double-edged swords, and at times modern media outlets wield them as deftly as Alexander. Two sentences uttered by Mattis to reporters in 2001 demonstrated this clearly: 'We now own a piece of Afghanistan. We can now give it back to the Afghan people'.[47] International media outlets dropped the second sentence and reported the first, which spawned mutterings of neo-imperialism and American colonialism – two of the grievances underlying the Salafi ideology of groups such as al-Qaeda.[48]

It is hard to overstate the significance of media coverage in modern warfare. Saddam's advisors, for instance, considered what they saw on CNN 'holy writ' according to Franks and his intelligence team.[49] The 'CNN effect', as Australian Defence Forces coined the phenomena in the 1990s, also drove the urge to send coalition forces into Fallujah so rapidly. After the televised barbaric killings of four U.S. contractors there in February 2004, senior U.S. officials were eager to show strength, even against the urgings of their ground commanders. The desire for favorable optics played to the coalition's disadvantage as AQI drew U.S. forces into Fallujah before they could set conditions for success. Subsequent indecision over how the city should be taken delayed the seizure of Fallujah for nearly the entire year of 2004, allowing insurgents to exploit any civilian casualties or damage to religious sites for recruiting purposes. Soldiers and marines finally cleared the city in November during a fierce and costly ground campaign involving house-to-house and hand-to-hand fighting.[50]

Ironically, after years of intense urban warfare, a people-centric approach to the Anbar Province like the one envisioned earlier by Mattis toppled AQI during the 2007 Anbar Awakening, as discussed in Chapter 2. Entering Fallujah with a heavy hand in 2004 was a tactical solution to a political problem spawned by the news cycle that allowed AQI to choose the time and place of battle. Though it may have been the wrong decision, once it was made, a failure to commit forces decisively only increased confusion on the ground.

For millennia, the challenge put to commanders before and during battle revolved around acquiring enough information to make decisions with relative confidence. In Alexander's time, that clarity often came from myths, which is arguably no more effective than allowing the twenty-four-hour news cycle to drive operations today. Plutarch tells us that Alexander wrestled with the options of building combat power in the coastal regions or pursuing Darius after his defeat at Granicus.[51] A bronze tablet foretelling Persia's fall to Greece supposedly convinced Alexander to choose the latter option.

Today, with the vast scope of collection tools deployed around the world from undersea cables to the far reaches of space, information overload is more of a problem than information deficit. This abundance can lead to frustrating practices in which leaders demand even more information to ensure they are making the right decisions. An old Italian proverb popularized in French by Francois Voltaire may have characterized this tendency best by reminding the reader that 'the perfect is the enemy of the good'.[52] If ever there was an enterprise in which good might be the best one can hope for, it is war. In other words, deciding with fifty percent certainty could produce better results than holding out for ninety percent certainty, at which point the enemy might have made the decision for you. Gen. George Patton is also famous for his command philosophy of surprise and speed. On 19 December 1944, he told Eisenhower that he would rather attack the southern flank of the Bulge with three divisions now than wait for six as Eisenhower suggested and lose the initiative.[53] It worked, of course. Lesser known is Patton's insistence that orders should be no more than a page of typewritten text, whereas today they can be

100 or more.⁵⁴ This process of sorting through floods of information to paint a coherent picture of the battlefield is one of increasing complexity.

British Maj. Gen. Thomas Copinger-Symes, CBE, clarified as much in his February 2020 speech at the world's oldest defence and security think tank, the United Kingdom's Royal United Services Institute (RUSI): 'We risk drowning in information; asphyxiated by a lack of understanding'.⁵⁵ He went on to highlight how populations are attacked in a perpetual information war taking place on their smart devices before the first shot of a physical war is ever fired, thus influencing both the speed of an army at war and a commander's ability to control public perceptions that impact political decisions. This can take the form of decision paralysis in which leaders are exposed to such a continuous deluge of information that decision-making is transformed into a guessing game or an exercise on the wrong problems altogether.⁵⁶ Modern leaders must adjust information requirements and decision-making thresholds in a way that exploits the benefits of technology without resulting in overload that imposes decision paralysis. Popular false narratives appeared to reach on apex during Russia's 2022 invasion of Ukraine, poisoning the information ecosystem with anti-Ukrainian and anti-American myths.⁵⁷ Exploiting open-source intelligence proved a double-edged sword there, for at times it thickened the fog of war as much as it offered clarity by overwhelming and confusing analysts and observers.⁵⁸

Many believe that modern information-sharing platforms are creating a 'post-truth' world. Yet if such technology existed millennia ago, a commander and leader like Alexander would surely have used it to fill the smart phones of his opponents with headlines that supported their pre-existing beliefs – just as he exploited the myth of the Gordian Knot to strike fear into his enemies and inspire his own men.⁵⁹ As a 2020 RAND Corporation study concluded, it is not necessarily the new platforms (Internet and social media) that create these opportunities for truth decay, but rather that there are more people willing to feed their personal biases and more outlets through which such biases might be confirmed.⁶⁰ In war, this array of options in the search for truth can impede understanding more than it offers clarity by encouraging leaders to favor certain assets, sensors, or people that tell them what they want to hear. It becomes much harder, then, to assess a situation and make rapid decisions as Alexander did amid a flood of conflicting information.

One might suggest that Alexander perfected this art of cutting through the fog by mastering the tempo, speed, and timing of something now called the OODA loop.⁶¹ Coined by U.S. Air Force pilot Col. John Boyd after the Korean War, the ability to observe, orient, decide, and act (OODA) faster than an opponent was a feature of the Macedonian king's military mind as much as Boyd suggested it contributes to a fighter pilot's effectiveness in air-to-air battle.[62] An intended effect of disinformation is the disorientation of an audience, which prevents recipients from establishing a baseline of reality and making sound decisions. Despite humankind's efforts to master Boyd's principles, the most frustrating characteristics of the initial phases of modern wars revolved around fluctuating indecisions that brought operations to a standstill – mostly due to a lack of trust between senior leaders and an onslaught of sensors and information that thickened the fog of war rather than diluting it as originally intended.

Artificial intelligence has emerged as both the source of and the answer to this conundrum, but even if advanced analytics systems become capable of organizing these streams of data in a comprehensive and comprehensible way, the great question remains: what will leaders do with that information? The U.S. military is attempting to answer this question with concepts such as joint all-domain command and control (JADC2) and 'convergence', each of which has led to as many challenges as solutions in their efforts to achieve 'battlefield singularity'.[63] These challenges exist even in simulated training environments without taking into consideration increasingly aggressive deception capabilities and information operations (IOs) crafted to disrupt understanding. At the strategic level, disinformation aims to influence and divide human populations because the will of the people still controls democratic governments and the war machines they employ.[64] Information operations is a popular tool because it is low cost and effective. It can produce effects below the threshold of violent conflict, and it allows a competitor to channel the ideas of Chinese strategist Sun Tzu by weakening an adversary without fighting.[65] As military and civilian leaders place increasing trust in machines and algorithms to make complex decisions that have greater influence on society, what will the age of AI-driven IO look like, and will it play out on the margins of human understanding?

It is perhaps fitting that most recommended countermeasures to the above problems involve training the human mind and improving the ways it seeks out, consumes, transmits, and processes information. Maj. Gen. Copinger-Symes identifies collaboration (thinking big and using interdisciplinary approaches), the willingness to assume greater risk (because the right answer will not always be evident when it's the right time to make a decision), and cultural shifts that recognise the strategic utility of data as the building blocks of effective future leaders.[66] Mattis might agree, as he expressed an affinity for mavericks and roguish thinkers with a bias for action upon whom he could rely to maintain tactical and operational momentum.[67] Leading thinkers and military professionals, in a time of unprecedented digital growth, remain advocates of building the intellectual means to harness and control that growth. This will become more essential, not less so, as institutions increase their reliance on digital systems for knowledge management, analysis, and information processing.

Despite monumental leaps in technological sophistication since the age of Alexander, transforming information into understanding is no less vexing. In many ways, the very systems created to cut through the 'fog of war' are becoming the platforms that could make that haze permanent. Many nations recognize the central role information will play in the future, such as the United States, United Kingdom, and even China with its 'systems warfare' concept in which the destruction of networked operational systems, not necessarily troops on the battlefield, is key to victory.[68] If the United States wishes to compete seriously in this arena, major institutional reforms are likely needed. Among them would be the creation of an undersecretary of strategic communications, the drafting of a national influence strategy, and significantly expanding the IO capabilities and authorities of the departments and individual military services. But ultimately, inhabitants of the free world will retain the right to seek out, process, and confide in the information they choose, and this very human problem is perhaps the most perplexing when examining clarity in modern warfare. Advanced technologies may assist in collecting some of these data, but how they are organized and incorporated into tactical plans and strategic outlooks will remain, as was the case in Alexander's time, a human responsibility driven by talent, experience, and intuition.

Losing Control

In the fall of 1944, as the Allies gained what seemed like terminal momentum toward victory in Europe, Gen. (later President) Eisenhower jotted down one of his last journal entries before the end of the war. He distilled the nature of his challenge into a single concept: 'The defeat of the German armies is complete, and the only thing now needed to realize the whole conception is speed'.[69] But operational speed must be accompanied by control. These two factors often pull commanders in opposite directions, as Eisenhower would soon discover with a logistical bog down caused by deteriorating road conditions at Aachen and Antwerp that extended the war into the following year. Maintenance issues brought convoys to a standstill as the Allies struggled to keep ports open and replacement parts coming. The boys would not be 'home by Christmas' as intended.

Characteristics of the twenty-first century, such as instantaneous communications, truth decay, and an overzealous faith in emerging weapons have frustrated this marriage even further. Too much control hampers speed, and too much speed eats away at control. The Russian Army learned this the hard way in March 2022 as its forty-mile-long convoy headed into Kyiv broke down and ran out of food and fuel, exposing it to attacks.[70] Modern technologies presented Russian officials with the illusion of control and the promise of speed, but without well-trained leaders and candid military advisors in Moscow, they guaranteed neither. Russia's notoriously Kremlin-centric command philosophy only enhanced its failures by propping up flawed expectations of a rapid Ukrainian collapse as the situation deteriorated on the ground.[71]

Wartime leaders tend to lose control the more desperately they attempt to master it through centralized systems, risk aversion, and micro-management. Alexander was required to use mission command and generally trust his subordinate commander's decisions because of his tendency to promote them based on personal observation of their valour.[72] His tactical philosophy was a combination of decisive intuition, speed, and mass designed to overwhelm an opponent and deny him the decision space to plan effectively in the fog of war. Liddell Hart called this 'strategic dislocation' that may lead to 'either the enemy's dissolution or his easier disruption in battle'.[73] Today, governments impose Alexandrian conundrums upon themselves.

A 2014 study by military historian Antulio Echevarria II critiquing Russell Weigley's research found that the American way of war is inherently risk-averse because of its political nature, which discourages each of the principles that defined Alexander's operational success.[74] The domestic political influence in American foreign policy is well-founded and, as some international affairs scholars argue, tied directly to the president's ability to exercise instruments of national power effectively.[75] Echevarria concluded that throughout its history, America 'rarely employed overwhelming or decisive military force' and often relied on indigenous allies or technological superiority to offset such shortcomings. Interestingly, he found that this penchant was not uniquely American but a common feature in the western world's application of modern military power. Gen. Franks' characterization of modern warfare is instructive here: 'Desert Storm had reinforced my conviction that maneuver, speed, and tactical surprise were the greatest force multipliers in war'.[76] Yet the principles of mass on the battlefield, mission command, and trust between political and military authorities were absent in America's recent wars.

The tactical problems that plagued modern operations in Iraq and Afghanistan were neither technological nor conceptual, and, in many respects, they mirrored what Alexander had faced. They revolved around clear and feasible mission guidance, well-trained commanders allowed to execute without interference, and the propensity to make rapid decisions even with access to incomplete or conflicting information. As with Alexander, human relationships, information, and a reliance on leaders to take initiative shaped the environment in Iraq. Here, we have the bedrock of mission command, what some modern generals consider 'the only approach to leading a winning army' – selecting and empowering leaders to make decisions and then leaving them be.[77] In this sense, tactical leadership is measured most fully by the ability of commanders to achieve objectives in the absence of information from their higher headquarters. Requisite to this formula's success is the higher headquarters understanding clearly what it wants to achieve.

Alexander's tactical principles of war were to some degree echoed in kinetic combat operations during the opening phases of the Iraq and Afghanistan wars, which removed the Taliban from power and toppled Saddam's regime rapidly. But the ensuing challenges of nation building and expeditionary counterinsurgency proved as daunting in both cases as they were for Alexander. Like modern operations in Iraq and Afghanistan, Alexander's early campaigns were punctuated by great tactical victories that stoked his confidence and blurred other challenges. He failed to recognize – or perhaps even did not care – how his treatment of disparate cultures and integration of them into his ranks might impact his strategic aspirations. He became increasingly paranoid of his companions and lacked humility as he pushed ever further into Asia, shifting his strategic priorities erratically. Increasingly – as is the concern of many nations today – Alexander commanded an army with the tools to win every battle, or perhaps even the war, but not the foresight to transform those victories into a means of controlling Central Asia.

Notes

1 Arrian 3.18.9.
2 The Blue Force Tracker, or BFT, saw first use with the U.S. military in 2002 and is now integrated into nearly 100,000 platforms. The most recent update, BFT 3, is scheduled to begin fielding by 2025: Lafontaine 2018.
3 O'Hanlon 2000, pp. 7–31; Freedman 2013, pp. 216–217.
4 Stoker and Whiteside 2020; Elkus 2015.
5 Blythe 2018, pp. 37–49.
6 Chandler 1966, p. 158.
7 Jomini, c.6, pp. 177–178.
8 From his 23 March 1944 journal entry. Having been relegated to the halls of educational institutions during the First World War, Ike had never served in combat, but he was a superior thinker who understood command relationships and strategy: Eisenhower 1981, pp. 114–115.
9 Bremer assumed the role as envoy to Iraq and took the reins from Lt. Gen. Jay Gardner even as combat operations continued, and an insurgency heated up. Gen. John Abizaid, who succeeded Franks at CENTCOM, became frustrated

with the conflicting guidance from CPA and Pentagon channels: West 2005, pp. 20–22; Ricks 2007, pp. 111, 158–161, 175, 203–213; Mazarr 2019, pp. 367–371, 375.
10 The Iraqi Stabilization Group took form in October 2003: West 2005, p. 23.
11 Mattis mentions Alexander by name five times in his memoirs, citing Xenophon and Fuller's work specifically, in no small part because his headquarters in Iraq sat roughly 500 meters from where Alexander stayed in Babylon: Mattis and West 2019, pp. 77–80, 257.
12 For more on hybrid warfare and the grey zone, see: Mazarr 2015; Dalton and Shah 2020, pp. 1–10.
13 Plato, *Laws* 1.625e–1.626a; Hanson 2001, p. 440.
14 West 2005, p. 190.
15 The term network-centric warfare, or variations of it, was also used by some to describe Secretary of Defense Donald Rumsfeld's style of control during the early phases of the Iraq and Afghanistan War: Cebrowski and Garstka 1998.
16 Shamir 2011; Mattis describes his philosophy of mission command: Mattis and West 2019, p. 29.
17 Creveld 1991, p. 40.
18 Arrian, 5.10.3–4.
19 Hanson 2001; Kroenig 2020.
20 Hanson 2001, p. 446.
21 This is confirmed in the memoirs of both Mattis and Franks.
22 Though most administration officials agreed that a 'light footprint' in Afghanistan was the right approach, Rumsfeld placed more faith in technology to compensate for mass than perhaps any other: Franks 2004, p. 271; Ricks 2007, pp. 75, 121–122, 128–129; Rice 2011, pp. 85–86, 91.
23 Committee on Foreign Relations in the United States Senate 2009.
24 Dick Clarke, a counterterrorism expert who worked in the White House for three presidential administrations, recorded this finding: Clarke 2004, p. 179.
25 Rice 2011, pp. 85–86.
26 At times, commandos launched upwards of 100 airstrikes a day on al-Qaeda fighters in Tora Bora: Committee on Foreign Relations in the United States Senate 2009, p. 2.
27 Owen and Maurer 2012.
28 According to Rice, Deputy Secretary of Defense Paul Wolfowitz was one of the first officials to propose acting against Iraq during the 15 September Camp David talks: Rice 2011, pp. 86–87.
29 Wolfowitz had publicly called for regime change in Iraq since at least December 1998, when he authored an article in *New Republic* outlining his goals: Ricks 2007, pp. 23, 35, 55–57; For further insight into Chalabi's role leading up to and after the invasion, and his relationship with Wolfowitz and other U.S. officials, see Woodward 2004, pp. 19–20, 284, 289; Weeks 2010, pp. 47, 59, 72–73; Gordon and Trainor 2013, p. 29.
30 Powell would later reverse his position during a 5 February 2003 speech at the U.N. Security Council, which he lived to regret. Franks 2004, pp. 393–394; Rice 2011, p. 87; Weeks 2010, pp. 72–73 (United Nations speech).
31 Donald Rumsfeld and Gen. Downing suggested such numbers in 2002: Ricks 2007, p. 37.
32 Franks 2004, pp. 393–397.

33 Ricks 2007, pp. 34, 79.
34 Roughly 800,000 troops were stationed in Saudi Arabia to support the war effort: Matthews, J. J. 2008, p. 254.
35 Belasco 2009.
36 Mattis and West 2019, p. 100.
37 Seventeen marines were killed during this lull: Mattis and West 2019, p. 100.
38 At the time, this was U.S. Army Central Command, the Service Component Command at Shaw Air Force Base, South Carolina, responsible for overseeing army operations in the Middle East; see Mattis and West 2019, pp. 70–71.
39 Mattis and West 2019, pp. 120–126, cautioned against rushing into Fallujah because of the likely collateral damage and propaganda potential it could create.
40 For a tactical view of the confusion on the ground, see Bolger 2014, pp. 171–191; Malkasian 2017.
41 West 2005, p. 184.
42 The NSC's Iraq Stabilization Group, proposed by Rice in September 2003 to bridge the gaps between CPA, Washington, and DOD, established another civilian-led council that influenced military movements and operations even as the Iraqi insurgency was blossoming. In essence, it was an additional layer of bureaucracy created to solve problems stemming from too many layers of bureaucracy: West 2005, pp. 22–25; Rice 2011, pp. 242–243; Mattis and West 2019, pp. 128–136.
43 Mattis and West 2019, p. 101.
44 Franks 2004, p. 501.
45 Franks 2004, pp. 500–505; this wasn't the only deception of the war. Mattis and West 2019 (p. 99) explains how then Col. Joe Dunford, who would later become the Chairman of the Joint Chiefs of Staff, led a feint near Bagdad during the opening months of OIF.
46 Arrian, 5.10.3–4.
47 Mattis and West 2019, pp. 67–68. Misinformation is a product of intentional deception, known as disinformation. For more on these concepts, see Ferguson 2018b, Ferguson 2020.
48 Calvert 2010, pp. 103–138, 197–228; Ferguson 2017, pp. 68–77.
49 Franks 2004, p. 342.
50 Williams and Schlosser 2014, pp. 33–37.
51 Plutarch, *Alexander* 17.
52 Voltaire included a French translation of the Italian article 'Art Dramatique' in *Questions sur l'Encyclopédie, par des Amateurs* (1770).
53 Patton 1947, p. 298.
54 Specifically, he wrote no more than a page and a half but clarified that a single page was preferred so the back could be used for a 'sketch map'. Patton 1947, p. 275.
55 Copinger-Symes 2020.
56 Liotta 2002, pp. 1–10.
57 Ferguson 2022c.
58 Journalists at *The Economist* found that such torrents of data could confuse as much as they can inform. Telegram became the 'single most important repository of data during the [2022] war in Ukraine' and geotagging was rampant on Russian social media applications, which exposed military positions to

targeting. 'Open-source intelligence is piercing the fog of war in Ukraine', *The Economist*, 13 January 2023.
59 Ferguson 2022a.
60 Kavanaugh and Rich 2018.
61 Luft 2020.
62 Coram 2004.
63 Eversden 2021.
64 Thorne 2020, pp. 25–30.
65 Sun Tzu 2002.
66 Copinger-Symes 2020.
67 Mattis and West 2019, pp. 46–47, 184.
68 Engstrom 2018; Wall Street Journal Editorial Board 2020; King 2020.
69 Eisenhower 1981, pp. 127–128.
70 Jones 2022, pp. 3–8.
71 Dalsjo, Jonsson, and Norberg 2022, pp. 7–28; Massicot 2023.
72 On how Alexander selected his commanders, see Roisman (forthcoming).
73 Liddell Hart 1954, pp. 324–327.
74 Echevarria 2014, pp. 2, 164, 167–169; The classic book referenced is Weigley 1973.
75 Milner and Tingley 2015, pp. 18–32.
76 Franks 2004, p. 368.
77 Throughout the first half of 2019, several senior U.S. Army officers published a three-part series on reinforcing the army's approach to mission command: Townsend, et al. 2019, pp. 1–9.

Part IV
Eastern Exposure

In this part, we look at Alexander in Central Asia and India and his final years. We challenge the assumption that Alexander had both command and control of his vast and expanding empire and propose that the two concepts often pulled him in opposite directions. Here, we conclude by addressing the social and psychological aspects of modern warfare within the context of culture shock and the enduring horror of war. We use Alexander's army as a framework to understand how these aspects of expeditionary wars have changed or remained the same, including the emotional toll of prolonged exposure to combat and the confusion that often besets invading armies in foreign lands. We primarily use the wars in Iraq and Afghanistan as our foundation, but also include other examples from the twentieth century. We conclude that no matter how the character of war evolves, policy-makers and military leaders must continue accounting for – and more carefully consider – these enduring realities in their plans and assumptions.

9 Alexander in Central Asia

In invading Bactria and Sogdiana, Alexander was certainly entering areas of the world that were relatively unknown to Greeks. Bactria consisted of what today is Afghanistan, Tajikistan, and Uzbekistan, north of the Hindu Kush (what the Greeks called the Caucasus), and south of the Oxus or Amu Darya River. Sogdiana (sometimes Sogdia) comprised Uzbekistan, Tajikistan, Kazakhstan, and Kyrgyzstan. The mountainous topography, rugged terrain, and then the deserts and plains tested the invaders to the utmost, especially as the natives anchored their resistance in guerrilla warfare and their cavalry could easily disappear across the vast steppes leaving the Macedonians behind. All these factors set the Bactrian campaign apart and challenged Alexander and his men more than anything they had encountered in Persia.[1]

Certainly, the king needed to end the threat from Bessus to legitimize his own rule and avenge Darius. But in tandem with that was his thirst for greater military glory and to eclipse the exploits of both his father Philip and a previous ruler of Asia, Cyrus the Great.[2] Those factors made the Bactrian campaign a different phase in the overall invasion of Asia.

The new phase brought about a change to the face and composition of the army, for in 330 its numbers were increased by 300 Lydian cavalry and 2,600 infantry. In 329, another 1,000 Lycian and Syrian cavalry and 8,000 infantry were added – these were the first of the youths in Lydia, Lycia, Syria, and Egypt that he had ordered to be trained in Macedonian tactics. The Macedonian troops were not impressed, and the new recruits were a factor in the mutiny at Opis in 324 (see Chapter 10). Although Alexander continued to exhibit the leadership qualities and gifted generalship skills when it came to planning and combat that mark him 'great', he began to lose touch with the rank and file of his army in Central Asia. His undoing was because he was following personal rather than strategic goals, which put his men's lives at risk for the wrong reasons.

DOI: 10.4324/9781003052951-14

It was also in Central Asia that we start to see disturbing changes in Alexander's personality in tandem with increasing brutality, including wholesale massacres, towards defiant native populations or anyone who personally crossed him. Certainly, Alexander had inflicted callous punishments before – on the people of Thebes in 335 and those of Tyre in 332, for example. Yet the increasing severity of punishments only stiffened resistance and exacerbated hatred of him as a foreigner and conqueror, something he never seems to have grasped. It cost him dearly in the end. Today the need to appreciate and understand the interplay of religion and politics in culturally dissimilar regions is the foundation of sound diplomacy, strategy, and even tactics. Where Alexander went wrong, and especially *how* he went about dealing with his multi-cultural subjects, are lessons for all of us.

Hunting Bessus

In Chapter 7, we left Alexander at Hecatompylus. A march north to Zadracarta (Sari), capital of Hyrcania (in Iran and Turkmenistan, southeast of the Caspian Sea), followed. His stay there was a busy one.[3] To begin with, Nabarzanes, one of Darius' assassins and now keen to earn the king's favour, surrendered and gifted Alexander the famous eunuch Bagoas, his soon-to-be lover.[4] It was also in Zadracarta that the king was said to have had a two-week dalliance with Thalestris, the Amazon Queen. The story goes that she had travelled over a month to visit him and have a child by him, only to find a man far removed from his reputation.[5] And it was from Zadracarta that Alexander invaded the territory of the Mardi peoples of the Zagros (not to be confused with the Mardi in southern Persis) in search of horses to replenish his cavalry numbers.

From Zadracarta, the army marched into Aria (western Afghanistan), where at its capital Artacoana (on or by the modern Herat) its satrap Satibarzanes, another of Darius' murderers, submitted to him.[6] He told the king of Bessus' plans to levy a large army including peoples beyond the Oxus (Amu Darya) River, prompting Alexander to leave a garrison of 40 javelin men in Artacoana under Satibarzanes and pursue Bessus at speed. He marched along the Kopet Dag massif (on the southwest border of Turkmenistan with Iran) but had gone only seventy miles when the news reached him that Satibarzanes had treacherously declared his loyalty to Bessus, murdered the Macedonian garrison at Artacoana, and brought about a revolt of Aria. Alexander immediately turned around with a contingent of troops and a forced march of two days brought him back to Artacoana, at which point Satibarzanes and 2,000 cavalry fled to Bessus.[7] The troops he left behind fled for refuge on a wooded hill, which Alexander set on fire, burning them alive.

The king installed Arsaces, another Persian nobleman, as satrap, and returned to his main army, but not before he embarked on a blitzkrieg of the region to ensure that no one dare copy Satibarzanes' disloyalty. Thus, in Drangiana and Arachosia (southwestern Afghanistan) he captured the satrap Barsaentes (another of Darius' assassins) as he tried to flee to India and executed him. As winter (of 330–329) was now upon him, Alexander decided to remain in the Drangianian capital, Phrada (Farah), where occurred a conspiracy allegedly involving Philotas, its origins perhaps in the king's growing orientalism.[8]

One of Alexander's royal bodyguards, Demetrius, decided to kill Alexander, though why is unknown. Philotas, commander of the companion cavalry and the son of Parmenion, was informed of the apparent plot, but did not inform the king. Eventually the man who had apprised Philotas managed to alert Alexander, who had the conspirators arrested. One of them, Dimnus, stabbed himself to death, but eight others (including Demetrius) were caught.[9] But then the king unexpectedly accused Philotas of treason for neglecting to tell him about the plot and of conspiring against him. He was put on trial the next day in front of at least 6,000 members of the army acting as a court for treason.[10] His defence was that he had investigated the claims and found them to be without foundation, so had not told Alexander.

Philotas was unpopular with his fellow generals because he was conceited, and they may well have egged on the king against him.[11] Nevertheless, no one was able to connect him to a plot, and he rebutted the accusation against him beyond any reasonable doubt for a court today. But Alexander was becoming a law unto himself. He decided to dispense with Philotas, despite the lack of evidence against him; the following day Philotas was stoned to death. Then Alexander ordered the execution of Parmenion, who was still in Ecbatana (800 miles away) and ignorant of events at Phrada. Under Macedonian law a traitor's family could be executed, but at this juncture of the campaign, and given Parmenion's status and experience, Alexander's action was inexcusable.

Still, he needed to be careful as Parmenion was popular with everyone and had 12,000 troops with him. We are even told that Alexander was fearful lest 'even if he had had no part in [the conspiracy], he would now be a dangerous man if he survived after his son had been brutally killed', because of the great respect in which he was held.[12] The king sent orders to the other generals at Ecbatana to kill Parmenion, which they did, and then had them read a letter to the men explaining Philotas' treachery, so they had little choice but to accept their general's fate.[13]

Whether there was even a plot in the first place is difficult to determine, though given the numbers of men involved it would have been hard to fabricate one. Even if there was, Philotas almost certainly was not involved in anything, and Parmenion certainly was not. More likely is that Alexander engineered their demises for personal reasons. They had long been critics of him, not to mention Parmenion was one of Philip's Old Guard, something Alexander despised.[14] In fact it was Philotas who in 337 informed Philip of Alexander's treachery in offering himself as husband to Pixodarus' daughter despite the king's arrangements – and Alexander held grudges for a long time. Hence the king perhaps exploited a situation and the law to rid himself of both. We will return to this episode in Chapter 13 for the light it sheds on Alexander's paranoia, and even his strategy of promoting divisiveness among his senior staff to ensure they did not try to overthrow him.[15]

Alexander now made some changes to his army, perhaps intended to disassociate it further from what his father had introduced and to keep his commanders loyal to him above all else.[16] More obviously, the move was to separate individual leaders from units of troops; in other words, a 'process of fragmentation'.[17] Philotas' position as commander of the companion cavalry was now split between Hephaestion and the veteran general Cleitus the Black (who had saved Alexander's life at the Granicus River) so the cavalry could not unite behind only one person.[18] In addition, he reorganized the cavalry squadrons (*ilai*) by creating cavalry regiments called hipparchies, each having two former *ilai* in it, and appointing his boyhood and close friends as hipparchs (cavalry commanders). More ominous was the creation of the 'unit of insubordinates', whose members had resented Parmenion's demise, sending out a clear message that Alexander would not take opposition from any level.[19] This was also the time when Ptolemy, one of Alexander's boyhood friends, was promoted to the royal bodyguard, taking the place so recently vacated by Demetrius.[20]

Not long after Alexander left Phrada, Satibarzanes provoked another revolt of Aria, this time with help from Bessus.[21] Its satrap Arsaces was obviously useless, but rather than move to end the insurrection himself, Alexander sent three commanders, Erigyius, Caranus, and the former Persian satrap Artabazus (who had surrendered before Alexander reached Zadracarta), to recover the satrapy.[22] They accomplished this by the spring of 329 and installed Stasanor as new satrap, but even then it took the latter over a year to gain control of the satrapy. Later in the same spring (of 329), after having had to wait for weather conditions to improve, Alexander and his men had battled the 11,000-feet-high Khawak Pass over the Hindu Kush.[23] For a fortnight, they suffered frost-bite, snow-blindness, and in the second week had to eat their pack animals raw because their supplies (especially grain collected from the rich areas of Iran) had run out, and there was no wood to build fires.[24] But one piece of good news for the king was that one of his commanders, Erigyius, had killed Satibarzanes in single combat – he chopped off his head and later sent it to Alexander in a box.[25]

Alexander's crossing of the Hindu Kush was a feat of great hardship and leadership. He emerged only about eighty miles from Bessus' position, who immediately fled north across the Oxus into Sogdiana with 7,000 to 8,000 cavalry, burning the boats and anything else that Alexander might use to cross the river after him.[26] His flight allowed Alexander to march to one of the capitals, Drapsaca (Kunduz in northeastern Afghanistan), and so take over virtually all Bactria. He now sent out word that his enemy was only Bessus and that he would make anyone who handed Bessus over to him his friend, a propaganda campaign that had every chance of success.[27]

The king pushed on to the Oxus via the desert, where the intense summer heat by day, freezing cold temperatures at night, and lack of water affected everyone dreadfully.[28] Alexander and his men, exhausted and dehydrated, reached the Oxus, probably at Kelif. They spent a week cobbling together rafts of skins and grass, which took them safely across the river and into Sogdiana. But before that, in June (of 329), he had to discharge the Thessalian troops and some of his veterans, who had clamoured to return home and threatened to mutiny. He gave them pay and bonuses and replaced them with local troops, thereby already altering the composition of the original army that had invaded Asia with him.

The crossing was the end for Bessus. Responding to Alexander's savvy propaganda appeal, two Sogdian chieftains, Spitamenes and Dataphernes, offered to deliver him to Alexander, but only if the king sent an official to receive him. Ptolemy, at the head of a substantial force of 4,000 infantry and 1,600 cavalry (perhaps as a caution in case he was walking into a trap), was tasked with this job.[29] He brought back Bessus, bound in a wooden collar, by leading him on the right-hand side of the road so that Alexander could ride up to him in a chariot, an action symbolic of a Great King.[30] Alexander ordered he be punished in Persian fashion for his crime of regicide: he was whipped, and sent to Bactra (Balkh; originally Zariaspa), the capital of Bactria, where his nose and ears were sliced off, and thence to Ecbatana for impalement. Thus, Alexander adopted Persian practice to claim revenge for the callous murder of Darius.[31]

With the threat to the security of his empire no more, hence mission accomplished, Alexander could have returned to Greece. That, however, was the furthest thing from his mind as for some time he had been planning a campaign in India for personal glory not strategic imperatives, which pushed his army to its limits and led to mutiny (Chapter 10).[32]

From Brutality to Atrocity

While Ptolemy was busy attending to Bessus, Alexander's men came across a town in which a group of Greeks, the Branchidae, lived. Their ancestors had been priests of the oracle of Apollo at Didyma (close to Miletus) but had supported the Persians during the Persian Wars, and for their safekeeping the Great King had relocated them to Sogdiana. Now, 150 years later, and despite surrendering to him, Alexander ordered all their descendants be executed and the town razed.[33] He may have been resurrecting the panhellenic revenge mission of the League of Corinth or sending out a message to cities in the region – or even giving his troops free reign; as Bosworth noted 'looting and murder were a cathartic release which Alexander could justify retrospectively by involving the theme of revenge'.[34]

Alexander continued towards the northern boundary of the Persian Empire, setting up garrisons in many of the mud brick forts to maintain control of the region. He made his headquarters at Maracanda (Samarkand in southeastern Uzbekistan), capital of Sogdiana. While there he and a foraging party were attacked by 30,000 local tribesmen, and during some bitter fighting he was shot in the leg by an arrow, breaking part of his fibula.[35] As the Macedonians gained the upper hand, the tribesmen fled to a fortress on top of a hill, but the king pursued them: 22,000 of them died, either in fighting or by throwing themselves off the top.

Leaving a Macedonian garrison in Maracanda, the king marched to the Jaxartes (Syr-Darya) River, the northern boundary of the Persian Empire, where he founded Alexandria Eschate (Alexander the Farthermost), the modern Khujand and former Leninabad. He had no time to rest, however, for news came to him that Spitamenes and Dataphernes had caused the whole of Bactria and Sogdiana to revolt, in the process massacring many of the Macedonians that the king had left behind. Their reason was simple: resistance to any invading army, let alone one from the west, was paramount.

There now followed three of the toughest years the Macedonians experienced in Asia because of the revolt of Bactria and Sogdiana. Spitamenes' guerilla raids several times overcame Alexander and the chieftain proved to be his most dangerous and ferocious opponent.[36] In his early campaigns in the Balkans in 335, Alexander had experienced the Illyrians' exploitation of adverse terrain against his men, but in Afghanistan he was up against foes far more experienced in subversion and hit-and-run guerilla tactics.[37] This is perhaps one of Alexander's hardest learned lessons, and most germane to the study of war today, in that such irregular approaches to warfare are typically employed by smaller or poorly equipped forces against larger, more sophisticated armies.[38] Clearly, the value of this type of warfare has not dissipated with time.

Terms such as 'revolt', 'rebellion', and 'insurgency' are now said to be wrongly applied to Alexander's campaign in Bactria and Sogdiana as the people did not view him as the Great King and thus felt no allegiance to him.³⁹ In essence, Bactrians could not be insurgents against what they saw as foreign invaders with no legitimate authority to impose laws over them. Hence querying whether we speak of a 'revolt' is a matter of semantics based on modern usage.⁴⁰ Alexander defeated enemies and tried to introduce a sustainable rule; then he repeatedly faced their defiance, which included killing his own men. He may well have understood the people's insubordination and even the idea of terrorism, but no matter the nomenclature, the defiant nature of the people always thwarted his attempts to govern, and he failed to bridge the divide between conqueror and conquered.⁴¹

Alexander and his men besieged several fortresses in the Jaxartes region, and faced stiff resistance at Memaceni and Cyropolis (Kurkath), which Cyrus the Great founded in 544.⁴² During that siege Alexander led his hypaspists, Agrianians, and a unit of archers one night along a dry (or nearly dry) river bed that ran under the walls and opened the gates for the rest of his army to pour into the city.⁴³ The defenders had left their posts to rush Alexander and his troops, so the walls presented no obstacle, and in the fighting 8,000 enemy were killed; the surviving men of fighting age were put to death, and the women and children enslaved, as had become the norm. Alexander, however, had been hit by a stone on his neck, affecting his voice for some time.⁴⁴

In the meantime, Spitamenes had overcome the Macedonian garrison in Maracanda and laid siege to the city. Since it was to be Alexander's main base in the region, he needed to regain control of it, but first he needed to neutralize a threat from the Sacae people, north of the Jaxartes and previous supporters of Bessus, who were encamped on the opposite bank of the river.⁴⁵ He sent 2,000 infantry and 300 cavalry with Pharnuches of Lycia (aided by three Macedonian commanders) to relieve Maracanda, while he himself crossed the Jaxartes against the Sacae. Apparently, he needed 12,000 boats, which took only three days to build.⁴⁶

To prevent his men being sitting ducks as they came within range of the Sacan arrows, Alexander set up catapults in his leading boats to bombard the Sacae and keep them at bay until his men landed safely and disembarked. But his cavalrymen were unprepared for the Sacan cavalry's tactic of galloping around an enemy while firing arrows into its midst, and as more of the Macedonians fell victim to this onslaught Alexander sounded the retreat. What had perhaps been considered a relatively minor campaign against these tribesmen had turned into a full-blown military conflict.⁴⁷

Alexander decided to dupe the Sacae into thinking he was readying for another frontal strike while preparing a three-pronged ambush. He planned to use a contingent of cavalry to engage the Sacae, a tactic like his pawn sacrifice at the Granicus River, and as they formed their customary circle, he would have his archers and javelin throwers attack them to disrupt their manoeuvre, at which time the Companions and the rest of the cavalry would charge them head on. His plan worked perfectly. The Sacae were overcoming the vanguard force when Alexander gave a prearranged signal, and the rest of his troops swung into action before the enemy realised it was a trap.

In the ensuing battle, 1,000 of the Sacae were killed and 150 captured; Alexander lost 60 cavalry and 100 infantry who were killed, with 1,000 wounded.[48] The king of the Sacae surrendered, but the battle had been a significant test of Alexander's generalship – as Fuller notes, he had many predecessors' experiences not to mention Xenophon to draw on, but 'for a battle on the plains against an enemy who possessed neither bases, nor communications, nor organization, he had no predecessor in tactics, even the great Cyrus had been defeated by the Scythians [Sacae]'.[49] That was why Alexander allowed the prisoners from the battle to return home without ransom, hoping to prevent reinforcements coming to the aid of defeated comrades, who presumably would not fall for the same trick.

The Sacan defeat ended the revolt in the north of Sogdiana. But Alexander was hardly able to celebrate as news reached him that the relief force to Maracanda under Pharnuches had been massacred. For once, Alexander had appointed the wrong man as commander. When the latter had arrived there, Spitamenes had fled westwards along the Zeravshan valley with Pharnuches hot in pursuit. It was a trap. Spitamenes had reinforced his numbers with 600 Sacan cavalry, which surrounded and killed as many as 2,000 infantry and 300 cavalry of Pharnuches' men; only 300 infantry and 40 cavalry escaped and fled back to Alexander.[50] Spitamenes again besieged Maracanda, this time supported by the people of the Zeravshan valley.

Although the king was not present, Pharnuches' rout was the greatest defeat Alexander suffered in Asia. He immediately marched the 180 miles south to Maracanda with half of his companion cavalry, the Agrianians, and other select infantry, reaching it in forced day and night marches only three days later according to Arrian.[51] Spitamenes fled west, and Alexander recaptured Maracanda, but he was furious with the people's support of Spitamenes. In revenge, he spent the summer of 329 storming citadels, burning crops, and massacring as many as 120,000 Sogdians in the valley.[52] Not everyone surely supported Spitamenes, but that mattered little.

For the winter of 329–328 Alexander headquartered at Bactra, where he planned a strategy to defeat Spitamenes, who was like a phantom, and to overcome the pockets of resistance that were still in existence in Bactria and Sogdiana. The chronology of the next several months is controversial, as our sources have little happening in 328 but an eventful 327, hence arguments have been made to move some events from the latter year to the former.[53]

The Murder of Cleitus the Black

After Alexander's winter at Bactra, in the following spring, presumably to combat the guerrilla warfare he was facing, he split up his army into four units, each under an individual commander to deal with resistance in different parts of Sogdiana before they all regrouped in Maracanda by the summer.[54] In its palace occurred one of the darkest episodes of Alexander's reign: the killing of Cleitus in cold blood.[55]

The setting was a drinking party after a religious ritual, where it appears that several of the king's supporters, young and old, were outdoing each other in sycophantic praise of him. Cleitus, the co-commander of the companion cavalry, whom Alexander had tapped to be the satrap of Bactria, was already aggrieved about his satrapal appointment as it marginalized him from the court.[56] This was probably Alexander's intention as Cleitus was increasingly critical of his orientalism and was another Old Guard general Alexander inherited from his father. Cleitus had known Alexander since he was born, and his sister Lanice had been one of Alexander's nurses. When, however, the Macedonian defeat at the hands of Spitamenes at Maracanda was mocked, and for some reason Alexander joined in, Cleitus became infuriated. Obviously, not all his army was present, so the rank-and-file soldiers would not have heard how Alexander was talking about their dead comrades, but it would surely have been impossible to keep what he said a secret, in which case he showed a serious error of judgement as a commander and king.

Then Alexander began to speak as though he was better than his father, and that victory at Chaeronea was thanks to him rather than Philip. Cleitus had had enough by then. He launched a tirade on the king, stressing that he was nowhere near as good as his father, and ended by reminding Alexander that he had saved his life at the Granicus River. The two men got into a furious argument, with Alexander shouting for Cleitus to be arrested, before a member of the royal bodyguard (*somatophylakes*), Ptolemy, apparently separated them and bundled Cleitus out of the room. But when Alexander yelled insults after him, Cleitus broke free and returned to confront the king, who grabbed a sword (or perhaps a spear) from one of his bodyguards and ran Cleitus through with it.[57]

Certainly, Cleitus had gone too far in his criticism of the king. But Alexander, whose reason had given way to drunken emotion, must be condemned for the murder, more so at such a critical point in the campaign. Considering the personal honour that underpinned his campaigns and which he expected of others, his action was anything but honourable.[58] Further, the removal of key leaders at pivotal moments must be weighed judiciously, as it can have debilitating effects on political perceptions, consistency of policy, and morale – indeed, Alexander's alcoholism was criticized as one of the 'things about Alexander that are not good' in the *Ephemerides* (daily records).[59]

Our ancient writers all agree that Alexander immediately regretted his unheroic action, apparently even trying to turn the weapon on himself.[60] Instead, he shut himself away in his rooms for three days. Eventually, Anaxagoras of Abdera, one of the court philosophers, persuaded him to emerge with the dubious argument that Cleitus' fate was part of a divine plan and Alexander was merely the agent of the gods. The relieved men accused Cleitus of treachery and refused him a burial, perhaps to further absolve Alexander of any wrongdoing.[61] Our sources also endeavour to exculpate the king, and that 'the fault was entirely on the side of Cleitus', with Arrian even saying that Alexander should be 'pitied for his misfortune'.[62]

The whole episode is worrying for several reasons, but two stand out that boded ill for the future: first, drinking parties were becoming more frequent as the army marched further east, and alcohol and arguments were deadly combinations. Second, Alexander had got away with murder so was above the law: Cleitus was even declared a traitor, in which case he would have been refused burial.[63]

The Sieges of the Sogdian Rock and the Rock of Chorienes

In the same summer (of 328), Alexander turned to mopping up operations as he consolidated his gains in the region. Probably now rather than before the Cleitus episode Alexander came across a fortress, built at the top of sheer cliffs nearly 20,000 feet high, ruled by the chieftain Ariamazes.[64] Various rebels and their families had fled there to escape Alexander's massacres; if we believe Arrian, they included Oxyartes of Bactria, whose young daughter Roxane Alexander would marry in spring 327.[65] Ariamazes refused to surrender to the king as he felt safe in his high fortress, which was also well-provisioned, and if necessary, he could melt snow for water. He taunted Alexander that he would need 'winged soldiers' to reach him. Of course, his response motivated Alexander even more to overcome him, and the king gave orders to besiege the Rock of Ariamazes, sometimes called the Sogdian Rock.[66]

Alexander knew he could only reach the defenders by scaling the sheer cliff face, which was unguarded as Ariamazes did not expect anyone to attack from that direction. Rock climbing was not part of the army's training; to make matters worse it had to be undertaken at night so no one in the citadel would spot anyone inching up, and the rock face would have been dangerously slippery because of the freezing conditions. This was virtually a suicide mission, as shown by Alexander offering the huge sum of twelve talents to the first man who made it to the summit. Still, 300 volunteered, though for once the king did not risk his life by taking part in the climb.

The climbers roped themselves together, like today, drove iron tent pegs into the rock face, and got to work. Thirty of the men fell to their deaths during the ascent, but the remainder eventually made it to the top and at dawn signalled to Alexander far below by waving white linen flags. Their ascent was an extraordinary achievement, given the atrocious conditions. It is probably going too far to claim that the climb was the ancestor of the modern rock climbing and military operations undertaken by the Special Forces Advanced Mountain Operations School. Yet after this mission rock climbing became part of military training. A modern example that echoes what Alexander's men faced is the U.S. Army Rangers' assault on Point du Hoc between Utah and Omaha Beach during the June 1944 invasion of Normandy, when Rangers scaled 100-foot-tall sheer cliff faces as the enemy hurled grenades and fired down upon them.

Back to Alexander's assault, the defenders in the citadel panicked and thought there were more climbers, as Alexander had intended, and laid down their arms. In this way the siege might be seen as another 'pawn sacrifice' approach because the fortress inhabitants could just as easily have fought the Macedonians off once they reached the top. As at Issus and Gaugamela, Alexander's psychological strategy had paid off, not to mention luck again smiling on him, especially as for once he had not been leading personally from the front. Now he mockingly told Ariamazes he had found his winged soldiers after all. He spared the lives of the defenders, though he put them to work in the fields in his new cities.

There remained one final pocket of resistance at the Rock of Chorienes in Nautaca – the same place where Ptolemy had taken Bessus into his custody. Since the fortress was situated at the far side of a deep chasm surrounded by thick woods, and with abundant water and supplies, the local ruler Sisimithres felt safe enough to defy Alexander.[67] He should have known better. The king again resorted to a psychological strategy of intimidation. Knowing that his men could hardly scale down one side of the ravine and up the other without suffering heavy casualties, he decided to build a bridge and storm the fortress frontally. Again, he chose the most direct and unexpected approach.

To this end, he had his troops climb down the sides and drive wooden stakes into them, on top of which they laid a series of wooden struts and piled earth on top of this foundation. He protected them from the defenders' arrows and other missiles by means of large wooden screens that acted as shields. By working day and night they completed the bridge to the point where Alexander could move his large siege engines into place. That did the trick. A terrified Sisimithres surrendered and was allowed to continue as ruler if he maintained loyalty to Alexander.

Elsewhere the Macedonians were gaining the upper hand especially when Coenus and a contingent of troops defeated Spitamenes and 3,000 Massagetae cavalry. Spitamenes lost all support; his former allies the Massagetae killed him and sent Alexander his head along with another rebel leader, Dataphernes, as a sign of their friendship.[68] In addition, Alexander received word that Stasanor had finally ended the ongoing discontent in Aria. The revolt of Bactria and Sogdiana was over, and Alexander combined them into one satrapy simply called Bactria, under Amyntas, which he garrisoned with 10,000 infantry and 3,500 cavalry.

Last Days in Bactria

In the spring of 327, Alexander married the young Bactrian princess Roxane (Roshanak, 'Beautiful Star'), reputedly the most beautiful woman in Asia, at Maracanda.[69] She had no say in the choice of husband, and even worse for her was that Barsine, who had been living with Alexander since Issus, was pregnant with their son Heracles. When Alexander saw Roxane among the captives at the Sogdian Rock, we are led to believe, he fell in love with her immediately, even perhaps marrying her to unite west and east in his empire. However, his reason was likely more pragmatic. By now he was planning to invade India and intended her father Oxyartes to be satrap of Bactria on the assumption that a Bactrian baron would be able to hold the satrapy in check.[70] The marriage to Roxane was therefore a political one, like his father's first six; try as he might, Alexander could not escape the shadow of Philip.

From Maracanda Alexander marched back to the capital Bactra where two events took place that reflect badly on his credibility as king and general. The first was his attempt to enforce the Asian custom of *proskynesis* (genuflection) on his men.[71] The Great King's subjects either kneeled or prostrated themselves fully as an act of subservience in his presence, and in return he seems to have blown them a kiss.[72] Greeks believed this custom was blasphemous as it was tantamount to worship of a living being, and some of Alexander's men even laughed at Persians' prostrating themselves before their king. At a symposium one night, someone pointed out to Alexander that Callisthenes, the court historian, was leaving but had not performed *proskynesis* before the king, so he was called back. Callisthenes adamantly refused, despite Alexander's growing anger, and left saying he would 'leave the poorer by a kiss'.[73] His stance resonated with the others and Alexander was forced to abandon the attempt.

Why Alexander tried to introduce the custom is unknown. Perhaps it was intended as a form of common greeting for his western and eastern subjects, yet he would have known how his men would react to it.[74] Perhaps it appealed to his vanity, as Justin comments the attempt 'was an exercise in vanity as practised by the Persian Kings'.[75] Alternatively, it might have been a way of having all his subjects worship him. Curtius believed this was so:

> [T]he time had come for the depraved idea that Alexander had earlier formed, and in deciding how he could give himself divine honours he ordered the Macedonians to follow the Persian custom of prostrating themselves on the ground, and so worship him.[76]

Whatever the reason, a gap was widening between the king and his men.

The second incident was a conspiracy of several of the royal pages.[77] Earlier, during a hunt, a page by the name of Hermolaus killed a boar even though Alexander as king had the right to kill the animal first. As was the custom, Hermolaus was publicly flogged, and his horse was confiscated. For some reason he persuaded several other pages to join him in killing Alexander when they next guarded his bed as he slept. According to Curtius, this was not for an entire month.[78] Alexander inadvertently foiled the plot by not going to bed that night as he stayed up drinking – as he was leaving a party, claims Aristobulus, a trusted Syrian prophetess, who 'was then being inspired by the god pleaded with him to go back and continue drinking all night'.[79]

This episode raises all sorts of questions. For one thing, Hermolaus had probably allowed his youth to get the better of him in killing the boar, and he may even have wanted to kill it, as has been argued, to satisfy the custom of killing a boar to recline at a symposium. But he was in the wrong and everyone would have known that. Was bruised pride therefore a reason for wanting the king dead, and why would other pages who had nothing to do with his error join him?[80] Perhaps Alexander's 'orientalism' was a reason for Hermolaus and his friends to conspire against the king, but if the pages had murdered a sleeping Alexander, they would of course have been the only suspects, and regicide was a capital crime punished by execution.

Here, Callisthenes may play a role. He was thought to have been the pages' tutor and, if Curtius is right, was said to have talked with them about the worrying changes in Alexander's character.[81] If so, this would introduce a political motive to any subterfuge. But perhaps closer to the truth is that Alexander had all the pages tortured for details of the conspiracy and to implicate Callisthenes in it. None did.[82] That did not stop Alexander – in similar fashion to his treatment of Philotas when no evidence existed – of accusing Callisthenes of participation and either executing him or imprisoning him where he died. Since Callisthenes was disliked at court anyway, his enemies may have influenced Alexander to bring him down.[83] But Alexander's rationale more plausibly may be traced back to Callisthenes' defiance of his *proskynesis* attempt. Significantly, Callisthenes was not put on trial at the time, a further instance of Alexander seeing himself above the law.

Guerilla warfare over the previous three years had challenged Alexander and the entire army more than the enormous battles and grand sieges in Persia. But they had overcome it, and now Alexander believed that Bactria was conquered. That was a miscalculation, not least because of his highhanded dealings with the native populations, which we will examine as part of the dilemma of west meeting east in Chapter 11. Alexander seemed to have followed a formula that presumed that an enemy defeated in battle was also conquered, but that was as untrue then as it is today. For now, though, India beckoned.

Notes

1 Alexander in Bactria and Sogdiana: Fuller 1960, pp. 234–245; Bosworth, 1988a, pp. 97–119; Ashley 1998, pp. 282–305; Lonsdale 2007, pp. 90–97; Worthington 2014a, pp. 211–235; especially Holt 1998, Holt 1999, Holt 2005; see too Bloedow 1991; Holt 1986, Holt 2015; Rtveladz 2007; Vacanta 2012; English 2011, pp. 158–174.
2 Cf. Brosius 2003.
3 Diodorus 17.73, 17.76.3–8; Arrian 3.24–25; Curtius 6.5.10–23; Plutarch, *Alexander* 44.
4 Ogden 2009, pp. 213–217, Ogden 2011, pp. 167–170, cautions accepting the homoerotic relationship at face value.
5 Curtius 6.5.29; Justin 12.3.5–7; cf. Ogden 2011, pp. 146–150.
6 Arrian 3.25.1–2; Curtius 6.6.13.
7 Diodorus 17.78.2; Curtius 6.6.22–23.
8 Diodorus 17.79–80; Arrian 3.26–27; Curtius 6.7.1–7.2.38; Plutarch, *Alexander* 48–49; Justin 12.5.1–8, with Bosworth 1988a, pp. 101–104; Heckel 2008, pp. 88–92; Worthington 2014a, pp. 216–220; deeper analysis: Badian 1960; Heckel 1977; Rubinsohn 1977; Adams 2003. On conspiracies generally, see Badian 1964, Badian 1996; cf. Heckel 2003a, Heckel 2009, especially on rivalries, conspiracies, and impact on leadership.
9 Curtius 6.7.15: Peucolaus, Nicanor, Aphobetus, Iolaus, Dioxenus, Archepolis, Amyntas, Demetrius, and Calis (the last 2 at 6.2.37).
10 Number: Curtius 6.8.23.
11 Heckel 1977.
12 Ptolemy, *BNJ* 138 F 13 = Arrian 3.26.4.
13 Diodorus 17.80.3; Arrian 3.27.3–4; Curtius 7.2.11–32; Plutarch, *Alexander* 49.13.

14 Badian 1964.
15 Heckel 2009.
16 English 2009a, pp. 113–114, 117–120.
17 Bosworth 1988a, p. 103.
18 Arrian 3.27.4.
19 Diodorus 17.80.4; Curtius 7.2.35–38.
20 Arrian 3.27.5.
21 Bosworth 1988a, p. 105; Ashley 1998, pp. 285–287; Worthington 2014a, pp. 220–221; see too Howe 2015, pp. 166–170.
22 Diodorus 17.81.3; Arrian 3.82.2; Curtius 7.3.2–3.
23 Arrian 3.28.4–291.
24 Curtius 7.3.21 on the duration.
25 Curtius 7.4.32.
26 7,000 cavalry: Arrian 3.28.8; 8,000: Curtius 7.4.20. Burning of boats: Arrian 3.28.9.
27 Ptolemy, *BNJ* 138 F 14 = Arrian 3.29.6–30.5.
28 Curtius 7.5.1–16.
29 Diodorus 17.5.36–42; Arrian 3.29–30.5 (from Ptolemy, *BNJ* 138 F 14); Curtius 7.5.36–42.
30 Heckel 2008, p. 95.
31 Arrian 3.30.4–5, Curtius 7.5.38–39.
32 Arrian 4.5.6.
33 Curtius 7.5.28–35, and see Parke 1985, though note Bosworth 1988a, pp. 108–109; cf. Howe 2015, pp. 172–173.
34 Bosworth 1988a, p. 109.
35 Arrian 3.30.10–11; Curtius 7.6.1–9.
36 Bosworth 1988a, pp. 110–117; Ashley 1998, pp. 292–294, 297–300; Vacante 2012.
37 Cf. Howe 2015, pp. 163–166.
38 See Boot 2013.
39 Howe 2015.
40 Here, see the excellent comments of Lonsdale 2007, pp. 95–97, on the pitfalls of a counterinsurgency approach.
41 On Alexander's attempts throughout the empire, cf. Anson 2015.
42 Curtius 7.6.17–23; Arrian 4.2; see too Vacante 2012.
43 Fuller 1960, pp. 234–236; Bosworth 1998, p. 110; Ashley 1998, pp. 296–297; Worthington 2014a, pp. 223–224.
44 Arrian 4.3.2–4.
45 Arrian 4.3.6.
46 Curtius 7.8.7.
47 Arrian 4.4–5.7; Curtius 7.9–10–13, with Fuller 1960, pp. 237–241; Bosworth 1988a, pp. 111–112; Worthington 2014a, pp. 223–224, on the clash.
48 Numbers: Curtius 7.9.16.
49 Fuller 1960, p. 241.
50 Arrian 4.5.2–9, 6.1–2; Curtius 7.7.31–39; cf. Plutarch *Alexander* 50.8.
51 Arrian 4.6.4.
52 Arrian 4.6.5.
53 See Bosworth 1981.
54 Cf. Arrian 4.16.1–3, with Bosworth 1988a, p. 276.

55 Arrian 4.8.1–9, Curtius 8.1.19–51; cf. Justin 12.6.1–12, Plutarch, *Alexander* 50–52.7 (Diodorus' version – assuming he wrote about it – is lost); on the episode: Bosworth 1996a, pp. 100–108; Heckel 2008, pp. 100–104; Worthington 2014a, pp. 225–228; in depth: Carney 1981; Bosworth 1996b; Tritle 2003.
56 Cf. Curtius 8.1.19, 35.
57 Curtius 8.1.48–51; Plutarch, *Alexander* 51.8.
58 Roisman 2003 – on the Cleitus incident, see pp. 288 and 319–320.
59 *Ephemerides*, *BNJ* 117 F 2a = Aelian, *Varia Historia* 3.23. See too *Ephemerides*, *BNJ* 117 F 2c = Plutarch, *Moralia* 623e, that Alexander could sleep for days at a time after drinking.
60 Arrian 4.9.2; Curtius 8.2.4; Plutarch, *Alexander* 5.11.
61 Curtius 8.2.12; cf. Justin 12.6.15–17.
62 Aristobulus, *BNJ* 139 F 29; Arrian 4.8.9, 4.9.1.
63 Curtius 8.2.12 (claiming that Alexander ordered him to be buried).
64 Bosworth 1988a, p. 113, for placing this attack before the murder of Cleitus.
65 Though Alexander may not have met Roxane until the following year.
66 Arrian 4.19.4–5; Curtius 7.11.28, with Fuller 1960, pp. 243–244; Bosworth 1988a, p. 113; Ashley 1998, pp. 301–302; English 2009b, pp. 105–109; Worthington 2014a, pp. 228–230.
67 Arrian 4.21.1–9 (who claims that Oxyartes acted as Alexander's envoy and persuaded Sisimithres to surrender), Curtius 8.2.19–33, Plutarch, *Alexander* 58.3–5, with Fuller 1960, pp. 244–245; Bosworth 1988a, p. 116; Ashley 1998, pp. 302–303; English 2009b, pp. 109–112; Worthington 2014a, pp. 229–230.
68 Arrian 4.17.4–7; Curtius 8.3.1–6.
69 Arrian 4.19.5–20; Curtius 8.4.21–30, Plutarch, *Alexander* 47.7–8, with Worthington 2014a, pp. 231–232.
70 Holt 1988, p. 66.
71 Arrian 4.10.5–12.5, Curtius 8.5.9–12; Plutarch, *Alexander* 54.3–6; Justin 12.7.1–3, with Bosworth 1998, pp. 284–287, Bosworth 1996a, pp. 109–112; Worthington 2014a, pp. 233–234; Matarese 2013; but see now Bowden 2013, for a sceptical approach to the whole incident (including Callisthenes' involvement).
72 Herodotus 1.134 says they prostrated themselves; the Persepolis Treasury reliefs illustrate bowing and blowing a kiss.
73 Chares, *BNJ* 125 F 14a (= Plutarch, *Alexander* 54.5–6); Chares, *BNJ* 125 F 14b (= Arrian 4.12.3–5).
74 See further Matarese 2013.
75 Justin 12.7.1.
76 Curtius 8.5.5–6.
77 Arrian 4.14, Curtius 8.6–8, Plutarch, *Alexander* 59, with Bosworth 1996a, pp. 112–114; Worthington 2014a, pp. 234–235; in depth: Carney 1980; Borza 1981; Golan 1988.
78 Curtius 8.6.11.
79 Aristobulus, *BNJ* 139 F 30 = Arrian 4.13.5.
80 Cf. Bosworth 1988a, p. 118.
81 Curtius 8.6.24; cf. Arrian 4.14.1, with Golan 1988, but against Callisthenes' involvement, see Bowden 2013.
82 Arrian 4.14.1; Curtius 8.6.24.
83 Borza 1981; cf. Badian 1996, pp. 71–72.

10 Alexander in India and His Final Years

The Indians in the Kabul valley had contributed only a small number of troops and war elephants to Darius' army at Gaugamela, so why did Alexander feel the need to invade India? His reasons were personal and imperial.[1] They ranged from curiosity to see whether Aristotle was correct about India being only a small triangular promontory on the Southern (Indian) Ocean, to the mythical, as his ancestral relative Dionysus had travelled with his panthers, grapes, and ivy from there to Greece, and his ancestor Heracles had performed some of his famous exploits in the country. Indeed, in India, Alexander openly took on the guise of the divinely born Dionysus, and Curtius even stated that he wanted the Indians to accept him as a god.[2] And of course, there was his ever-present *pothos* (a 'longing' or 'consuming need') to venture further and add to his military reputation.

Alexander's army now included an increasing number of oriental troops, first heard of in any real numbers at the end of his time in Bactria, though they remained in their own ethnic units.[3] In the spring of 327, he divided his invasion force of some 70,000 men into two halves, each one taking a different route to put down resistance on a wider scale, with both to rendezvous at the Indus River.[4] Hephaestion and Perdiccas commanded one half, which marched along the Cophen (Kabul) River via the Khyber Pass, while Alexander led the other half via the Choaspes (Kunar) River and the northerly Bajaur and Swat regions near the foothills of the Himalayas (in what is today Pakistan).[5]

Early Campaigns and the Siege of the Rock of Aornus

Hephaestion and Perdiccas captured the capital of the Gandhāra region Peucelaotis (Charsadda) but had to return when its prince revolted and besieged the city for thirty days, during which the prince was killed. Eventually, it capitulated, and the army was able to continue to the Indus without further trouble. At Taxila (about twenty miles northwest of Islamabad in the Punjab), they received food as a goodwill gesture from its ruler, prince Taxiles, who had already established diplomatic relations with the king in Sogdiana.[6]

Alexander had a tougher time on his route.[7] He was initially faced with resistance in the Kunar basin, which he overcame with what was becoming his 'new normal' of massacres or enslavements in retaliation for not submitting immediately – in other words, he already thought of the Indians as his subjects.[8] But in the Lower Swat valley, the independent Assaceni peoples (who were expert horsemen and whose king could muster an army of 30,000 infantry, 2,000 cavalry, and 30 elephants) fled on his approach to various strongholds.[9] These included Massaga, at the northern end of the valley near the Katgala pass, where the king and many of his troops, along with 7,000 mercenaries brought by his brother, took a stand.[10] Seeing the opportunity to demoralize the rest of the natives in the region, Alexander ordered the siege and capture of Massaga. For four days his siege engines bombarded the mudbrick and stone walls; as more of the defenders were killed, including the king, the queen asked Alexander for terms. He swore he would spare everyone if the fortress surrendered and the mercenaries joined his army.

For some reason, he reneged on his promise, perhaps thinking that the Indians could pose a future threat and callously had them gather on a hill outside the fortress where he had every single one slaughtered. Their shocked wives rushed out and fought the invaders, but they too were cut down. Even our ancient writers condemned Alexander's treachery.[11] His action caused widespread distrust of him and his word, while the remaining Assaceni in other fortresses were spurred to resist him even more. Thus, the inhabitants of Bazira (Barikot), for example, put Coenus, who was besieging them, under so much pressure that Alexander was forced to march to his aid. Along the way he took the mountain fortress of Ora (Odigram), which gave those in Bazira the chance to escape via the Shang-la pass to Aornus (probably Pir-Sar), a few miles west of the Indus River.[12] There, all the surviving Assaceni made a last stand.

The fortress at Aornus was on the eastern summit of 10,000-feet-high cliffs and had abundant natural resources to provision it. Alexander had to secure it to gain control of the entire Cophen valley as well as to prevent the Indians from claiming any victory over his army. But on top of that strategic reason was the personal: during his famous Twelve Labours, Heracles had twice tried to take Aornus (actually this was Krishna, the Indian equivalent of Heracles) and both times failed.[13] Here, then, was the opportunity for Alexander to trump his divine ancestor.[14]

It was impossible to scale the rock without being seen. However, Alexander noted that the peak's western summit overlooked the citadel on the eastern summit but was separated from it by a ravine. He therefore decided to build a bridge across the ravine upon which he would set up his siege engines – a similar strategy as at the Rock of Chorienes in Nautaca against Sisimithres (see pp. 191–192). After installing garrisons in Massaga, Ora, and Bazira and ordering Craterus, then at Ecbolima, the town closest to Aornus, to collect and store grain in case of a lengthy siege, Alexander sent Ptolemy to establish a base on the western summit. In the meantime, the king and some battalions of the phalanx and light infantry, including the Agrianians, followed a local guide for two days to a high ridge overlooking the 800-feet deep Burimar-Kandao ravine (about eighty miles south of Abottabad) and their target beyond it.[15] After only four days the bridge was nearing completion; when the siege engines were wheeled into place, the defenders panicked and requested terms.

Alexander was willing to negotiate, but the defenders, remembering the fate of the mercenaries at Massaga, wanted to buy time so they could escape that night down the slopes of Aornus. As they did so Macedonian scouts spotted them; the king with 700 men made his way to the fortress and attacked them from the rear, killing many of their number. Aornus was now his: he had outperformed Heracles, and to celebrate he built victory altars to Nike and Athena. The remaining Assaceni in the valley now fled across the Indus into the lands of Prince Abisares in Kashmir, but the Macedonians could not claim long-term success in this region as one year later it revolted.[16]

The Battle of the Hydaspes River

Shortly after, Alexander resumed his progress to the Indus where the force under Hephaestion and Perdiccas had constructed a bridge for his crossing, probably at Udabhandapura (Hund, fifty miles east of Peshawar).[17] He celebrated the reunion with athletic games and sacrifices, and then the entire army moved to Taxila, arriving there by the spring of 326.[18] Other rulers also expressed their friendship to Alexander, including Abisares of the neighboring region.[19] But the Macedonians' hopes of a lengthy rest and recreation period were soon shattered. Porus, the ruler of Paurava, a large area of the Punjab between the Hydaspes (Jhelum) and Acesines (Chenab) rivers with supposedly 300 cities in it, was preparing to block Alexander moving east.[20] Perhaps also a motive in opposing Alexander was that Porus and Taxiles were rivals: the former had no wish to see a conquering army support Taxiles. Alexander thus encountered the problems of dealing with local rivalries and how the flipside of making friends was making enemies, something we discuss in Chapter 12. Regardless, in keeping with his character, Alexander immediately marched 100 or so miles to do battle.

Porus had mustered a large army at the Hydaspes River, perhaps close to Bhera or Rasul, planning to use it as his line of defence. For 100 miles, Alexander led an army of probably 34,000 infantry (including 5,000 Indian troops from Taxila) and 7,000 cavalry across the Salt Range to the Nandana Pass that overlooked the Hydaspes river at Haranpur, from where they could see Porus' army. The sources give different numbers for the latter: 20,000 infantry (Plutarch), 30,000 (Arrian) or even 50,000 (Diodorus), and either 2,000 cavalry (Plutarch) or 4,000 (Arrian).[21] Further, Plutarch states that Porus had 1,000 chariots (more likely 300) and other writers that he had a substantial number of war elephants: 85 (Curtius), 130 (Diodorus), or 200 (Arrian).

Porus could see he was outnumbered, hence he aimed to prevent the attackers crossing the river at Haranpur and to use the size and smell of his elephants to terrify the enemy horses while stomping enemy soldiers to death. He stationed the elephants fifty feet apart, which would have made his line anything from three-quarters of a mile to 1.5 miles long and his infantry eight to sixteen men deep, occupying the gaps between the elephants.[22] Elephants were still novel to the Macedonians, though once Alexander incorporated them into his army, they would become a staple of Hellenistic formations.[23]

In 334, the narrowness and shallowness of the Granicus River had posed few problems for Alexander. But the Hydaspes was far wider and even had several small islands in midstream. It was also fast flowing and swollen from the seasonal melting snow of the Himalayas and the onset of the monsoon rains. These would not abate until about September, but Alexander could not afford to wait them out in case other princes joined Porus. Therefore, he devised a two-pronged strategy to take his enemy by surprise by using the river against him as well as his customary psychological trickery.

Porus had already drawn up his line by the time Alexander arrived. In full view of his foe, Alexander established a base camp and sent out his men on foraging parties to stockpile supplies as though he was intending to sit out the monsoons.[24] To keep Porus guessing about his actual intention, Alexander moved his men up and down the riverbank, and every so often made sallies, day and night, into the river as though they were whiling away time because of the monsoons.[25] As a result, Porus was forced to dedicate parts of his army to shadow the Macedonian movements along the riverbank and keep his men on standby in case Alexander suddenly struck. The

Indians grew frustrated with these manoeuvres and eventually succumbed to complacency by relaxing their guard – as Alexander intended.

All of this was a feint on Alexander's part to distract Porus while he searched for a more advantageous place to cross the river out of sight, sending his scouts as far east as what became Jalalpur. They found a densely forested headland of the Salt Range, eighteen miles upstream from his base camp, with a wooded island (probably Admana) lying off it that would screen his boats from any Indian observers as they ferried his men across the river. In the meantime, Alexander's men constructed a motley fleet from small rafts made of skins to 30-oared galleys with Porus none the wiser.

One dark night, Alexander decided that the time had come to fight.[26] He left Craterus at the base camp with orders to make it look like the entire army was present and even to station mercenaries and other infantry and cavalry under the command of Meleager, Attalus, and Gorgias along the riverside.[27] The king himself with a strike force of 6,000 infantry and 5,000 Bactrian and Sacan cavalry set off for the hidden headland and embarked on the boats, their cover helped by a sudden thunderstorm.[28] They were past the midstream island when the storm abated, but then Alexander's luck ran out. For once, he had not undertaken a proper reconnaissance of his landing site. As his men struggled onto what they thought was the opposite bank of the river, they discovered it was another island, beyond which was another channel of the Hydaspes. It was too narrow for the boats so the men and horses would need to wade across it, but the water was still deep and fast flowing. By the time they had reached the actual shore dawn was breaking, and enemy scouts spotted them.

Leading thousands of men across the river in such conditions was a considerable feat at the best of times, but given the obstacles they faced Alexander's leadership stands out even more – as does the stamina of his troops, who must have been exhausted but nonetheless persevered against the odds. His horses must also have struggled in crossing. Then came the stress of losing the element of surprise with the onset of dawn and the enemy alerted to Alexander's presence. Through it all, he pushed his men on, suffering himself, yet despite the considerable numbers clambering onto shore and dripping wet, he managed to form a line.

Luck now returned to him. The scouts did not rush to Porus but to a nearby contingent of troops led by one of his sons, who immediately took 2,000 cavalry and 120 six-men chariots against Alexander. Porus of course had not expected Alexander to cross the river at that location, so, in contrast to the detailed instructions provided by the invaders to his commanders, he had not given the scouts or indeed his son any orders about what to do if they saw Alexander. Had he anticipated Alexander's move, he might well have made plans to obstruct his enemy while he led his army against him, hence not unexpectedly the scouts reported to the nearest Indian contingent. Alexander put his cavalry, including the Companions and 1,000 horse archers, at the front, and the hypaspists under Seleucus behind.[29] When the two sides clashed, the Indians were hopelessly outclassed, and the mud from the rains bogged the chariots, so they were useless. The cavalry charge smashed their line followed by the infantry; Porus' son along with 400 Indian cavalry were killed. The survivors managed to make it back to Porus at the main camp, but they mistakenly told him that the entire invasion army had crossed, so the Indian raj must have thought that Craterus had only a few troops with him on his side of the river.

Porus set up his long line on the sandy plain, which would enable him to deploy his cavalry more effectively. On each flank were 150 chariots and 2,000 cavalry, in between his infantry ten-men deep, with the elephants ranged along the line at fifty-feet intervals. Like Alexander, he could also resort to morale boosts and bravery as he sat on an elephant in full view of his men – and since he was five cubits (seven feet or 2.1 metres) tall, he would have been equally visible to the enemy. Alexander's line had the king on the right flank heading the largest contingent of cavalry, Coenus on the left flank commanding 1,000 cavalry, and the infantry massed in between. Alexander had a plan for neutralizing the threat from the elephants – an indication that he and his men were getting used to them – by making them turn to stampede their own line, and in the ensuing disarray and panic, the Macedonian phalanx would overcome it.

Alexander made the first move (Figure 10.1). His stratagem was that of 'convergence', attacking and trapping an enemy between two offensive lines, those of Alexander and Craterus, who was to cross the river to take Porus by surprise. Whichever line Porus faced first would expose his rear to the other, at which time Alexander wanted to kill or capture him as was his objective with Darius in the Persian battles.

To begin, Alexander ordered a unit of horse archers against the Indian left, which crumpled and allowed him to move against it, forcing Porus to reinforce it with infantry from his right. This move put the troops behind the elephants, as Alexander had hoped. In the meantime, Craterus and his cavalry from the base camp had crossed over the river. The Indians expected him to join Alexander, but instead he suddenly wheeled around their flank and charged their rear. Caught between these two fronts, the Indians panicked and began to give way, leaving Porus with no choice but to launch his elephant attack earlier than planned to save his left flank.

This was the decisive point in the battle – the moment that Alexander knew would win the day for him. As the elephants met the Macedonian line,

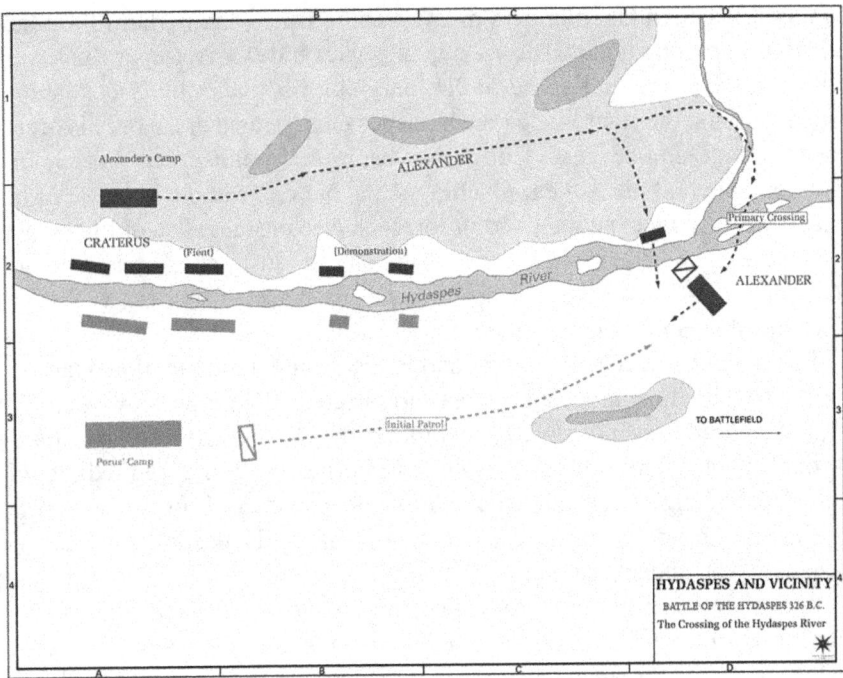

Figure 10.1 Battle of the Hydaspes River. Credit: Frank Martini, Department of History, United States Military Academy.

trampling some of his men underfoot and impaling others on their tusks, he gave his customary prearranged trumpet signal and the phalangites moved quickly to their left and right opening gaps in their line, into which the elephants plodded. As they did so, the Macedonians attacked them with their sarissas, slashing their trunks, blinding them, and dislodging the mahouts; out of control and in agony, the giant beasts turned back onto their own line, killing the Indians.[30] The tactic was the same as he had used against Darius' scythed chariots at Gaugamela, and again, we cannot emphasize enough how prepared his troops were in executing this manoeuvre despite the noise and chaos around them. Alexander's infantry, with their superior training and weaponry, next overpowered Porus' troops, who were trying to escape the elephants, while the cavalry encircled the Indian line and in the chaos all but massacred it. All the Indian chariots were then destroyed and the elephants either killed or incorporated into the army.

According to Arrian, Alexander lost 280 infantry and 35 cavalry to the Indians' 20,000 infantry and 3,000 cavalry, whereas Diodorus' figures are 700 infantry and 280 cavalry, with 12,000 Indians killed and 9,000 men captured.[31] The Indian numbers must be embellished and perhaps the Macedonian ones downplayed to exaggerate Alexander's victory, which was unnecessary as the battle, the preliminary skirmish, and the issues he had faced crossing the river made the Hydaspes engagement arguably his greatest challenge and success. But as has been well pointed out, his victory had gone beyond his tactical planning skills but came about because of his adaptability to meet sudden and unforeseen circumstances, 'confusing and compressing the enemy to a point at which they lost cohesion and ceased to be an effective military force'.[32] In the parlance of modern U.S. joint doctrine, Alexander *disintegrated* Porus' army.

Porus had suffered a javelin wound to his shoulder, but – unlike Darius – he stayed with his soldiers and refused to surrender. When he was eventually brought before Alexander, who was impressed by his bravery and asked him – through interpreters – how he wished to be treated, Porus replied laconically 'like a king'. Alexander spared him and even reconfirmed him as ruler of Paurava, giving him more territory east of the Hydaspes, although he was now Alexander's vassal.

Alexander's treatment of Porus presumably did not sit well with his men, but it was strategically sensible. In effect, even at this late stage of the campaign, Alexander treated him as he had the Persian and Bactrian nobility to help maintain Macedonian rule in conquered areas. To commemorate his victory, the king held games and planned the building of two new cities on opposite sides of the river. The first was Nicaea ('Victory City', perhaps Jalalpur) on the battle site. The second, probably at the site of his base camp, was Bucephala (Jhelum), honoring his beloved horse Bucephalas, which had died from wounds to its side and neck.[33] In addition, for propaganda reasons, he had his mint in Babylon strike two commemorative coins (the 'Porus medallions'). The first were tetradrachms, with an elephant on the reverse and an Indian bowman (holding the characteristic body-length bow) on the obverse. The other were decadrachms, showing a mounted Alexander with a sarissa attacking two Indians on an elephant on the obverse and the goddess Nike (Victory) crowning Alexander on the reverse. These coins depict the first encounter between east and west that we have – and the first representation of Alexander on a coin with a thunderbolt as Son of Zeus.[34] The famous ones of Alexander wearing an elephant scalp to identify him with his Indian victory were struck by Ptolemy in 319 when he was ruler of Egypt.[35]

From a propaganda viewpoint, the Porus medallions were meant to proclaim that Alexander had symbolically conquered India as coins were circulated widely in the ancient world.[36] But in fact the battle was the zenith of Alexander's invasion of India; from then on, the king faced only defiance, eventually a mutiny of his own men, and a revolt forcing him to quit the country rapidly. Paradoxically, his most impressive victory was the beginning of the end.

The Hyphasis River Mutiny

Alexander continued east, easily overcoming minor resistance until he crossed the Hydraotes (Ravi) River and was faced by a cousin of Porus, also named Porus.[37] Cousin Porus had surrendered to Alexander before the battle at the Hydaspes, but now he had changed his tune. Alexander, with the support of Porus the vassal, seized his lands and besieged the town of Sangala (near Lahore).[38] After an initial sally by the defenders was repelled, Alexander tried to use his siege towers, but the monsoon rains prevented them from operating properly. For two days he attacked the brick walls of the town, with as many as 1,200 of his troops wounded, until the defenders surrendered. Alexander's army brutally massacred 17,000, captured 70,000, and razed Sangala; those who managed to flee were pursued, and any stragglers who had fallen behind from sickness, exhaustion, or even old age were ruthlessly killed. This continued pattern of barbarity only stiffened the determination of the Indians to oppose him.

By now the monsoon rains were in full soaking force, and the men were tired and jaded. For seventy days they marched through the drenching rains, suffering from dysentery, trench foot, exhaustion, probably depression, with some even dying from the bites of cobras.[39] Eventually, they struggled to the Hyphasis (Beas) river, the second-to-last river of the Punjab. Across it lay the warlike people of the Nanda dynasty, said to number in the hundreds of thousands, of which 400,000 lived in their capital Pataliputra (at the confluence of the Son and Ganges rivers by modern Patna).[40] This information came from locals, who of course had every reason to exaggerate anything they could to demoralize the enemy.[41]

Alexander was probably intent on reaching the Ganges as he was learning about the Gangetic plain from the locals. He had also taken with him the Brahman philosopher Calanus when he left Taxiles, who would have been an invaluable guide to geography and customs. But when he gave orders to cross the river the men refused, despite his appeals; they had had enough of his plans for a worldwide empire.[42] Although in 329 at the Oxus, Alexander had faced defiance from his Thessalian troops, there had been no mutiny. But now Coenus became something of a spokesperson for the rebellious troops; he stressed their loyalty to Alexander as king but was adamant they wanted to return home and see their families again after being away so long.[43] Coenus had commanded a *taxis* in the phalanx and even held the important post of hipparch so his word carried weight.[44] Adding to their psychological state, arguably, was that their armour had been falling to pieces over the years, perhaps along with increasingly deficient equipment. Surely as a morale boost, after the mutiny Alexander ordered 25,000 new panoplies, which the men were ecstatic to receive.

Alexander went to his tent, and for two days there was a stalemate. It must have dawned on him that he needed to do something. Therefore, on the third day, he took the auspices, as was his duty as king, but interpreted them unfavourably as a sign that the gods wanted them all to return westwards.[45] The men probably suspected that his reasoning was to try to save face, but still, they and Alexander now reconciled. The king had twelve stone altars built, each eighty feet high, as a thank-offering to the twelve Olympian gods for his successes to date and to mark the eastern boundary of his empire and then gave orders to break camp and return to Nicaea.

The term 'mutiny' might not be appropriate as Alexander was not deposed, but the incident clearly was a vote of no confidence in him during a combat situation. As king and general he should have been more attuned to his men's attitude and limits. We have said before that once anyone crossed Alexander, redemption was impossible. Shortly after Alexander ended the insurrection, Coenus, the voice of the opposition and respected commander, was found dead. There is no evidence that Alexander had anything to do with his death but given the way he had dealt with opponents in the past, like Philotas, Parmenion, and Callisthenes, the coincidence is striking. Even some of our ancient writers treated it with suspicion.[46]

The Siege of Malli

By September of 326, Alexander was back at Nicaea on the Hydaspes, where he assembled a fleet of either 800 or 2,000 vessels to be commanded by his boyhood friend Nearchus of Crete.[47] The king may have been thwarted of his dream to reach the Ganges, but he still intended to realize another goal: to sail down the Indus into the Southern (Indian) Ocean. The fleet set off in November, heralded by trumpets and the applause of the natives. The land army marching alongside on both banks of the river – Hephaestion on the left and Craterus on the right, separated because their hatred of each other was growing every day. At the confluence of the Indus and Acesines rivers, the fast-flowing water wrecked and sank several vessels.[48]

Alexander by now was hearing of potential defiance from a union of the fierce Oxydracae (Ksudrakas) and Malli (Malavas) peoples in the lower Punjab region, so while his ships were being repaired, he decided on a surprise blitzkrieg of the Mallian lands from different directions, again relying on local knowledge.⁴⁹ He led 6,500 infantry and 2,000 cavalry fifty miles in only thirty-six hours, while Craterus and the satrap of northern India, Philip (the son of Machatas), marched down the river's west bank, Hephaestion down its east, and Nearchus with some ships sailed down the Acesines to the borders of the Malli's lands. Ptolemy was to follow three days later and mop up any Mallians who managed to escape the surprise attack.

The campaign was brutally successful. Many towns west of the Hydraortes succumbed to the attackers, and, in keeping with Alexander's pattern by now, their inhabitants were slaughtered. Any surviving Mallians fled to the citadel in the strongest city of the region – also called Malli (perhaps Multan) – to make a last-ditch stand, prompting Alexander to besiege it. The mud bricks of the city quickly gave way, but it was a different story with the fortified citadel, not so much for its height but for the enthusiasm of the Macedonians. They attempted only a lacklustre assault on it, perhaps tired from all their long marches and fighting, so to inspire them, Alexander climbed a scaling ladder to the battlements.[50] His example of leading from the front rallied the men, but in their zeal the hypaspists climbed the ladders *en masse*, which broke under the soldiers' weight. Suddenly Alexander, with perhaps only three others (said to be Peucestas, Leonnatus, and Abreas), were stranded on the parapet of the citadel wall.

Without hesitation, the king leapt down into the citadel, deciding that he would rather die a heroic death fighting his enemy than be shot as a sitting duck. The others with him followed suit, and in fierce fighting Abreas was killed. The Mallians backed Alexander against a fig tree, where an arrow penetrated his armour and came out of his neck.[51] It may even have punctured a lung as Ptolemy states that 'breath and blood came out from the wound'.[52] Peucestas protected him with the Shield of Achilles, which the king had taken from Troy, while the frenzied men outside smashed through the gates and stormed the citadel. When they saw Alexander lying in a pool of blood, they thought he was dead and became so incensed they massacred all the defenders.[53]

Fortunately, Alexander's doctor, Critobulus of Cos, removed the arrow and sewed up the hole, saving his life. Even so, he was terribly weak; he had to be carried to a ship and transported to the main camp, where he waved to reassure his panicked troops and then in a display of true grit akin to movie superheroes it was said he mounted a horse and rode in front of them.[54] It is telling that the men's delight was because he was alive and – ominously – that they did not have to serve under one of the other senior staff who showed no united front.[55] It took Alexander several weeks to recover from his near fatal wound, but luckily the widespread slaughter of the Malli led to many of their survivors, along with the Oxydracae, surrendering to him.

The Final Years

When Alexander had recovered sufficiently, he conducted some minor and successful campaigns, though if we can believe our sources, 80,000 Indians were killed during them.[56] They included one against Musicanus, a prince on the border of northern and southern India on the lower parts of the Indus, who surrendered and was allowed to continue as ruler. But while Alexander was campaigning against Sambus, to the west of the Indus, Musicanus rebelled, and the king sent Peithon (his new satrap of all southern lands to the Ocean) to deal with him, who ended up crucifying him along with several Brahman advisers.[57] Despite their ascetic life, the Brahmans acted as advisers to Indian rulers and even fought for them when need be.[58] Peithon treated them as rebels as they had encouraged Musicanus to revolt, but his callous treatment of them had terrible consequences. Likewise, despite his contacts with them, Alexander never seemed to have grasped – or perhaps ignored – that, like today, the Brahmans represented the highest order of the four *varnas* (social classes) in Indian society.

In the meantime, Alexander had marched to Patala (perhaps Bahmanabad, about fifty miles northeast of Hyderabad), arriving there in July of 325.[59] This was where he tasked Nearchus with an expeditionary voyage of 1,000 miles along the Makran Coast of the Southern Ocean to the Persian Gulf, mapping the entire coastline, which took him sixty days.[60] From Patala, Alexander set sail down the western arm of the Indus. After some abortive attempts thanks to the southwest monsoon winds, he finally sailed down the river and into the ocean, where he sacrificed bulls to Poseidon and built altars on a small island to Ocean and Earth to mark the southern boundary of his empire.[61] This achievement was all the more extraordinary as only a little over nine years ago, he had first set foot on foreign soil in Turkey – and he was still only thirty-one years old.

The sailing of the Indus was the high point of Alexander's final years. Hatred for the brutal activities of the invading army had been causing Porus the vassal to plan a revolt of all conquered Indian lands for some time. Now, with the urging of the fiercely independent Brahmans, he did just that, giving Alexander a lesson for history that invaders would always be despised and mistrusted.[62] He teamed up with a young rebel leader in the Punjab named Chandragupta Maurya (Sandrocottus) to undo every Macedonian success in India and to kill and expel the invaders. Philip, the satrap, was murdered, and the Indians turned on the Macedonians around Patala while Alexander was sailing the Indus. Nearchus managed to leave only in the nick of time, although he was supposed to have waited there until Alexander returned.[63]

Despite a campaign against the Oreitae people, who lived close to the modern Lasbela in Baluchistan, Alexander had no choice but to leave India despite the adverse weather. His campaign in India was a strategic failure, but he would be long remembered – the *Visnu Purana* (second half of the first millennium AD), for example, talks of *yavanas* (Greeks) still living in western India, whose ancestors may well have been Alexander's men. And he had opened India (and Bactria too) to the west as never before.[64]

Perhaps to save face, or more likely to seize the final opportunity to outdo two legendary predecessors, Semiramis, Queen of Assyria, and Cyrus the Great of Persia, he chose to take around 30,000 men, along with their Asian wives, families, and belongings, and march through the Gedrosian Desert (Makran in Baluchistan). Alexander knew that Semiramis and Cyrus had all but failed in their attempts, surviving only with a fraction of their initial forces: the challenge to better them was too great for him. He sent the rest of his army via the Mulla Pass to Carmania and set off via present-day Karachi and the Lasbela plain, over the Kirthar Range, and then across the desolate desert.

This march was arguably Alexander's biggest military blunder.[65] The hostile landscape, with its searing hot days and freezing cold nights, saw many of his men die from heatstroke or exhaustion. Adding to his woes were unforeseen catastrophes, such as one night while the soldiers were camped in a dry river bed, a sudden flash flood washed away most of their wives and children as well as the baggage train. Arrian speaks of the trek, which took sixty days from early October to early December (325) as worse than all the fighting of the last decade.[66] Alexander lost roughly one-third of his men before eventually making his way to Gedrosia's capital Pura (perhaps Iranshahr).

Yet at the same time, the march brought out the best in Alexander's leadership skills, and again showed that he willingly suffered along with his men and inspired them. When all the Macedonians were parched from lack of water, some of them found a small spring. They collected some water, put it into a helmet, and took it to Alexander 'as if it were a valuable gift'. In full view of everyone, the king unselfishly emptied it out on the ground, which 'reinvigorated the entire army to such an extent that it was as if everyone had drunk the water that Alexander had poured away'.[67] Nevertheless, despite the losses, a blot on his entire campaign much like Napoleon's retreat from Moscow in 1812, Alexander believed he had outdone his predecessors.

The final year of Alexander's life saw no more major battles or sieges but a host of diplomatic and other events, many controversial. At Pura, he received word that fourteen of his twenty-three satraps and governors had led extortionate lives while he was in India, thinking he would be killed there, so he conducted a purge and ordered all satraps and governors to disband their mercenary armies – the so-called 'Dissolution Decree'.[68] He may have intended these ex-mercenaries to join his army, and some clearly did. But thousands of others roamed the eastern half of the empire, pillaging and looting, and causing security issues that Alexander had to deal with when he was in Susa (see below). In addition, we can add the flight of the corrupt imperial treasurer, Harpalus, from his headquarters at Babylon to Athens, intending to incite a revolt of the Greeks against Macedonia, but in this attempt he failed dismally.[69]

At Salmus (capital of Carmania), a disheveled and at first unrecognizable Nearchus appeared before Alexander with triumphant tales of his voyage along the Makran Coast.[70] Alexander was overjoyed that his boyhood friend had survived and celebrated his return. However, he was furious when he arrived at Pasargadae (the ancestral capital of Persis) and found the tomb of Cyrus the Great smashed and plundered. He tortured the Magi who were supposed to have guarded it, but they could tell him nothing, therefore he ordered it to be rebuilt.

The army next arrived in Persepolis. There, the Brahman sage Calanus fell ill and opted to die by ritual self-immolation. He was led to a large funeral pyre in the presence of the entire army, the elephants farewelling him with their trumpet cries. Calanus sat rigid and silent as the flames devoured him.[71] Afterwards, Alexander held games in his honour, including a drinking contest, during which forty-one of the contestants died, and the winner (who drank four quarts of wine) died four days later.[72]

By March 324, Alexander arrived at Susa, where he held a mass marriage. He and 91 members of his staff married Persian royal women in a ceremony lasting one week, although five days were spent on entertainment provided by conjurors, rhapsodes, harp-players, flute-players, and tragic and comic actors.[73] Alexander took two wives, Stateira, the eldest daughter of Darius III (whom he had encountered with her family after Issus), and Parysatis, the youngest daughter of Artaxerxes III. Darius' other daughter, Drypetis, was married to Hephaestion. The rank and file of the army was not neglected: Alexander paid off all their debts, which personally cost him over 20,000 talents.

Probably also at Susa, Alexander issued a directive known as the Exiles Decree to address the problem of the marauding robber bands composed of ex-mercenaries, the result of his Dissolution Decree.[74] His solution was simple: he unilaterally sent them home regardless of whether their cities wanted them back or not. The enforced return of thousands of former exiles would cause socio-economic chaos in Greece, hence cities sent embassies of protest to Alexander, but he seems not to have bothered much about affairs on the mainland.

From Susa it was an easy march to Opis (on the Tigris, a little above Babylon), with the army arriving there by the midsummer of 324. Opis would be the scene of his second army mutiny.[75] Despite the men's desire to return home, Alexander was already intent on invading Arabia, a sign of his 'never-ending thirst for fresh conquests', as Arrian puts it.[76] He planned to launch his new campaign from Babylon and had even given orders to build a fleet and to have it ready by the time he arrived there. Arabia had a lucrative spice trade spread even as far as Yemen, but for Alexander there was a personal reason for his missions: 'the Arabs were the only barbarians of these areas that had not sent an embassy to him or done anything in terms of their position and they had showed him no respect'.[77] Since Bactria he had viewed this type of behaviour as rebellion and a pretext for war.[78] In addition, the Arabs worshipped Uranus and Dionysus, but Alexander believed he had performed deeds on a par with Dionysus and so should be worshipped by the Arabs as a third god.[79]

At Opis, he ordered Craterus to lead back to Greece 10,000 veteran and wounded infantry and 1,500 cavalry, to whom he granted an honorable discharge and pay for their return journey. His move made sense, given that the upcoming Arabian campaign was likely to be arduous, but for some reason the entire army mutinied. The men seemed to think that he was going to replace them with foreign soldiers, given that many of these had already been absorbed into the army, and that at Susa 30,000 joined the army, with Alexander calling them *epigonoi* (successors) and a new outfit or counterbalance (*antitagma*) to the Macedonian phalanx.[80] On top of that, the men were unhappy that non-Greeks comprised four of the cavalry hipparchies and another one was mixed.[81] Alexander's pretensions to personal divinity also seem to have been a factor, for the men mockingly told him that if he wanted to go to Arabia he could go with his father Zeus since he clearly did not respect his men's wishes.[82]

Alexander immediately executed thirteen of the more vocal protesters, but to no effect. He delivered an impassioned speech, which Arrian records though it was likely a rhetorical piece, praising Philip for his accomplishments, as well as his own in building the great empire and eclipsing his father in glory.[83] The men were unmoved, so he withdrew into the palace. He could not resort to the trick he had played at the Hyphasis by reading omens, so he decided on a more abrupt approach. On the third day, he began to transfer traditional Macedonian military titles to Persian soldiers and units, which had the effect he anticipated. He thus placed transactional value on Macedonian tradition and by extension Macedonian honour, which separated him even further from the great army that brought him to this point. Ashamed, his men, in tears, begged forgiveness, which Alexander granted, holding a great banquet, at which he prayed for 'harmony and unity for both Macedonians and Persians in the empire'.[84] We shall return to this prayer as an apparent example of Alexander's idealism in Chapter 11.

Alexander's Death

After the Opis banquet, Craterus began the long journey to Greece with the discharged veterans after all. In the meantime, Alexander marched to Ecbatana, arriving in the autumn of 324 and staying throughout the winter. There, after a drinking party, Hephaestion fell ill. His doctor, a man named Glaucias, put him on a meagre diet, and he was recovering until he disobeyed medical orders and consumed a whole chicken and half a gallon of chilled wine in one sitting, causing his death.[85] The king executed the unfortunate doctor, and then, still evoking his image as a second Achilles, he mourned for Hephaestion as Achilles had grieved for his lover and fellow warrior Patroclus.[86] Among other things, he ordered the empire to be in mourning for three days and for the Persian sacred fires to be extinguished, which infuriated the Persians. The excess is understandable, given the bond between Hephaestion and Alexander, whose death left the king feeling increasingly isolated: the loneliness of power.[87] To take his mind off his grief, according to Plutarch, Alexander conducted a forty-day campaign (which turned out to be his last) against the Cossaeans of the Zagros Mountains, bordering on Media (in Luristan), who controlled important communications routes.[88] He starved them into surrender, but they reasserted their independence after he died.

Finally, in early 323 Alexander moved to Babylon, where he attended to embassies from the Greek states on various matters (including the Exiles Decree, all of which he refused), as well as from Carthage (potentially flagging his interest in the western Mediterranean after Arabia), and supposedly Rome, and turned to matters to do with the Arabian expedition.[89] Before his arrival in Babylon, however, several soothsayers had predicted his death, but the king largely ignored them.[90] After a drinking party one night, he was getting ready to leave when Medeius of Larissa persuaded him to stay. Never one to say no, he toasted 'the health of everyone at the dinner, as many as twenty altogether, and he received the same number of toasts from everyone'.[91] Then after some violent spasms he collapsed and died less than a fortnight later.[92]

His last days were purportedly recorded in his *Royal Diaries* (*Ephemerides*), a daily journal supposedly written by his secretary Eumenes of

Cardia.[93] He first suffered a fever, which worsened over the next six days, confining him to his bed. Two days after that he was unable to speak and lapsed into a semi-comatose state. His troops filed past him to pay their final respects, and two days later he fell into a coma and died in the later afternoon of 11 June 323.[94]

The cause of Alexander's death is unknown. The belief that he was poisoned at Antipater's instigation lacks credibility, and was perhaps put out by his mother Olympias, who was often at loggerheads with Antipater in Pella.[95] All too often in history, the deaths of prominent figures are associated with murder and conspiracy theories abound. More likely is that Alexander's excessive drinking, punishing lifestyle, and numerous wounds, especially his near-fatal one at Malli, combined to bring about his end. The general opinion is that he died from acute alcoholic pancreatitis.

Alexander's final plans, supposedly including a monument to Hephaestion in Babylon, building a fleet of 1,000 ships to operate in the western Mediterranean, constructing a tomb for his father to rival the pyramids, and a transpopulation policy from Asia to Europe and vice versa 'to establish harmony and familial unity in the largest continents by means of intermarriage and family ties' were all abandoned.[96] These plans are considered spurious anyway. Given the men's reaction to Alexander's orientalism and the rapidity of divorces after the enforced Susa marriage, the wholesale transfer of populations looks especially doubtful. In Central Asia, many of the people Alexander had settled in his new cities, weary of the isolation and perhaps even holding a distaste for local practices, took advantage to leave and return to Greece.[97]

Back on the mainland, the Athenian orator Demades quipped that if Alexander were dead, the whole world 'would smell of his corpse'.[98] Once, however, the news was confirmed, and especially that Alexander had not left an heir, for Roxane was pregnant when he died, the Greeks revolted from the Macedonian hegemony in the so-called Lamian War, which Antipater ended the following year (322).[99] By then Alexander's senior staff had carved up his hard-fought empire among themselves, beginning a forty-year period of warfare known as the Wars of the Successors, and leading to the establishment of the kingdoms of the Hellenistic era: Ptolemaic Egypt, Seleucid Syria, and Antigonid Greece[100] We will return to Alexander's legacy and its implications for his 'greatness' as a king and general in Chapter 13.

Notes

1 Bosworth 1996a, pp. 154–165.
2 Curtius 8.8.15. Alexander and Dionysus: Bosworth 1996a, pp. 119–126.
3 Arrian 4.17.3. Orientals in the army: Bosworth 1988a, pp. 271–273.

4 Alexander in India: Bosworth 1988a, pp. 119–139, Bosworth 1996a; Ashley 1998, pp. 306–341; Heckel 2008, pp. 112–131; Worthington 2014a, pp. 235–261. See too Narain 1965; Bosworth 1983, Dobbins 1984; Bosworth 2003; English 2011, pp. 175–215.
5 Arrian 4.22.7.
6 Diodorus 17.86.4; Curtius 8.12.5.
7 Arrian 4.23.5–24.1., 24.8–10, 27.1.5–6, 28.7–8.
8 Bosworth 1988a, p. 121.
9 Numbers: Arrian 4.25.5.
10 Fuller 1960, pp. 245–246; Bosworth 1988a, pp. 122–123; Ashley 1998, pp. 311–313; English 2009b, pp. 115–120.
11 Diodorus 17.84; Arrian 4.27.3–4; Plutarch, *Alexander* 59.3–4.
12 Ora: Arrian 4.27.9. Note Fuller 1960, pp. 251–252, on the accuracy of Arrian's topographical details.
13 Arrian 4.28.2; Curtius 8.11.12.
14 Siege: Diodorus 17.85; Arrian 4.28–30.4; Curtius 8.11; Plutarch, *Alexander* 58; Justin 12.7.12–13, with Fuller 1960, pp. 247–253; Bosworth 1988a, p. 123, Bosworth 1996a, pp. 49–53; Ashley 1998, pp. 313–317; English 2009b, pp. 122–129, Worthington 2014a, pp. 241–242.
15 Diodorus 17.85.3–17.61.1; Arrian 4.29.1–4.30.4.
16 Revolt: Arrian 5.20.7.
17 Bosworth 1988a, p. 125.
18 Games: Diodorus 17.86.3; Arrian 5.3.5.
19 Curtius 8.12.12.
20 Cities: Strabo 698.
21 Diodorus 17.87.2; Arrian 5.15.4; Curtius 8.13.6; Plutarch, *Alexander* 62.2. Numbers on Alexander's line: English 2011, pp. 186–188, and on the sources, see pp. 180–182.
22 Bosworth 1996a, p. 16.
23 Charles 2010.
24 Arrian 5.9.3–4.
25 Cf. Arrian 5.9.3.
26 Battle: Diodorus 17.87–89.3; Arrian 5.8.4–19; Curtius 8.13–14; Plutarch, *Alexander* 60; Justin 12.8.1–7, with Fuller 1960, pp. 180–199; Devine 1987; Bosworth 1988a, pp. 126–130, Bosworth 1996a, pp. 9–20; Ashley 1998, pp. 318–329; Holt 2003, pp. 49–53; Lonsdale 2007, pp. 86–90; Heckel 2008, pp. 115–120; English 2011, pp. 192–215; Worthington 2014a, pp. 243–250. Location: Arrian 5.11.1.
27 Arrian 5.12.3–12.1; Curtius 8.18.22.
28 Size: Arrian 5.14.1. Crossing: Arrian 5.12.3–4; Plutarch, *Alexander* 60.3–4.
29 Arrian 5.14.3–15.2; Curtius 8.14.2–8.
30 Diodorus 17.88.2–3; Arrian 5.17.3; Curtius 8.14.16.
31 Diodorus 17.89.1–3; Arrian 5.18.2–3.
32 Lonsdale 2007, p. 90.
33 Chares, *BNJ* 125 F 18; Onesicrius, *BNJ* 134 F 20; Arrian 5.19.4; Curtius 9.1.6; Plutarch, *Alexander* 61.1; Justin 12.8.8. Alexander getting the horse as a young boy: Plutarch, *Alexander* 6 (open to doubt on several issues).
34 Dahmen 2007, pp. 6, 109–110; cf. Heckel 2008, p. 125.

35 Worthington 2016, p. 107.
36 Bosworth 1996a, pp. 6–8; Dahmen 2007, pp. 6–9, 109–110. There are ten surviving medallions: see in detail Holt 2003 (but arguing that Alexander gave them to his men as a reward; *contra* Dahmen 2007, pp. 6–9). See too Bhandare 2007.
37 These campaigns: Bosworth 1988a, pp. 130–132; see also on Sangala, Fuller 1960, pp. 255–258; English 2009b, pp. 129–135.
38 Arrian 5.24.
39 Seventy days: Diodorus 17.94.3.
40 Arrian 5.25.1; cf. Diodorus 17.93.2–4; Curtius 9.2.2–7.
41 Bosworth 1996a, pp. 74–80.
42 Diodorus 17.94.5; Arrian 5.25–27; Curtius 9.2.11–3; Justin 12.8.10–16. See Heckel 2003b on Alexander's supposed plans.
43 Bosworth 1988a, pp. 132–134 (downplaying the episode as an actual mutiny); Worthington 2014a, pp. 251–253; see too Holt 1982; Carney 1996; Howe and Müller 2012, on Alexander allegedly manipulating the mutiny so he could retreat, which seems unlikely.
44 Arrian 4.28.8, 5.12.2, 5.21.1 (phalanx), 5.16.3 (cavalry).
45 Omens: Arrian 5.28.4 (from Ptolemy).
46 Arrian 6.2.1; Curtius 9.3.20, with Worthington 1999; in disagreement, see Holt 2000.
47 Date: Aristobulus, *BNJ* 139 F 35. Fleet: 800: Nearchus in Arrian, *Indica* 19.7; 2,000: Ptolemy in Arrian 6.2.4.
48 Diodorus 17.97.1–3; Arrian 6.4.5–6.5.4.
49 Diodorus 17.98–9; Arrian 6.6–11; Curtius 9.4.26–5.21; Plutarch, *Alexander* 63.2–14; Justin 12.9.1–4, with Fuller 1960, pp. 259–263; Bosworth 1988a, pp. 135–137, Bosworth 1996a, pp. 133–145; Ashley 1998, pp. 333–338; English 2009b, pp. 135–140; Worthington 2014a, pp. 253–256.
50 Arrian 6.9.2–3; Curtius 9.4.30; Justin 12.9.5–13. Alexander climbing up himself: Arrian 6.7.5.
51 Aristobulus, *BNJ* 139 F 46 = Plutarch, *Moralia* 341c.
52 Ptolemy, *BNJ* 138 F 25 = Arrian 6.10.1; cf. Diodorus 17.99.3; Curtius 9.5.9–10; Plutarch, *Alexander* 63.6.
53 Diodorus 17.99.4; Arrian 6.11.1; Curtius 9.5.20.
54 Arrian 6.13.2–3.
55 Arrian 6.12.2–3.
56 Cleitarchus, *BNJ* 137 F 25 (= Curtius 9.8.15); cf. Diodorus 17.102.6.
57 6.17.1–2; Curtius 9.8.16, with Bosworth 1988a, pp. 137–138; Ashley 1998, pp. 339–341.
58 Cf. Nearchus, *BNJ* 133 F 23. On the Brahmans, see Stoneman 1994, Stoneman 1995; cf. Bosworth 1996a, pp. 92–97.
59 By the rising of the Dog Star: Aristobulus, *BNJ* 139 F 35.
60 Detailed mapping: Arrian, *Indica* 32.11.
61 Diodorus 17.104.1; Arrian 6.18.5–6.19.5; Curtius 9.9.1–27; Plutarch, *Alexander* 66.1–2.
62 Bosworth 1998.
63 Cf. Arrian 6.18.1.
64 Woodcock 1966, p. 45. On Alexander's legacy in India, see the essays in Ray and Potts 2007.

65 Bosworth 1988a, pp. 142–146; Ashley 1998, pp. 342–343 and 345–348; Worthington 2014a, pp. 261–263. March and presentation in the sources: Bosworth 1996a, pp. 169–183 – hardly a 'hiccup in the career of conquest' (p. 169).
66 Aristobulus, *BNJ* 139 FF 49a and 49b = Arrian 6.24; Strabo 15.2.5–7; cf. Plutarch, *Alexander* 66.
67 Aristobulus, *BNJ* 139 F 49a = Arrian 6.24.
68 Diodorus 17.106.3, 17.111.1, with Worthington 2014a, pp. 263–264.
69 Worthington 2013, pp. 310–324.
70 Bosworth 1996a, pp. 184–185; Worthington 2014a, pp. 269–270.
71 Onesicritus, *BNJ* 134 F 18; Nearchus, *BNJ* 133 F 4.
72 Chares, *BNJ* 125 F 19a = Athenaeus 10.437a-b; see too Diodorus 17.107.2–5; Arrian 7.3.1–6; Plutarch, *Alexander* 69.6–70.1.
73 Chares, *BNJ* 125 F 4 = Athenaeus 10.538b-539a. See further Diodorus 17.107.6; Arrian 7.4.1–8; Plutarch, *Alexander* 70.3; Justin 12.10.9–10, with Bosworth 1988a, pp. 156–158; Worthington 2014a, pp. 275–277.
74 Diodorus 18.8.4, with Bosworth 1988a, pp. 220–228, 223–224; Dmitriev 2004; Worthington 2014b.
75 Diodorus 17.109.2–3; Arrian 7.8.1; Curtius 10.2.13–3; Plutarch, *Alexander* 71.2–9; Justin 12.11–12.10, with Bosworth 1988a, pp. 159–162; Worthington 2014a, pp. 277–281.
76 Arrian 7.19.6.
77 Aristobulus, *BNJ* 139 F 55 = Arrian 7.19.3–6.
78 Bosworth 1996a, pp. 152–154.
79 Aristobulus, *BNJ* 139 F 55 = Arrian 7.20.1. Other reasons: Worthington 2014a, pp. 270–271.
80 Diodorus 17.108.1–3; Arrian 7.6.1; Curtius 7.5.1; Plutarch, *Alexander* 71.1, but note Heckel 2008, pp. 140–141. *Antitagma*: Diodorus 17.108.3. Changing composition of the army: Bosworth 1980, pp. 13–20; cf. Bosworth 1988a, pp. 271–273.
81 Arrian 7.6.4.
82 Diodorus 17.109.2; Arrian 7.8.3; Justin 12.11.6.
83 Arrian 7.9.6–10–7. On the speech, see Nagle 1996.
84 Arrian 7.11.9.
85 Diodorus 17.110.7–8; Arrian 7.14.1; Plutarch, *Alexander* 72.2; Justin 12.12.11–12 with Worthington 2014a, pp. 282–283.
86 Arrian 7.14.2–3.
87 Badian 1964.
88 Plutarch, *Alexander* 72.3–4; cf. Diodorus 17.111.5–6.
89 Diodorus 17.113.1–2; Arrian 7.19.1–2; Justin 12.13.1–3; stay in Babylon: Bosworth 1988a, pp. 166–173; Worthington 2014a, pp. 288–297.
90 Cf. Diodorus 17.112-.2–6; Arrian 7.17.1–4; Justin 12.13.3–6. He did enter Babylon by a different gate to be on the safe side: Aristobulus, *BNJ* 139 F 54 = Arrian 7.16.1.
91 Nicoboule, *BNJ* 127 F 1 = Athenaeus 10.434c; cf. Ephippus, *BNJ* 126 F 3 = Athenaeus 10.434a-b.
92 Bosworth 1988a, pp. 171–173; Worthington 2014a, pp. 293–297.
93 *Ephemerides*, *BNJ* 117 F 3b = Plutarch, *Alexander* 76–77.1; cf. Diodorus 17.117.1–3; Arrian 7.25–26.3; Justin 12.13.7–16.1. On the document, see Samuel 1965; Badian 1967; Bosworth 1971; Hammond 1988, Hammond 1989d; Chugg 2005.

94 Date: Depuydt 1997.
95 Poison: Arran 7.27.2 (from Medius, *BNJ* 129 T 4); Justin 12.14.6–9; cf. Nearchus, *BNJ* 133 T 10(d).
96 Diodorus 18.4.1–6. Likely forged by Perdiccas later: Bosworth 2000; cf. Heckel 1998.
97 See Fraser 1996, for example pp. 177 and 193–195.
98 Plutarch, *Phocion* 22.3.
99 Lamian War: Hammond and Walbank 1988, pp. 107–117.
100 Wars of the Successors: Hammond and Walbank 1988, pp. 117–244; Bosworth 2002; Bennett and Roberts 2008–2009; Waterfield 2011; Anson 2014.

11 West Meets East: Command *and* Control?

Alexander's imperial administration hardly captures the imagination like his battles, and he has been criticized for not establishing a more durable and stable administrative structure.[1] Yet his empire was not a static one with clearly defined and permanent borders as he was never satisfied with territorial gains. In addition, there had never been a king of Macedonia who was also ruler of Asia, so Alexander had to make decisions on how to govern on almost a daily basis, which became doubly challenging when he encountered peoples largely unknown to Greeks in Afghanistan and Pakistan.

Although Alexander's rule was based on military superiority, he gave serious consideration to the governance of his empire, given its inherent problems and the opposition he faced, for which he deserves a better press. He may well have pursued policies that illustrate the modern concept of nation building and had such a notion in mind, but if we apply the theory of command and control to Alexander, he is found wanting. In Central Asia in particular, despite superior military tactics and capabilities, his conquering did not bring with it controlling, something the west must consider when attempting to construct a united and national identity in culturally dissimilar regions of the world.[2]

Administering the Empire

Alexander rightly kept the satrapal divisions of the Persian Empire that Darius I had introduced in 513 to improve the efficiency of administering the vast empire.[3] Each satrapy was under the control of a satrap, subservient only to the Great King, who was expected to levy troops when needed and collect taxes payable to the King. We see Alexander's use of the satrapal system as early as 334, after the battle of Granicus River, when he sent Parmenion to occupy Dascylium, capital of Hellespontine Phrygia, and oversee the payment of taxes to him. Alexander had in the meantime marched to take over Sardis, capital of the satrapy of Lydia, and before leaving tapped a certain Asander (perhaps Parmenion's brother) to govern Lydia. In addition, he appointed Pausanias, one of his companions, as garrison commander and a Greek named Nicias to superintend taxation. Alexander went even further when he left Caria in 334, allowing its ruler, Ada, to retain her position for her loyalty and even to be adopted by her as her son. Again, though, one of Alexander's men, Ptolemy (not the later bodyguard and king of Egypt), was put in charge of a military force of 3,200 men.[4]

This tripartite arrangement in managing a satrapy was entirely novel but necessary and shows us Alexander's forward thinking even at this early stage of the campaign. As he intended to maintain the various satrapies as part of his own administration, he could hardly allow the native satraps to exercise the same power – military and financial – they had enjoyed under the Persian Kings. He therefore appointed his own men in these two key areas, making the actual satrap more of a titular or civil office. At the same time, keeping local satraps in his administration would make him be seen as embracing Greek and non-Greek populations and so, he hoped, help promote acceptance of his rule.

All cities of Asia Minor were to pay their tribute to him, changing the name from *phoros* (tribute) to *syntaxeis* (contributions), a euphemism that surely fooled no one.[5] He supposedly granted them their freedom, yet there was never a doubt that they were subject to his rule now and that he decided their futures.[6] Then again, in deliberately casting himself as different from Persian rule, we should note that the Carians were the first to send him needed reinforcements of 2,600 infantry and 300 cavalry in 330.[7] Also, in 334 and 333, he installed Macedonian garrisons in Halicarnassus, Side, Soli, Ephesus, Aspendus, Priene (probably), Mytilene, Chios, and Rhodes, which flew in the face of a war of liberation. On the other hand, given the activities of the powerful Persian fleet, the garrisons may have protected security along the coastline and prevent civil strife (*stasis*) in these cities as Alexander encouraged their democratic exiles to return. As such, the garrisons were envisioned as short-term ventures, for by 331 they had all been removed (apart from those at Ephesus and Rhodes) when the Persian fleet no longer threatened his lines of communication to Greece.[8]

A major change to Alexander's administration occurred as he prepared to leave Babylon in 331 and was maintained all the way to India.[9] He continued with his practice of satraps having only civil authority while Macedonians were put in charge of military and financial affairs, but in Babylon, he began to appoint natives who had previously been his enemies as satraps. The first was Mazaeus, who had commanded the right flank at Gaugamela and had been the previous satrap of Cilicia and Syria; he was now made satrap of Babylonia. Although his new appointments were often former enemies, it made sense to keep them in their high positions to give some sense of continuity of rule and for them to play a liaison role between king and people; they also had the same customs and spoke the same language and local dialects, which were unknown to the invaders the further east they marched. The appointments therefore seemed logical.

If Alexander had hoped his satraps would show him loyalty since they depended on him for their positions, he was mistaken. On his return from India in the winter of 325/4, he was forced to take punitive measures against about fourteen of them for their treachery while he had been away, removing some and issuing his 'Dissolution Decree' ordering all to disband their mercenary armies.[10] In addition, even though foreign satraps held only titular positions, Alexander's men were not impressed at seeing former enemies and the conquered wield such influence – and the native satraps were likewise unhappy with their dilution of power.[11] The human aspect of all this should not be overlooked, particularly in the context of the two mutinies the king faced in 326 and 324. Alexander's army had to watch enemy commanders who had killed fellow Macedonian soldiers assume positions of power in the expanded empire.

Alexander also streamlined his financial administration.[12] At some point, he introduced the office of imperial treasurer. Given the amount of money and treasure Alexander was accumulating, it made sense to appoint an official who would oversee taxation collection and management rather than the satraps independently trying to manage financial affairs. Originally two men had shared the position, but after 331 his boyhood friend Harpalus took on the role. Unfortunately, Harpalus, who eventually made his headquarters in Babylon, exploited the native peoples and lived a life of luxury, which included keeping two expensive Athenian courtesans. When Alexander returned from India and began his purge of satraps, Harpalus' grand lifestyle and especially calling his courtesans 'queens' made him a target, so he fled to Athens. He tried to persuade the Athenians to lead a Greek revolt against Macedonia hoping it would distract Alexander enough to lose interest in him, but the Athenians rejected his advances, and Harpalus was eventually murdered in Crete.[13]

Another aspect of Alexander's administration, intended to benefit trade, communications, and security, was the foundation of cities, of which the most famous was Alexandria in Egypt, which shot to prominence in the Mediterranean under Ptolemy I.[14] Plutarch speaks of seventy cities, but the vast majority were really military outposts, populated by garrison troops, veteran soldiers, and locals which helped to keep the peace in their areas.[15] Since most were founded in troublesome Bactria and Sogdiana – such as Alexandria in Areia (near Herat); Alexandria in Arachosia (Kandahar);

Alexandria in Caucaso (Begram); Alexandria Eschate (Khodjend, formerly Leninabad); and Alexandria on the Oxus (Ai-Khanoum) – they clearly did have a defensive role and afforded protection and the chance of prosperity.[16] Again, however, Alexander's policy backfired on him. His people resented being made to live in these remote unfamiliar areas, and the locals resented these foreign foundations and that Greek culture was so dominant in them. When Alexander died, some 20,000 inhabitants left to return to their original homes.[17]

Whatever Alexander did, or did not do, there would always be someone objecting. The same holds true today if we think of U.S. foreign policy after the Cold War, which was anchored in bettering its own interests despite offending or causing suspicion in others. Alexander was astute enough to know that for the greater good of Macedonian rule, he had to press on with his administrative policies regardless of hostile reaction. He was not swayed by his former teacher Aristotle's argument to treat non-Greeks as nothing more than plants or animals. Yet at the same time, as we shall see, Greek conventions and culture were always preferred over native ones, and it was Alexander's men who were in charge of everything – hardly a recipe for social stability and feelings of mutual respect and equality.[18]

Social Customs

If Alexander had given thought to nation building, his moves to integrate foreigners in his administration can be taken as support. So too might his deliberate changes in appearance while at Babylon in 331. There, he abandoned wearing only the functional Macedonian clothing in favour of a hybrid of Macedonian and Persian, such as a purple tunic with white stripes, a girdle with the Macedonian cloak, and the Persian blue and white royal diadem instead of a *kausia*, the flat, wide-brimmed hat. In addition, he began using two seals – a Macedonian one for the western or European half of his empire and Darius' signet ring for matters to do with Asia – as well as keeping a harem of 365 women (the same number as the Great Kings) and being attended to by several Persian court personnel, including a royal usher (*eisangeleus*) and a food and drink taster (*edeatros*).

The king may have been trying to devise a ceremonial dress to unite his western and eastern subjects under him as King of Asia. He could not refer to himself as Great King because he did not have the spiritual bond that Achaemenid rulers had with Ahura Mazda, the God of Light, which legitimized their rule.[19] Yet to be called, or at least considered, the king of Macedonia was increasingly inappropriate the further eastwards he marched, which Alexander himself realized as after Issus he began calling himself

King of Asia, which still made him an absolute monarch.[20] Yet his actions when it came to dress and nomenclature emphasized rather than diminished cultural differences. The Persians were aggrieved that he did not wear traditional Persian long-sleeved robes and trousers, and his men did not take kindly to his growing orientalism – they thought he was more like one of the conquered than the conqueror.[21]

Nor did he please both sides with his marriage in spring 327 at Maracanda to Roxane, the daughter of the Bactrian nobleman Oxyartes.[22] Curtius claims that as well as being taken by her beauty, Alexander saw the marriage as 'a means of uniting his empire, for only in this way could the conquered lose their shame and the conquerors their pride'.[23] More plausibly, given his pragmatism, he wanted to win over her father and have him keep the peace in Bactria as satrap once the Macedonians left for India.[24]

The marriage was celebrated in Macedonian fashion, perhaps so as not to upset his troops, with Alexander slicing a loaf of bread with his sword and sharing it with Oxyartes.[25] But that custom must surely have offended the Bactrians, and it did not endear himself to his own men as they were already unhappy with the inter-racial marriage, given that any sons from it would alter the makeup of the Argead line. When Roxane gave birth to a son (Alexander IV) after her husband's death in 323, the boy was never taken seriously as king, and he was put to death in 310.

Alexander's plan to ensure the passivity and longevity of his new satrapy of Bactria came to nothing in terms of his governance, administration, and even politics. The reason had nothing to do with his military policy or generalship but stemmed from a total disregard, in fact rejection, of Bactrian customs – if indeed he ever tried to understand them – that conflicted with his own.[26] Take, for example, the Bactrian practice described by Onesicritus that:

> those who have become helpless because of old age or sickness are thrown out alive as prey to dogs kept expressly for this purpose, which in their native tongue are called 'undertakers', and that while the land outside the walls of the metropolis of the Bactrians looks clean, most of the land inside the walls is full of human bones; but Alexander broke up the custom.[27]

Having dogs eat elderly and sick people alive and leaving their corpses unburied is to us an abhorrent ritual. It was also that to the Greeks, who believed among other things that proper burial was the only way for the deceased to have a happy afterlife. But Alexander's unilateral decision to end this Bactrian convention simply because it jarred with his beliefs was at best inconsiderate and at worst a glaring example of his military power and Greek moral pretensions, further accentuating social and cultural differences between the invaders and the invaded.

Arguably, his action was also an example of hypocrisy, for in India he allowed the practice of killing parents and family members, 'just as they would sacrificial victims before age or disease eat away at them; then they feast on the entrails of the slain. That is not a crime there but a symbol of piety'.[28] Nor did he stop other unsettling or degrading (to us) customs there, such as killing weak or deformed babies or fathers publicly displaying their naked daughters, when they reached marrying age, to attract husbands.[29] Possibly here he was swayed by Greek traditions. Marriages, for example, were arranged ones, whereby a daughter (usually in her very early teens) was given by her father to a much older man (usually in his late twenties or even thirties) as his wife, and in Sparta a tribal elder determined whether a newborn baby was strong enough to live; if not, it was exposed to die (with the parents' approval). Nonetheless, Alexander should have had a uniform attitude to all his subjects.

Some of Alexander's worst military atrocities took place in India, with wholesale slaughtering of enemy combatants and even civilians. These included the Brahman philosophers and naked ascetics (hence their Greek name of *gymnosophistai* or 'naked thinkers'), who may have reminded Alexander of Diogenes the Cynic living in his barrel in Corinth.[30] Unlike Greek philosophers, the Brahmans were not just philosophers but also political advisers to Indian rulers as well as soldiers who fought alongside regular troops, and they were greatly venerated in Indian society – warrior-scholars in every sense of the term. During his campaign against the Mardi in 325, Alexander massacred an entire population of Brahmans in a city in Sindh, shocking all Indians, and leading the Brahmans in tandem with Porus to organize a revolt of India. Alexander had not understood – or had not bothered to understand – the interplay of politics, longstanding traditions, and beliefs, and it cost him dearly.

Relevant to Alexander and nation building is the belief that he intended to establish a brotherhood of mankind, an idea first mooted centuries after his death by Plutarch.[31] Today, this notion endures in the form of universal values and multinational alliances comprised of states that already agree on fundamental issues, such as NATO. Mention has already been made in previous chapters of various episodes and approaches that seem to support his intention – his integration of foreigners into the army and administration; his marriage to the Bactrian Roxane; his attempt to introduce *proskynesis* at Bactra in 327; the mass marriage at Susa in 324; and the banquet at Opis and prayer for concord after the mutiny there in 324.

It has been well argued that Alexander never had such a policy, and that in everything he was a pragmatist rather than an absolute idealist.[32] Foreign troops were used to boost his reserves as Alexander soon realized that Macedonia and Greece could not furnish the troops he needed to rule an empire, including Persia and Egypt, hence his desire also to liberate as many peoples from Persian rule so they would come over to him.[33] If such foreigners had military skills his men lacked (such as mounted archers and javelin men), they were kept in their own ethnically segregated units. It was not until late in the reign, when he was changing the face of the army in light of its mutiny and his future planned offensives, that he added Arachotians, Bactrians, and Sogdianians to the companion cavalry and nine Persians to the royal bodyguard.[34] Alexander's use of foreigners in the administration was to help its functioning at local levels, as we have seen, given that he had curtailed native satraps' military and financial powers, and his marriage to Roxane was more a means of winning her father's support than of uniting the races despite Curtius' statement.

Often seen as part of an attempt to create a unity of mankind, the *proskynesis* attempt reveals a dangerous side to Alexander's character.[35] The king certainly would have known how the custom was viewed by his men, so it is stretching credulity that he thought of it as a common social protocol. The only other explanation is that he saw it as a way for everyone to acknowledge his personal divinity. That he must have anticipated the men's reaction to this side of his character yet still attempted to enforce the practice reveals his megalomania and disconnect with his own people.

Likewise, the mass marriage at Susa has nothing to do with any idealistic unity of mankind.[36] Although it followed Persian fashion with the bridegrooms sitting on high-backed chairs receiving a toast, and then their brides entering and kissing their respective husbands, it is significant that no Greek women were brought across from the mainland to marry Persian noblemen. When Alexander discharged his troops at Opis a short while later, he forbade them to return with their Asian wives and children. The inter-racial unions were meant to produce a mixed Irano-Macedonian nobility so Alexander – or a successor – would never be challenged by an actual Persian pretender. Moreover, the racial resentment was shown after Alexander's death, when as far as we know only Seleucus stayed married to his wife.

Finally, we have the famous banquet of reconciliation (with over 9,000 present!), after the Opis mutiny in 324, at which Alexander prayed for 'various blessings and especially that the Macedonians and Persians should enjoy harmony as partners in government'.[37] A prayer for concord (*homonoia*) among the races is significant, but in this instance any prayer was directed towards the smooth running of his administration and especially unity in the army. We should remember that Alexander ended the mutiny by playing on his men's suspicion, perhaps even dislike, of the Persians. Further, the seating arrangement at the banquet demonstrates a clear order of importance: the king at the head table, flanked by senior Macedonian military and civilian officials; next to him were Persians, and next to them were members of other races. The prayer thus becomes as practical as his other measures and had no idealistic nature to it. On the eve of his campaign to Arabia, Alexander needed to ensure the continued adherence of his Persian territories, given the recent revolts of India and Bactria as he had left them and promote harmony among his increasingly diverse troops.

Pragmatism was at the core of Alexander's dealings with his subject peoples, but it was a pragmatism that ended up offending everyone as he never embraced nor recognized local customs, and he stifled powers that satraps had enjoyed for almost two centuries. Perhaps if he had personally engaged more with the natives and tried to understand and respect their rituals – even if he did not agree with them – things would have been different. But that was an approach he did not follow – not simply because he was busy elsewhere, but because he believed that defeated in battle meant conquered. In his eyes, this allowed him to impose what he wanted on his subjects regardless of their beliefs or traditions.

Religion

Religion is one of the most polarizing aspects in any society and as much a challenge for leaders of multi-cultural subject populations then as it is now. Alexander was careful to acknowledge and even allow differing religious traditions, but only as and when needed, and again, his misunderstanding or even disregard of native religions brought repercussions.

Greeks and Macedonians worshipped the same gods (Zeus being the most important to the Macedonians), but the east had a proliferation of deities with attributes foreign to Greeks.[38] At the same time, many foreign gods were equated with Greek ones – Melquart with Heracles at Tyre, Zeus with Amen-Ra in Egypt, perhaps Dionysus with Indra or Shiva in India, for example. At times the native people exploited the associations of foreign deities with Greek ones to play on Alexander's divine pretensions. Thus, shortly after he arrived in India in 326 and was marching through the Kunar valley, an embassy came to him from the town of Nysa.[39] The envoys told him that the townspeople were descendants of men who had travelled with Dionysus, that their local god Indra or Shiva was the Greek Dionysus, and that they had named their town after his nurse. The king, now identifying himself with Dionysus, believed them, especially when he thought he saw ivy, Dionysus' symbolic flora, growing there (it was scindapsus, which is like ivy), he allowed Nysa to retain its autonomy though he did take hostages with him.[40]

In Egypt, Alexander granted the Egyptians freedom to worship their own deities. When he first entered Memphis in 332, he even sacrificed a bull to the native god Apis and funded temple restoration projects including that of Amun-Re at Thebes and of Thoth at Hermopolis.[41] His reason, however, was again pragmatic as opposed to spiritual: he wanted to make it plain that he was not like previous Persian rulers (such as Cambyses, who had killed the sacred bulls), and rally the people to him. In this he was successful, for Egypt remained passive throughout his reign. The tolerance of Egyptian religion, as well as other customs, was noted: when Ptolemy took over the country in 323, he was careful to maintain the same conciliatory attitude, which brought him popularity and established the Ptolemaic dynasty.

Alexander exploited religion to appeal to the people. For example, he promised to rebuild Egasila, the temple of Babylon's patron deity Marduk, which the Persians had destroyed, and he never called himself Great King. Yet he failed to grasp other important aspects of Persian belief, such as the religious and secular functions of Persian capitals. Thus, whenever he gained a capital, he was more interested in its repository of money than treating it with the respect of a religious centre. And his attempts at fusing Greek and Persian religion failed badly, as with the silver tetradrachms he struck after Issus. On them, Alexander identified himself with Heracles on the obverse and, by means of a seated Zeus on the reverse, with the god Ba'al.[42] The Persians detested the combination, but they were especially scandalized in 324, after Hephaestion died, when Alexander ordered a series of measures in memory of his friend, including extinguishing all the sacred fires over a three-day mourning period.[43] These fires were only put out when a Great King died. The idea of a conqueror, out to dominate his empire militarily and culturally, being sensitive to local cultures is perhaps a modern construct; even so, it is no surprise why Alexander was always seen as a conqueror because of his unthinking – or uncaring – acts and could never reconcile the people to his rule.

Cultural Life

Like his predecessors, and probably most Macedonians, Alexander was a genuine philhellene (lover of Greek culture and learning). When he left for Asia in 334, he took with him a retinue of philosophers (including Pyrrho of Elis, the first Sceptic thinker and founder of Pyrrhonism), poets, artists, actors, athletes, and investigators (charged with recording the topography, fauna, flora, and other features of the areas through which the army marched). These men reflected Alexander's intellectual pursuits and curiosity and enjoyment of debate, although it has been pointed out that they gained much from associating with him in terms of reputation and income.[44]

However, their presence and Alexander's predilection for all things Greek highlighted another sharp division between conqueror and conquered even in cultural life: his frequent festivals and competitions deliberately featured Greek cultural and athletic performances to the exclusion of native ones.[45] At Tyre, for example, the king held a festival of athletic games and performances of Greek tragedies to Heracles, with the foremost actors of the time Thessalus and Athenodorus taking part in them. Yet everything at them was Greek, and nothing changed the further Alexander moved east.

Indeed, when Alexander restored buildings or donated to other projects, he ordered that they be completed in Greek style.[46] His cities likewise were Greek foundations, which had another purpose of helping to spread Greek culture throughout his empire. Thus, the military outpost of Ai Khanoum (Alexandria on the Oxus) in Afghanistan became a flourishing and prosperous city, with Greek temples and a theatre. He also insisted that his subjects learn Greek and study Greek literature – especially Homer, Aeschylus, Sophocles, and Euripides – but we do not hear of the Macedonians and Greeks learning Aramaic or Old Persian with the exception of Peucestas, who spoke Persian.

We have no evidence to tell us what Alexander thought of local cultural traditions or art, but clearly it did not move him enough to embrace it. It is therefore easy to understand why the native peoples felt slighted, and why his promotion of a cultural gap only stiffened native resentment. Plutarch praised Alexander as the bringer of civilization to foreign peoples, and Greek culture certainly did spread throughout the entire empire: but at what cost?[47]

Then and Now?

The Persians, Bactrians, and Indians always perceived Alexander as the invader. They resented all his policies and strove to resist him at every opportunity they could. His own men also became discontented with their king, not just from his continual marching with no end in sight, but also because he was transforming himself from changing before their eyes from a traditional warrior king to a self-serving oriental potentate, who even believed in his own personal divinity.[48] As Arrian says, 'It looked as if Alexander was developing a completely barbarian mentality and placing Macedonian culture and the Macedonians themselves at a low level of esteem'.[49] The comment does not apply only to the army on campaign. Back home in Macedonia, the people might well have relished being an imperial power, and the income they were receiving from Alexander's conquests, yet they seemed to have held Philip in higher regard.[50]

Could Alexander ever have successfully ruled these culturally dissimilar peoples and reconciled them to being part of the same empire? Could there ever have been 'command *and* control'? Perhaps – with time, careful diplomacy, the gaining of trust, a thorough understanding of different beliefs, and interest in cultural traditions rather than all things Greek. But Alexander did not have the time; or if he did, he did not have the inclination it seems. To be fair, as we have said before, he had no precedent to follow, so he was trying to be as practical as possible in dealing with constant new challenges. Perhaps, then, it is too harsh to speak of his successes or failures. Then again, we should concentrate on, and try to learn from, the strengths and weaknesses of his overall statesmanship.

Alexander's use of foreigners in administration and the value of personal relationships were arguably seen in 2007 at Ramadi, the capital of Iraq's Anbar Province. After wresting control of the city from al-Qaeda through force between 2004 to 2006, coalition forces gained the confidence of local sheiks and their compatriots and worked with them to build unity and even prosperity.[51] Although the situation did not last long because of the western withdrawal from Iraq and the rise of ISIS, what we notice, though, is that locals' powers were not denuded in any way, as the United States had done previously during the initial 2003 invasion of Iraq and as Alexander had done to the native Iranians. How Alexander dealt with conquered peoples and why his personal relations and diplomacy succeeded or failed are valuable lessons for the western world today when it involves itself in the east.

Notes

1 Badian 1965; Higgins 1980; Bosworth 1988a, pp. 229–250; Hammond 1992a, pp. 205–236; Briant 2010, pp. 67–138.
2 Worthington 2010b; see too Worthington 2014a, pp. 196–201; cf. Anson 2015.
3 Bosworth 1988a, pp. 229–241.
4 Ada: Arrian 1.23.7–8. Ptolemy: Arrian 1.23.6. See too Bosworth 1988a, p. 230.
5 Kholod 2013. But Bosworth 1988a, p. 254, argues that it is wrong to accuse Alexander of 'cynical semantic manipulation' as they may not have been annual payments but levied to meet situations as they arose.
6 Cf. Arrian 1.17.4, 7.
7 Curtius 6.6.35.
8 Kholod 2010. On Alexander and the cities of Asia Minor, see further Ehrenberg 1938; Badian 1966; Hammond and Walbank 1988, pp. 72–76; Bosworth 1988a, pp. 250–258; Faraguna 2003, pp. 109–115; Nawotka 2003.

9 Worthington 2014a, pp. 193–196.
10 Diodorus 17.106.3, 17.111.1, with Bosworth 1988a, pp. 240; Worthington 2014a, pp. 263–264.
11 Heckel 2008, pp. 164–165 (Appendix 3) lists Alexander's satraps and their successors.
12 Boworth 1988a, pp. 241–245.
13 Worthington 2013, pp. 310–324.
14 Worthington 2016, pp. 133–146.
15 Plutarch, *Moralia* 328e, with Bosworth 1988a, pp. 245–50 and especially Fraser 1996 (Alexander founded only nine actual cities).
16 Holt 1986.
17 Diodorus 18.7.1.
18 Aristotle would not have been impressed with his former tutee, although presumably not to the extent of urging Antipater to kill him: Plutarch, *Alexander* 8.3–4 and 78.2.
19 Brosius 2003, pp. 179–181.
20 Fredricksmeyer 2000.
21 Curtius 6.6.1–10; Plutarch, *Alexander* 45.1–4. Alexander's orientalism: Worthington 2014a, pp. 214–216.
22 Arrian 4.19.5–20; Curtius 8.4.21–30, Plutarch, *Alexander* 47.7–8, with Worthington 2014a, pp. 231–232.
23 Curtius 8.4.21–26.
24 Holt 1988, p. 66.
25 Custom: Curtius 8.4.27–29; cf. Renard and Servais 1955.
26 Worthington 2014a, pp. 239–241.
27 Onesicritus, *BNJ* 134 F 5 = Strabo 11.11.3.
28 Archelaus, *BNJ* 123 F 1 = Solinus 52.18–23.
29 Aristobulus, *BNJ* 139 F 42 (= Strabo 15.62); cf. Nearchus, *BNJ* 133 F 11 (= Arrian, *Indica* 16–17): some girls are given as prizes to winners of wrestling matches.
30 Stoneman 1994, 1995; cf. Bosworth 1996a, pp. 92–97. Alexander may not have met them beforehand: Arrian 7.1.5–2.1 clams that he did, whereas Onesicritus, *BNJ* 134 F 17a (= Strabo 15.1.63–64), says that the king sent him to visit them.
31 Plutarch, *Moralia* 329c.
32 Badian 1958; Bosworth 1980; Borza 1991; cf. Worthington 2014a, pp. 275–277.
33 Hammond 1992a, pp. 205–206.
34 Arrian 7.6.4–5 (the arrival of the 30,000 Macedonian-trained native youths at Susa in 324 was 'like Alexander was doing as much as he could to become less reliant on his own men'); see further Bosworth 1980, pp. 13–20.
35 Arrian 4.10.5–12.5, Curtius 8.5.9–12; Plutarch, *Alexander* 54.3–6, with Bosworth 1998, pp. 284–287, Bosworth 1996a, pp. 109–112; Worthington 2014a, pp. 233–234.
36 Chares, *BNJ* 125 F 4 = Athenaeus 10.538b–539a. See further Diodorus 17.107.6; Arrian 7.4.1–8; Plutarch, *Alexander* 70.3; Justin 12.10.9–10, with Bosworth 1988a, pp. 156–158; Worthington 2014a, pp. 275–277.
37 Arrian 7.11.9.
38 Macedonian religion: Christesen and Murray 2010.
39 Arrian 5.2.5–7; Curtius 8.10.15–17; Justin 12.7.6–8; cf. Bosworth 1988a, pp. 121–122, 1996a, pp. 121–126.

40 Woodcock 1966, pp. 21–23, on the identity of the Nysans, with an analogy to present-day Kafirs in Chitral (Pakistan), whose men wear hats like the *kausia*, are viticulturalists, and hold an annual festival in honour of the god of wine.
41 Worthington 2014a, pp. 179–180.
42 Cf. Bosworth 1988a, pp. 244–245, on coinage; *contra* Briant 2010, pp. 96–100.
43 Arrian 7.14.2–3, with Worthington 2014a, pp. 282–283.
44 Tritle 2009.
45 Worthington 2014a, pp. 185–187.
46 Arrian 2.5.8, 7.14.1.
47 Plutarch, *Moralia* 328b.
48 Cf. Hammond 1992a, pp. 226–231, on his orientalism.
49 Arrian 7.6.2–5; see too Briant 2010, pp. 101–138.
50 Worthington 2014a, pp. 300–309.
51 See Smith and MacFarland 2008; Abed Al-Jabouri and Jensen 2010, pp. 3–18.

12 The Trials and Tolls of Expeditionary Warfare

Alexander began his invasion of Asia in 334 as a liberator of the Greek cities of Asia Minor from Persian rule. He tended to dismantle oligarchies and install democracies, and when Macedonian loyalists in Ephesus began to slaughter those who resisted, Alexander, understanding such acts could lead only to future insurrection, forbade the killing. It is evident that he understood sociopolitical cause-and-effect among the Greeks, but the further east he ventured, the more his enemies challenged his assumptions. For example, when the Sogdian leader Spitamenes besieged Maracanda in the summer of 329, Alexander sent a contingent of 2,000 infantry and 300 cavalry under his interpreter Pharnuches to relieve the city. According to Arrian, Pharnuches was intended to liaise with the barbarians rather than take command of battles.[1] Since he was supported by three military commanders, Arrian's comment presumably reflects Alexander's intention to bring about a diplomatic settlement using his interpreter, and then if that failed, resort to a military strike headed by his experienced officers. But he erred by appointing Pharnuches as overall commander, for he fell victim to a surprise enemy attack, and his men were massacred. Alexander himself then pursued Spitamenes to the River Helmand (Etymandrus), a name that might sound familiar to veterans of Afghanistan's recent wars, but his foe escaped him.[2]

Since Alexander's march through Bactria and Sogdiana, there has been no shortage of imperial and democratic powers charting the same paths for numerous reasons. The 'great game' period was coined by Rudyard Kipling and chronicled most notably by journalist and author Peter Hopkirk. It involved intense competition between the Russian, British, and French Empires for control over Central Asia's resources and territories in the eighteenth and early nineteenth centuries.[3] Characteristics of this game, such as advanced cartographic methods and the liberal employment of spies, gave rise to some of the first formally recognized national intelligence architectures – most notably in the form of England's Persian Office as a central intelligence directorate between 1790 and 1820.⁴ Information was currency, ethnocentrism often drove information processing, and the urge to understand and control foreign cultures consumed the imperial mind.

At times, understanding and control pulled invaders in opposite directions. Much of what the British Empire and others gathered in Asia during this period contributed more to their own confusion, as flawed intelligence or outright falsehoods came to fill knowledge gaps in their 'imperial archives'.⁵ Like Alexander, the rate at which they encountered new civilizations far exceeded their capacity to process and understand the previous one before they attempted to control another. Sir John W. Fortescue, who wrote one of the most authoritative histories on the British Army's first tragic jaunt into Afghanistan (1837–1842), surmised that it was English naiveté of the Afghan chiefs with whom they negotiated that led to the slow and excruciating annihilation of roughly 12,000 European forces during their retreat from Kabul in 1842.⁶ Those who weren't hacked to pieces simply froze to death.

Imperialistic control, access to resources, and conquest since Alexander's age long motivated expeditionary warfare – that is, wars waged in lands generally far removed from one's own. It is a somewhat recent phenomenon, then, that expeditionary wars have been presented as toils of altruistic liberation, international justice, or global security (an entirely foreign and uninteresting idea to much of the world's rural populations concerned with subsistence alone).⁷ This philosophy arguably reached a crescendo under the presidency of George W. Bush (2001–2009), who believed that all people yearned for a western style of freedom, and it was the duty of stronger nations to give it to them.⁸ Interestingly, most military conflicts of the twenty-first century have been cast in such a light, from NATO's spread of democracy in Kosovo, Iraq, and Afghanistan to, far more loosely, Russia's alleged 'liberation' of ethnic Russians in Ukraine during its 2014 and 2022 invasions there.⁹

On the surface, it might appear as though failures to bring decentralized cultures in Asia under some sort of centralized national authority were the result of misdiagnosed ways and means. The surge of post-mortem Afghan war analyses in 2021 is one such example, most of which pointed fingers at either military leaders or politicians for 'failing' to turn the country into a functional democracy with a regimented military in twenty years.¹⁰ The inspector-general report on the collapse of the Afghan government placed the blame almost squarely on the Trump Administration's February 2020 U.S.–Taliban agreement and President Joe Biden's decision to withdraw in August the following year.¹¹ Notwithstanding this report, Andrew Bacevich's comment shortly after the war may be more on the mark, when he wrote that creating 'an army comprised of non-Americans that will advance US policy objectives is a daunting proposition'.[12] Indeed, Craig Whitlock's *Afghanistan Papers* makes the Afghan Defense Forces' implosion seem all but predestined. While there is certainly enough blame to go around, a more realistic theory proposes that the roots of these failures could have been the desired end – rapid and fundamental social and political change – that most beguiled each attempt, from Alexander's march through Asia to the Global War on Terrorism. All the while, the social and psychological costs of such wars on society remain staggeringly high.

Why, then, do nations continue to wage them? Is the cost often worth the reward? And have leaders gotten any better at fighting expeditionary wars since Pharnuches met his demise in 329? Although the challenges of this form of warfare are legion, for the purposes of this chapter, we have condensed them into three core problems: the effects of culture shock, the disadvantages of the offense in urban warfare, and the enduring horror of war. But before exploring the impacts of culture shock, it is important to first understand the nature of foreign military occupations.

A New Expedition

One must begin any discussion on expeditionary warfare by acknowledging its characteristics and its nature. Namely that it is a tool wielded almost exclusively by great powers to pursue their interests through the long-distance projection of military power, during which time the political nervous system of the warring country remains virtually unexposed to risk. Maintaining domestic social order and economic stability during such an endeavor requires immense wealth and military strength to extend logistical networks that keep pace with the speed of war. It is therefore a privileged form of warfare.

The purposes of it are many, beginning of course in Alexander's time with expansionism, which he later attempted to connect to Macedonian national security, as demonstrated by his speech at Hecatompylus imploring his men to invade Bactria to end the threat from Bessus. His logic was as follows: if the Macedonian king ruled all of Asia, thus turning neighbor kingdoms into fiefdoms, surely that would be in the interest of Macedonia's defense.[13] He was wrong then, as are Russia's leaders now who use similar justifications for their twenty-first century expansionism in Georgia and Ukraine.[14] There is no evidence that Moscow's numerous incursions have increased its security – in fact, the opposite is likely true. Since Vladimir Putin's 2007 Munich speech that laid bare his intentions, each act of imperial aggression has hardened NATO's resolve, increased military spending of its members, and boosted the presence of NATO troops on Russia's border.[15] This exchange is nothing new.

Expressions of expeditionary warfare evolved most significantly in the seventh to thirteenth centuries with the introduction of a new religion. The rise of the powerful Islamic caliphates sought to turn the world toward the Muslim faith, which led to the infamous Catholic Crusades designed to return control of various regions to Anglo rulers and restrict the influence of Muslim armies in Gaul (modern France).[16] The colonial eras of the sixteenth to early twentieth centuries saw imperial powers sending armies abroad to quash rebellions in colonized regions, establish governance, or annex an unruly or strategically critical territory, such as those of the 'great game' period in colonial India or British North America.[17] A trend of decolonization and imperial disintegration after 1918 blunted the use of imperial militaries abroad, which ultimately met its end with the Allied victory in 1945; the culmination of what was, for the United States, arguably the most virtuous and consequential expeditionary war.[18]

World War II changed the dynamics of modern warfare by proving that waging war far from one's borders was not only possible, but also in many ways strategically beneficial. The Second World War reshaped the international order by establishing the United States as a global power when it had previously enjoyed only a fraction of such influence. Nowhere was this reshaping more evident than in the growth of defense capacity, considering the U.S. Army ranked an astonishing seventeenth among the world's armies in the 1930s behind Portugal and Belgium.[19] In contrast, other great powers saw their influence dwindle into a shadow of what it had been in prior centuries.[20] Just war thereby became a viable and even obligatory policy for a great power, as the western world sought to replicate the positive effects of the Second World War around the globe through various, often limited, military engagements.[21]

These approaches were typically designed to curb the spread of an opposing political ideology or a competitor state's sphere of influence in a specific region, such as the United States in Korea (1950–1953) and Vietnam (1965–1975), or the Soviet Union in Afghanistan (1979–1989). Complicating matters was the explosion of information systems witnessed near the end of the twentieth century, which meant the justification for and conduct in war became connected to a global discussion that influenced political will and public perception in real time.[22] Concepts of global security and international stability came into focus as the world became more diplomatically and economically interconnected throughout the twentieth century. This reached a climax as the United States emerged from the Cold War as a unitary superpower. The aperture of a liberal nation's interests, driven by momentous political change and a deepening sense of transnational interdependence, was therefore widened.

Information age expeditionary warfare, then, has emerged as somewhat of a historical anomaly. Campaigns are still carried out in the national interest of a great power, but most contemporary missions are framed as just wars, wars of liberation, or even altruistic wars that help populations because it is the morally correct thing to do.[23] During his 2002 commencement speech at the U.S. Military Academy at West Point, President George W. Bush made clear that it was America's duty to build this just peace, and it could not do so on the defense while 'hoping for the best'.[24] Considering the rather nascent spirit of such operations – on the heels of centuries of colonial expansionism no less – it is not hard to understand why many populations might view these endeavors with a skeptical eye. This is especially germane considering the long memories of most European, African, and Asian cultures compared to those of younger countries such as the United States.

The Soft Imperialism of Nation Building

Political scientists and social historians describe the above method of foreign policy as postmodern or soft imperialism – the process by which a stronger nation seeks to impose new forms of governance or thinking on a weaker state through security cooperation, diplomacy, or limited military means as opposed to oppression, annexation, and domination.[25] The key difference is that soft imperialism deploys persuasion through economic and information dominance rather than coercion by force. Although the application of military force often remains present, in contrast to conventional warfare, soft imperialism relies on the diplomatic, information, and economic instruments of power.[26] Attempts to reform foreign governments through limited force are peculiar considering the lessons learned from the imperial age. One of which is that the political and religious ideals of imperial powers rarely survived, whereas the real triumph of European civilization abroad was its technological influence. In what might be a controversial statement, Daniel Headrick argued that 'western industrial technology has transformed the world more than any leader, religion, revolution, or war'.[27] And yet soft imperialism and its expressions, such as expeditionary counterinsurgency, remain incredibly popular in the twenty-first century.

Examples of this form of warfare include France's experience in the First Indochina War (1946–1954); foreign involvement in Iranian regime change (1953 and 1979); the Vietnam War (1965–1975); NATO incursions into South America (1983 and 1989); the United States countering warlords in

Somalia (1993); NATO's Balkan Wars (1999) and invasion of Afghanistan (2001) and Iraq (2003); and to a lesser extent Russia's invasion of Georgia (2008).[28] In the case of the wars in Iraq and Afghanistan, NATO sought to do more than depose a tyrant and achieve limited military objectives; it wanted to establish a new and more stable western-style government after forcibly dissolving the old one – known colloquially as regime change and nation building, typically in that order.[29]

After an inglorious end to the twenty-year-war in Afghanistan, many experts predicted that the world would witness a reduction in these efforts due to their unpopularity, at least in the near term.[30] This might be true, but nation building is rarely an explicit policy – governments sink into it slowly – so it stands to reason that it could nevertheless reappear. As mentioned in Chapter 8, for instance, White House officials in 2002 were overwhelmingly opposed to a large, long-term military occupation of the Middle East. Shortly after the 2001 invasion of Afghanistan, President Bush made this clear by insisting that his country would not be stuck with the burden of nation building.[31] Deputy National Security Advisor Stephen Hadley later confessed that the administration did not want to do nation building in Afghanistan, but after ousting the Taliban, they did not want to throw away that progress either.[32] President Barrack Obama ran for office in 2008 on a mandate to end the war in Iraq within his first 100 days in office. Instead, he committed a massive troop surge to Afghanistan as nation building continued in Iraq for nearly three years. While campaigning in 2016, President Donald Trump pledged to bring troops home but then doubled down on operations in Afghanistan once in office.[33] Alexander's army would surely empathize with this dilemma, having set out to merely topple the Persian Empire but finding themselves in India with a king asking them to press on ever further.[34]

Nation building in Afghanistan was ironic if only for use of the word 'nation' in a region awash with tribal populations that do not recognize national borders as depicted by the 1648 Treaty of Westphalia or the 1916 Sykes–Picot agreement. To draw from the research of Benedict Anderson, a nation is an 'imagined community'.[35] In places like Afghanistan, Oman, Yemen, and Saharan and Sub-Saharan Africa, many peoples – particularly those on the periphery of major cities – identify less by their nationality and more by their ethnicity or tribe. The Pashtuns of Afghanistan, Ibadis of Oman, or Tuaregs of the Sahara are examples.[36] Alexander's Bactrian and Indian satraps often became oppressive in their efforts to control this environment and bring decentralized tribal cultures to heel under a centralized state – particularly a foreign one. Because expeditionary warfare and nation building are policies exercised by privileged states almost exclusively within nations lacking such privilege, the potential for culture shock is high. Technological progress aside, these challenges continue to hamstring the military operations of modern armies as much as they did Alexander's. This brings us to the first and most crippling challenge associated with expeditionary warfare.

Culture Shock

Within twenty-four hours of the 11 September 2001 terrorist attacks on the United States, NATO invoked its collective defense article for the first time in its history.[37] Many western soldiers soon found themselves drawn into a stretch of land known as the 'graveyard of empires'.[38] What they found outside Afghanistan's major city centers of Kabul, Herat, and Kandahar was a world untouched by time, where some seventy percent of the population lived in mud houses with no access to running water or electricity.[39] Not only were there material barriers to mutual understanding, but these populations also followed their old ways. Pashtunwali, a centuries-old tribal code, exposed coalition forces to notions such as blood-for-blood and obligatory shelter for those in need – both of which would help or hinder coalition efforts depending on the circumstance.[40] The former placed a duty of revenge on Afghans whose family members had been killed by the coalition, while the latter saved the life of U.S. Navy SEAL Marcus Luttrell who came to be known as the 'lone survivor'. A local Afghan man risked his life to harbor Luttrell after his team was killed by Taliban fighters in 2005. His story was told first in a book and later as a major motion picture.[41]

In 2006, Saudi officials ran al-Qaeda's affiliate in the Arabian Peninsula out of the country after a series of attacks triggered a feud with the local tribal and religious leaders.[42] The group moved its operational base to Yemen, where it remains as of this writing. Across the Red Sea, pastoralist Tuaregs in half a dozen African countries fought a civil war for their independence against the Mali government in 2012, the consequences of which are ongoing.[43] The aversion to being governed in whole or in part by external powers is a core element of tribal identity. This reality stems from millennia of imperial suppression and pastoral lifestyles that made independence non-negotiable. One need not peer deeply into history for this knowledge. Afghan tribal leader Haji Daoud told journalist Jack Fairweather that he did not want the Afghan police or the Taliban to have authority over him because he preferred to rule himself.[44] An old Arabic proverb contributes to this logic: 'He who rules over you emasculates you' and is therefore your master. To most Afghans, their only master is God.[45]

While tribalism and xenophobia remain characteristic of the rural landscape, the added factor of religion further complicates matters of expeditionary warfare – especially concerning secular nations that wage war among those who prioritize nothing higher than adherence to their religious principles. Though Islam did not emerge for some 900 years after Alexander's campaigns, even he struggled to find common ground with Persian and Indian cultural norms of the time.[46] Modern liberal democracies pride themselves on ideas such as social inclusion and religious plurality, but the political organizations stewarding Afghanistan's future after the Taliban's 2001 ouster were purely Islamic, and they recognized no separation between faith and politics. This observation personifies challenges secular alliances encounter when forced to hype the benefits of ethnic inclusion and religious plurality among cultures that view religious homogeneity as an essential cog of any ruling system.[47]

Indeed, expeditionary wars – particularly expeditionary counterinsurgencies – are rarely successful in the long term.[48] They are often plagued by cultural hang-ups that preclude understanding and political stability due to conflicting interests. Like the tragedy of Alexander's interpreter, Russian Tsar Peter the Great made similar mistakes just east of the Caspian Sea in 1717 when he sent one of his commanders – a Muslim prince named Alexander Bekovich who had converted to Christianity – to parlay with the Khan of Khiva. The nearby River Oxus was flush with gold ore, and any caravan routes from Russia to India would have to pass through the Khan's lands. Bekovich's trusting nature led to the systematic slaughter of his entire brigade – some 4,000 men. His severed head and that of his officers were stuffed with straw and put on display while the few remaining survivors were sold into slavery.[49]

British officers experienced the same culture shock in 1842 and later in 1864, in each instance encountering an incalcitrant Afghan opponent who refused to abide external influence no matter its form.[50] In Kabul, several days before Christmas 1841, Akbar Khan lured British officer Sir William Hay Macnaughten into a trap with promises of parlay before a mob of Afghan men cut him to pieces.[51] Even when trying to identify with local customs, though, foreign militaries faced challenges.

Alexander was genuinely bewildered – one might even say troubled – by Bessus' ignoble acquiescence in Darius' murder, in part because Alexander was obsessed with honor, but also, perhaps, because it forced him to recognize his own mortality as Darius' successor.[52] For this, Alexander had Bessus' nose and rims of his ears cut off in accordance with local Persian custom, an act that Arrian condemned as evidence of Alexander becoming seduced by barbarian culture.[53] Curtius reinforced this sentiment with his account of Coenus expressing shame that Alexander forced Macedonians to wear foreign clothing.[54] This cultural appropriation became a reoccurring grievance, especially during the obeisance debates in which Alexander's most pious aides insisted he take the moniker of 'god' as other Persian Kings had done.[55]

Balancing respect for a foreign culture with the interests of the warring state remains a challenge even for seasoned expeditionary warriors. Lawrence of Arabia, arguably the most effective foreign officer to ever embed with Arab tribes, was often met with derision by fellow English officers who mocked him for donning the traditional dress of his Arab counterparts in the early twentieth century. In one instance reminiscent of Coenus' complaint, this deference for local customs – a primary source of Lawrence's effectiveness – prompted another British officer to suggest that Lawrence be shot for carrying himself in such a disgraceful way.[56] But it is not only one's fellow countrymen who pose a threat when dealing with the culture shock of expeditionary wars.

A century later, President Obama's 2009 troop surge in Afghanistan led to a spike of green-on-blue attacks as Afghan security forces turned on their American advisers for one of two reasons: they felt disrespected by western soldiers or they had been recruited into an extremist camp.[57] The death toll from such attacks rose from two in 2008 to forty-five by 2012, accounting for a total of 152 American military deaths between 2008 and 2017.[58] In 2015 alone, a year with very few U.S. casualties, green-on-blue attacks were responsible for eighty percent of American combat-related deaths.[59]

Some of the most successful expeditionary operations, such as the British mission to support Sultan Qaboos bin Said during Oman's Dhofar Rebellion (1962–1976), were the result of covert military forces applying the smallest footprint possible based on the understanding that in tribal regions 'less is more'.[60] Smaller forces also tend to develop specialized skills that soften the blow of culture shock, such as foreign language proficiency and a deeper understanding of other cultures and their traditions. Others have observed that most western militaries are not organized to fight long-term irregular wars and must either restructure their forces appropriately or manage their expectations regarding what is possible in such conflicts.[61] President Dwight Eisenhower appeared to understand this. He approached the Middle East and far east with profound restraint in the 1950s. Examples of this caution were evident in his administration's policies toward Oman and Egypt, which recognized that direct involvement of a foreign military in volatile political situations could make matters worse.[62] British Maj. Gen. Tony Jeapes would later reach similar conclusions when he stated that Vietnam showed the world that 'there is no future for a foreign army of intervention in a national revolutionary war'.[63]

Colin Powell drew upon these experiences when in 1991 he advised against pushing the U.S. military into Baghdad after expelling Saddam Hussein's forces from Kuwait, which gave rise to what is now known as the Weinberger–Powell Doctrine.[64] Initially codified in 1984 by U.S. Secretary of Defense Caspar Weinberger, the philosophy states that military force should only be used decisively and with the full support of Congress and the American public for clear objectives.[65] Only then would the use of *force* become an effective instrument of national *power*.[66] Powell's interpretation of Weinberger's philosophy during the Gulf War left his mark on the policy, which reinforced the importance of strategic restraint and clearly defined exit plans when using the military as an arm of U.S. policy abroad.

Congressional reports later identified the abandonment of this doctrine as a major flaw in the planning and execution of the Iraq and Afghanistan wars.[67] It was not that American officials failed to recognize these lessons, only that they did not adhere to them over time. Principles that defined early successes in Operation Enduring Freedom (OEF), such as the use of small SOF teams to avoid the perception of western invaders, were eventually abandoned.[68] Notions of presentism explored in the Introduction and Chapter 2 gave rise to dismissive attitudes toward lessons of the Cold War era.[69] One of those lessons was the importance of recognizing that western forces, when tasked to combat a foreign adversary, must first understand him.

A Cultural Crash Course

Geopolitical realities make the above lessons that much more sobering for the United States, Australia, and United Kingdom, as most of their wars are expeditionary. Over the last century, these nations demonstrated a remarkable capacity to improvise and succeed in the material and tactical realms of expeditionary warfare. That is, getting the army *over there* and fighting.[70] But the more vexing and common thread woven into expeditionary wars throughout history is that of militaries fighting distant enemies they do not understand to change them radically through mirror imaging – whether politically, socially, or economically. Palestinian-American literary scholar Edward Said contributed to this discussion, as did Indian author Ibn Warraq who offered a counterpoint to Said's thesis depicting the culturally aloof westerner.[71] Despite these conversations ongoing in the academic community since at least the 1960s, many western nations remain hamstrung by a general lack of cross-cultural empathy in modern war. Although religion certainly plays a role in this deficiency, particularly within secular armies tasked by their governments to influence what are inherently tribal and religious populations, the challenges of expeditionary war go deeper.

Former U.S. Secretary of Defense Robert Gates oversaw some of the most sensitive military decisions of President Barack Obama's administration (2009–2017). In his memoirs, Gates admitted that his government was 'profoundly ignorant about our adversaries and about the situation on the ground [in Iraq and Afghanistan]'. He added that the United States 'entered both countries oblivious to how little we knew'.[72] Gates amplified his comments with an account of an officer reading a book called *Islam for Dummies* on early flights into Afghanistan, a knowledge gap that the United States never managed to fill. Ten years into the war, soldiers at Bagram Airbase accidentally burned copies of the Quran, and five years later national military strategies still refused to mention the Salafi-Jihadist ideology at the heart of groups with which the United States was supposedly at war.[73] Gates' observations reflect a trend.

More than 100 years before America's war in Afghanistan, President William McKinley deployed forces into the Philippines that suffered from a widespread ignorance of local culture and geography.[74] Analysis of various approaches to most population-centric wars – that is, wars in which the perceptions and beliefs of the local civilian population play a central role in their outcome – has produced similar conclusions immaterial to the era in which the analysis occurred.[75] It is worth noting, however, that prior to entering Afghanistan and Iraq in 2001 and 2003, there were indeed experts who served as the exception to Gates' observation. The problem is that their voices were either not pursued or not amplified sufficiently once found – a trend that endured throughout the war.[76]

In addition to literature from military historians and regional analysts, the experiences of the British and Soviet armies in Afghanistan are well-documented, as is the intractable nature of religious tribalism associated with the parts of Central Asia in which NATO found itself.[77] Soldiers on mission there in 2008, such as the author Mike Ferguson, were forced to relearn many of the hard-won lessons documented by the French, Russian, and British armies in the eighteenth century – including those related to notions of dishonor over which many tribal populations were and still are willing to kill.

The outcome of this negligence to educate invading forces on such sensitive issues was western militaries that in large part could not explain what Salafists believe and why, even though they had been at war with them for nearly a generation. As of this writing, many service members remain unfamiliar with the differences between the two major denominations of Islam, much more so regarding the nuances of Salafism.[78] In population-centric wars that rely on the trust and goodwill of locals to succeed, this demonstrates a lack of respect for, or interest in, the most influential feature of the local population.

Though Alexander possessed a deeper understanding of Persia's culture and political affairs than most in his time, he was, like many Greeks, rather ignorant of India and Bactria, having only myths passed down through the generations to feed his imagination. Despite modest efforts to adopt an Asiatic wardrobe – which might be considered a manner of negotiating culture shock by patronizing new subjects – he wound up offending conquered populations more than endearing himself to them.[79] His conquest was so rapid that he could not understand the nature of one culture before conquering another. Perhaps he did not care to understand. The British Empire experienced a similar 'imperial fatigue' during its years in colonial India, which resulted in flawed analysis designed to reach predetermined conclusions in its struggle to understand new environments.

Democracy in the Middle East has certainly had sparks of hope in the form of exceptional leaders like Afghanistan's Gen. Abdul Raziq and Iraq's Hisham al-Hashimi, a top security analyst and government advisor who worked out of Baghdad. Tragically, both have since been assassinated; the former by a Taliban infiltrator in 2018 and the latter by unknown assailants potentially linked to Hezbollah in 2020.[80]

Centuries of nation building in the region often reached the same ends through miscommunication and cultural disconnects reminiscent of Alexander's attempt to bring the Bactrians to heel permanently under his empire. Such ideological disharmony might be the most systemic problem facing expeditionary militaries, but it is not necessarily the deadliest. As Alexander pressed further east, he discovered that much of Asia was less nomadic and more dependent upon city centers or fortifications to defend their armies and connect their supply chains. This presented both risk and opportunity to Alexander, the exploitation of which became a trademark of his success with lessons for leaders today. We now turn to the second trial in expeditionary wars.

Return of the Siege

By its nature, expeditionary warfare pits a mobile force against a predominantly static one; the former occupies unfamiliar territory while the latter operates on home terrain. But this was not always so. Since Alexander's time, pastoralist societies in Central Asia were accustomed to defending on the move before many of them were forced into city centers and mutual defense pacts by sultanates who centralized control of security and commerce.[81] When in combat with Macedonians, the Scythians fought fiercely until they saw favor turning against them, at which time they would flee deep into the desert where Alexander's army could not follow. This resulted in the Macedonians refusing to pursue their foes into the vast desert, where the lack of resources and open terrain allowed the Scythians to scatter and take evasive action. Defeat of any forces was not decisive, consisting of small pockets of resistance here and there. Arrian captures their *modus operandi*: 'These Scythians are easily recruited into one war after another: they live in conditions of extreme poverty, and theirs is a nomadic way of life without the permanent settlements which would make them fear consequences for their families'.[82] The same tactics proved as deadly for British soldiers some 2,100 years later when the Nepalese and Hindu Gurkhas deployed them in the mountainous regions of Central Asia.[83]

In India, however, Alexander encountered cultures that were less nomadic and more agrarian and therefore static. They were reliant upon cities as a means of protection from external threats, which became a significant tactical dilemma for them. At Massaga, for example, Alexander drew his enemy far enough away from their city walls to trick them into believing that his army had begun a withdrawal (see Chapter 10). In the process, he denied them a swift return to safety as he wheeled his forces around in a bold maneuver and advanced toward them at speed, resulting in a rout. Indians not killed in the melee retreated to the city where they became not only vulnerable to defeat in a central location, but they also inhabited key terrain that provided subsistence to an invading force once it had breached the walls.

Although sieges eventually became a hallmark of Alexandrian warfare, they gave him an exceptionally hard time early in his campaigns, specifically at Myndus.[84] But through the innovative application of his engineer corps, he transformed siege warfare into an advantage that gave him strategic goalposts to refit, consolidate forces, and accrue materiel for the next leg of his journey.[85] Mastering the siege was perhaps one of the most essential elements of Alexander's military success, beginning in Tyre and continuing later at Gaza, where he tasked his army to build massive dirt mounds that allowed his siege engines to be brought in level with the city walls.[86] The same conditions emerged at Bazira when Alexander captured several smaller towns on the city's perimeter, forcing the remaining citizens to seek refuge at the Rock of Aornus. This placed the preponderance of Alexander's enemies in one place, thereby making their destruction that much more complete.[87] Other sieges, like that of the Sogdian Rock in winter, were non-negotiable – Alexander needed these forts not only as a means of material recuperation for his fatigued army, but also as a way of establishing communication nodes and cementing his authority over the region. Aornus, for example, gave Alexander control over the roads through the Cophen valley – a critical communications route.

Sieges remained common up to and throughout the Middle Ages, but the emergence of heavily fortified stone castles and additional physical security measures, such as moats and drawbridges, made sieges more complex. This reality gave way to less aggressive and more passive approaches in which the occupants of the city were isolated, cut off from external support and resources, and forced to surrender once supplies ran thin.[88] The tendency to rely on fortified structures as passive rather than active security measures contributed to the strategic theory of a 'castle paradox'. Although the castle's inhabitants are relatively safe, they have little influence on or visibility of the events transpiring outside the safety of their walls. Siege parties could burn crops and terrorize local municipalities with impunity while waiting for a castle's inhabitants to submit, as Alexander did on numerous occasions. The spirit of the castle paradox re-emerged on a larger scale in the form of twentieth-century political constructs such as isolationism and retrenchment in which strong nations chose to disengage from the world to avoid becoming entangled with the unpleasantries far beyond their borders.[89]

The inherent flaws of political retrenchment remain unchanged, as isolated nations tend to develop a false sense of security and a decreased awareness of and influence on events taking place outside their boundaries. Modern states negotiate this paradox by maintaining diplomatic posts and a sophisticated yet small forward military presence that avoids triggering the perception of a foreign occupation.

While castles now serve more as tourist attractions than defense mechanisms, megacities and urban living are on the rise. According to a 2018 United Nations estimate, sixty-eight percent of the world will live in cities by 2050.[90] This includes the migration of roughly 2.5 billion people to urban areas, ninety percent of which will likely occur in Africa and Asia, with the preponderance in India and Nigeria alone. These densely populated urban areas remain dependent upon their rural peripheries to provide essential means of subsistence, such as food, labor, and natural resources. The risk of a 'city paradox' is as dangerous as any experienced by past inhabitants of castles, and the perils are far from theoretical.

Urbanization, as it is often characterized, is a growing security challenge that defense analysts are watching closely.[91] Modern warfare has produced many important lessons, but one of the most profound is that poorly organized and ill-equipped forces can resist sophisticated militaries in urban

Figure 12.1 Image of Ramadi's urban landscape. Credit: Michael P. Ferguson.

areas by deploying guerrilla tactics that favor improvised explosives, disinformation, and manipulation of the local populace and international law.[92] For this reason, several nations began studying megacity warfare or the potential for war to erupt in cities with a population of a million or more.[93] Such conditions would degrade or negate many of the technological assets upon which modern armies rely to conduct operations, such as air strikes, persistent aerial reconnaissance, armour platforms, and long-range precision fires. Each of these capabilities faces significant challenges in the form of proportional damage, destruction of infrastructure and legally protected sites (such as religious and medical facilities), and subterranean networks beneath developed urban areas. Paris alone has more than 200 miles of labyrinthine chambers, tunnels, and rooms under its tourist-filled cobblestone streets.[94] Consequently, the ability to seize major cities could be as pivotal to modern war as siege warfare was to Alexander.

Conflicts in Grozny (1994, 1999), Fallujah and Ramadi, Iraq (2004–2007), Georgia (2008), Ukraine (2014), Marawi (2017), Nagorno-Karabakh (2020), Syria (2015-current), and Kyiv (2022) have all shown the devastating consequences of cities under siege just within the last quarter century, yet there remain more questions than answers to the problem of urban warfare.[95] As demonstrated by Russian tactics in Grozny and Crimea, the most effective urban campaigns are sometimes the most merciless – an approach that western armies rightly shirk from entertaining. If an attacking force isolates an urban area inhabited by an adversary, the risk of harm and starvation to civilians increases, which erases the foundation upon which stability operations rely to achieve success. If, on the other hand, the military attacks an opponent held up in a megacity, the risk of destroying infrastructure and civilian casualties could be equal or greater. We see here the nature of the dilemma proposed to Gen. Mattis in his 2004 clearance of Fallujah discussed in Chapter 8.

Nomadic tribes today still shun the dependency of city life because they know that such dependency can be manipulated by those in political power.[96] Like the aforementioned sultanates who made nomads reliant upon their armies for protection and production lines to survive, when urban areas are cut off from their lines of rural supply, chaos ensues. Displaced persons scatter, often leading to refugee crises with consequences extending far beyond the borders of conflict. Russia alone supplies roughly two-thirds of Ukraine's natural gas and half of Germany's.[97] In the event of an urban siege, these resources could be cut off and, if timed during the winter, might lead to a widespread humanitarian crisis. These risks became a reality in 2022 as Russia launched a full-scale invasion of Ukraine, which sent Kyiv officials scrambling to find new energy suppliers as millions of refugees flooded eastern Europe.[98]

Combating the urban siege might require some form of Alexandrian expeditionary warfare – what U.S. Chairman of the Joint Chiefs of Staff Gen. Mark Milley saw in 2020 as the future of war.[99] Always on the move with meager support networks, operating far beyond friendly forward lines to protect their headquarters placed out of range of increasingly capable enemy fires, this vision considers many of the challenges discussed in Chapter 4. To be effective in this projective context, militaries of the future may need to fight more like Alexander and less like the enemies he conquered who relied upon their grand city walls to protect them. This requires cultural shifts in contemporary defense formations that have become technologically bent and overly reliant upon established command posts or well-supplied forward bases to conduct operations far from their borders. Finding balance between isolationism and costly expeditionary wars calls for greater investment in forward positioned diplomatic and special purpose forces who build and maintain trusted relationships with foreign partners. This investment, however, remains fraught with risk.

The Human Toll

Western militaries have stretched their forces thin in the twenty-first century. This became particularly acute for the United States, even though foreign U.S. military presence reached a sixty-year low in 2017.[100] Most overseas service members are stationed in countries with well-established bases in Germany, Japan, and South Korea, not combat zones. But at any time during the early years of the Iraq and Afghanistan wars, the United States had upwards of 250,000 troops in various theaters of conflict – roughly twenty percent of its active-duty force.[101] This was more than all other allied coalition forces combined and nearly twice the size of the United Kingdom's Armed Forces.[102] After two decades of conflict, some U.S. military service members spent half of that time deployed to a foreign theater of war, which is equal to the time Alexander's armies marched eastward in their attempt to conquer Asia. But unlike Macedonians, modern soldiers had to deploy, return home, acclimate to their environment, and then return to war again. Thousands of them – even the most hardened and specialized – have succumbed to their demons upon return through destructive behaviors like substance abuse or suicide.[103] Warfare changes drastically, but the toll it extracts from its participants less so.

Overcome by the emotions associated with this toll, and specifically a loss of comrades, the Macedonian army at times descended into slaughter. At the Mallian citadel in 325, fear that Alexander had been killed led to the death of every man, woman, and child there, which in turn intensified the locals' hate for Alexander.[104] But Alexander cannot bear all responsibility for these crimes. U.S. Army Lt. Col. Dave Grossman's 1995 study on the psychology of killing in war examines the concept of 'group absolution' by reinforcing Konrad Lorenz's famous quip: 'Man is not a killer, but the group is'. Grossman argues that the phalanx likely offered ancient soldiers a form of mob anonymity similar to that experienced by participants in a riot, which led to escalating fits of violence especially as enemies began to flee a battle.[105] More recently in Iraq and Afghanistan, battle fatigue, poor discipline, and frustrations associated with fighting an ambiguous enemy gave way to misconduct that tarnished hard-won relationships and eroded gains made with the local populace.[106] Some of these acts are just coming to light.

Numerous investigations into potential war crimes committed by American, British, and Australian forces are ongoing.[107] To make matters worse, as the U.S.-led coalition pulled out of Afghanistan in summer 2021, a poorly planned drone strike killed ten civilians, including seven children.[108] In her study of war's impact on society, Margaret MacMillan observed: 'The delicate balance is between training recruits to overcome the normal human inhibitions against killing – otherwise they will not be useful in combat – and reining them in from going too far'.[109] In Alexander's time there were much fewer checks on that balance. But, as MacMillan writes, 'we cannot pretend that we are not part of the same family, with the same potential for fighting'.[110]

Soldiers of antiquity are often lionized with herculean tales of battlefield achievement, leading to perceptions from scholar and laymen alike that they possessed near superhuman courage, tenacity, and strength. Modern military units adopt imagery of the ancients on their regalia to connect with an age in which warriors fought with unusual valor. Monikers of gladiators or Spartans or images of Greek armour from antiquity adorn unit patches and headquarters buildings throughout western military organizations.[111] Although many ancient warriors achieved significant feats that should be recognized and admired, they were still human and so equally susceptible to the toll of expeditionary warfare.

Certainly, there is much we do not or cannot know about the ancient mind, but all that we can know about the psychological effects of prolonged exposure to death and killing tells us it is harmful.[112] Our ancient sources prove that Alexander's contemporaries were thinking, sentient beings in possession of powerful emotions – perhaps none more so than Alexander. The overwhelming display of emotion from Macedonian troops at the Hyphasis River in 326, many of whom had not seen their families in eight years, was perhaps one of the more sobering instances connecting Alexander's army to those of today. Their children who, upon embarking on this grand expedition, were either unborn or infants were nearly adolescents by the time Alexander reached the Hyphasis River.

Alexander navigated Asia at times without knowing what the next crest of a hill or far side of a river would present to him, as was noted in the Introduction. His army had fought without hesitation in close combat against trained war elephants and foes far outnumbering them in battle, seeing their commanders and comrades die honorable yet horrible deaths. They had faced challenges in sieges and overcome them, thanks often to Alexander's audacity, with ingenious engineering feats that would strike awe into the hearts of any modern industrialist. With minimal clothing and a thinly stretched baggage train, they had passed through the towering mountain ranges of the Hindu Kush on foot, and in India many of the troops succumbed to exotic snake bites.[113] They suffered all this and more while their families remained thousands of miles away in Greece and Macedonia. The overwhelming display of emotion from Macedonian commanders at the Hyphasis when Alexander agreed to return home was evidence of the psychological, physical, and emotional toll that this campaign extracted from even the most hardened warriors. It is one thing to ask that a man die

The Trials and Tolls of Expeditionary Warfare 249

Figure 12.2 Image of Afghan mountains near Kabul. Credit: DoD Staff Sgt. Michael L. Casteel, U.S. Army.

defending what is clearly his homeland, but quite another to ask that he die a world away defending someone else's. This brings us to the third and final challenge of expeditionary warfare: the psychological toll of fighting a foreign war.

A Sweet Death in a Strange Place

Today, troops sent to fight protracted wars in faraway lands are not tangling with elephants or freezing to death on snowcapped mountains – though they are often very cold – but similar tolls on the human condition endure. Service members not returning with lost limbs and bullet wounds often suffer from post-traumatic stress, traumatic brain injuries from proximity to explosive overpressure, and other unseen scars with which Alexander's men likely struggled.[114] There is something to be said about the concept of posttraumatic growth; the process by which members of a team obtain greater clarity and organizational cohesion after enduring a traumatic experience together.[115] This is true for some, including Ferguson who believes that his combat experiences in Iraq and Afghanistan had a clarifying influence on his priorities in life. But for many others, those memories eat away at them as they struggle with depression, alcoholism, or suicidal ideations in a world they feel does not understand them or appreciate the sacrifices they made at the behest of their country.

Posttraumatic growth should be reinforced in modern armies to engender a fighting spirit, but it could be deceptive or even counterproductive to planners and senior decision-makers who determine the prudence and parameters of war. The idea should not glorify war or dilute its nature, thus turning armed conflict into a euphemism of itself and making the decision to wage it a less deliberative process.[116] Between 2001 and 2021, nearly 10,000 service members from dozens of NATO countries died in strange lands still understood only superficially by the nations that sent them there – often mangled by rifle fire, mines, or improvised explosive devices. The human toll of protracted war is hard to overstate, and its long-term effects on society not easily calculated. Those effects could become evident in the coming years.

Like most warriors of his time, Alexander believed in the glory of a battlefield death, reminding his brigade commanders at the River Hydaspes 'how sweet it is to live courageously and die with a legacy of immortal fame'.[117] It was at this moment, however, that the king's most trusted followers began to question how extending any further east would serve Macedonian interests. They also likely experienced doubt as to whether this immortal glory of which their king spoke was in fact theirs to grasp – perhaps it was Alexander's only. In this light, while the sardonic title of Wilfred Owen's poem *Dulce et Decorum est pro patria mori* is attributed to a quote from the Roman poet Horace (65–8 BC), it could just as easily have been attributed to Alexander.[118]

Owen, who was killed in 1918 during the First World War, used a poison gas attack to describe the horrors of war as they were and still are: the pale faces; the lifeless open eyes; the animal-like cries of a man in his death throes.[119] His point was that it is not sweet and right to die for one's homeland in such a way, principally because the justification for war had yet to convince him that enduring these horrors abroad would bear proportional benefits at home. Within several years of Owens' account, far from the European killing fields of which he wrote, Col. T. E. Lawrence, better known as 'Lawrence of Arabia', often awakened trembling in cold sweats, haunted by memories of bodies suffering from the 'ultimate degradation' on the Arabian Peninsula. His masterful advising of Arab counterparts was not without cost, as he admitted that 'anyone who had, like me, pushed through to success a rebellion of the weak against their masters, must come out of it so stained that nothing in the world would make him clean again'.[120]

The most solemn decision a head of state can make is one that involves sending a military abroad to fight, kill, and die in such ways. Even the most resilient Macedonian soldiers reached a breaking point and implored Alexander to cease his eastward campaign. Though their king had pushed them into Asia and was prepared to push them ever further, he ultimately conceded to turn back toward Macedonia, if only temporarily. The same challenges plague leader-led dynamics today inasmuch humanity cannot seem to shake its obsession with the myth of cheap, effective, and toll-free military engagements.

Promises of bloodless or decisive wars that regularly accompany discussions on emerging military technologies can blind leaders to the harsh realities beyond these rosy horizons.[121] As they always have been, the lives of soldiers are the currency with which nations purchase respect for their most valued interests, and that currency is exchanged when those interests are threatened in a way that diplomacy, economic pressure, and information transactions are incapable of deterring. Understanding clearly which national interests are non-negotiable, and how those interests might be defended in the swiftest and most cost-efficient manner, ensures that this precious currency is not squandered. Such calculations do not warrant a return to isolationism or retrenchment, but the decision to deploy military forces into harm's way will be influenced increasingly by the convergence of highly skilled military formations augmented with the latest technologies. Such augmentation will make the prospects and potential rewards of expeditionary warfare more alluring in the future, which could goad nations into making the same mistakes in new and more spectacular ways.

Moderation in the Midst of Success

A mélange of post-Cold War military strength, astute thinking from the likes of Gen. Colin Powell, and clever campaign planning led to blisteringly quick victories against the Iraqi army in 1991, the Taliban and al-Qaeda in Afghanistan circa 2001, and Saddam Hussein's regime in 2003. The challenges that soon emerged, however, were not rooted in manoeuvre warfare, precision fires, or human–machine integration. Rather, they involved consolidating those tactical and operational gains into strategic success, a resoundingly human endeavor cemented in relationships, trust, and a historical understanding of foreign cultures and their political dynamics. Stopping short of taking Baghdad in 1991 was probably the right decision at the time, but it was also one that came back to haunt the United States when an enraged Hussein liquidated elements of Iraq's Kurdish and Shia populations for assisting the coalition.[122]

An eventual democratic election in post-2003-invasion Iraq put a Shia government in power after decades of Sunni rule, creating the appearance of a U.S.-assisted religious coup that created damaging ripple effects in the region to this day. It did not help that Ahmad Chalabi, one of the sources U.S. officials used to prop up the invasion lobby, was a Shia exile who had spent much of his life working to depose Saddam Hussein.[123] One side effect is the now entrenched presence of Iranian militias that would have otherwise been less likely to appear under a Sunni regime. Between 2017 and 2021, western officials accused these Iranian proxies of supplying weapons to local militias and conducting no less than four rocket attacks on U.S. bases there.[124] This escalation not only expanded the scope of conflict in Iraq to a regional perspective, but it also moved policy beyond the realm of counterinsurgency and stability operations to interstate competition between the United States and Iran.

By 2023, the contours of a new Cold War between the United States and the People's Republic of China became clearer, as great powers seemed poised to learn hard lessons in expeditionary operations once more. Strategic documents from the United States commanded its departments to expand their aperture far beyond the Middle East and into Africa and the Indo Pacific where competing powers were already encroaching.[125] In African states such as Ethiopia, Sudan, Somalia, and Mali, ethnic tensions began to spill over. As of this writing, Ethiopia is undergoing a full-fledged civil war with its Tigray population that spawned claims of widespread human rights abuses, including ethnic prison camps and pits filled with mutilated bodies.[126] Targeting of 'others' has tragically become more common in a century when such tactics appear anachronistic.

In Xinjiang, the Chinese Communist Party's oppression and alleged genocide of its Muslim Uighur population continues to draw condemnation.[127] Meanwhile, the Russian Federation shows no signs of slowing its military or paramilitary influence in Syria and central Africa, and in February 2022 it began further expanding its territory into Ukraine through military force.[128] By April of that year, several western institutions accused the Russian military and its Chechen proxies of war crimes, including the mass killing of civilians based on their ethnicity in cities such as Bucha and Izium.[129] Such heinous acts do not bode well for ethnic Russians in Ukraine, which was perhaps Vladimir Putin's goal: to force Kyiv's hand against its ethnic Russian population in a way that confirmed Putin's specious justifications for war in the first place.[130] As Russian artillery barrages wiped out entire cities, U.S. ambassador to the U.N. Linda Thomas-Greenfield told the U.N. Security Council that Putin aimed to dismantle Ukraine and dissolve it from the world map.[131] These tragedies serve as a reminder that the drivers of conflict since Alexander's time have been rooted less in asymmetrical military capabilities or even flawed policies and more in ethnic and cultural heterogeny.

There are no easy answers to such fissures in a world that seems terminally interconnected through forms of information technology that stoke confusion more often than understanding.[132] Leaders tasked with bridging these divides must appreciate the limits of military force and diplomacy in a 'post-truth' world while nurturing cross-cultural and strategic empathy among their diplomatic and military cadres.[133] These problems will not go away. On the contrary, they are likely to become more acute as the realities of first-world nations become ever more divergent from those of the regions in which their soldiers are often sent to fight.

In an age of instant gratification, it is tempting to offer hindsight critiques about missed opportunities regarding what leaders should have done to achieve success in recent wars. Few care to entertain the idea that even if these recommendations were taken into consideration at the time, they may have produced the same results.[134] Fewer still want to be the leader who is forced to make and ultimately take responsibility for such choices. For even the greatest superpower with the most abundant resources at its disposal, the ends of expeditionary wars are finite. They remain limited by the same constraints that shackled Alexander in Asia: political will, cultural heterogeny and its related misunderstandings, geopolitical realities, and human interest.

A rather unpleasant but perhaps realist notion to entertain is that foreign wars will never be clean or easy because it is in the interest of the disadvantaged side to prevent them from becoming so. Indeed, the enduring cultural and ethnic drivers of conflict explored in this chapter make the future of war appear as protracted and complex as its past. This is especially true considering the challenges of the offense in urban warfare and the diffusion of small, cheap, and smart technologies for use in the defense. It is in war's nature to take its toll from humankind, and it is in humankind's nature to convince itself that war's toll can be avoided through political disengagement or the application of advanced military technologies. Leaders must select objectives that allow expeditionary wars to conclude as swiftly as possible and align all available means to achieve those ends.[135] Despite his brilliant military mind, this was something even Alexander struggled to comprehend. When a powerful nation sees its grandest military objectives as simply won with limited means against a numerically or technologically inferior foe, the brave words supposedly spoken by Coenus to Alexander at Hydaspes should give any leader pause: 'As fine a quality as any, your majesty, is moderation in the midst of success'.[136]

Notes

1. Arrian 4.6.1–2.
2. Arrian 4.6.6.
3. Kipling 2002; see too Hopkirk 1992.
4. The East India Company played a significant role in establishing and nurturing these networks: Bayly 2000, p. 89, 145.
5. Thomas Richards' sobering take argues that an empire is at its core a fantasy sustained only by force of knowledge because it is 'by definition and default a nation in overreach . . . that has taken over too many countries too far away from home to control them effectively': Richards 1993, pp. 1–9.
6. Fortescue 2016, p. 235.
7. As late as 2012, some claimed that high end wars were not 'the future', which echoed sentiments of the 2012 U.S. Defense Strategic Guidance: see Bennett, T. 2004.
8. Woodward 2004, p. 284; Brands 2014, pp. 162–164.
9. In his 2007 speech, Putin portrayed NATO expansion as imperialist and not a manifestation of the national self-determination of individual European states that in fact reduced instability on Russia's borders: Putin 2007.
10. Afzal 2021; Schogol 2021.
11. Special Inspector-General for Afghanistan Reconstruction 2022, pp. 1–70. Some rightly criticized the report's conclusions: Schroden 2022.
12. Bacevich 2021.
13. Curtius' account of the speech at 6.3 offers potential insight into Alexander's logic.
14. Vladimir Putin's speech of 'little Russia' and 'white Russia' in late 2021 preceded his invasion of Ukraine. For analysis see Kofman 2022; Ferguson 2022a, Ferguson 2022b.
15. One might conclude that this was Putin's objective: to use periodic invasions as a means of forcing NATO to enlarge its military presence in Eastern Europe, thus validating his narrative. Finland became NATO's newest member on 4 April 2023, and as of this writing Sweden was set to break more than seventy years of neutrality and join NATO.
16. Kennedy 2007, 2016; For an alternative view on the Crusades, see Stark 2009.
17. The 'great game' is a nod to Kipling's classic novel 'Kim' that takes place during the same period: Kipling 2002.
18. Albertini 1969, pp. 17–35.
19. O'Hanlon 2015, p. 10.
20. This reduction of European military power has only continued: see Meijer and Brooks 2021, pp. 7–43.
21. Korean War (1950–1953); Vietnam War (1965–1975); Iranian Revolution (1979); Soviet-Afghan War (1979–1989); Balkan Wars (1999); Iraq and Afghanistan Wars (2001–2021); Syrian campaign (2014-present); and the Libyan campaign (2014) are some examples.
22. Pherson, Ranta, and Cannon 2021, pp. 316–341; Barclay 2022.
23. Ehrhardt 2022, pp. 11–32. Notions of policing the world, democracy through force (Libya, Bosnia), and policies that emerged in the immediate aftermath of 9/11 contributed to the American neoconservative movement and its underlying philosophy.

24 Relevant comments between 11:30–13:00 and 16:00–17:15 minutes: Bush 2002.
25 Walberg 2011. Granted, it is not only western powers potentially engaged in this practice: Mead 2018.
26 Richards 1993, p. 23.
27 Headrick 1981, p. 3–4.
28 In 1964, French officer and military theorist Roger Trinquier saw expeditionary counterinsurgency as representative of a new form of modern warfare to which the world must adapt (Trinquier 1964).
29 For more on nation building and Foreign-Imposed Regime Change or FIRC, see Downes and O'Rourke 2016, pp. 43–89.
30 Luhnow and Seib 2021. See also H. R. McMaster's take on Vietnam Syndrome after Afghanistan in McMaster 2020a, pp. 434–435.
31 Whitlock 2021, pp. 29–39.
32 Whitlock 2021, p. 14.
33 Whitlock 2021, pp. 158–168, 230, 241–243.
34 Curtius 9.2.8–30.
35 See Benedict Anderson's explanation of the origins of national consciousness: Anderson 1983, pp. 37–46.
36 Oman's Ibadis date back to the late eighth century and still have a hold on succession laws there. There are nearly three million nomadic Tuaregs in Niger and Mali alone: Barrett 2011, pp. 5–8.
37 The collective defense Article 5: see Kaplan 2004, pp. 1–8.
38 Rice made such observations while looking at a map of Afghanistan at Camp David just days after the attacks: Rice 2011, p. 84; see also Jones 2009. The fifth NATO article covers obligations of its members regarding collective defense in which all members must contribute to a war effort if one of them is attacked.
39 Ahmadzai and McKinna 2018, pp. 435–469.
40 See Rashid 2000, p. 112.
41 Luttrell and Robinson 2007; see also Williams 2011.
42 Riedel and Saab 2008, pp. 37–38; Committee on Foreign Relations in the United States Senate 2010.
43 Kone 2017, pp. 53–75.
44 This conversation took place in Afghanistan's Sangin Valley. Fairweather 2014, p. 320.
45 Salzman 2008.
46 See Chapters 10 and 11.
47 Sharma 2009, pp. 33–42.
48 Brookings Institution senior fellow Michael O'Hanlon once assessed that the United States had anywhere from two to ten years of successful counterinsurgency in its history: O'Hanlon 2009. See also Ucko and Engel 2014, pp. 11–22; the work of T. X. Hammes is also useful.
49 Hopkirk 1992, pp. 16–19.
50 Dalrymple 2013, pp. 412–420; Fortescue 2016, pp. 230–235.
51 Fortescue 2016, p. 222.
52 Arrian 3.30.4–5; On honor, see Roisman 2003.
53 Arrian 4.6.6.
54 Curtius 9.3.10.
55 Arrian 4.11.8.

56 Lawrence 1962, c.122 (p. 682).
57 Bolger dedicates an entire chapter to green-on-blue attacks: Bolger 2014, pp. 396–415.
58 Roggio and Lundquist 2017; Whitlock 2021, pp. 213–225.
59 Roggio and Lundquist 2017.
60 The British military's experience in Oman is a useful case study for reflecting on missteps in Iraq and Afghanistan: Barrett 2011, pp. 52–62.
61 Cleveland and Egel 2020, pp. 9–12, 186–194; Summary of the Irregular Warfare Annex to the 2018 National Defense Strategy of the United States 2020, p. 2.
62 Lenczowski 1990.
63 Jeapes 1996, p. 30.
64 Some challenge this decision, but most agree it was the failure to support Kurdish resistance forces in Iraq after the war that proved most damaging: Powell 2003, p. 219, 221; DeYoung 2006, p. 216; Ricks 2007, pp. 4–6.
65 Allison 2012, pp. 60–61.
66 Gail Yoshitani's research examines the relationship between force and power that underpins the Weinberger Doctrine: Yoshitani 2012, pp. xiii–xiv, 131–133.
67 Committee on Foreign Relations in the United States Senate 2009.
68 President Bush and his national security team agreed that the Afghan War would not be a large ground war and would instead rely on small SOF footprints to avoid the image of a foreign invasion. This policy, of course, did not last: Rice 2011, p. 86.
69 For a conversation on the pitfalls of abusing history, see Howard 1961; MacMillan 2008; Barnes 2022 examines how governments see recent events as rudders to the future.
70 Hoffman 2021.
71 Said 1979; Warraq 2007. Warraq is notably critical of Islam and writes under a pen name for fear of his personal safety; see also Burdick and Lederer 1958.
72 Gates 2014, p. 589.
73 Whitlock 2021, pp. 67–76, 215. U.S. Special Operations Command pressured the Pentagon to name Salafi Jihadism as the doctrine behind most extremist groups in 2016, including al-Qaeda and Islamic State: see Scarborough 2016.
74 From 1899 to 1902, U.S. Marines sent to fight an insurgency in the Philippines admitted that they entered the conflict oblivious to the geography, culture, and traditions of the area: Jones 2013, p. 117.
75 In addition to the history of U.S. interventionism in the Philippines, soldiers deployed to North Korea in 1950 were also at an information disadvantage. Fehrenbach 1963, p. 27.
76 Gates admitted that during his tenure leading the Pentagon, critical thinkers were shunned in the White House and Defense Department: Gates 2014, p. 590. This pattern of sidelining regional experts endured. After the Taliban took control of Afghanistan within weeks of the 2021 withdrawal, former U.S. Army Europe commander Lt. Gen. Ben Hodges wrote that a failure to include Pakistan in the Afghan strategy was a result of suppressing or ignoring experts with dissenting views: Hodges 2021. See also Ricks 2007, pp. 42–43, 64–65, 71–73.
77 Hopkirk 1992; Huntington 1996; Grau and Gress 2002; Dalrymple 2013; Fortescue 2016.

78 These knowledge gaps endured despite worthy efforts, such as the Pentagon's Human Terrain System and the Robert Gates-era Minerva Program that funded academic study of the Islamic world: Ackerman 2011; McFate and Laurence 2015; Sims 2015, Sims 2016.
79 For example, lighting the torches after Hephastion's death, as explained in Chapter 10.
80 Mashal and Gibbons-Neff 2018; Coles 2020.
81 This transformation took place over centuries in Iraq, Egypt, Afghanistan, and Iran, but most notably between the late eighteenth century and the decolonization and nationalist period that blossomed after the First World War. As borders were drawn, cities were erected that encroached upon tribal territories and encouraged dependency on the state, which subsequently broke the power of many tribes: Quataert 2000, pp. 118–119, 131; Salzman 2008, pp. 49–100, 175–196.
82 Arrian 4.17.5.
83 Hopkirk 1992; Fortescue 2016.
84 Arrian 1.20.6.
85 Arrian 4.26.1–4.
86 Arrian 2.26.3.
87 Arrian 4.28.1.
88 Alexander was no stranger to this technique. He isolated and starved the Cossaeans in the Zagros Mountains, yet they still declared independence upon his death: Diodorus, 17.111.5–6; Plutarch, *Alexander* 72.3–4.
89 Policies of isolationism under Woodrow Wilson in the United States and Neville Chamberlain in England later gave charge to what some coined 'Vietnam syndrome', or the reluctance to become mired in overseas troubles because of the unpopularity of the Vietnam War.
90 United Nations 2018.
91 There is even a chair of urban warfare studies at the Modern War Institute at the U.S. Military Academy at West Point, headed by U.S. Army veteran Maj. John Spencer.
92 For example, see the Algerian War (1954–1962), NATO's wars in Iraq and Afghanistan (2001–2021), and Russia's 2022 invasion of Ukraine.
93 Megacity warfare studies are somewhat of a spiritual successor to French strategist Roger Trinquier's *Modern Warfare* in 1964 in which he described the advantage of irregular forces in urban areas.
94 Macfarlane 2019.
95 Ukraine's ability to resist Russia's advances in its cities proved formidable: Marson 2022. For additional reading on urban warfare in the twenty-first century, see Rozman 2019, pp. 1–12; Collins and Spencer 2022.
96 Boudali 2007, pp. 4–5.
97 Menon and Rumer 2015, p. 153.
98 Data published by the United Nations High Commissioner for Refugees recorded 7.1 million Ukrainian refugees in Europe as of October 2022, 4.2 million of whom applied for temporary residence in another country. United Nations 2022.
99 Milley made clear that despite advanced technologies, future wars would be as brutal as ever during his May 2022 commencement speech to the graduating class at the U.S. Military Academy at West Point: Milley 2022.

100 Bialik 2017.
101 Total active-duty U.S. military personnel as of 2018 was 1.3 million. The U.S. military presence peaked in Afghanistan in 2011 (82,174) and Iraq in 2007 (218,500): Bialik 2017.
102 As of 2022, the number of trained and untrained full-time U.K. Armed Forces was just under 158,000; see Kirk-Wade 2022, p. 8.
103 Vincent 2020.
104 Arrian 6.11.1–3.
105 Grossman 1995, pp. 149–154.
106 Human Rights Watch 2013; Public Broadcasting System 2008.
107 Gaynor 2020; Bensouda 2020; Philipps 2021.
108 Aikins 2021; Romo 2021.
109 MacMillan 2020, p. 148.
110 MacMillan 2020, p. 150.
111 For instance, the 3rd Brigade Combat Team of the U.S. Army's 10th Mountain Division is known as the 'Spartan Brigade', England's main battle tank post-WWII was the Centurion, and France's Foreign Legion uses a word dating back to ancient Rome's military organization. After the United States Army activated its 11th Airborne Division on 9 June 2022, the unit commissioned an artist to paint a mural in the headquarters building in Alaska. It included a Spartan shield and helmet.
112 Grossman 1995, pp. 44–45, 74.
113 Plutarch, *Alexander*, 70, records a drinking competition hosted by Alexander after the funeral pyre of Calanus that resulted in the deaths of forty-two officers and companions. The winner, Promachus, is said to have drunk twelve quarts of neat wine and died three days later.
114 John Keegan wrote what is perhaps the foremost work on the human toll of war in *Face of Battle*; one study found that more soldiers committed suicide in the United States between 2012 and 2017 than died overseas – by a ratio of three to one. Yet even these numbers might be low: Montgomery 2022.
115 For more on the concept of posttraumatic growth, see Boynton 2008, pp. 69–86.
116 Chief of Staff of the Air Force and Chairman of the Joint Chiefs of Staff nominee Gen. Charles Q. Brown Jr. suggested that casualties and conditions could resemble those of WWII in future wars: Brown 2020.
117 According to Arrian's account of Alexander's speech: Arrian 5.26.4.
118 Translated, Wilfred Owen's poem reads: 'It is sweet and fitting to die for the homeland'.
119 Owen 1921.
120 Lawrence 1962, c.122 (p. 682).
121 For decades, literature that examined emerging military technology has entertained the notion of posthuman wars in which machines do all the fighting. The human nature of war precludes this vision from likely ever becoming a reality. See for instance Shaker and Wise 1988; Coker 2002.
122 Clarke 2004, p. 66; For details on the 1988 Halabja Massacre, see U.S. Department of State 2009; Human Rights Watch 1992.
123 Iraqi security forces raided Chalabi's Baghdad home in May 2004 after U.S. officials accused him of leaking intelligence to Iran. Chalabi denied this, though he admitted to meeting with Iranian intelligence officers: Ricks 2007,

p. 35, 55–57, 388; Gordon and Trainor 2013, p. 157, 270, 473; Mazarr 2019, pp. 34–35, 51, 144, 209–211, 224.
124 Kube, Lee, and De Luce 2022.
125 Biden 2021, Biden 2022.
126 Roth 2022.
127 Scherer 2021; Wong and Buckley 2021.
128 Weapons from Moscow were even seized at Khartoum Airport on 4 September 2021. For additional context, see Ramani 2022.
129 United Nations investigators found mass graves at Bucha and Izium: McLaughlin, Abbasi, and O'Reilly 2022; Human Rights Watch 2022.
130 Kirillova 2022; Troianovski 2022; Ferguson 2022c.
131 Lederer 2022.
132 See Chapter 8 for examples of how technology can lead to greater confusion in war.
133 Post truth and strategic empathy are concepts described by H. R. McMaster in *Battlegrounds*, an excerpt of which he published in *The Atlantic* on 20 May 2020 under the title 'What China Wants'.
134 Malkasian 2020.
135 Kolenda's research on the fallacy of zero-sum victory contributes to this imperative. Nations that adopt an all-or-nothing approach to expeditionary wars more often end up with the latter: Kolenda 2021.
136 According to Arrian, Coenus spoke these words to Alexander at Hydaspes River. Arrian 5.27.9.

Part V

The Human Domain

The final part of this book analyzes Alexander's relationship with his subordinate commanders and his strategic education and grand strategic shortcomings. We place them within the context of similar lessons the western world relearned during its wars in Vietnam, Iraq, and Afghanistan. Alexander's critical flaws were strategic overreach and a failure to identify an heir or train a pupil, thereby turning himself into Macedonia's COG. Drawing lessons from these flaws involve looking at the nature and nurture of strategic thinkers in Alexander's time and our own. We find that western nations tend to assume war changes far more often than it does, which leads governments to make the same conceptual forecasting mistakes in their strategies – only with new weapons and military capabilities. Hubris and overreach are often the result. This intellectual trap bleeds into modern military education and further complicates the process of connecting tactical actions to strategic objectives.

13 Alexander's Generalship

Alexander was a first-rate general, a superb leader of men in the field, and a brilliant strategist and practitioner of psychological warfare. Yet as commander of his troops he suffered two mutinies and committed the blunder of the Gedrosian Desert march, with Arrian claiming the death rate for the latter was worse than all the fighting of the previous decade.[1] Alexander was also a king and a man, but here too he had his failings, not least his pretensions to personal divinity.[2] We can also add a declining popularity with his own people towards the end of his reign as he was an absent king who showed no signs of returning home.[3] All of this is a stark reminder that today's military leaders and policy-makers need to be rational, strategic, diplomatic, informed, and free from delusions of grandeur. Although Alexander as commander, leader, and king often overlap, this chapter focuses on his great generalship.

Maj. Gen. Fuller has this to say on Alexander's strategic and tactical genius:

> Genius is a baffling word. It is neither high talent, nor outstanding intelligence, nor is it the product of learning, or of discipline or training. It is, so it would seem, a creative gift, intuitive and spontaneous in its manifestations, that endows its possessor with a god-like power to achieve ends, which reason can seldom fathom. It is neither capable of analysis or explicable, it is solely demonstrative, and from the very opening of Alexander's reign we are brought face to face with genius in its highest flights.[4]

It would be hard to argue against Fuller's view, as we have seen throughout this book, while the circumstances, benefits, and disadvantages of Alexander the grand strategist are discussed further in Chapter 14.[5] Though we might query the wisdom of acting on the notion that success in anything is predestined, there is no doubt that Alexander had an inherent military genius matched by few commanders after him – Caesar and Napoleon are the obvious examples.[6] Even then, these later – and much older – emulators were not able to eclipse him as he had conquered the Persian Empire and sailed into the Southern (Indian) Ocean by the time he was thirty-one and died shortly before his thirty-third birthday in Babylon in 323.

Alexander as Leader

In his chapter about Alexander's generalship, Fuller returns to the concept of genius, arguing that individual generalship, rather than an army per se, is responsible for victory – he cites Napoleon, who himself singled out Alexander and Asia, Caesar and the Gauls, and Hannibal and the Romans as examples of commanders whose skills brought about victory.[7] If we are to attribute great military victories to brilliant generalship as Napoleon and Fuller insist, then conversely we must interpret failures as a product of poor leadership. Yet we cannot discount the role that Alexander's formidable army played in his successes. This serves as a sobering reminder to those who see permanence in the present world order and its power balance, considering the United States has enjoyed its role as global hegemon for less than half as long as Macedonia remained unbeaten in war, and the emerging dominance of China's potential to disrupt the current order of things.[8]

The Macedonian army was thus Alexander's greatest asset – 'without it, and in spite of his genius, his conquests would be inconceivable', admits Fuller.[9] When we consider Alexander's engagements, from his earlier campaigns in the Balkans in 335 to the great battles and sieges in Asia, we can appreciate how his infantry phalanx and cavalry arms worked together under his tactical direction to overcome enemy forces often far outnumbering his own. At Issus in 333, for example, Darius' army numbered probably 100,000 to 150,000 and Alexander's 40,000, yet at battle's end, and accepting distortions in our sources, the Persians were said to have lost 100,000 infantry and over 10,000 cavalry to Alexander's 500 casualties. At Gaugamela in 331, Persian numbers were probably the same as those at Issus against Alexander's 47,000, but again the king won a decisive victory, losing probably 300 men to the Persians' 40,000.[10] His successes are perhaps not surprising, for it was evident even in his campaigns of 335 that he had 'attained full maturity as a general at a remarkably early age'.[11]

Alexander used cavalry and infantry offensively in a combined arms fashion. His troops moved, like their king, at speed, and obeyed his dangerous and audacious orders without hesitation, often not knowing what he had in mind for he certainly did not have 'a one-size-fits-all approach'.[12] At Gaugamela, Darius staked his strategy on his cavalry and his 200 scythed chariots disrupting the Macedonian formation. But Alexander overcame his cavalry and as the chariots thundered towards his men a trumpet blast rang out; his infantrymen immediately leapt to their left and right with split-second precision, opening gaps in their line through which the chariots raced. Now at the mercy of the Macedonians, their horses and riders were shot and killed from the back and flanks.[13]

We saw a similar tactic used with devastating success against Porus' elephant *corps* at the battle of the Hydaspes River. It is with justification that the battles of Gaugamela and Hydaspes River have been described as Alexander's 'masterpieces'.[14] Like the modern Japanese martial art aikido that allows smaller fighters to manipulate the momentum of larger opponents, rather than meeting force on force, Alexander turned his enemies' apparent strengths against them.

A lesser army could not have maintained the rapidity of movement, distances marched, fighting spirt, and battle order that Alexander expected. In return, he bravely led from the front, deliberately conspicuous to his own and enemy armies, often at his own peril. Thus, at the battle of the Granicus River in 334, he was nearly killed when his helmet was sheared off his head in close combat. He was saved only by the quick action of Cleitus, who sliced off the arm of the Persian Spithridates as he was about to decapitate the king.[15] The same courage was shown in the sieges, especially at Malli in 325, when Alexander raced up scaling ladders to spur on his men and, when the ladders broke behind him, jumped into the enemy midst to fight on, suffering a near fatal wound.[16] These were heroic actions, intentionally on a par with his ancestor Achilles.

Alexander was a great general and leader of men, never expecting them to do or suffer what he was not prepared to do or suffer – arguably the greatest example here was his refusal to drink water during the crossing of the Gedrosian Desert in 325.[17] Likewise in his forced marches, he pushed himself as hard as his troops no matter the harshness of the terrain and climate. For example, in his pursuit of Darius in 330, Alexander marched alongside his men for over ten days across the 200 burning miles of the Great Salt Desert to Rhagae (Rey, south of Tehran); many of his men collapsed from dehydration and heat exhaustion, but Alexander inspired the rest to continue by his own example.[18]

Equally inspiring was that before battles Alexander rode up and down the line calling on some men by name and emphasizing everyone's bravery, mettle, and their role in Macedonia's greatness, thereby exhorting them to fight all the harder despite being outnumbered.[19] He identified with them and even made himself, in effect, one of them, endearing them to him all the more, just as in the modern era troops are fiercely loyal to trusted and competent commanders. In addition, he valued honour as much as bravery, giving his high expectations of honour from himself and from his men a Homeric quality.[20] Yet we cannot overlook that he was guilty of dishonorable acts, of which his cold-blooded killing of the unarmed Cleitus in 328 is an obvious example.

Still, it was his positive attributes that spurred his men to march thousands of miles under him into hostile and increasingly unknown territory, to battle armies far greater than their own, and to endure personal suffering and losses. In Asia, they fought practically every year – often several times in one year – from mere skirmishes to full-scale pitched battles, sieges, and guerilla warfare. We do not know about the troops' experience in the field of course.[21] Attempts have been made to shed light on their battlefield experiences by drawing on those of surviving soldiers and their families of the Vietnam War, but these types of analogies are open to doubt. For one thing, we cannot interview survivors or their families from the ancient world and just because soldiers in more recent eras have been adversely affected by battle does not mean their ancient counterparts were impacted similarly.[22]

Philip refashioned the army for sure, but it was Alexander who led and inspired the troops. To Fuller, Alexander's genius 'gave soul to his army' and bound the troops to him with 'invisible and unbreakable moral ties'.[23] Yet as the king marched eastwards, he began to change as a person and leader, in the process losing the confidence of his army and suffering two mutinies in 326 and 324.

Alexander as Strategist

'Alexander's grasp of strategy stands rightly in place alongside his many attributes as a commander'.[24] When he invaded Asia in 334, his act of throwing a spear into its soil showed he had come to conquer.[25] His entire strategy was anchored in this aim. He was not interested in simply overcoming the Great King, allowing him to retain power, and then returning home covered in military glory – his rejection of Darius' offer of terms when he returned from Egypt proves that.[26] He was solely focused on seizing Persia: anything less was not acceptable. In this respect, his invasion was a far cry from the Gulf War of 1991, when U.S.-led forces successfully repelled the Iraqi Army for its invasion of Kuwait the previous year, yet President George H. W. Bush allowed Saddam Hussein to remain in power, with both local and regional consequences.[27]

To achieve his goal Alexander adhered to the strategic objectives that Clausewitz (influenced by Napoleon) later applied to any type of warfare: overcoming the enemy, seizing all assets, and winning over the people.[28]

He succeeded in the first two, but not the third as we have seen. Folded into these objectives were Clausewitz's strategic principles of using all force at the decisive place and time; launching the maximum force in battle at the points that would bring victory even if it brought disadvantage elsewhere; moving rapidly and not wasting time; using the element of surprise; and ensuring an enemy is pursued or captured.[29] Alexander's successes were thus Clausewitz's principles in action, in particular speed and decisive manoeuvre.

Darius was a more than competent commander and strategist, although it has been said he blundered in trying to defeat Alexander in battle.[30] The Great King's reaction at Issus and Gaugamela may support this view: he was taken aback and chose to flee when Alexander did not attack his flanks as Darius had anticipated but forced his way with daring speed through the Persian centre to attack the Great King and demoralize his army. Still, Darius commanded substantial manpower and had plentiful resources at his disposal: Alexander would have his work cut out for him.

The king's strategy as he marched through Asia was anchored in battling Darius and either killing or capturing him as well as winning over the locals and ensuring he had adequate resources and safe supply lines. To this end, when he first landed on Asian soil in 334, he undertook a rapid campaign to liberate the Greek cities in Asia Minor from Persian rule, earning their goodwill and, equally important, their tribute, which was now paid to him rather than the Great King.[31] In the same year and into the next (333), among other things, he defeated a Persian army at the battle of the Granicus River, successfully besieged Miletus and Halicarnassus, wreaked psychological havoc on his enemy by undoing the Gordian knot, and defeated Darius and his army at Issus in 333.

The following two years saw Alexander take Tyre and Gaza in brilliant sieges, annex Egypt, defeat Darius at Gaugamela, and seize the great palace centres and treasuries of Babylon, Susa, and Persepolis, along the way defeating the satrap Ariobarzanes at the Persian Gates. He had not captured or killed Darius, but by the time Alexander took control of Persepolis that was no longer necessary: the Great King had lost all his support after Gaugamela and was assassinated at Hecatompylus in 330.[32] With him died the Achaemenid dynasty; Alexander had already been calling himself King of Asia, but now there was no doubting that title.

Logistics have been and still are the most daunting challenge of any military campaign, and Alexander was always careful to maintain his supply line. His control of the eastern Mediterranean coastline protected his rear and meant he could receive supplies by ship. But he had a large army of at least 40,000 men under him all the time, together with the personnel needed to look after the men and their arms and armour, not to mention horses for cavalry and pack animals. It would have been impossible for his army to carry its own provisions and water over the thousands of miles he marched, and supplies brought by ship would have taken days to reach him. He must have arranged supply dumps along his route. That would explain his sensible reliance on the Royal Road, from Sardis to Susa, which was well provisioned. Further east, however, there must have been times when he sent out advance parties to collect supplies, maintain communication with them, and set up guards to ensure locals did not loot any of his depots – perhaps even making use of a royal road in the eastern areas of the empire.[33]

In addition, Alexander was quick to learn from his mistakes and adopt a 'once bitten twice shy' approach. He built a new fleet after disbanding his previous one after the siege of Miletus and nearly succumbing to the Persian counter-offensive at sea. Then, rather than chase down Darius after Issus, he moved to control the entire eastern Mediterranean coast down to Egypt, thereby protecting his lines of communication to Greece as he marched deeper into the Persian Empire. The same regard to future rule was evident in his not pursuing Darius after Gaugamela: he realized the Great King was now a spent force, and it was more strategically sound to seize the remaining Persian capitals and their treasuries. This was a rare glimpse of Alexander the restrained general, for once consolidating his gains as his father would have done.

In spite of Alexander's planning, we cannot discount another factor that any general had to have: luck. If, for example, the Macedonians had faltered crossing the Granicus River (or if Mennon's scorched earth policy had been adopted); if Darius had stood his ground at Issus or Gaugamela and rallied his men; if that hidden track had not been revealed to Alexander at the Persian Gates enabling him to move behind his enemy and win the element of surprise; if the Indians had overcome their enemy as they struggled ashore at the Hydaspes River, soaked, tired, and in some disarray, the outcomes of all those battles would potentially have been very different. We can add other episodes, not least Alexander almost dying in close combat at the Granicus River or when he swam in the Cydnus River or in the siege of Malli in India. Alexander was indeed a brilliant strategist – but he was also a lucky one.

Alexander and His Commanders

Luck was also with Alexander when it came to his officers, although he was careful in how he went about choosing them as we have noted elsewhere in this book.[34] He inherited first-class generals such as Antipater, Parmenion, and Cleitus from his father, along with Parmenion's son Philotas, who was commander of the companion cavalry until his demise in the so-called Philotas conspiracy in 330. Parmenion especially proved his mettle many times, most obviously at Gaugamela when the left flank under his command also gave way to a Persian assault, but news of the Great King's flight enabled him to rally his men and push back the Persians for victory.

Although Antipater did not accompany Alexander on campaign, for the king had appointed him deputy hegemon of the League of Corinth, he nevertheless played a pivotal role in the security of the western half of the Macedonian Empire.[35] He provided the king with reinforcements when needed, and always ensured that Greece remained passive, swiftly bringing an end to Agis III of Sparta's abortive war against Macedonian hegemony by defeating and killing the Spartan king in battle in 330.[36] Other officers proved their worth on campaign, like Coenus, who held senior infantry and cavalry ranks, fought in every battle in Asia, and distinguished himself as commander of a cavalry contingent on the Macedonian left at the battle of the Hydaspes River.

Yet Alexander's relations with his senior staff grew strained as his reign progressed, and he often feuded with Philip's former generals even in combat. He did not necessarily follow his officers' advice, as was certainly the case with Parmenion, whom Alexander may have personally disliked despite the general's obvious military prowess. It seems that everything Parmenion advised was disregarded, whether it be waiting to engage the Persian army at Granicus, accepting Darius' offer of money and territory at Tyre, or setting fire to the palace at Persepolis. Sometimes Alexander was right to do so, as after the siege of Miletus when Parmenion wanted to battle the Persian fleet.

Arguably Alexander's view of Parmenion was evidenced at the battle of Gaugamela when the hard-pressed general sent an urgent appeal for help to Alexander. Possibly Alexander did not receive it, or he viewed his own objective to kill or capture Darius as decisive and was therefore willing to sacrifice Parmenion for the greater good of the mission. A commander must make these hard decisions when circumstances demanded it, and at the Granicus River Alexander had no second thoughts about sending Amyntas and his troops across the river as a pawn sacrifice to draw Persian fire away from his line.

A more sinister scenario is that the king ignored Parmenion's message hoping the Persians would kill him, given the tension between the two of them and Parmenion's popularity with the men. Certainly, Parmenion came into ridicule for his vulnerability in the battle. Callisthenes, the court historian and Alexander's mouthpiece, called Parmenion 'lazy and ineffectual because either his courage was marred to an extent by old age or he was jealous and resented the arrogance and display ... of Alexander's power'.[37] Nothing could be further from the truth, as we saw, for Parmenion had been able to regroup his men and save his left flank.

Alexander's increasing paranoia may have led him to view all his senior staff with suspicion, in turn exploiting their personal animosities towards each other to bring about enough divisiveness among them to ensure they never banded together against him.[38] It is with good reason that the contemporary writer Ephippus spoke of those in Alexander's presence towards the end of his life either keeping silent or saying 'only words of good omen, out of fear. For he was a very violent man, with no regard for human life'.[39]

The two major conspiracies (one allegedly involving Philotas and the other of the Pages) against him did not help. Anger at criticisms by the likes of Parmenion and Cleitus over his growing orientalism led to their removal, for once anyone had crossed Alexander personally redemption was all but impossible. From Persepolis Alexander had sent Parmenion to Ecbatana, effectively removing him from court while Alexander chased down Darius. But Parmenion's popularity with the men and the forces at his disposal aroused Alexander's suspicions, and it is possible that he engineered the old general's downfall by implicating him in a conspiracy at Phrada involving his son Philotas in 330 so he could have both put to death.

Likewise, making Cleitus satrap of Bactria removed him from court once Alexander had marched into India. But the drunken quarrel at Maracanda in 328 that led to Alexander murdering Cleitus in an emotional rage robbed Alexander of his satrap and likely influenced his marriage to Roxane to win over her father as satrap. Stepping away from the immediate circumstances of the deaths of Parmenion, Philotas, and Cleitus is the inescapable fact that despite his leadership qualities Alexander had removed – permanently – generals he needed at crucial points of his campaign in hostile Bactria, and mostly for personal reasons. In their place he promoted his boyhood friends, who could not match the years of experience of the Old Guard. Hephaestion, for example, was made co-commander of the companion cavalry on the execution of Philotas, yet Hephaestion's first significant command had been of a hypaspist detachment at Gaugamela, only one year previously.

These men, however, would not rebuke Alexander, which is what the king intended, though not everyone learned this lesson. Coenus' brave and singular defiance of the king in the Hyphasis River mutiny of 326 may have brought about his death.[40] In modern parlance, this process of destabilizing subordinate leaders and institutions is called coup-proofing.[41] We see here that despite his military genius, Alexander's greatest flaws were those involving human emotion and fractured relationships, which are as germane today as they were then. Alexander the leader in the 320s was very different from the one of the 330s; his insatiable ambition 'of ever acquiring fresh territory' rebounded on him.[42]

Problems with Alexander's Generalship

In the end, Alexander is a textbook case of meeting Clausewitz's three strategic principles as mentioned above. All that is, apart from gaining the loyalty of the conquered peoples by appointing locals and his own men to govern satrapies. Still, he had achieved the objectives of the invasion, revenge on the Persian Empire, as endorsed by the League of Corinth.

The march into Central Asia and India casts a shadow over Alexander's victories despite flashes of his genius in battle. True, he needed to hunt down Bessus, who had defiantly called himself Great King when Darius was treacherously killed and who potentially jeopardized the security of the eastern half of Alexander's empire. But once Alexander had achieved the strategic objective of eliminating the threat of Bessus, consolidation of that massive political gain was far from his mind. For the next two years brutal guerilla warfare ensued, as the Macedonians faced a formidable foe in the shape of Spitamenes, who often had Alexander on the back foot. The king's erroneous belief that a defeated enemy was a conquered one came back to haunt him in India. Despite a spectacular victory over Porus at the Hydaspes River, Alexander's disregard of local customs, ignorance of local religions, and massacres of civilian populations, coupled with the unsurprising hatred of a foreign invader, came together in the revolt of India that Bactria quickly joined as Alexander marched back west.

Alexander did live up to Clausewitz's principles of the engagement and the attack, such as moving rapidly, using the element of surprise, and pursuing an enemy, but most tellingly is that once Bessus was captured, any strategic objectives in Central Asia disappeared.[43] Alexander marched eastwards to extend the shadow of his own military glory over those great commanders who came before him, eager to see how far he could get, and to indulge his love of fighting. In the process he lost touch with his men, who showed what they thought of his personal campaigns when they mutinied on him. These personal reasons expose his flaws as a man and a king, thus impacting his generalship.

If there had been no historical Alexander and we were watching a Hollywood movie about a fictitious conqueror, we would surely find all his exploits, victories, bravado, and narrow escapes far-fetched. Even more so when we consider his breathtaking pace and momentum over the thousands of miles he marched – for example the distance from the most westerly

Persian capital, Sardis (Sart in Turkey), to the most easterly, Persepolis (northeast of Shiraz in Iran), is the same as Los Angeles to Chicago; from Shiraz to the Hyphasis (Beas) River in Pakistan is almost as far as London to Athens. But Alexander was no fictional action hero; he was a real person whose actions were larger than life.

His generalship demonstrates his prowess at understanding even modern military constructs of combat operations including mission command; communicating and transportation between his forces; speed of march; and skillful use of information. He invaded Asia in 334 with determination and a clear plan in mind, sweeping all before him in an awesome display of brilliant generalship, speed, and sheer fighting prowess and tenacity. The empire he forged did not survive his death, but thanks to his strategic and tactical skills overcoming impossibly high odds, we can agree with Keegan's comment: 'All or nothing: Alexander played for all, and won'.[44]

Alexander the *Great*?

Alexander's death in 323 ushered in the Hellenistic era, which came to an end only when Rome finally asserted its dominance over the entire Mediterranean and near east with the fall of Egypt in 30. His pioneering campaign opened east to west as never before in terms of trade, communications, social and cultural exchange, and travel, and the period was also one of great artistic, literary, and scientific achievements especially in the intellectual epicenter of the Mediterranean, the Museum and Library at Alexandria.[45] We can say with confidence, then, that Alexander's accomplishments and his influence on the world were great – but great does not always equal better, nor are great achievements concomitant with great men.

The king's death brought about the collapse of the Macedonian Empire that he and his father had worked so hard to craft, and when we compare the legacy of Philip to Alexander, certainly for the kingdom of Macedonia, the differences are striking.[46] On Alexander's death, Roxane was still pregnant, and he had named no successor – when his senior staff crowded around his deathbed at Babylon and asked to whom he was leaving his empire, he apparently said 'to the best'.[47] Of course, each man thought he was the best, and they went on to carve up his empire while paying only lip service to his son Alexander IV (born a few months after his death) and, at the army's insistence, his co-king, Alexander the Great's half-brother, Arrhidaeus, known as Philip III.

The ambitions of the rival generals soon led to warfare between them, during which time the kings were killed and the Argead dynasty ended in 310. When the so-called 'Wars of the Successors' ended in the first quarter of the third century BC, the Hellenistic dynasties of the Ptolemies in Egypt, Seleucids in Syria, and Antigonids in Macedonia were entrenched. There would never be a unified, large-scale Macedonian Empire again.

Alexander is best known throughout history for his genius on the battlefield. He led his men over thousands of miles of enemy territory, won many victories, and established an empire that for its time was unparalleled. As Diodorus remarks, he 'accomplished greater deeds than any, not only of the kings who had lived before him but also of those who were to come later down to our time'.[48] Despite his shortcomings and character flaws – with which modern leaders still struggle – he inspired his men to follow him across inhospitable lands and over freezing mountain passes, until his yearning for personal glory at the cost of everything else finally proved too much. He certainly did defeat his enemies in epic battles and sieges, but he did not conquer them, nor could he impose prolonged economic and political stability, showing that a great conqueror does not necessarily make a great king. His 'greatness' as commander is unassailable, but as ruler and man it is questionable.

How troubling it is, then, that 2,300 years later, the world's free nations often excel in conflict but struggle to negotiate a lasting peace. From ill-conceived grand strategies to a persistent inability to connect military actions to strategic and political objectives, western powers continue to grapple with Alexander's most perplexing challenges, and the complexity of modern geopolitics only adds fuel to the fire.

Alexander's grand strategy, or perhaps more specifically, his deviation from Philip's original vision, provides modern strategists and policy-makers some of antiquity's most instructive lessons. The following chapter discusses these lessons in various modern contexts.

Notes

1 Arrian 6.24.1.
2 Bosworth 1988a, pp. 278–290; Worthington 2014a, pp. 265–269.
3 Worthington 2014a, pp. 300–302. A sign of his unpopularity is that the Macedonian mints at Pella, Amphipolis, and Philippi produced no coins of Alexander after Issus: Bosworth 1988a, pp. 244–245. It speaks volumes that his coinage was struck either personally by him in the east or by his successors for political reasons: Meeus 2009.
4 Fuller 1960, p. 82.
5 See also Lonsdale 2007, especially pp. 45–78, on grand strategy, and see too our Chapter 14. Lonsdale 2007 is really a book about the art of strategy using Alexander as the case study, but Lonsdale's discussion of the king's strategy and tactics, acute observations, and parallels with the modern era make the book essential reading.

6 Generalship: see for example Fuller 1960, pp. 281–305; Burn 1965; Keegan 1987, pp. 13–91; Cartledge 2003, pp. 157–188; Strauss 2003, Lonsdale 2007, pp. 45–158.
7 Fuller 1960, pp. 281–283; Here, Fuller subscribes to Thomas Carlyle's 'great man' theory.
8 Swaine 2021; Jentleson 2021: Hartung 2021 but see now Ferguson 2021f, pp. 48–65.
9 Fuller 1960, p. 292; cf. Lonsdale 2007, p. 137: 'it is difficult to overestimate the significance of having a professional Macedonian core to the army, and the combined-arms approach developed by Alexander and his father'. Further on the army, see Chapter 3, with Fuller 1960; pp. 292–301; Burn 1965, pp. 140–146; Keegan 1987, pp. 33–40; Cartledge 2003, pp. 162–167; Strauss 2003, pp. 142–147; Lonsdale 2007, pp. 37–42 and 136–144.
10 See Hammond 1989b, pp. 57–62, on casualty figures.
11 Cartledge 2003, p. 173. On the military operations as examples of strategy, see too Lonsdale 2007, pp. 79–144.
12 Lonsdale 2007, p. 47, also discussing Alexander' non-military measures in this light: pp. 44–78.
13 Arrian 3.13.5; Curtius 4.15.4.
14 Burn 1965, p. 150, and see Fuller 1960, pp. 147–263; Burn 1965, pp. 146–154; Strauss 2003, on the battles.
15 Diodorus 17.20.1–7, Arrian 1.15.7–8, Curtius 8.1.20, Plutarch, *Alexander* 16.7–11.
16 Arrian 6.9.2–3; Curtius 9.4.30; Justin 12.9.5–13.
17 Aristobulus, *BNJ* 139 F 49a = Arrian 6.24. Leadership here: Fuller 1960, pp. 301–305; cf. Burn 1965, p. 140.
18 Worthington 2014a, pp. 209–210, with references.
19 Iglesias-Zoido 2010; see too Keegan 1987, pp. 54–59, and cf. pp. 44–47.
20 Roisman 2003.
21 Worthington 2014a, pp. 283–288, citing bibliography, on the experience of war and battle.
22 Shay 1994; Tritle 2000. See too Hanson 1989; Rawlings 2007, pp. 203–222.
23 Fuller 1960, pp. 281, 301.
24 Lonsdale 2007, p. 156.
25 Diodorus 17.17.2, with Degen 2019.
26 Diodorus 17.39.1–2; Arrian 2.14; Curtius 4.1.7–14.
27 Locally, minority Iraqi populations that supported the U.S.-led effort to expel Saddam from Kuwait suffered at the hands of a dictator left in power. Saddam was not only shamed for his defeat but also emboldened on the world stage for having survived an encounter with the American military, which became one of the west's justifications for invading Iraq after 9/11 as his brazenness increased: Stoker 2019, pp. 79–80, 113.
28 Clausewitz 1976, p. 121, and see Fuller 1960, pp. 286–287.
29 Clausewitz 1976, pp. 210–211; see also Lonsdale 2007, pp. 108–110, 136–144, on the principles of war and complexity of strategy (not always agreeing with Clausewitz).
30 Nylander 1993; Badian 2000 on Darius' military capabilities. Strauss and Ober 1990, pp. 103–131, are too critical, though they are right to emphasize that the Great King's loss of his subjects' support played into Alexander's hands;

at pp. 124–131, they argue he should have adopted a scorched earth policy to defeat Alexander not relied on pitched battle.
31 Kholod 2013.
32 Diodorus 17.73.3; Arrian 3.21.10; Curtius 8.16–17; Justin 11.15.5, with Worthington 2014a, pp. 209–211.
33 On logistics, see Engels 1978; cf. Borza 1977. Eastern royal road: Briant 2012 (I owe this reference to Nick Sekunda).
34 Cf. Strauss 2003, p. 138. See too Keegan 1987, pp. 40–44 and Roisman (forthcoming).
35 Diodorus 17.17.4–5; on Antipater, cf. Gilley and Worthington 2010, pp. 199–205.
36 Agis' war: Bosworth 1988a, pp. 198–204; Hammond and Walbank 1988, pp. 76–78; Worthington 2014a, pp. 206–208.
37 Callisthenes, *BNJ* 124 F 37 = Plutarch, *Alexander* 33.9–11.
38 Heckel 2009.
39 Ephippus, *BNJ* 126 F 5 = Athenaeus 12.537e.
40 Arrian 6.2.1; Curtius 9.3.20, with Worthington 2014a, pp. 251–253.
41 Rabinowitz and Jargowsky 2018, pp. 322–346.
42 Aristobulus, *BNJ* 139 F 55.
43 Clausewitz 1976, 4.2 (pp. 266–268), 7.2–4 (pp. 634–638).
44 Keegan 1987, p. 44.
45 Hammond 1993b; Burstein 2003, for example.
46 Worthington 2008, pp. 204–208, Worthington 2010c, Worthington 2014a, pp. 302–309.
47 Ptolemy, *BNJ* 138 F 30 = Arrian 7.26.3; see too Diodorus 18.1.4; Justin 12.15–8. On the last words, see Antela-Bernárdez 2011.
48 Diodorus 17.117.5.

14 Alexander's Grand Strategy: Model or Model Failure?

The word 'strategy' has become an overused and often misunderstood term in a fast-paced digital world, where results come quickly, and weapons of war demonstrate a sophistication that lends to allegedly phenomenal capabilities.[1] There is clearly, as previous chapters explored, an enduring relevance of technical, tactical, and cultural factors in Alexander's life, but nowhere are his lessons more germane to a world immersed in information technology than in the realm of strategic theory. Consequently, the political theory of grand strategy has proven even more esoteric despite efforts to promote understanding in academia and senior military service colleges – as authors from Clausewitz to Hew Strachan have couched strategy within a military framework.[2] In his seminal work covering Alexander's generalship, Fuller relied heavily on Clausewitzian and Napoleonic thought to shape his methodology, which in the same way presented strategy as a military construct involving a nexus of combat engagements.[3] Fuller was, however, one of the first to codify the notion of grand strategy as the process by which one employs both military and nonmilitary activities to subdue an opponent. In comparison, B. H. Liddell Hart labeled grand strategy as simply 'war policy' or how policy extends beyond war 'into the subsequent peace', echoing the Aristotelian view that 'peace is the final end of war, and leisure the final end of work'.[4]

Still, the character of war in the time of Clausewitz and Hart led them to tether strategy to, and therefore measure its success or failure by, the waging of what constitutes a conventional war involving a series of engagements. Strategy and its grander political expression, grand strategy, are thereby intertwined in that they both support the political object of peace. More recent grand strategies, such as that envisioned by U.S. diplomat George Kennan and Secretary of State George Marshall to contain the Soviet Union during the Cold War, were designed to keep the peace as much as win a war.[5] Grand strategies must therefore transcend the realm of conflict by addressing periods of long-term strategic competition between states not

DOI: 10.4324/9781003052951-20

at war with each other. Failing to account for this reality is crippling to the development of frameworks that extrapolate utility from past strategic approaches.[6] Grand strategy should be understood more as a means of gaining advantage while deterring or preventing war rather than winning one – wartime strategy and operational plans become an outgrowth of that existing framework.[7] In other words, campaign strategies must be couched within the larger bucket of grand strategy to account for conditions that impact war before its inception and after its termination.

As explained in the previous chapter, Alexander erred in this regard. Though he certainly viewed strategy as more than a matter of battles and subjugated populations, the other elements of his strategy, such as infrastructure development, political warfare, and his marriage to Roxane, were ways of supporting his desired end of absolute military conquest. Indeed, the mass marriage at Susa was an attempt to link Alexander's conquest to long-term political stability, but instead it exposed the fragility of coerced unity after many of the alliances disintegrated.[8] Though Alexander's unifying initiatives may have borne fruit had they had generations to mature, the fact that their legitimacy was tied to his physical presence implies that he rarely imagined his empire beyond the prism of his mortal frame, which certainly does not lend well to a grand strategy. This failure to connect wartime activities to peacetime realties turned his campaign into an endless march as his personal military ambitions outgrew the original grand strategy set into motion by his father to topple the Persian Empire.

This perception of strategy as a military theory may be attributed to the word 'strategy' deriving to some degree from the Greek term *strategos*, meaning 'general'. Kings in Alexander's time were generals also, and thereby responsible for wielding all instruments of national power, to include the implementation of those instruments at war. Implied within the scope of a general's power was the need to devise methods of synchronizing, prioritizing, and applying those various levers of power in a holistic manner that allowed the king to gain or maintain a favorable position over an opponent – a propensity that waned the further east Alexander marched.

Colin S. Gray contributed to the definition of strategy with a more expansive interpretation of its meaning as the glue that holds together the purposeful activities of state by synchronizing political ambition and military activity.[9] His definition calls to mind both the essence and flaws of Alexandrian strategy within the context of modern warfare. Alexander's initial holistic approach transcended whole-of-government efforts into what might be called a whole-of-influence strategy that applied every available resource and not simply those affiliated with government. This is exceptionally relevant to the modern world in which several private corporations hold more capital than some countries, and thereby exert influence over policy and military capability, which makes public–private cooperation essential to crafting viable strategies. Space X and Tesla owner Elon Musk alone is worth more than the GDP of Romania or Portugal, for instance.[10]

Adopting such a wider conceptual lens is necessary if one accepts that Clausewitz's understanding of war as a continuation of policy by other means was in fact an inverse of the reality in which political warfare is ongoing between states whether their individual policies recognize it or not.[11] As American writer and futurist Alvin Toffler once proffered, if you do not have a strategy, then you are part of someone else's.[12] Policy therein becomes a continuation of war by other means.[13] Recognizing that armed conflict existed long before the emergence of monarchies or democracies, and diplomacy for ages was only favored by weaker powers that viewed war as imprudent under current circumstances, this expression holds particular weight.[14] The Athenian orator Demosthenes accused Philip II of using this approach of war by other means while chastising the ecclesia for their indifference toward Philip's advances. Though Athens went to war with Macedonia eventually, Demosthenes once proclaimed that Philip was at war with Athens, but Athens was not at war with him.[15]

Like Adolf Hitler's earlier years in power and more recently the Chinese Communist Party's approach to foreign policy this century, Philip's grand strategy in Greece sought domination primarily by means other than war. In other words, conquest by way of politics as opposed to direct military engagement was favorable when feasible.[16] Devising clever means of leveraging political, economic, legal, and psychological influence to gain advantage and knock an opponent off balance with what Hart called the 'indirect approach' could at times avoid war altogether.[17] Military doctrines and strategic concepts emerging from Russia, China, and the United States, such as integrated deterrence and the theory of three warfares, have been interpreted as embryonic constructs that delay or avoid open war by achieving objectives with other means.

As Hart's claim suggests, however, all strategies are by nature indirect because they are multifaceted, and therefore cannot be defined by or limited to the application of military force. Fuller assessed as much by comparing the indirect nature of Philip's strategy to Hitler's, which both sought to consume an opponent from within before delivering a *coup de grace*.[18] More recently, American defense theorists Brad Roberts and Frank Hoffman framed the notion of strategy as a 'theory of victory' or 'theory of success' whether applied in war or peace.[19] Information warfare, political warfare, and economic warfare are each and all integral facets of grand strategy, but they have no clear alpha or omega. Similarly, under such circumstances, there can be no clear victor or 'post-war' armistice pursued in their aftermath. They are policies that pursue war-like effects, thereby eroding the classical western perception of war as a binary construct that can be turned on or off by formal declarations.

To powers such as China and Russia, foreign policy is war. All foreign affairs are a competition by any means to gain advantage over an opponent in every domain, from information to economic. Policies remain hinged upon manipulation, deception, and disinformation to create a tail-wagging-the-dog effect where the public opinion of democracies becomes the very mechanism through which their powerful governments are controlled.[20] Perhaps then it is the western understanding of what constitutes a war that needs revision if we hope to extract value from Alexander's strategic experience. Clausewitz defined war as a 'duel on a larger scale' involving an 'act of force to compel our enemy to do our will'.[21] Over time, the characteristics of such acts of force have changed, but the words 'compel' and 'will' tell us that war and strategy remain fundamentally human endeavors.

For the purposes of this chapter, it is more accurate and perhaps more helpful to refer to grand strategy as a theory of long-term success that employs or at least considers every available instrument of power. In other words, all strategies are theoretical. John Gaddis suggests, 'the test of a good theory lies in its ability to explain the past, for only if it does can we trust what it may tell us about the future'.[22] The assumptions underpinning any strategic theory can only withstand scrutiny when rooted in historical precedent, a realistic appreciation of the resources at one's disposal, and an understanding of the leader or group toward which the theory is directed. From this perspective, the timeless value of strategy and its grand counterpart should be axiomatic.

Critics who doubt the relevance of grand strategy in liberal democracies tend to highlight past failures or suggest that the scope of grand strategy limits the options available to decision-makers when responding to emerging threats.[23] Notwithstanding these critiques, presidents and prime ministers engage in grand strategy whether they choose to acknowledge so or not. Their vision while on political campaign defines a role for their nation in the world, and, if only loosely, how that role might be achieved during their tenure by exercising the resources at their disposal.

Grand strategy is therefore a theoretical construct for understanding geopolitical realities, forecasting likely conditions, and setting long-term national goals – the basis of political and military interstate competition in Alexander's time as much as any other. Other authors have provided valuable analysis of Alexander's strategic decisions and juxtaposed them with modern judgements – an approach that limits Alexander's enduring utility to *what* he did within the confines of his own theater and character of war.[24] Instead, this chapter seeks to understand *why* Alexander made those decisions and *how* current institutions might develop strategic thinkers who can emulate his successes and avoid his blunders in the pursuit of a better peace.

Alexander the Grand Strategist

Napoleon, Clausewitz, and Hart all studied Alexander because he was a capable one-man grand strategist – capable, not perfect. At any given time, he directed battlefield maneuvers, foraging expeditions, diplomatic engagements, courier letters, satrap deposals, and the distribution of captured treasure simultaneously.[25] Most kings assumed similar responsibilities, but few carried them out while at the frontline of persistent and distant battles for as long as Alexander. In this way, the king demonstrated not only an exquisite eye for combat but also a skill for what modern theorists refer to as strategic competition, where governments pursue objectives against competitors short of conventional war. This style of competing can at times involve conflict through the nuanced manipulation of diplomatic, economic, and informational levers of power.[26] Michael Mazarr submits that developing effective countermeasures to such 'gray zone' strategies is inherently challenging for the United States because the long-term, unwavering effort they require cuts against the mercurial political nature of democratic systems.[27] Luckily for Alexander, he had no such limitations. This kind of sharp power was as much a facet of Alexander's victories as the phalanx – a skill likely passed down by his father, a master of political warfare.[28]

As he waged battles, Alexander commissioned the building of roughly a dozen cities and as many dockyards, including one to connect his supply trains and maintain his fleet as far east as Sogdiana in 325 while returning to Greece.[29] He also demonstrated a profound knowledge of spontaneous engineering by tasking the assembly of various structures that proved decisive during battles and between them.[30] Alexander merged the tactical with the strategic, the military with the political, the economic with the diplomatic along a seamless continuum driven by his grand vision, as we have seen in other chapters. Uniquely, he was also at the point of friction that placed his theories into practice through tactical and operational decisions in battle. The disintegration of his eastern empire after his death despite his brilliant strategic mind is evidence of how complicated the actualization of a grand strategy can be – a reality that has spawned criticism of Alexander's strategic coherence for generations.[31]

The flaws in Alexander's theory were human in nature. Because of this, they are as prevalent today as they were then, made most apparent when viewed through the Clausewitzian lens of ends, ways, and means – the connective tissue of any strategy.[32] Gaddis points out that the theoretical ends of strategy can give life to infinite ambitions. He describes grand strategy as 'the alignment of potentially unlimited aspirations with necessarily limited capabilities'.[33] To account for the limitless nature of ends, strategies must therefore be tied to a nation's inherently finite *means*, consisting of available resources, such as materiel, weapons, personnel, or even the will to fight. Likewise, a nation's *ways*, or the tactics and plans devised by the makers of strategy and wagers of operations, must also support the political end if they are to have any chance of being strategically coherent.

Suffering two mutinies in 326 and 324 is an expression of Alexander's material ways and means not connecting with the desired ends of his strategy. If his aim was to rule all of Asia, he clearly miscalculated the means available (the spirit of his army) and the ways in which he could achieve his political aim – for instance, by simply marching further east and requesting additional reinforcements from Antipater. This misjudgment is also what prompted him to further integrate Asian units into his military, a key point of friction between him and his men. These flawed assumptions in his theory of success were not lost on Curtius, who observed that, at times, 'Alexander's ambition prevailed over reason'.[34] Consequently, the capricious nature of human ambition remains fatal to sound grand strategy.

This penchant notwithstanding, the king's legacy as a great commander and strategist is secure. Alexander is not remembered as great only because he purportedly descended from Zeus or Heracles, or because he inherited a great army from his father, but because he dedicated his life to studying the myriad arts, sciences, and interdisciplinary complexities that support the practice of strategy. By the time he assumed the throne in 336, he showed an understanding of what Lawrence Freedman would describe in 2016 as a fundamental characteristic of strategy: the art of creating power.[35] Alexander's deep knowledge of Asia's geography and the Persian military mind paired with his magnetic personality to exude a confidence that generated degrees of power otherwise unattainable to a less studied general. Granted, as his campaign continued, particularly after taking Persepolis in 330, his prudence diminished.

Still, like the devilishly clever yet mentally unstable Col. Walter Kurtz portrayed by Marlon Brando in Francis Ford Coppola's 1979 film *Apocalypse Now*, Alexander had a gift of 'seeing clearly what there is to be done and doing it directly – quickly'.[36] Kurtz describes what Clausewitz and French military theorists refer to as *coup d'oeil*, an innate strategic vision possessed by figures such as Alexander.³⁷ Translated literally, the term reads *stroke of the eye*, alluding to a rapid glance that awards valuable insight into a given scenario.

Lawrence of Arabia, who saw the relationship between tactics and strategy as a false antithesis, channeled the idea in 1926 when he wrote that 'nine tenths of tactics were certain enough to be teachable in schools; but the irrational tenth was like the kingfisher flashing across the pool, and in it lay the test of generals'.³⁸ Several military theorists and historians of the eighteenth century referred to this skill simply as genius, such as Clausewitz's mentor Gerhard von Scharnhorst, Henry Lloyd, and George Heinrich von Berenhorst.³⁹ Clausewitz even dedicated portions of *On War* to the notion of military genius, explaining *coup d'oeil* as an 'inward eye' capable of recognizing truth in tactical and strategic situations.⁴⁰ Though elements of this gift are likely rooted in hereditary intelligence, Alexander fueled his *coup d'oeil* with best practices that modern leaders can apply in their own lives, which is the focus of this chapter.

Alexander's tutelage under Aristotle may have influenced his views of the outside world and so may be an underappreciated contributing feature of the general's thinking. Philip provided through word and deed enough guidance to instill military competence, yet Alexander's power came not only in the form of soldierly acumen, but rather in his ability to understand and influence people, at times against their own interests! It is here that the value of an academic mentor (Aristotle) as well as a military example (Philip and Leonidas) in the life of a strategist becomes evident, as both had an influence on Alexander's strategic thought. The ability to think deeply, research broadly, and understand the needs and desires of the opposing army was as central to Alexander's success as any weapon or tactic. Without such diverse figures in his life, it is unlikely that he would have developed the mind that fueled his trek across Asia. Modern technology has expanded the world's access to information in unimaginable ways, but by no means has this led to a deeper understanding of, or greater clarity in, matters of war, conflict, and strategy.⁴¹

Alexander's Strategy in Practice

Tyre was a Persian center of gravity because it housed the Phoenician navy, a key weapon in Darius' arsenal. It also served as a logistical hub that connected and supported Egypt and Cyprus, which remained under Persian control.⁴² Pursuing Darius in great number deep into Persia without first severing his naval capability and seizing Tyre would place the Macedonian army at risk. Alexander was also concerned with the potential for Darius to exploit political fault lines between Macedonia, Sparta, and Athens should the Macedonian army bypass Tyre. Arrian claimed that Alexander saw his hold over Athens as fused together more by fear than sympathy.[43] Yet Alexander's knowledge of his opponent's culture, history, and capabilities meant his mind dwelled in the realm of second and third-order effects. According to Arrian, Alexander's grand strategy was articulated simply – as any grand strategy should be – in the form of a question while speaking to his commanders three miles away from the Persian frontline at Gaugamela: 'Who should rule all of Asia?'[44] This inquiry alone meets several of the requisite conditions for a viable grand strategy – specifically that it establishes a role for a nation play and an identity that it seeks to either gain or maintain in relation to the world.

In the same speech, Alexander purportedly made clear that his engagement criteria – where, when, and how he would fight – was not guided by brute military strength but rather by consideration for public perception and Greek opinion. This passage is essential to understanding Alexander's thinking considering the misconception that public opinion or 'optics' in war were of no import to rulers of antiquity with absolute power.[45] Further, the prevalence of information operations and online disinformation campaigns designed to shape public perception in the modern world is often viewed as a relatively new consideration in strategic decision-making. Although other challenges certainly existed, Alexander did dedicate intellectual energy to the notion of perception, or how his actions might be interpreted by friends or exploited by foes. One example is found in him emphasizing this point to his commanders by refusing to conduct a night assault at Gaugamela because it could be construed as acting from a position of weakness, thus dulling the splendor of any potential victory.[46] Arrian explains:

> Alexander was accustomed to taking risks in battle, but he could see that night was treacherous. Moreover, if Darius were again defeated, their stealthy attack by night would excuse him from conceding that he was an inferior leader of inferior troops.[47]

Alexander's victory at Gaugamela in 331 set off a cascade of surrenders and shifting loyalties in his favor, including those of Babylon, Susa, Persepolis, and the Uxians. Along with them came the acquisition of their treasure and troops.[48] When viewed from a functional perspective, Alexander's experience demonstrates three points of interest. The first is his strategic identity or vision for Macedonia's future expressed during his speech at Gaugamela. The second is his strategic mind and the way he went about its development as he matured from student to king, but still failed to mentor a successor capable of stewarding his legacy. The third and final is his tendency to overreach and fall victim to what Alistair Horne described as strategic hubris; when the certainty of his own right to absolute victory became the very factor that prevented it from coming to pass.[49] The following chapter uses these three frameworks as a guide to examining characteristics of the modern strategic environment.

Strategic Identity in the Twenty-First Century

What, then, can leaders take away from Alexander's hard-earned lessons in strategic identity, strategic thought, and strategic humility? The answer to this question is vital, considering literature critical of western strategic literacy has blossomed in the decade since NATO's presence of combat troops in Iraq and Afghanistan began to dwindle.[50] Such analyses reached a climax in August 2021 after the hurried and rather clumsy withdrawal of all American forces from Kabul.[51] While these offerings remain essential to understanding where the western world has been and where its strategies may need to go, many of them adopt a methodological approach that assumes future wars are likely to mirror those of the immediate past. More specifically, they offer prescriptions for strategic ailments related to limited wars and counterinsurgencies since the Korean War (1950) based on the assumption that these conflicts represent a sort of 'new way of war' that will endure throughout the twenty-first century.[52] It is true that so-called irregular wars are ironically more common than conventional ones, but this does not mean they are equally consequential.[53] Because modern democracies have never encountered a large-scale war for which they were well-prepared, they have an obligation to maintain a capability to meet the demands placed upon them by low-intensity conflicts as much as high-intensity warfare. This, of course, is easier said than done.

Gen. George Marshall wrote in his World War I memoirs that because of America's culture and internal politics, it will always pursue a policy of unpreparedness for war that results in poorly trained and poorly equipped militaries at the onset of conflicts once deemed unlikely.[54] More recent studies have reached similar conclusions. In 2014, Antulio Echevarria assessed that America's inherently political way of war means it will always struggle to balance popular support with the force strength and mass required to win wars. This leads to risk averse, incremental approaches to wars that protract their existence and frustrate the realization of strategic objectives.[55] Even the Korean War, arguably the last large-scale conventional ground war in which the United States engaged, was a conflict into which U.S. forces waded with less than optimal preparedness.[56] Western powers such as France and the United States were likewise forced to relearn in this century many discarded counterinsurgency lessons from their twentieth-century Indochina and Vietnam Wars.[57]

Grand strategy, then, is as much about identity as it is policy, beginning with an understanding of the nature of war and the relationship between humanity's propensity for organized violence and a state's role in the world. Because of this relational paradigm, the way a nation goes about interacting with the outside world defines its strategic identity. For most countries, this involves the application of foreign policy through diplomacy, economic exchange, and security cooperation or military operations. The size of the U.S. military and its central role in recent conflicts around the world make it particularly relevant to any study of modern war. A single base in the United States, such as Fort Liberty, North Carolina, is home to more federal employees than the United Kingdom's Army.[58] Because of its primarily foreign means of implementation, the structure and purpose of a nation's military are emblematic of its strategic identity, and by extension its ability to generate desirable effects through deterrence and the application of force or its credible threat.

Despite its varying degrees of intensity, the object of any war remains the same as it was in Alexander's time: the forceful submission of a human opponent and the peaceful transition of governance in war's aftermath. Liddell Hart crystallized this truism in his Aristotelian characterization of grand strategy: 'The object in war is to attain a better peace – even if only from your own point of view'.[59] Hart clarified that if one focuses only on victory, it is likely that any resulting peace will contain the germs of another war.[60] Even Alexander desired such ends for his subjected populations, if only because it was in his interest to prevent insurrection in his acquired territories as he campaigned eastwards and later may have intended to move against Carthage and into the western Mediterranean.

It is important to reiterate that grand strategies are not always tied to a war, which means the terms of victory may vary. Strategy must therefore begin by defining what success looks like broadly to determine how one might approach it through policy and force design. This, as we saw with Alexander, begins with an agreed-upon national identity as hegemon and an army capable of expanding his empire and solidifying his role as the dominant regional power. The question of identity seems opaquer to modern western armies bombarded by the demands of a rapidly changing security environment.

Contemporary research from Barry Posen, Erica Borghard, and Ganesh Sitaraman recommends a grand strategy of restraint or resilience as the solution to what ails the western way of war.[61] But if faced with an act of war from another great power, conservative approaches to defense strategy would quickly become irrelevant. Moreover, grand strategies defined by reductionist theories have been met in the past by enterprising authoritarians who capitalized on such passive approaches. Adolf Hitler's response to European disarmament policies endorsed by the United States in the 1930s or more recently the CCP's remarkable military buildup as the western world focused on 'small wars' in Iraq and Afghanistan come to mind.[62] The unpopularity of these protracted wars in the Middle East and the associated lack of strategic results make a modest approach to the region seem obvious in hindsight. Apart from the most ardent hawks, few would argue in favor of a strategy in which the west remains susceptible to ambiguous, decades-long conflicts against non-state enemies in hyper-religious tribal areas. That said, the future of limited war is not preordained. Given the strategic direction outlined in recent national security documents from Britain, France, and the United States, it is not even the most pressing concern.[63]

As discussed in Chapter 2, the United States declared in 2017 that, for the first time since 2001, countering violent extremist organizations would not be the primary focus of its national security apparatus. The U.S. Marine Corps even vowed to abolish tanks from its formations in 2020, opting for a more agile maritime force augmented with remotely piloted aerial and seaborne crafts and a more robust suite of artillery assets.[64] Similarly, talks are underway in the United Kingdom to remove tank battalions from its army in favor of a lighter military that would exploit emerging technologies and rely heavily on small special operations units to realize its strategies.[65] Building a force tailored for more rapid and less enduring deployments resembles the punitive expeditions Alexander launched near Sogdiana in 325 when Oxicanus failed to send envoys surrendering and declaring fealty.[66] It appears as though the United States and United Kingdom are at an impasse regarding strategic identity, with the former predicting a return to interstate competition between major powers and the latter envisioning a world similar to that described in earlier twenty-first century U.S. defense reviews that focused on violent extremist groups and counterterrorism operations. Authoritarian regimes, however, seem less conflicted.[67]

Autocracies do not necessarily practice better grand strategies than democracies, but they certainly have fewer restrictions on their implementation. Exchanging political leadership every four to eight years in a democracy typically results in the unearthing of the previous administration's priorities.[68] For this reason and others, such as the horrors of war and ongoing nuclear deterrence efforts, since the mid-twentieth century limited war employed as a strategic shaping tool has held a certain appeal and spawned massive expansions of units comprised of small teams that specialize in this type of warfare. In 2001, U.S. Special Operations Command (SOCOM) had 2,900 personnel deployed globally, but by 2010 that number had tripled to 8,700 deployed every week. Roughly eighty percent of these forces operated in U.S. Central Command's Middle East area of responsibility, yet even after SOCOM's missions were reduced there, others simply increased in Europe, Africa, and Asia.[69]

By its nature, low-intensity conflict implies that strong nations can afford to withhold military resources in pursuit of their associated political and military objectives. It follows, then, that the terms of victory are negotiable because those goals are not essential to the survival of the nation choosing to wage limited war.[70] This is precisely what occurred in Afghanistan in 2021. The Taliban did not defeat NATO in a traditional sense – NATO member nations and their constituencies got simply tired of fighting the Taliban. In such grinding wars of attrition, an insurgency must only keep fighting in some capacity to win.

Small or even covert military outfits have been most successful in limited campaigns, which peels back the layers of complexity associated with sending large conventional armies to wage limited wars during the first quarter of the twenty-first century.[71] In essence, the United States chose to fight an unconventional war with conventional forces that were not trained or equipped to do so, and then attempted to adapt to this mismatch under fire. Some analysts and practitioners have acknowledged this by calling on their militaries to boost investments in special operations, technology acquisition programs, and long-range precision munitions.[72] One British Army officer, Col. Denis James, proposed just such a strategy for his Ministry of Defence.[73] As the reader might recall, however, by 2017 some western nations began shifting away from low-intensity conflicts to train for high-intensity war with a peer or near-peer competitor. In such conflicts, mass has its place.

Perhaps the most successful wartime strategy nested within a grand strategy of the last seventy-five years was that of the Gulf War, which gave birth to what is known as the Weinberger–Powell Doctrine. It focused on clear and attainable political objectives, overwhelming combat power, and a well-defined exit strategy.[74] The employment of mass force is of particular interest amid recent calls for leaner militaries augmented with sophisticated technologies. Mass is a sobering challenge for European armies that have on average reduced their tank fleets by sixty-six percent and surface fleets by twenty-five percent between 1999 and 2014.[75]

The danger in building strategies around smaller, specialized militaries geared toward limited conflicts of the near past is three-fold. The first is that such strategies serve as prescriptions for the military ills of recent wars and pay no regard to the reality that nations considered in competition with the west, such as China and Russia, do not share this vision of perpetual limited war. Some of them are in fact maintaining or expanding their conventional formations of infantry, armour, surface and subsurface vessels, and ballistic missile units.[76] Along with these material examples, Beijing and Moscow officials have each released statements regarding both the inevitability of Taiwan's 'return' to the Chinese state and questioning the sovereignty of Russia's neighbors, such as Ukraine, Moldova, and Lithuania.[77] Historical grievances and enduring geopolitical disputes present opportunities to revisionist powers not bound by faddish western predictions of new forms of war supplanting old ones.[78]

The second issue is that such strategies call on a nation to assume a permanent and rather clandestine role as a liminal war-fighting apparatus. This train of thought assumes a great deal that is entirely unknowable by presuming small wars are the future, and therefore small armies are the solution. Descriptions of this philosophy on future war are prevalent in military and foreign policy literature, painting a future rife with non-state-actor conflicts where 'conventional force on force is no longer the way in which warfare is conducted', and powerful opponents 'avoid direct conflict' to achieve global dominance.[79] Michael O'Hanlon found that this way of thinking could be a precarious gamble if such sweeping predictions about the changing character of war prove ill-imagined.[80] Chief of staff of France's armed forces, Gen. Thierry Burkhard, expressed similar concerns in 2021 when he stated that France must 'win the war before the war' by preparing for 'high intensity warfare'.[81] As a result, between 2019 and 2025, France's military intends to experience what its army chief of staff characterized as the 'most important modernization undergone since World War II'.[82] A grand strategy built around the national capacity to fight at least one conventional war can still support various forms of limited war if necessary. The inverse is not true.

Third, building high-tech militaries expands requirements for public–private industry partnerships, and, with that, amplifies their related interdependencies. Security policies of private tech corporations can impact the foreign policies of governments and the general security of their citizens by altering the lens through which the public filters information and therefore casts votes.[83] As these industries become further intertwined, in the interest of their own security, governments may come to rely on the goodwill and cooperation of private entities over which they have little control, such as Amazon, Google, and Microsoft.[84] Satellite constellations and AI programs that support the defense plans of most democracies are examples of such interdependencies. Consumers and stakeholders in private companies have expectations of transparency that feed into the strategic coherence of governments. The already widespread reluctance of certain American private corporations to enter defense contracts is in many ways linked to public opinion.[85] Organizations rely on the business of customers who may be turned away from their products based on the company's military contracts and the associated actions of the said government. This give and take is an inverse of the Cold War's technological environment where government research led to profound breakthroughs in science and technology that benefitted private industry, such as the Internet.

These realities make the deceptively simple task of settling upon a national identity to steer grand strategy more complex in the twenty-first century. Even if a military *should* draw its identity from leaner formations empowered by technological domination, that does not mean that it *can* if that dominance is wed to fashionable conditions in the environment or the obligations of private corporations that serve the interests of a fickle consumer. Yet western militaries can ill afford to settle exclusively on one or the other – conventional mass or unconventional specialization – because as the war in Ukraine has demonstrated, the United States, for one, must be able to teach and support resistance even as its joint force trains for conventional war. Strategic identity, however, is not one dimensional. It must also account for the identities of other nations and how they might expand, contract, or influence one's own theory of success. Strategic empathy thereby becomes a centerpiece of grand strategy, and cultivating this trait requires a passion for learning that is uncommon in the human condition, but present within history's greatest strategists, such as Philip II and Alexander.

As a young teenager Philip II was a hostage in Thebes. There he met and was apparently influenced by the generals Epaminondas and Pelopidas and lived in the house of the politician Pammenes.[86] One might also imagine the many colorful discussions that Alexander likely had with Aristotle while under his tutelage. Mentoring deep strategic thinkers who also possess practical military experience was a priority for political bodies on the Greek peninsula 2,400 years ago. Is it now?

Alexandrian Strategic Education

At the height of the Vietnam War in January 1970, journalist Ward Just asked superintendent of the U.S. Military Academy at West Point, Maj. Gen. Samuel Koster, why the United States had never produced a Clausewitz. 'We're more interested in the "doer" than the thinker', he responded.[87]

One faculty member at the academy confirmed as much, telling Just that there was 'no time to sit and wonder'.[88] Having spent eighteen months as a war correspondent in Vietnam, Just had his doubts about the efficacy of this approach.

Alexander was by all accounts a doer, but he thought just as much. Plutarch tells us that the king was devoted by nature to all kinds of learning and was a lover of books.[89] After particularly long battles, he would retire to his tent, sleeping at times the entire following day and taking time to reflect on his decisions. In certain moments he was filled with contrition for his actions, such as after his treatment of Thebes. In others he surely felt pride, but he thought, nonetheless. It is even likely that he devised clever ways of challenging his thinking and displayed a keen interest in semantic games of critical thought, which recent studies have identified as an essential component of lucid strategic thinking.[90] Plutarch offers one such account of Alexander's critical analysis, when in India the king supposedly captured and questioned ten philosophers who had incited revolt against him, threatening punishment of death for incorrect answers.[91] Of the sixth philosopher Alexander asked how long a man should live, to which he replied: 'Until he has stopped regarding death as better than life'. Their lives were spared.

Although glorification of death in Alexander's time fostered generations of warriors, it did little to promote strategic continuity between those generations if every king adopted an existentialist philosophy. Notions of legacy and remembrance did, however, weigh heavily on Alexander's mind. The inscription on Cyrus' grave asking travelers to not 'grudge me this little earth that covers my body' supposedly had such an impact on Alexander that he had it translated into Greek.[92] The Spartan epitaph at Thermopylae also affected Alexander with its short but biting statement: 'Go tell the Spartans, stranger passing by, that here obedient to their laws we lie'. Despite contemplation of his own mortality, Alexander's reluctance to marry until late in his reign, even against the urgings of his generals, indicates that he became so enthralled with his grand objective that he dedicated insufficient time to thinking about what might happen to his empire upon his passing.[93] Perhaps, then, he did too much.

There has been no shortage of doers in the twenty-first century – some might even say there is a surplus of military things being done all over the world, from Africa to the Indo-Pacific. But the lingering perception that deep thinking is incongruent with the military man or woman appears to be as strong today as it was in 1970.[94] Curiously, this philosophy is a rather nascent phenomenon. With few exceptions, history's greatest military leaders were the product of academic rigor long before their battlefield exploits, and there is no finer example of this than Alexander, who was raised in the shadows of his politically cunning father Philip and his tutor Aristotle.

Alexander exhibited savant-like qualities in the intellectual arena even as a teenager, which he eventually developed into a phenomenal strategic mind by his early twenties. As a reader of Homer and student of history, he could call to mind the geographic details of far-flung regions and their supposed correlating anthropological factors.[95] The wisdom Alexander displayed was not merely a gift from the gods, so to speak, but a result of his work ethic and insatiable hunger for knowledge fed by experienced teachers for years before he took the throne. Aristotle's influence helped transform Alexander into the type of king who traveled with books in his baggage caravan and slept with a copy of the *Iliad* under his pillow.[96] Though they eventually drifted apart, Plutarch tells us that Alexander was closer to Aristotle than his own father Philip, which speaks volumes about Alexander's personality.[97] The worth of an academic mentor to military professionals has not eroded with time.

In 1801, Prussian officer Gerhard von Scharnhorst had already established himself as a respected military theorist when he requested transfer to an instructor position at the Berlin Institute in the Military Sciences for Young Infantry and Cavalry Officers.[98] It was here that he met and began to invest time developing a young lieutenant named Carl von Clausewitz. Over time, Clausewitz evolved from a struggling student to graduate first in his class, which ultimately gave him the confidence to later write *On War*.[99] According to Clausewitz's wife Marie, the world may never have received what is possibly the greatest written work on military theory and strategy if it were not for Scharnhorst's mentorship.[100] When Scharnhorst died of wounds suffered at Lützen in 1813, Clausewitz wrote that he had lost the dearest friend of his life, but more than that, he admitted no person had had a greater influence on his thinking, with the exception of Marie.[101]

Though Clausewitz's name is revered in military circles, he is a man known more for his mind than his method. It is fitting, then, that centuries after Clausewitz's passing, the man who led the Allies to victory as Supreme Commander in World War II lacked frontline combat experience and had yet to command so much as a regiment when the war began.[102] Eisenhower was, however, well-traveled and well-read, purportedly reading *On War* three times, and he had a knack for implementing strategy at the human level instead of simply in the theoretical realm.[103] Gen. George C. Marshall was similarly an iconoclast. The man who reformed the U.S. officer corps as Army Chief of Staff during World War II and later devised the strategy to rebuild Europe, contain the Soviet Union, and ultimately end the Cold War, never commanded in battle but rather dedicated himself to studying policy in his nation's capital.[104] This chain of remarkable strategic leadership was not an undirected process.

Gen. John J. Pershing saw potential in Marshall during the First World War, and thus took a keen interest in his career. Marshall likewise perceived Eisenhower's somewhat dormant abilities and nurtured them, just as Eisenhower later appointed Gen. George Patton commander in Tunisia, who would go on to lead the Third Army to victory across Europe.[105] A sequence of thoughtful stewardship put into motion by mentors and spread across nearly a half-century was linked directly to the Allied victory. The expression coined by George Bernard Shaw, 'he who can, does. He who cannot, teaches', is a contorted paraphrasing of a quote often falsely attributed to Aristotle: 'Those who know, do. Those who understand, teach'.[106] The derision held in some circles towards the academic profession is an outgrowth of the curiously novel philosophy that deep learning should be a peripheral endeavor for military professionals, if not altogether shunned in favor of tactical commands.[107]

Others have more recently captured this disposition through assessments of modern military cultures that venerate tactical experience at the cost of broadening assignments or advanced academics. This is in part a product of the west's relentless military campaign launched against global terrorist groups in 2001.[108] An environment of constant but relatively narrow military activity against non-state actors in the Middle East left little time for reflection on the grander schemes of state competitors and the concomitant effects of technological modernization within their borders. The extent to which this operational environment has influenced the western military mind is only now beginning to reveal itself. Many of the identified shortfalls relate more to a lack of imagination regarding the scope and complexity of tomorrow's challenges than an ability to target and kill today's adversaries. The problems endemic within western military education identified by Maj. Gen. Robert Scales in 2010 have perpetuated despite commendable efforts, such as the U.S. Army's Advanced Strategic Planning and Policy Program or ASP3.[109] Among those issues was a cultural bias toward action rather than reflection that permeated a doer-centric military. The previously mentioned idiom on doing and teaching therefore ignores the fact that doers owe their skill to the wisdom passed off by instructors, many of whom – once doers themselves – took up teaching to prevent others from relearning their hard-earned lessons.

Gen. Eisenhower was a thinker if ever the United States had one. He rose to become one of the most successful generals and presidents in American history. As mentioned above, before taking command in North Africa and later of the Allied invasion of Europe in 1944, he had spent a lifetime on staff or teaching in the classrooms of various military institutions.[110] Gen. Marshall and U.S. diplomat George Kennan, heroes of the Cold War and masterminds of arguably the most successful grand strategy of the last century, never commanded during World War II – Kennan never even wore a uniform.[111] Yet their ideas and policies shaped the western world as we know it today. Half a century later, some derided Gen. Colin Powell as a 'Washington general' who familiarized himself early with strategic thinking in the nation's capital.[112] Yet he rose to become one of the most effective and respected wartime generals in modern history after evicting Saddam Hussein's army from Kuwait.[113] Lt. Gen. H. R. McMaster, whose Ph.D. dissertation grew into the highly acclaimed book *Dereliction of Duty*, was critical of decisions made by senior leaders during the Vietnam War, which, not unlike the actions of a young Marshall, nearly ended his career.[114] Yet he wound up serving as National Security Advisor to President Donald Trump from 2017 to 2018 where he played a central role in shaping the nation's foreign policy toward the looming threat of an ascendent Chinese military power.

Building strategic thinkers with practical experience and placing them where they can have the greatest impact is a problematic system for modern militaries.[115] Contemporary career paths often force soldiers to choose between the identity of warrior or scholar – although some governments pay lip service to those who pursue both on their own terms – but history's greatest strategists were both. Modern military training and career development methodologies have not addressed this sufficiently. In certain instances, these skills can be sharpened in the crucible of combat, but one would have a hard time arguing that Alexander's strategic acumen was any sharper in India than it was in Persia. Perhaps the opposite was true.

Alexander's battlefield triumphs blinded him to the strategic reality of the means at his disposal, cajoling perpetual action when deep thinking and restraint would have better served his interests. The aftermath of Tyre is a prime example of this logical fallacy. Darius made sweeping concessions to Alexander as the siege carried on, offering favorable terms to end the war, but of course the Macedonian denied them.[116] Had Alexander accepted, he could have consolidated his immense gains, reconstituted his forces to form an even larger army, and delivered a death blow to Asia, perhaps never meeting an untimely death or offending his troops to the point of mutiny.

Much like the trap into which Alexander fell, the factors outlined above have dissuaded deep strategic thinking and encouraged action for action's sake. To a rifleman in a firefight this kind of can-do attitude is valuable – elsewhere, it is dangerous. Leaders in modern western militaries frequently spend the entirety of their careers unexposed to the operational or strategic level of war in a major geographic command, joint staff, or academic institution, and instead seek or are wedged into tactical leadership positions that conform to their service's developmental models. Ironically, or perhaps tragically, the use of western military force since at least the late twentieth century has revealed both a mastery of tactics and an inability to connect those actions to a clearly defined and feasible strategic end-state. Though military leaders today are not the architects of grand strategies, they advise their civilian leaders on them and prepare and execute the plans that support them. As numerous western nations shift their focus from insurgencies in the Middle East onto a more nuanced and multifaceted competition with peer states in contested domains, the importance of understanding interstate power dynamics, historical continuities, and strategic shaping through tactical action has become more apparent.[117] This shortcoming has been highlighted by others, but the solutions are complex.[118]

The Russian Federation, for instance, exposes its officers to the strategic environment on an expedited career timeline, but this exposure typically comes at the price of a holistic grasp of tactical integration and the operational art that connects tactics to strategy.[119] Moscow's disastrous 2022 invasion of Ukraine laid bare this shortcoming. For Alexander, his practical combat experience injected a shade of realism into his strategy uncommon among theorists who must infer best practices from the experiences of others only. His upbringing consisting of strenuous historical, geographical, and political study, paired with philosophical debate and military theory, set the foundation for what evolved into one of history's most decisive military minds. Though every soldier cannot be Alexander, a more balanced distribution of these qualities in the development of military leaders, while strengthening the relationship between defense and academia, is sure to narrow the divide between theories that win campaigns and the grand strategies that secure peace in their aftermath.[120]

Alexander's victories, great as they were, also represented the climax of Macedonian power, thus calling into question the grander aspects of his strategy. His success was made possible by a nexus of Macedonian customs that stewarded the profession of leadership and strategic thinking among its leaders. The king's greatest blunder was his failure to invest time in a pupil and thereby pass his wisdom to a successor as Philip, Leonidas, and Aristotle had done with him. As U.S. Lt. Gen. Ronald Clark said in an April 2022 interview, 'there's no such thing as success without successors'.[121] Potential reasons for this shortcoming – the *why* – have been described in these pages, but it is also likely that the exceptional fortune Alexander experienced early in life imbued him with delusions of invincibility, which over time matured into feelings of personal divinity and a belief that success for his army was preordained so long as he remained in command. His brilliant mind, shaped by the experiences of his mentors as much as his own, died with him in 323, leaving only his unborn child and handicapped half-brother as potential heirs.[122] This failure led to the tumultuous years following his death, during which time every potential successor fought to match the influence that Alexander held over his army. None met the challenge.

The Curse of Success

Despite its many forms, a consistent bane of any strategy is its theoretical nature – it seeks to attain some measure of control over future conditions by predicting events, actions, and decisions of others who have crafted their own strategies that remain under constant revision. 'Trend spotting is easy', according to Colin Gray, but it is 'the guessing as to the probable meaning and especially the consequences of trends that is the real challenge'.[123] Lawrence Freedman drives this point home:

> As in the past there will be a stream of speculative scenarios and anxious warnings, along with sudden demands for new thinking in the face of an unexpected development. Whether couched in the language of earnest academic papers, military appreciations or fictional thrillers, these will all be works of imagination. They cannot be anything else because the future is not preordained.[124]

Strategic phenomena therefore frustrate the best laid plans, as the unpredictability of human agency and convergence of the unholy trinity of friction, chance, and uncertainty tend to uproot assumptions.[125] Knowing this, notions of certainty and hubris within the human condition tend to beguile the practice of strategic forecasting. When faced with doubt from his commanders, Alexander offered them a theory of inevitable victory supported by their battlefield triumphs, at times questioning their courage: 'Are you afraid that there are barbarians out there who will finally stop your advance? How so?'[126] In doing this Alexander was defending his theory of victory, but not necessarily a theory of success. Coenus answered the question skillfully by suggesting that the vast scale of Alexander's achievements was reason enough to 'put a limit to the labours we undergo and the dangers we face'.[127] Arrian writes that Coenus further advised his king that, should he insist upon pushing further into Asia, he would 'not find [his army] as ready as they were to meet the dangers, when they have lost their own will for the battle'.¹²⁸ Alexander had many opportunities to halt his campaign victoriously, but he did no such thing. Strategic overreach is an especially intoxicating elixir when taken in the throes of success.

In 2001 and 2003 respectively, the United States achieved its primary objectives in Afghanistan and Iraq within a year. Special operations forces dismantled the Taliban in Afghanistan and incised its al-Qaeda infection with a textbook display of irregular warfare, leaving only the third and final objective at play: preventing the country from becoming a future haven for international terrorists.¹²⁹ In Iraq, coalition forces stormed Baghdad and toppled Saddam's regime in six months, arresting Hussein himself not long after that. Seeking to transition rapidly to stability operations and build a democracy, the United States established a provisional authority and appointed diplomats to lead the effort, even as combat operations continued and insurgencies escalated in both theaters, presenting asymmetric challenges to technologically superior western forces.¹³⁰

As discussed in the Introduction, many leaders viewed the Iraq and Afghanistan campaigns as an opportunity to showcase the state of American military might as a sort of 'science fiction' made reality, not dissimilar to the employment of the AH-64 Apache helicopter and F-117A Night Hawk stealth fighter during the Gulf War.¹³¹ Coalition forces ravaged Saddam's military in 1991 with technology far inferior to that which NATO brought to bear in 2003, which contributed to the theory that western military ways and means were on the cusp of becoming capable of achieving any strategic end. Ironically, it was the Iraqi Army's ability to push Iranian forces back in their bloody decade-long war (1979–1989) that breathed life into plans for annexing Kuwait a mere year after its conclusion.¹³² Saddam Hussein wanted to transform Iraq into the helm of Sunni power in the Middle East. His strategists told him what he wanted to hear and his major offensives against Iran toward the end of the war propped up their favorable assessments.¹³³

Gaddis suggests that many strategic theorists who manage to reach the apex of popular influence are often prisoners of their own preeminence, unable to imagine a future from which their theories are detached.¹³⁴ Alvin Toffler explained this flaw as an abuse of the verb 'will' when anticipating future conditions – as in, wars of the future *will* or *will not* possess certain characteristics.¹³⁵ Just such a phenomenon emerged after the West's triumphant performance in the Cold War and its scattering of Saddam Hussein's forces in Kuwait the following year (1991), prompting a litany of flawed assumptions about the strategic utility of military coercion in the coming century, as described in Chapter 2. These victories promoted increasing confidence in the ability of western governments to control complex situations involving intelligent beings pursuing goals below and above the threshold of declared war. In his account of military failures in Iraq and Afghanistan, Lt. Gen. Daniel Bolger concluded that, in addition to mission creep and a poor understanding of the enemy, it was America's initial successes that undid its progress.[136] Hubris has a way of crippling the most well-crafted grand strategies, which, according to Gaddis, can result in strategic estimates that create nice soundbites but ultimately prove inaccurate.[137]

Both Alexander and Darius were the benefactors of great victories, and so suffered from the advice of ingratiating aides who fed their hubris to the extent they became accustomed to analysis that was pleasing to their ears.[138] Notwithstanding his brilliant military mind, it was Alexander's certainty in his right to rule Asia that ultimately stretched thin his means, and certainty is an emotion that humans tend to feel more often and more intensely than doubt.[139] The curse of success was so potent that Alexander came to perceive as unimaginable any future in which his vision was unattainable. In line with Gaddis' above observation, Alexander was at the pinnacle of strategic achievement and therefore unable to envision a world from which his own theory of victory was detached. In the realm of forecasting, this is a precarious situation.

Today, decision-makers are eager to hear predictions that are pleasing to the ears: the possibility of bloodless wars; the capacity to alter the social and political fabric of ancient peoples in a single generation; the potential to achieve war-like ends without the need to convince a public that there is a steep human cost in doing so; and so forth. Perhaps just as many are eager to believe that these things are, or soon will be, possible through the application of advanced technologies or the right weapons. To an extent, a lack of appreciation for historical tragedy lay at the heart of such fantasies.

Gen. Tommy Franks referred to the 9/11 terrorist attacks as a crease in time; a moment in which the defining characteristics of the future became separated in perpetuity from those of the past.[140] But it was not so much the 2001 attacks on the United States that disrupted a peaceful norm as it was the comparatively tranquil decade prior to those attacks that interrupted an otherwise tragic course of human events. The post-Cold War geopolitical sea change was so striking that it eroded the western world's sense of tragedy almost entirely. This erosion was so profound that in the months leading up to the 9/11 attacks, most Americans could not call to mind a single foreign policy concern.[141] Western strategies took shape amid such a backdrop at the close of the twentieth century, when policy-makers had an unprecedented sense of control over the future. Conflict was viewed as a controllable action through lenses built of logic, science, and reason. But war is anything but; it is messy, unpredictable, violent, illogical, and characterized by human suffering, desperation, and surprise.

The United States, in that respect, has never suffered a defeat that warrants deep reflection on notions such as national identity, purpose, and existential survival. China's century of humiliation beginning with its loss to Britain in the opium wars in 1842 still weighs heavy on the minds of Chairman Xi Jinping and other CCP officials.[142] Germany's failure in 1918 stoked the fires that ultimately spread into the next global conflict some thirty years later. In a different way, Japan's willingness to 'embrace' a truly catastrophic defeat in 1945 was what allowed it to become one of the world's leading technology innovators after centuries of imperial oppression and civil war.[143] In this way it is also hard to overstate the impact of the Soviet Union's demise on Russia's current leaders and their view of the world, many of whom served in government at the time of its fall.[144] But Russia did not lose a conventional war, which made the pill of failure that much harder to swallow for those in power. It is often failure, then, that reveals the clearest grand strategy. Yet after twenty years at war in Afghanistan, the American people and even their military moved on quickly in 2021, thereby missing the opportunity to engage in a substantive national discussion on its broader implications.[145]

Much like the United States, Alexander was never afforded the clarity of a crippling defeat. His early campaigns certainly exhibited glimmers of a brilliant strategic mind, even grand strategic. But numerous factors contributed to Alexander's strategic atrophy – the curse of success, hubris, and advice that placated to his preferences rather than his environment are examples. Each of these is a human flaw to which leaders today remain equally vulnerable. Alexander's success gave way to an insatiable thirst for conquest that he deemed feasible so long as he was the one pursuing that end.

Success breeds confidence. Too much confidence leads to certainty; certainty courts hubris; and hubris is the bedfellow of strategic failure. Alexander knew nothing but success until his final exhale. He therefore had little reason to entertain plans or take deliberate measures to account for the potential failure to see his grand objective to the end. Modern leaders might take note of this. Western experts can make predictions and advise policymakers confidently from a position of safety. In recent memory, the western world's large armies and advanced military technologies have proven sufficient compensators for poor or non-existent strategies against inferior opponents, inasmuch as they have avoided societal collapse in the west.[146] This hypothesis may not be as reliable in the future, especially when contextualized by competition between opponents in possession of similar means, which makes the curse of success even more perilous for western policy-makers. The sting of true defeat is a humbling and therefore clarifying blow with which the modern liberal world order is unfamiliar. If it is not careful, it could fall victim to the Alexandrian curse of success and wade into its next war woefully underprepared to meet the challenges of a major conflict that defies popular assumptions.

Model or Model Failure?

To characterize Alexander as a strategic failure would require disregarding the sources upon which we rely to understand his life and legacy. It would also come as a surprise to those who knew him and to the world he inhabited, including those who wrote of him long after his death, which further demonstrates the profound influence his strategies had on the world he left behind.[147] But it is also true that the Macedonian Empire reached its apex during Alexander's short rule largely because of the army bequeathed to him, and his human flaws led predictably to a post-mortem decline of Macedonian power. If the efficacy of a king's grand strategy should be measured by the stability and strength of his kingdom and not the reach of his name, then there is room to question how the world views Alexander in modern memory. It stands to reason, then, that there is as much to admire about Alexander's strategic acuity as there is to avoid, particularly in the realm of grand strategy. He mastered operational art, but in keeping with Hart's definition of grand strategy as a system that connects wartime actions to favorable peacetime conditions, it was here that Alexander met his match. If a strategy does not account for one's own mortality, it can hardly be considered grand. Edward Luttwak offers insight into this characteristic: 'Brilliant victories at the technical, tactical, operational, or theater-strategic level, or for that matter diplomatic blunders, may have the opposite effect or even remain without consequence in the confluence of grand strategy'.[148]

The power of Alexander's personality became the very glue that held his grand strategy together. As a result, his campaign (military) strategy overshadowed and thus became dislodged from his father's grand strategy to unseat Darius and rule Persia. Liddell Hart characterized this way of thinking as confusing the national object with the military aim, a nod to Clausewitz's analysis of political aims and military objectives.[149] The all-consuming Iraq and Afghanistan wars had a similar narrowing effect on strategic thought in the twenty-first century, as campaign strategy supplanted grand strategy in the western world – a shortfall that the 2017 and 2022 U.S. National Security Strategies aimed to rectify by focusing efforts on a specific challenge in the form of the CCP.[150]

Alexander was the alpha and omega of Macedonian prestige. He was simultaneously its zenith and its twilight, the acme of a generation of grand strategy initiated by his father decades before him. Young, talented, and impetuous, he could not wait for the world to come to him – he would take it. Alexander's tale bolsters the theory that most strategic change is generational. It demands a kind of patience, consistency, and farsightedness uncommon in the human condition even in Alexander's time, but exceedingly rare in a technocratic world accustomed to instant gratification and plagued by attention deficits.[151]

Portable information systems that shrink attention spans and shape global opinions are no longer a first-world phenomenon. Such devices have proliferated widely in the third world, placing further burdens on governments to provide steady streams of evidence to justify a chosen strategy and maintain legitimacy among the international community.[152] These characteristics of the modern world are likely to force societies and by extension their governments to lean toward strategic theories propped up by advanced technologies that promise quick wins in accordance with the culture's trajectory. Regardless of the scope of technological revolution, certain military objectives might demand generational efforts coordinated across multiple administrations and a nexus of successors to make a reality. Other goals could remain unattainable or eventually fail to achieve a better peace in war's aftermath despite incredible advances in a nation's tools of warfare.

Successful grand strategy is rooted in and therefore measured by the chain of human existence on the margins of war – more aptly, the quality of life that any such strategy cultivates and ultimately leaves in its wake. Strategy must revolve around these human elements, depicted in the form of Alexander's three pillars of strategy formulation: identity, consistency, and humility. The enduring value of Alexander's strategic legacy consists of three correlating maxims. First, grand strategy must be driven by a national identity that defines the state's role in relation to the world and lays out clearly the cost deemed acceptable to achieve that vision. The public must accept that cost as part of their social contract with the state. This cost was neither clearly articulated by Alexander nor accepted by his army once apparent. The same is true for America's inter-generational war in the Middle East. Second, if grand strategies are to have any sense of historical perspective, senior leaders and educators should come to view taking on mentors as an obligation and not a burden. Aspiring strategists must likewise seek mentors both inside and outside of their profession, paying special attention to thought leaders in academia. If grand strategy is a generational practice, then limiting strategic wisdom to the current generation or within certain professions is a road map to failure. Third, critical thought, strategic empathy, and humility must always guide the strategic formulation process. Past victories should not factor significantly into theories of future success, as the character of war can change drastically once the fighting begins. Underestimating the will of an opponent to act brazenly often leads to surprise. Ironically, Alexander's refusal to accept counsel that contradicted his own assumptions was one of his downfalls – a flaw that plagues decision-makers of modern governments and their expert advisors all too frequently.[153]

Had Alexander crafted more carefully his grand strategy toward Persia and Asia by recognizing limitations, identifying and mentoring a potential successor, and consolidating his gains after the Siege of Tyre or death of Darius, his grand theory may have become a reality. Even so, the fact that many still debate Alexander's greatness despite his flawless record in battle and stunning rate of march across Asia is proof that grand strategies can fail even during remarkable success. Alexander's strategic experience offers valuable insights that should not be ignored by modern scholars and practitioners, even if those pearls of wisdom never matured over time to a point when Macedonia regained the splendor it enjoyed in the age of Alexander.

Notes

1. Colin Gray suggests that the tendency to misunderstand strategy derives from its conceptual rather than material nature, and the vast number of behaviours and even objects that claim to be strategic: Gray 2015, p. 110.
2. Hal Brands even hosted a program on grand strategy at Duke University in North Carolina. Clausewitz defined strategy as 'the use of engagements for the object of the war'. Clausewitz 1976, 2.1, 3.1 (p. 146, 207).
3. Fuller 1960.
4. Brands 2014, p. 2, drawing on Aristotle, *Politics* 7.15, 1334a11.
5. Kennan's essay became known as 'the long telegram': Kennan 1947; Eisenhower 1965; Roll 2019.
6. Containment and Mutually Assured Destruction theory, for instance: see Gaddis 2012; Brands 2022, pp. 60–74.
7. One of the architects of the 2018 U.S. National Defense Strategy characterizes strategy as a framework, not a master plan, 'for making choices and simplifying a world that would otherwise be bewildering': Colby 2021, p. xi.
8. Diodorus 17.107.6; Arrian 7.4.1–8; Worthington 2014a, pp. 275–277.
9. Gray 2015, p. 23.
10. Elon Musk's estimated worth as of winter 2022 was $245 billion.
11. More specifically, Clausewitz wrote 'that war is simply a continuation of political intercourse, with the addition of other means': Clausewitz 1976, 8.6.B (p. 731); in February 2023, the Pentagon signed its Joint Doctrine Note 1–22, codifying strategic competition as an "infinite" struggle: Joint Doctrine Note 1–22 (February 2023).

12 Toffler was the unofficial progenitor of American futurism, or the formal study of the future and the development of appropriate strategies. This popular but frequently misstated quote is from a 1999 interview: 'But if you don't have a strategy and you rely on agility, you will be permanently reactive and will wind up as part of somebody else's strategy': Toffler, Johnson, and Benningson 1999, pp. 4–10; see also Toffler 1970.
13 This philosophy is an outgrowth of Mao Tse Tung's 1938 proclamation that 'politics is war without bloodshed while war is politics with bloodshed'. Since then, the idea has been paraphrased and used to influence western policies and strategies that tend to prioritize being 'ready' for wars rather than competing aggressively between them. See Ferguson 2021c, Ferguson 2021d.
14 Keegan 1993, p. 3.
15 It is important to mention that Athens went to war with Phillip twice, but Demosthenes' point was that it was too little too late: Trevett 2011, p. 158.
16 The obvious reference here is Sun Tzu's famous but contested allusion to winning without fighting. For an enlightening take on the quote, see Sullivan 2020. For more on the CCP's indirect approach, see O'Hara 2020; Economy 2022.
17 Liddell Hart 1954, pp. 5–6.
18 Fuller 1960, pp. 308–309.
19 Hoffman 2020b, pp. 55–63; Roberts, B. 2020.
20 Ferguson 2020.
21 The opening chapter of *On War* is appropriately titled, 'What is War?' – Clausewitz 1976.
22 Gaddis 2018, p. 10.
23 Brands 2012; Avey, Markowitz, and Reardon 2018, pp. 28–51; Fuchs 2019.
24 For instance, Fuller and Lonsdale provide valuable insight into Alexander's enduring strategic utility in relation to the policies of more modern nations.
25 For instance, in winter 327, while Alexander set up camp in the Indian city of Arigaeum, he tasked Craterus to fortify the city's defences and find volunteers for service, deployed Lagus on a foraging expedition that also served as a scouting mission, and sent the finest cattle seized in battle with the barbarians back to Macedonia to work the farms: Arrian 4.24.6–9, 4.25.4.
26 Collins 2021; see too Kilcullen 2020, pp. 115–164 (liminal warfare derives from the Latin term for 'threshold'), see also limited war and hybrid war.
27 Mazarr 2015, p. 125.
28 Clausewitz defined the 'political object' as the 'original motive' of war, thereby making the application of military force a political act. George Kennan would later define political warfare as 'the employment of all the means at a nation's command, short of war, to impose its national objectives'. See too Clausewitz 1976, 1.11 (p. 90); Kennan 1996; for further insight into measures short of war, see Rid 2020.
29 Arrian 6.15.4; Patala: Arrian 6.18.2. Cities: Fraser 1996 (Alexander founded only nine cities but many military outposts).
30 To scale the walls at the Rock of Chorienes, for instance, Alexander directed the building of a fortification in a ravine while under attack: Arrian: 4.21.1–10.
31 Grainger 2007.
32 Clausewitz 1976, 1.1.23–28 (pp. 98–100); 2.2 (pp. 164–166); Freedman 2013, p. xi.
33 Gaddis 2018, p. 21.

34 Curtius 9.2.12.
35 Freedman 2013, p. xii.
36 Francis Ford Coppola, *Apocalypse Now*. In the film, Kurtz describes his philosophy on war and killing in a note to his son.
37 Clausewitz explores this term in *On War* while describing Napoleon's strategic genius: Clausewitz 1976, 1.3 (pp. 118–120); William Duggan expanded upon the idea in *Napoleon's Glance*: Duggan 2002.
38 Lawrence of Arabia perceived tactics and strategy as more matters of the art and science of war than separate forms of military thought: Lawrence 1962, c.33 (pp. 197, 199).
39 Stoker 2014, p. 263.
40 Clausewitz 1976, 1.3 (p. 118), 8.1 (p. 698).
41 See Chapters 2, 4, 8, and 12 for further examination of this problem.
42 For Clausewitz's definition of a COG, see Clausewitz 1976, 8.4 (pp. 720–721).
43 Arrian 2.17.2.
44 Arrian 2.17.2.
45 A notion made popular in no small part by Machiavelli's conclusion that it is better to be feared than loved because a prince has more control over fear in his subjects: Machiavelli 2014, c.17 (pp. 87–92).
46 Arrian 3.10.1–4.
47 Arrian 3.10.3–4.
48 Arrian 3.14.3.
49 Horne 2015.
50 Ricks 2007; Miller 2010, pp. 26–65; Bolger 2014; Fairweather 2014; Brands 2018, pp. 133–148; Mazarr 2019; Stoker 2019; McFate, S. 2020.
51 Demirjian et al. 2021; Ferguson 2021a; Haas 2021; Jones 2021a; Risch 2022.
52 Boot 2006; McFate, S. 2019; Galeotti 2022; Brose 2020; also see Chapter 2.
53 Boot 2013.
54 Tom Ricks reminded students of this important lesson during his Nimitz Lecture at U. C. Berkeley in 2011. The title of his speech was 'Why our generals were more successful in World War II than in Korea, Vietnam or Iraq/Afghanistan'.
55 Echevarria 2014, pp. 164–173.
56 T. R. Fehrenbach's classic, *This Kind of War*, is required reading for most U.S. military officers, as it demonstrates the profound philosophical disconnect between post-WWII soldiers and those of the North Korean and Chinese armies: Fehrenbach 1963.
57 Metz and Millen 2004.
58 More than 90,000 U.S. service members and civilians are stationed on Fort Liberty, North Carolina, whereas the British Army as of April 2022 was on track to maintain a 73,000 strong force: Kirk-Wade 2022, p. 6.
59 Liddell Hart 1954, p. 353.
60 After NATO spent twenty years killing terrorists in Afghanistan in pursuit of victory, one wonders if Hart's warnings were heeded. The Taliban filled its cabinet with the world's most-wanted extremists, including those aligned with the Pakistan-associated Haqqani Network: Liddel Hart 1954, p. 353.
61 See Posen 2014; Sitaraman 2020; Borghard 2021.
62 Ferguson 2018a, pp. 78–83; Maizland 2020.

63 See Chapter 2 on the 2017 National Security Strategy and 2018 National Defense Strategy. France began pursuing similar reforms: Delaporte 2021; Shurkin 2022.
64 South 2021.
65 Ministry of Defence of the United Kingdom 2021; Carleton-Smith 2021, pp. 13–25.
66 Arrian 6.16.1–2.
67 Tobin 2020.
68 Brands 2014, pp. 12–13.
69 Ellis, Black, and Nobles 2016, pp. 112–114.
70 This crystallizes the arguments of scholars such as Stoker 2019.
71 See Chapter 12 for more on the utility of small forces in limited campaigns.
72 Haynes 2019; Cleveland and Egel 2020; Ferguson 2021c, Ferguson 2021d; Oakley 2021.
73 Col. Denis James of the British Army made such an argument: James 2020.
74 Allison 2012, pp. 60–61, 158–159; Ferguson 2021a.
75 A report from the French Institute for International Relations on mass in the French army released these numbers (Delaporte 2021).
76 Ashley 2019, pp. 23–45; Austin 2021, pp. v–vii, 35–37, 43–96; Ferguson 2021f, pp. 48–65.
77 In September 2022, China's Foreign Minister Wang Yi made clear yet again that 'only when China is fully reunified can there be true peace across the Taiwan Strait': Anthony 2022. See also Putin's 2007 Munich speech, his 2016 Presidential Address to the Federal Assembly, and numerous speeches prior to the 2022 invasion.
78 Hammes 2020, p. 135.
79 As suggested by Col. Denis James: James 2020; for another take on the perils of SOF-centric strategies, see Haynes 2019: The 'myopic use of U.S. special operations forces as a foreign policy "easy button" divorced from the hard work required to make lasting progress toward strategic objectives' precludes national leaders from making a convincing case to the public for the necessity of their use. For predictions on future war being less about 'force-on-force', see Bernsen 2021.
80 O'Hanlon 2000, O'Hanlon 2015, p. 172.
81 Adding to this grim assessment is Gen. Eric Laval who pondered whether France could hold out for even forty-eight hours in a high-intensity conflict: Delaporte 2021.
82 Delaporte 2021.
83 Zegart 2020.
84 Chapter 4 offers further context on these relationships.
85 Wakabayashi and Shane 2018.
86 Hammond 1997b; Worthington 2014a, pp. 27–29.
87 Two months after this interview, a military commission charged Maj. Gen. Koster with failure to obey regulations and dereliction of duty for his role as division commander of the unit that carried out the 1968 *My Lai* massacre: Just 1970, pp. 20–24.
88 Just 1970, p. 31.
89 Plutarch, *Alexander*, 8.
90 Vencil 2020; Coleman 2022.

91 Plutarch, *Alexander*, 64–65.
92 Plutarch, *Alexander*, 69; Arrian 6.29.4–11.
93 This shortcoming recalls Liddell Hart's definition of grand strategy as war policy that extends into the subsequent peace highlighted in the chapter's opening: Liddell Hart 1954, pp. 353–360.
94 The Pentagon's own strategic document recognized this shortcoming in 2018, admitting that U.S. professional military education had 'stagnated' and the development of leaders 'competent in national-level decision-making' demanded broad talent management reforms across the Armed Services involving fellowships and civilian education: Mattis 2018, p. 8.
95 Arrian 2.7.3–4; 2.17.1–5. Alexander forecasted Uxian redoubts based on terrain analysis, enabling him to position Craterus where he made quick work of them, many in their sleep: Arrian 3.17.4–6. For Alexander's purported insights into geography and hydrology, see Arrian 5.26.1–2 and 6.1.2–6.
96 From a young age, Alexander supposedly was fascinated with books and asked clever questions of visiting dignitaries. Plutarch writes that Alexander's copy of the *Iliad* included notes from Aristotle himself. Plutarch, *Alexander*, 8.
97 Plutarch, *Alexander* 8.
98 Stoker 2014, pp. 29–31.
99 Stoker 2014, p. 263.
100 Stoker 2014, p. 30.
101 Stoker 2014, p. 165.
102 Eisenhower, a Lt. Col. in 1940, was handpicked by Gen. Marshall to lead the war in Europe, which saw him promoted to major general by March 1942 and notified of his appointment as Supreme Allied Commander of Operation Overlord (five-star general) by President Roosevelt in early December 1943. Eisenhower 1981, p. 53, 103–110; Ricks 2012, pp. 40–45.
103 Ricks 2012, p. 42.
104 President Roosevelt denied Marshall command of Operation Overlord because he did not feel that he could sleep at ease with Marshall away from Washington: Roll 2019, p. 294. For the Marshall Plan that earned Gen. Marshall a Nobel Peace Prize, see Roll 2019, pp. 478–480.
105 Eisenhower 1981, p. 84.
106 See 'Maxims for Revolutionists' in Shaw 1967. The second quote is likely confused with a paper by Stanford University faculty member Lee S. Shulman entitled, 'Those Who Understand: Knowledge Growth in Teaching': Shulman 1986, pp. 4–11.
107 Joyner 2018; Perez 2018.
108 Dr. Leonard Wong of the U.S. Army War College's Strategic Studies Institute used a now popular analogy to examine this problem by likening the reluctance of officers to broaden their career paths through graduate study or fellowships to a refusal to update one's wardrobe. He attributed the trend to the army's selection preferences for senior officers which, since 1995, had increasingly favored tactical command and staff positions: Wong 2006.
109 Scales 2010; Lushenko 2020; the United Kingdom faces similar challenges: Steve Maguire 2021; see also Brands 2022, pp. 237–253.
110 Eisenhower missed combat in WWI because the War Department wanted him to teach in the United States. By 1939 he was a Lt. Col. serving in the Philippines, but he was promoted to Maj. Gen. on 27 March 1942, and the following

year FDR made him the five-star Supreme Allied Commander: Eisenhower 1981, pp. 38–52, 104–107.
111 President Roosevelt informed Marshall on 23 April 1939 that he would serve as Army Chief of Staff, where he remained throughout the war working mostly out of the capital to reform the army. As Secretary of State, Marshall, along with Kennan, later formulated the initial strategy to contain the Soviet Union: Roll 2019, pp. 121–122; Gaddis 2012.
112 Some saw Colin Powell as a Washington general, but Caspar Weinberger considered his leadership during the Gulf War invaluable and saw Powell as one of the most knowledgeable officers he knew: Weinberger 2001, p. 294; Allison 2012, p. 44; Matthews, J. J. 2008, pp. 231–262.
113 There is much more to be said about the gap between military strategy and grand strategy in the Gulf War. Robert Gates, who was a senior planner in Bush 41's administration at the time (later Secretary of Defense), saw the decision to leave Hussein in power as a strategic mistake. He believed the United States could have removed Saddam without invading Baghdad by arresting him at the surrender site, potentially saving thousands of Iraqi lives: Gates 2014, p. 26.
114 As a captain on the French front in 1917, Marshall once grabbed Gen. Pershing's arm to explain to him in greater detail the challenges his unit faced. Rather than ending his career, Pershing took a keen interest in Marshall's success because of his candor and moral courage: Ricks 2012, pp. 20–21; McMaster 1997.
115 This does not necessarily mean the world needs more strategists, only that more officers need to understand how to connect their tactical actions to their nation's strategic objectives: Milley 2020; Thornhill 2022; Terino Jr. 2021, pp. 101–105.
116 Arrian 2.25.1–3.
117 For shortcomings in liminal warfare, see Kilcullen 2020, pp. 115–166; Cleveland 2020; Ferguson 2022d.
118 David, Acosta, and Krohley 2021.
119 Russian officers such as Valery Gerasimov and Inspector General Makarov advanced from tactical to operational or strategic assignments at a rate approximately three times faster than their American counterparts: Grau and Bartles 2016, pp. 11–12.
120 Building bridges between academia and the military has silently contributed to many successes in recent wars: see De Witte 2020.
121 Lt. Gen. Ronald P. Clark, then commanding general of U.S. Army Central Command, made this statement during an interview with the Association of the United States Army on 20 April 2022.
122 Diodorus 18.1–3; Plutarch, *Eumenes* 3.
123 Gray 2005, p. 38.
124 Freedman 2017, p. 287.
125 As worded by Gray in Gray 1999, p. 41; see also Clausewitz 1976 1.1.28 (p. 101), 1.7 (pp. 138–140); Gray 2014, p. 124; Taleb 2010.
126 Arrian 5.25.6.
127 Arrian 5.27.4.
128 Arrian 5.27.4.

129 The ironically subtitled 2009 book, later turned major motion picture, describes the initial operation to unseat the Taliban and oust al-Qaeda from Afghanistan in 2001: Stanton 2009; see also the Introduction and Chapter 8 for objectives in Afghanistan.
130 The invasion began in March 2003, and coalition forces seized Baghdad by October. The hard work then began.
131 Allison 2012, p. 60.
132 Though according to the UN the war ended in stalemate, Iraq's series of offensives toward the end led to more favorable assessments in Baghdad, which fed the curse of success and ultimately forced Hussein down a path that led to his ousting and execution in 2003: Murray and Woods 2014, pp. 337–338.
133 Georges Sada, an Assyrian Christian and general in the Iraqi Air Force, recorded these observations in his memoirs – a rare public inside account of Saddam's regime: Sada 2006.
134 Gaddis 2018, p. 27.
135 Toffler 1970, pp. 1–6.
136 Bolger 2014, pp. 428–431.
137 Gaddis 2018, pp. 8–10.
138 Darius: Arrian 2.6.3–5 and 3.8.7.
139 For more on this, see Burton 2009; Schultz 2011; Liddell Hart 2019.
140 Franks 2004, p. 539.
141 Brands 2014, p. 148; Brands and Edel 2019, pp. 96–103.
142 Schuman 2020, pp. 241–264; Wang 2020, pp. 38–42; For a western policy analysis perspective, see McMaster 2020a, pp. 89–125.
143 Dower 1999, pp. 536–540.
144 Laqueur 2015; Ostrovsky 2015; Sarotte 2021.
145 Karlin 2022, pp. 1–22.
146 Freedman 2022.
147 Curtius 10.5.17, for example, despite the many reservations he held toward Alexander, writes that upon his death the Persians 'admitted they had never had a worthier ruler'.
148 Luttwak 2001, p. 211.
149 Liddell Hart 1954, pp. 338–352; Clausewitz 1976, 8.6.A (pp. 728–730).
150 See Chapter 2 and Colby 2021.
151 Duffy M. T. 2022.
152 In certain African countries, access to cell phones and Internet is more readily available than running water (Ferguson 2021e).
153 See Bolger 2014, pp. 428–431; Eliot Cohen and T. X. Hammes have also highlighted the failures of senior U.S. leaders to take advice; also see McMaster 1997; Ricks 2007 for numerous examples of policy-makers brushing off sound military advice since the 1960s.

Conclusion

Lt. General H. R. McMaster

American actor Alan Alda once said that our assumptions are windows into the world, and we need to wipe them clean occasionally to let the light in. Michael P. Ferguson and Ian Worthington have done just that. Readers will look through the window of Alexander the Great's military history to view a contemporary world that is uprooting conventions and challenging expectations. In 1992, at the end of the Cold War and as the Soviet Union collapsed, few would have believed predictions that thirty years later Russia would make veiled nuclear threats toward the west while leveling European cities, the size of China's navy would eclipse that of the United States, or a NATO military coalition would withdraw from Afghanistan in self-defeat after fighting the Taliban for two decades.

In the 1990s, after victory in the Cold War and a lopsided victory over Saddam Hussein's Iraq in a hot war, three fundamentally flawed assumptions clouded windows through which we surveyed the future. First, that an arc of history guaranteed the primacy of free and open societies over authoritarian and closed societies. The expansion of liberal democracy was inevitable. Second, that the old rules of international relations and competition were no longer relevant. Global governance and a great power condominium would displace great power rivalry. And third, that America's unmatched military prowess would guarantee 'full-spectrum dominance' over any potential enemy. Military competition was over. The western world seemed to be in a position of terminal advantage in political influence, cultural allure, and military power. The history of Alexander and the history of recent decades demonstrate that the present can have a charm of permanence that is dangerously intoxicating to great powers.

As the United States fights off the hangover from the post-Cold War unipolar moment and competes with revanchist authoritarian powers China and Russia, leaders should reflect on the historical observations the authors make in *The Military Legacy of Alexander the Great*. The authors demonstrate that the history of the ancient world can inform our understanding of the present and help us make projections into the future. Their analysis highlights continuities in human nature and the nature of war. And it reveals that the greatest challenges leaders face are agnostic to time and technology. Those include the need to cope with uncertainty, establish trust between political and military leaders, connect tactical actions to strategic objectives, develop cultural understanding, and ensure that the desired end in war is consistent with the means employed.

Whether or not one agrees with all of the authors' conclusions, this book provides a valuable example of how to use historical inquiry to think about contemporary challenges. In recent decades, preoccupation with technological change and neglect of continuities have undermined our strategic competence. This is a book to be read and debated because the stakes are too high for its lessons to lie inert within its cover.

Finally, *The Military Legacy of Alexander the Great* is an argument for the reinvigoration of history in higher level education. Many universities do not teach military and diplomatic history or teach it only in relation to social history. After the Vietnam War, many gave into the anti-war movement's tendency to confuse the study of war with militarism. But thinking clearly about the problems of diplomacy, national security, and defense, however, is both a necessity and the best way to prevent war. The analogy drawn by the late historian Dennis Showalter is apt: no one would ever accuse an oncologist of being an advocate for the disease he or she studies. Moreover, many courses in diplomatic and military history have been displaced by theory-based international relations courses that tend to mask the complex causality of events and obscure the profound cultural, psychological, social, and economic elements that distinguish cases from one another. Theories encourage students to force complex problem sets into frameworks that create only the illusion of understanding.

Thus, the story of Alexander reveals that the study of history is an exercise in humility that allows for a clearer understanding of our world today when viewed through the window of his vices and virtues. Hubris, jealousy, and pride continue to haunt humanity in this century as much as they did Alexander. Learning from his reign can thereby help modern leaders navigate these flaws, if they are willing to listen.

Bibliography

Alexander the Great

Abed Al-Jabouri, N. and S. Jensen, 'The Iraqi and AQI Roles in the Sunni Awakening', *PRISM* 2, no. 1 (December 2010), pp. 3–18

Adams, W.L., 'The Episode of Philotas: An Insight', in W. Heckel and L. Tritle (eds.), *Crossroads of History, the Age of Alexander* (Claremont, CA: 2003), pp. 113–126

Allen, L., *The Persian Empire* (Chicago, IL: 2005)

Anson, E.M., 'Macedonia's Alleged Constitutionalism', *CJ* 80 (1985a), pp. 303–316

Anson, E.M., 'The Hypaspists: Macedonia's Professional Citizen-Soldiers', *Historia* 34 (1985b), pp. 246–248

Anson, E.M., 'The Evolution of the Macedonian Army Assembly (330–315)', *Historia* 40 (1991), pp. 230–247

Anson, E.M., 'The Introduction of the Sarisa in Macedonian Warfare', *Ancient Society* 40 (2010), pp. 51–68

Anson, E.M., *Alexander's Heirs: The Age of the Successors* (Malden: 2014)

Anson, E.M., 'Counter-Insurgency: The Lesson of Alexander the Great', in T. Howe, E. Garvin and G. Wrightson (eds.), *Greece. Macedon and Persia: Studies in Social, Political and Military History in Honour of Waldemar Heckel* (Philadelphia, PA: 2015), pp. 94–106

Antela-Bernárdez, B., 'Simply the Best: Alexander's Last Words and the Macedonian Kingship', *Eirene* 47 (2011), pp. 118–126

Ashley, J.R., *The Macedonian Empire: The Era of Warfare Under Philip II and Alexander the Great, 359–323 B.C.* (Jefferson, NC: 1998)

Aymard, A., 'Philippe II de Macedoine otage à Thébes', *REA* 56 (1954), pp. 15–36

Badian, E., 'Alexander the Great and the Unity of Mankind', *Historia* 7 (1958), pp. 425–444

Badian, E., 'The Death of Parmenio', *TAPhA* 91 (1960), pp. 324–338

Badian, E., 'Alexander the Great and the Loneliness of Power', in E. Badian (ed.), *Studies in Greek and Roman History* (Oxford: 1964), pp. 192–205

Badian, E., 'The Administration of the Empire', *G&R*^{2} 12 (1965), pp. 166–182

Badian, E., 'Alexander the Great and the Greeks of Asia', in E. Badian (ed.), *Ancient Society and Institutions: Studies Presented to V. Ehrenberg on his 75th Birthday* (Oxford: 1966), pp. 37–69

Badian, E., 'A King's Notebooks', *HSCPh* 72 (1967), pp. 183–204

Badian, E., 'The Battle of the Granicus: A New Look', in *Ancient Macedonia 2* (Institute for Balkan Studies, Thessaloniki: 1977), pp. 271–293

Badian, E., 'Alexander the Great and the Scientific Exploration of the Oriental Part of His Empire', *Ancient Society* 22 (1991), pp. 127–138

Badian, E., 'Conspiracies', in A.B. Bosworth and E. Baynham (eds.), *Alexander the Great in Fact and Fiction* (Oxford: 1996), pp. 60–92

Badian, E., 'Darius III', *HSCPh* 100 (2000), pp. 241–268

Baynham, E., 'Why Didn't Alexander Marry a Nice Macedonian Girl Before Leaving Home? Observations on Factional Politics at Alexander's Court in 336–334 BC', in T. Hillard (ed.), *Ancient History in a Modern University 1* (Sydney: 1997), pp. 148–155

Baynham, E., *The Unique History of Quintus Curtius Rufus* (Ann Arbor, MI: 1998)

Bennett, B. and M. Roberts, *The Wars of Alexander's Successors, 323–281 BC 1–2* (Barnsley: 2008–2009)

Bhandare, S., 'Not Just a Pretty Face: Interpretations of Alexander's Numismatic Legacy in the Hellenistic East', in H.P. Ray and D.T. Potts (eds.), *Memory as History, the Legacy of Alexander in Asia* (New Delhi: 2007), pp. 208–256

Bloedow, E.F., 'The Siege of Tyre in 332 BC: Alexander at the Crossroads in His Career', *La Parola del Passato* 301 (1990), pp. 255–293

Bloedow, E.F., 'Alexander the Great and Bactria', *PP* 46 (1991), pp. 44–80

Boot, M., *Invisible Armies: An Epic History of Guerrilla Warfare from Ancient Times to the Present* (New York, NY: 2013)

Borza, E.N., 'Fire from Heaven: Alexander at Persepolis', *CPh* 67 (1972), pp. 233–245

Borza, E.N., 'Alexander's Communications', *Ancient Macedonia 2* (Institute for Balkan Studies, Thessaloniki: 1977), pp. 295–303

Borza, E.N., 'Anaxagoras and Callisthenes: Academic Intrigue at Alexander's Court', in H.J. Dell (ed.), *Ancient Macedonian Studies in Honour of C.F. Edson* (Thessaloniki: 1981), pp. 73–86

Borza, E.N., 'Ethnicity and Cultural Policy at Alexander's Court', *Ancient World* 22 (1991), pp. 21–25

Bosworth, A.B., 'The Death of Alexander the Great: Rumour and Propaganda', *CQ^2* 21 (1971), pp. 112–136

Bosworth, A.B. 'Alexander and the Iranians', *JHS* 100 (1980), pp. 1–21

Bosworth, A.B., 'A Missing Year in the History of Alexander the Great', *JHS* 101 (1981), pp. 17–39.

Bosworth, A.B., 'The Location of Alexander's Campaign Against the Illyrians in 335 B.C.', in B. Barr-Sharrar and E.N. Borza (eds.), *Macedonia and Greece in Late Classical and Early Hellenistic Times* (Washington, DC: 1982), pp. 74–84

Bosworth, A.B., 'The Indian Satrapies under Alexander the Great', *Antichthon* 17 (1983), pp. 37–46

Bosworth, A.B., *Conquest and Empire: The Reign of Alexander the Great* (Cambridge: 1988a)

Bosworth, A.B., *From Arrian to Alexander* (Oxford: 1988b)

Bosworth, A.B., *Alexander and the East: The Tragedy of Triumph* (Oxford: 1996a)

Bosworth, A.B., 'The Tumult and the Shouting: Two Interpretations of the Cleitus Episode', *AHB* 10 (1996b), pp. 19–30

Bosworth, A.B., 'Alexander, Euripides and Dionysos: The Motivation for Apotheosis', in R.W. Wallace and E.M. Harris (eds.), *Transitions to Empire: Essays in Honor of E. Badian* (Norman, OK: 1996c), pp. 140–166

Bosworth, A.B., 'Calanus and the Brahman Opposition', in W. Will (ed.), *Alexander der Grosse: Eine Welteroberung und ihr Hintergrund* (Bonn: 1998), pp. 173–203

Bosworth, A.B., 'Ptolemy and the Will of Alexander', in A.B. Bosworth and E.J. Baynham (eds.), *Alexander the Great in Fact and Fiction* (Oxford: 2000), pp. 207–241

Bosworth, A.B., *The Legacy of Alexander: Politics, Warfare and Propaganda Under the Successors* (Oxford: 2002)

Bosworth, A.B., 'The Indian Campaigns, 327–325 BC', in J. Roisman (ed.), *Brill's Companion to Alexander the Great* (Leiden: 2003), pp. 59–68

Bowden, H., 'On Kissing and Making Up: Court Protocol and Historiography in Alexander the Great's "Experiment with Proskynesis"', *BICS* 56 (2013), pp. 55–77

Briant, P., *From Cyrus to Alexander: A History of the Persian Empire*, trans. P.T. Daniels (Philadelphia, PA: 2002)

Briant, P., *Alexander the Great and His Empire*, trans. A. Kuhrt (Princeton, NJ: 2010)

Briant, P., 'From the Indus to the Mediterranean Sea: The Administrative Organization and Logistics of the Great Roads of the Achaemenid Empire', in S.A. Alcock, J. Boden and R.J.A. Talbert (eds.), *Highways, Byways, and Road Systems in the Pre-Modern World* (London: 2012), pp. 185–201

Briant, P., *Darius in the Shadow of Alexander*, trans. J.M. Todd (Cambridge: 2015)

Brosius, M., 'Alexander and the Persians', in J. Roisman (ed.), *Brill's Companion to Alexander the Great* (Leiden: 2003), pp. 169–193

Brosius, M., *A History of Ancient Persia: The Achaemenid Empire* (Malden: 2020)

Brunt, P.A., 'Alexander's Macedonian Cavalry', *JHS* 83 (1963), pp. 28–32

Brunt, P.A., 'The Aims of Alexander', *G&R*^{2} 12 (1965), pp. 205–215

Brunt, P.A., *Arrian, History of Alexander*, Loeb Classical Library, 2 vols. (Cambridge: 1976 and 1983)

Burn, A.R., 'The Generalship of Alexander', *G&R*^{2} 12 (1965), pp. 140–154

Burstein, S.M., 'Pharaoh Alexander: A Scholarly Myth', *Ancient Society* 22 (1991), pp. 139–145

Burstein, S., 'The Legacy of Alexander: New Ways of Being Greek in the Hellenistic Period', in W. Heckel and L.A. Tritle (eds.), *Crossroads of History: The Age of Alexander* (Claremont, CA: 2003), pp. 217–242

Carney, E., 'The Conspiracy of Hermolaus', *CJ* 76 (1980), pp. 223–231

Carney, E., 'The Death of Clitus', *GRBS* 22 (1981), pp. 149–160

Carney, E.D., 'Macedonians and Mutiny: Discipline and Indiscipline in the Army of Philip and Alexander', *CPh* 91 (1996), pp. 19–44

Carney, E., 'The Role of the *Basilikoi Paides* at the Argead Court', in T. Howe and J. Reames (eds.), *Macedonian Legacies: Studies in Ancient Macedonian History and Culture in Honor of Eugene N. Borza* (Claremont, CA: 2008) pp. 145–164

Carney, E.D., 'Women and Symposia in Macedonia', in T. Howe, E.E. Garvin and G. Wrightson (eds.), *Greece, Macedon, and Persia. Studies in Social, Political, and Military History in Honour of Waldemar Heckel* (Philadelphia, PA: 2015), pp. 33–40

Cartledge, P., *Alexander the Great: The Hunt for a New Past* (London: 2003)

Cawkwell, G.L., *Philip of Macedon* (London: 1978)
Cawkwell, G.L., The End of Greek Liberty', in R.W. Wallace and E.M. Harris (eds.), *Transitions to Empire: Essays in Honor of E. Badian* (Norman, OK: 1996), pp. 98–121
Charles, M., 'Elephants, Alexander and the Indian Campaign', *Mouseion* 10 (2010), pp. 327–353
Christesen, P. and S.C. Murray, 'Macedonian Religion', in J. Roisman and Ian Worthington (eds.), *A Companion to Ancient Macedonia* (Malden: 2010), pp. 428–445
Chugg, A., 'The Journal of Alexander the Great', *AHB* 19 (2005), pp. 155–175
Cloché, P., *Histoire de la Macedoine jusqu' à l'avènement d'Alexandre le Grand* (Paris: 1960)
Cohen, A., *The Alexander Mosaic: Stories of Victory and Defeat* (Cambridge: 1997)
Collins, A., 'Alexander's Visit to Siwah: A New Analysis', *Phoenix* 68 (2014), pp. 62–77
Dahmen, K., *The Legend of Alexander the Great on Greek and Roman Coins* (London: 2007)
Dandamaev, M., *A Political History of the Achaemenid Empire* (Leiden: 1989)
Daskalakis, A., *The Hellenism of the Ancient Macedonians* (Thessaloniki: 1965)
Degen, J., 'Alexander III., Dareios I., und das speererworbere Land (Diod. 17,17,2)', *Journal of Ancient Near Eastern History* 6 (2019), pp. 53–95
Depuydt, L., 'The Time of Death of Alexander the Great: 11 June 323 B.C. (-322), ca. 4:00-5:00 PM', *Die Welt des Orients* 28 (1997), pp. 117–135
Devine, A.M., 'Grand Tactics at Gaugamela', *Phoenix* 29 (1975), pp. 374–385
Devine, A.M., 'The Strategies of Alexander the Great and Darius III in the Issus Campaign (333 BC)', *Ancient World* 12 (1985a), pp. 25–38
Devine, A.M., 'Grand Tactics at the Battle of Issus', *Ancient World* 12 (1985b) pp. 39–59
Devine, A.M., 'Demythologizing the Battle of the Granicus', *Phoenix* 40 (1986a), pp. 265–278
Devine, A.M., 'The Battle of Gaugamela: A Tactical and Source-Critical Study', *Ancient World* 13 (1986b), pp. 87–115
Devine, A.M. 'The Battle of Hydaspes; A Tactical and Source-Critical Study', *Ancient World* 16 (1987), pp. 91–113
Devine, A.M., 'A Pawn-Sacrifice at the Battle of the Granicus: The Origins of a Favorite Stratagem of Alexander the Great', *Ancient World* 18 (1988), pp. 3–20
Devine, A.M., 'Alexander the Great', in J. Hackett (ed.), *Warfare in the Ancient World* (New York: 1989a), pp. 104–129
Devine, A.M., 'The Macedonian Army at Gaugamela: Its Strength and the Length of Its Battle-Line', *Ancient World* 19 (1989b), pp. 77–80
Dobbins, K.M., 'Alexander's Eastern Satrapies', *Persica* 11 (1984), pp. 74–108
Dmitriev, S., 'Alexander's Exile's Decree', *Klio* 86 (2004), pp. 348–381
Dreyer, B., 'Heroes, Cults, and Divinity', in W. Heckel and L. Tritle (eds.), *Alexander the Great: A New History* (Malden: 2009), pp. 218–234
Ehrenberg, V., *Alexander and the Greeks* (Oxford: 1938)
Ellis, J.R., *Philip II and Macedonian Imperialism* (London: 1976)
Ellis, J.R., 'The First Months of Alexander's Reign', in B. Barr-Sharrar and E.N. Borza (eds.), *Macedonia and Greece in Late Classical and Early Hellenistic Times* (Washington, DC: 1982), pp. 69–73

Engels, D., *Alexander the Great and the Logistics of the Macedonian Army* (Berkeley and Los Angeles, CA: 1978)

Engels, J., 'Macedonians and Greeks', in J. Roisman and Ian Worthington (eds.), *A Companion to Ancient Macedonia* (Malden: 2010), pp. 81–98

English, S., *The Army of Alexander the Great* (Barnsley: 2009a)

English, S., *The Sieges of Alexander the Great* (Barnsley: 2009b)

English, S., *The Field Campaigns of Alexander the Great* (Barnsley: 2011)

Errington, R.M., 'The Nature of the Macedonian State Under the Monarchy', *Chiron* 8 (1978), pp. 77–133

Errington, R.M., *A History of Macedonia*, trans. C. Errington (Berkeley and Los Angeles, CA: 1990)

Faraguna, M., 'Alexander and the Greeks', in J. Roisman (ed.), *Brill's Companion to Alexander the Great* (Leiden: 2003), pp. 99–130

Ferguson, M.P., 'The Taliban Didn't Change – It Adapted to the (Dis)Information Age', *The Hill*, 27 September 2021, https://thehill.com/opinion/technology/574025-the-taliban-didnt-change-it-adapted-to-the-disinformation-age

Ferguson, M., 'Strategic Imperative: A Competitive Framework for US-Sino Relations', *Strategic Studies Quarterly* 15 (2021), pp. 48–68

Finn, J., 'Alexander's Return of the Tyrannicide Statues to Athens', *Historia* 63 (2014), pp. 385–403

Fraser, P., *Cities of Alexander the Great* (Oxford: 1996)

Fredricksmeyer, E.A., 'Alexander, Midas, and the Oracle at Gordium', *CPh* 56 (1961), pp. 160–168

Fredricksmeyer, E.A., 'On the Final Aims of Philip II', in W.L. Adams and E.N. Borza (eds.), *Philip II, Alexander the Great, and the Macedonian Heritage* (Lanham, MD: 1982), pp. 85–98

Fredricksmeyer, E.A., 'Alexander and Philip: Emulation and Resentment', *CJ* 85 (1990), pp. 300–315

Fredricksmeyer, E.A., 'Alexander the Great and the Kingship of Asia', in A.B. Bosworth and E.J. Baynham (eds.), *Alexander the Great in Fact and Fiction* (Oxford: 2000), pp. 136–166

Fredricksmeyer, E.A., 'Alexander's Religion and Divinity', in J. Roisman (ed.), *Brill's Companion to Alexander the Great* (Leiden: 2003), pp. 253–278

Frei, P., 'Der Wagen von Gordion', *Museum Helveticum* 29 (1972), pp. 110–123

Fuller, J.F.C., *The Generalship of Alexander the Great* (repr. New Brunswick, NJ: 1960)

Gabriel, R.A., *Philip II of Macedon: Greater than Alexander* (Washington, DC: 2010)

Garlan, Y., *Recherches de poliorcétique grecque* (Paris: 1974)

Gilley, D. and I. Worthington, 'Alexander the Great, Macedonia and Asia', in J. Roisman and I. Worthington (eds.), *A Companion to Ancient Macedonia* (Malden: 2010), pp. 186–207

Golan, D., 'The Fate of a Court Historian: Callisthenes', *Athenaeum* 66 (1988), pp. 99–120

Grainger, J., *Alexander the Great Failure: The Collapse of the Macedonian Empire* (London: 2007)

Green, P., *Alexander of Macedon* (Harmondsworth: 1974)

Greenwalt, W.S., 'Polygamy and Succession in Argead Macedonia', *Arethusa* 22 (1989), pp. 19–45
Griffith, G.T., 'Alexander's Generalship at Gaugamela', *JHS* 67 (1947), pp. 77–89
Hamilton, J.R., 'Alexander and His "So-Called" Father', *CQ*² 3 (1953), pp. 151–157
Hammond, N.G.L., *A History of Macedonia 1* (Oxford: 1972)
Hammond, N.G.L., 'Alexander's Campaign in Illyria', *JHS* 94 (1974), pp. 67–87
Hammond, N.G.L., 'The Campaign of Alexander Against Cleitus and Glaucias', in *Ancient Macedonia 2* (Institute for Balkan Studies, Thessaloniki: 1977), pp. 503–509
Hammond, N.G.L., 'Training in the Use of the Sarissa and Its Effect in Battle 359–333 BC', *Antichthon* 14 (1980a), pp. 53–63
Hammond, N.G.L., 'The Battle of the Granicus River', *JHS* 100 (1980b), pp. 73–88
Hammond, N.G.L., *Three Historians of Alexander the Great* (Cambridge: 1983)
Hammond, N.G.L., 'The Royal Journal of Alexander', *Historia* 37 (1988), pp. 129–150
Hammond, N.G.L., *Alexander the Great: King, Commander and Statesman 2* (Bristol: 1989a)
Hammond, N.G.L., 'Casualties and Reinforcements of Citizen Soldiers in Greece and Macedonia', *JHS* 109 (1989b), pp. 56–68
Hammond, N.G.L., 'The Battle Between Philip and Bardylis', *Antichthon* 23 (1989c), pp. 1–9
Hammond, N.G.L., 'Aspects of Alexander's Journal and Ring in His Last Days', *AJPh* 110 (1989d), pp. 155–160
Hammond, N.G.L., 'Royal Pages, Personal Pages, and Boys Trained in the Macedonian Manner During the Period of the Temenid Monarchy', *Historia* 39 (1990), pp. 261–290
Hammond, N.G.L., *The Macedonian State: Origins, Institutions, and History* (Oxford: 1992a)
Hammond, N.G.L., 'Alexander's Charge at the Battle of Issus in 333 B.C', *Historia* 41 (1992b), pp. 395–406
Hammond, N.G.L., 'The Archaeological and Literary Evidence for the Burning of the Persepolis Palace', *CQ*² 42 (1992c), pp. 358–364
Hammond, N.G.L, *Sources for Alexander the Great* (Cambridge: 1993a)
Hammond, N.G.L., 'The Macedonian Imprint on the Hellenistic World', in P. Green (ed.), *Hellenistic History and Culture* (Berkeley and Los Angeles, CA: 1993b), pp. 12–23
Hammond, N.G.L., *Philip of Macedon* (London: 1994)
Hammond, N.G.L., *The Genius of Alexander the Great* (London: 1997a)
Hammond, N.G.L., 'What Philip May Have Learnt as a Hostage in Thebes', *GRBS* 38 (1997b), pp. 355–372
Hammond, N.G.L. and G.T. Griffith, *A History of Macedonia 2* (Oxford: 1979)
Hammond, N.G.L. and F.W. Walbank, *A History of Macedonia 3* (Oxford: 1988)
Hanson, V.D., *The Western Way of War: Infantry Battle in Classical Greece* (New York, NY: 1989)
Hanson, V.D. (ed.), *Hoplites: The Classical Greek Battle Experience* (London: 1991)
Hanson, V.D., *Warfare and Agriculture in Classical Greece* (Berkeley and Los Angeles, CA: 1998)

Hardiman, C.L., 'Classical Art to 221 BC', in J. Roisman and I. Worthington (eds.), *A Companion to Ancient Macedonia* (Malden: 2010), pp. 505–521

Hartung, W., 'Exaggerating Challenge from China Threatens U.S. Security', *Forbes*, 22 January 2021

Hatzopoulos, M.B. (ed.), *Macedonia from Philip II to the Roman Conquest* (Princeton, NJ: 1994)

Hatzopoulos, M.B., *Macedonian Institutions Under the Kings*, 2 vols. (Athens: 1996)

Hatzopoulos, M.B., *L'organisation de l'armée macédonienne sous les Antigonides: Problèmes anciens et documents nouveaux* (Athens: 2001)

Hatzopoulos, M.B., 'Macedonia and Macedonians', in R. Lane Fox (ed.), *Brill's Companion to Ancient Macedon* (Leiden: 2011a), pp. 43–50

Hatzopoulos, M.B., 'Macedonia and Macedonians', in R. Lane Fox (ed.), *Brill's Companion to Ancient Macedon* (Leiden: 2011b), pp. 43–50

Hatzopoulos, M.B., 'Macedonians and Other Greeks', in R. Lane Fox (ed.), *Brill's Companion to Ancient Macedon* (Leiden: 2011c), pp. 51–78

Hatzopoulos, M.B., *Ancient Macedonia* (Berlin: 2020)

Heckel, W., 'The Conspiracy *Against* Philotas', *Phoenix* 31 (1977), pp. 9–21

Heckel, W., 'Alexander at the Persian Gates', *Athenaeum* 58 (1980), pp. 168–174

Heckel, W., *The Last Days and Testament of Alexander the Great* (Stuttgart: 1998)

Heckel, W., 'King and "Companions": Observations on the Nature of Power in the Reign of Alexander', in J. Roisman (ed.), *Brill's Companion to Alexander the Great* (Leiden: 2003a), pp. 197–225

Heckel, W., 'Alexander the Great and the "Limits of Civilised World"', in W. Heckel and L. Tritle (eds.), *Crossroads of History, the Age of Alexander* (Claremont, CA: 2003b), pp. 147–174

Heckel, W., *The Conquests of Alexander the Great* (Cambridge: 2008)

Heckel, W., 'A King and His Army', in W. Heckel and L. Tritle (eds.), *Alexander the Great: A New History* (Malden: 2009), pp. 69–82

Heckel, W., T. Howe and S. Müller, 'The Giver of the Bride, the Bridegroom, and the Bride: A Study of the Murder of Philip II and Its Aftermath', in T. Howe, S. Müller and R. Stoneman (eds.), *Ancient Historiography on War and Empire* (Oxford: 2017), pp. 92–124

Higgins, W.E., 'Aspects of Alexander's Imperial Administration: Some Modern Methods and Views Reviewed', *Athenaeum* 58 (1980), pp. 129–152

Holt, F., 'The Hyphasis Mutiny: A Source Study', *Ancient World* 5 (1982), pp. 33–59

Holt, F., 'Alexander's Settlements in Central Asia', in *Ancient Macedonia 4* (Institute for Balkan Studies, Thessaloniki: 1986), pp. 315–323

Holt, F., *Alexander the Great and Bactria: The Formation of a Greek Frontier in Central Asia* (Leiden: 1988)

Holt, F., *Thundering Zeus: The Making of Hellenistic Bactria* (Berkeley and Los Angeles, CA: 1999)

Holt, F., 'The Death of Coenus', *AHB* 14 (2000), pp. 49–55

Holt, F.L., *Alexander the Great and the Mystery of the Elephant Medallions* (Berkeley and Los Angeles, CA: 2003)

Holt, F., *Into the Land of Bones: Alexander the Great in Afghanistan* (Berkeley and Los Angeles, CA: 2005)

Holt, F.L., *The Treasures of Alexander the Great* (New York, NY: 2016)

Howe, T., 'Alexander and "Afghan" Insurgency: A Reassessment', in T. Howe and L.L. Brice (eds.), *Brill's Companion to Insurgency and Terrorism in the Ancient Mediterranean* (Leiden: 2015), pp. 151–182

Howe, T. and S. Müller, 'Mission Accomplished: Alexander at the Hyphasis', *AHB* 26 (2012), pp. 21–38

Iglesias-Zoido, J.C., 'The Pre-Battle Speeches of Alexander at Issus and Gaugamela', *GRBS* 50 (2010) pp. 215–241.

Jentleson, B.W., 'Be Wary of China Threat Inflation', *Foreign Policy*, 30 July 2021

Kalléris, J.N., *Les anciens Macédoniens. Etude linguistique et historique*, 2 vols. (Athens: 1988)

Kalléris, J.N., 'L'armee macedoine sous Alexandre I, Le Philhellene', in J. Servais, T. Hackens and B. Servais-Soyez (eds.), *Stemmata: Melanges de philologie, d'histoire et d'archeologie grecques offerts Jules Labarbe* (Liege: 1987), pp. 317–331

Karunanithy D., *The Macedonian War Machine: Neglected Aspects of the Armies of Philip, Alexander and the Successors 359–281 BC* (Barnsley: 2013)

Keegan, J., *The Mask of Command* (London: 1987)

Keyser, P.T., 'The Use of Artillery by Philip II and Alexander the Great', *Ancient World* 15 (1994), pp. 27–49

Kholod, M.M., 'The Garrisons of Alexander the Great in the Greek Cities of Asia Minor', *Eos* 97 (2010), pp. 249–258

Kholod, M.M., 'On the Financial Relations of Alexander the Great and the Greek Cities in Asia Minor: The Case of *Syntaxis*', in A. Mehl, A.V. Makhlayuk and O. Gabelko (eds.), *Ruthenia Classica Aetatis Novae: A Collection of Works by Russian Scholars in Ancient Greek and Roman History* (Stuttgart: 2013), pp. 83–92

Kilcullen, D., *The Dragons and the Snakes: How the Rest Learned to Fight the West* (Oxford: 2020).

King, C.J., 'Kingship and Other Political Institutions', in J. Roisman and I. Worthington (eds.), *The Blackwell Companion to Ancient Macedonia* (Malden: 2010), pp. 374–391

King, C.J., *Ancient Macedonia* (London: 2018)

Kuhrt, A., 'Alexander in Babylon', *Achaemenid History* 5 (1990), pp. 121–130

Lane Fox, R., *Alexander the Great* (London: 1973)

Lane Fox, R. (ed.), *Brill's Companion to Ancient Macedon* (Leiden: 2011a)

Lane Fox, R., 'Philip of Macedon: Accession, Ambitions, and Self-Presentation', in R. Lane Fox (ed.), *Brill's Companion to Ancient Macedon* (Leiden: 2011), pp. 335–366

Lloyd, A.B., 'Philip II and Alexander the Great: The Moulding of Macedon's Army', in A.B. Lloyd (ed.), *Battle in Antiquity* (London: 1996), pp. 169–198

Lonsdale, D.J., *Alexander the Great: Lessons in Strategy* (London: 2007)

Maclean Rogers, G., *Alexander: The Ambiguity of Greatness* (New York, NY: 2004)

Marsden, E.W., *The Campaign of Gaugamela* (Liverpool: 1964)

Marsden, E.W., 'Macedonian Military Machinery and Its Designers Under Philip and Alexander', in *Ancient Macedonia 2* (Institute for Balkan Studies, Thessaloniki: 1977), pp. 211–223

Matarese, C., 'Proskynesis and the Gesture of the Kiss at Alexander's Court: The Creation of a New Elite', *Palamedes* 8 (2013), pp. 75–85

Matthews, R., *Alexander at the Battle of the Granicus: A Campaign in Context* (Stroud: 2008)
Meeus, A., 'Alexander's Image in the Age of the Successors', in W. Heckel and L. Tritle (eds.), *Alexander the Great: A New History* (Malden: 2009), pp. 235–250
Millett, P., 'The Political Economy of Macedonia', in J. Roisman and I. Worthington (eds.), *A Companion to Ancient Macedonia* (Malden: 2010), pp. 472–504
Milns, R.D., 'Philip II and the Hypaspists', *Historia* 16 (1967) pp. 509–512
Milns, R.D., 'The Army of Alexander the Great', in E. Badian (ed.), *Alexandre le Grand: Image et réalité* (Geneva 1976), pp. 87–136
Müller, S., 'Philip II', in J. Roisman and I. Worthington (eds.), *A Companion to Ancient Macedonia* (Malden: 2010), pp. 166–185
Murison, C.L., 'Darius III and the Battle of Issus', *Historia* 21 (1972), pp. 399–423
Nagle, B., 'The Cultural Context of Alexander's Speech at Opis', *TAPhA* 126 (1996), pp. 151–172
Narain, A.K., 'Alexander and India', $G\&R^2$ 12 (1965), pp. 155–165
Nawotka, K., 'Freedom of Greek Cities in Asia Minor in the Age of Alexander the Great', *Klio* 85 (2003), pp. 15–41
Noguera Borel, A., 'L'évolution de la Phalange Macédonienne: Le Cas de la Sarisse', *Ancient Macedonia* 6 (Thessaloniki 1999), pp. 839–850
Nogueira Borel, A., 'L'armée macédonienne avant Philippi II', in *Ancient Macedonia* 7 (Institute for Balkan Studies, Thessaloniki: 2007), pp. 97–111
Nylander, C., 'Darius III – The Coward King: Point and Counterpoint', in J. Carlsen et al. (eds.), *Alexander the Great: Reality and Myth* (Rome: 1993), pp. 145–159
Ogden, D., 'Alexander's Sex Life', in W. Heckel and L. Tritle (eds.), *Alexander the Great: A New History* (Malden: 2009), pp. 203–217
Ogden, D., *Alexander the Great: Myth, Genesis and Sexuality* (Exeter: 2011)
Olbrycht, M., 'The Military Reforms of Alexander the Great During His Campaigns in Iran, Afghanistan and Central Asia', in C. Galewicz, J Pstrunińska and L. Sudyka (eds.), *Understanding Eurasia from Ancient Times to the Present Day* (Kraków: 2007), pp. 309–321
Paliadeli-Saatsoglou, C., 'The Arts at Vergina-Aegae, the Cradle of the Macedonian Kingdom', in R. Lane Fox (ed.), *Brill's Companion to Ancient Macedon* (Leiden: 2011), pp. 271–295
Parke, H.W., 'The Massacre of the Branchidae', *JHS* 105 (1985), pp. 59–68
Papazoglou, F., *The Central Balkan Tribes in Pre-Roman Times* (Amsterdam: 1978)
Paspalas, S.A., 'Classical Art', in R. Lane Fox (ed.), *Brill's Companion to Ancient Macedon* (Leiden: 2011), pp. 179–207
Peters, H. M., 'Department of Defense Contractor and Troop Levels in Afghanistan and Iraq: 2007–2020', *Congressional Research Service*, 22 February 2021, https://sgp.fas.org/crs/natsec/R44116.pdf
Rawlings, L., *The Ancient Greeks at War* (Manchester: 2007)
Ray, H.P. and D.T. Potts (eds.), *Memory as History, the Legacy of Alexander in Asia* (New Delhi: 2007)
Renard, M. and J. Servais, 'A propos du mariage d'Alexandre et de Roxane', *L'Ant Class* 24 (1955), pp. 29–50
Roisman, J., 'Honor in Alexander's Campaign', in J. Roisman (ed.), *Brill's Companion to Alexander the Great* (Leiden: 2003), pp. 279–321

Roisman, J., 'Royal Power, Law and Justice in Ancient Macedonia', *AHB* 26 (2012), pp. 131–148

Roisman, J., 'Alexander's Expectations of Commanders and Friends', in K. Nawotka and A. Wojciechowska (eds.), *The Ancient Near Eastern Legacy and Alexander vs. Alexander's Legacy to the World* (Vienna: forthcoming)

Roisman, J. and I. Worthington (eds.), *A Companion to Ancient Macedonia* (Malden: 2010)

Roller, L.E., 'Midas and the Gordian Knot', *Class Antiquity* 3 (1984), pp. 256–271

Romane, P., 'Alexander's Siege of Tyre', *Ancient World* 16 (1987), pp. 79–90

Romane, P., 'Alexander's Siege of Gaza', *Ancient World* 18 (1988), pp. 21–30

Rtveladze, E.V., 'Alessandro in Battriana e Sogdiana', *Parthica* 9 (2007), pp. 153–204

Rubinsohn, W.Z., 'The "Philotas Affair" – a Reconsideration', in *Ancient Macedonia 2* (Institute for Balkan Studies, Thessaloniki: 1977), pp. 409–420

Ruzicka, S., 'War in the Aegean, 333–331 BC: A Reconsideration', *Phoenix* 42 (1988), pp. 131–151

Ryder, T.T.B., 'The Diplomatic Skills of Philip II', in I. Worthington (ed.), *Ventures into Greek History: Essays in Honour of N.G.L. Hammond* (Oxford: 1994), pp. 228–257

Samuel, A.E., 'Alexander's Royal Journals', *Historia* 14 (1965), pp. 1–12

Sancisi-Weerdenburg, H., 'Alexander and Persepolis', in J. Carlsen et al. (eds.), *Alexander the Great. Reality and Myth* (Rome: 1993), pp. 177–188

Sawada, N., 'Macedonian Social Customs', in J. Roisman and I. Worthington (eds.), *A Companion to Ancient Macedonia* (Malden: 2010), pp. 392–408

Sears, M.A. and C. Willekes, 'Alexander's Cavalry Charge at Chaeronea, 338 BCE', *Journal of Military History* 80 (2016), pp. 1017–1035

Sekunda, N.V., 'The Sarissa', *Acta Universitatis Lodziensis, Folia Archaeologica* 23 (2001), pp. 13–41

Sekunda, N.V., 'The Macedonian Army', in J. Roisman and I. Worthington (eds.), *A Companion to Ancient Macedonia* (Malden: 2010), pp. 446–471

Sekunda, N.V., *The Antigonid Army* (Gdansk: 2013)

Sekunda, N.V., 'Alexander and Demaratus of Corinth at the Battle of the River Granicus', *Anabasis, Studia Classica et Orientalia* 9 (2018), pp. 47–61

Sekunda, N.V. and A. McBride, *The Army of Alexander the Great* (London: 1984)

Sekunda, N.V. and J. Warry, *Alexander the Great: His Armies and Campaigns, 334–323 BC.* (Oxford: 1998)

Serhan, Y., 'The Taliban Is Just as Bad as It Always Was', *The Atlantic*, 16 October 2021

Shay, J., *Achilles in Vietnam: Combat Trauma and the Undoing of Character* (New York, NY: 1994)

Smith, N. and S. MacFarland, 'Anbar Awakens: The Tipping Point', *Military Review* (March–April 2008), pp. 41–52

Speck, H., 'Alexander at the Persian Gates: A Study in Historiography and Topography', *AJAH* 1 (2002), pp. 15–23

Stewart, A., *Faces of Power: Alexander's Image and Hellenistic Politics* (Berkeley and Los Angeles, CA: 1993)

Stoker, D., *Why America Loses Wars: Limited War and US Strategy from the Korean War to the Present* (Cambridge: 2019)

Stoneman, R., 'Who Are the Brahmans?', CQ^2 44 (1994), pp. 500–510

Stoneman, R., 'Naked Philosophers: The Brahmans in the Alexander Historians and the *Alexander Romance*', *JHS* 105 (1995), pp. 99–114

Strauss, B.S., 'Alexander: The Military Campaign', in J. Roisman (ed.), *Brill's Companion to Alexander the Great* (Leiden: 2003), pp. 133–156

Strauss, B.S. and J. Ober, *The Anatomy of Terror: Ancient Military Disasters and Their Lessons for Modern Strategists* (New York, NY: 1990)

Sullivan, P.L., 'Does Security Assistance Work? Why It May Not Be the Answer for Fragile States', *Modern War Institute at West Point*, 15 November 2021, https://mwi.usma.edu/does-security-assistance-work-why-it-may-not-be-the-answer-for-fragile-states/

Swaine, M.D., 'China isn't That Big of a Threat to the United States', *Foreign Policy*, 21 April 2021

Thompson, M., *Granicus 334 BC: Alexander's First Persian Victory* (London: 2007)

Tritle, L., *From Melos to My Lai: A Study in Violence, Culture and Social Survival* (London: 2000)

Tritle, L., 'Alexander and the Killing of Cleitus the Black', in W. Heckel and L. Tritle (eds.), *Crossroads of History, the Age of Alexander* (Claremont, CA: 2003), pp. 127–146

Tritle, L., 'Alexander and the Greeks. Artists and Soldiers, Friends and Enemies', in W. Heckel and L. Tritle (eds.), *Alexander the Great: A New History* (Malden: 2009), pp. 121–140

Vacanta, S., 'Alexander the Great and the "Defeat" of the Sogdianian Revolt', *AHB* 26 (2012), pp. 87–130

Van Wees, H. (ed.), *War and Violence in Ancient Greece* (Swansea: 2000)

Van Wees, H., *Greek Warfare: Myths and Realities* (London: 2004)

Waterfield, R., *Dividing the Spoils* (Oxford: 2011)

Weber, G., 'The Court of Alexander the Great as Social System', in W. Heckel and L. Tritle (eds.), *Alexander the Great: A New History* (Malden: 2009), pp. 83–98

Wiseman, D.J., 'Hoplite Warfare', in Hackett, J. (ed.), *Warfare in the Ancient World* (New York, NY: 1989), pp. 54–81

Woodcock, G., *The Greeks in India* (London: 1966)

Worthington, I., 'Alexander the Great and the "Interests of Historical Accuracy": A Reply', *AHB* 13 (1999), pp. 136–140

Worthington, I., 'Alexander, Philip, and the Macedonian Background', in J. Roisman (ed.), *Brill's Companion to Alexander the Great* (Leiden: 2003a), pp. 69–98

Worthington, I., 'Alexander's Destruction of Thebes', in W. Heckel and L.A. Tritle (eds.), *Crossroads of History: The Age of Alexander the Great* (Claremont, CA: 2003b), pp. 65–86

Worthington, I., *Philip II of Macedonia* (New Haven, CT: 2008)

Worthington, I., 'Intentional History: Alexander, Demosthenes and Thebes', in L. Foxhall and H.-J. Gehrke (eds.), *Intentional History: Spinning Time in Ancient Greece* (Stuttgart: 2010a), pp. 239–246

Worthington, I., 'Alexander the Great, Nation-Building, and the Creation and Maintenance of Empire', in V.D. Hanson (ed.), *Makers of Ancient Strategy: From the Persian Wars to the Fall of Rome* (Princeton, NJ: 2010b), pp. 118–137

Worthington, I., 'Worldwide Empire vs Glorious Enterprise: Diodorus and Justin on Philip II and Alexander the Great', in E. Carney and D. Ogden (eds.),

Philip II and Alexander the Great: Lives and Afterlives (New York, NY: 2010c), pp. 165–174

Worthington, I., *Alexander the Great: A Reader*, 2nd ed. (London: 2011)

Worthington, I., *Demosthenes of Athens and the Fall of Classical Greece* (New York, NY: 2013)

Worthington, I., *By the Spear: Philip II, Alexander the Great, and the Rise and Fall of the Macedonian Empire* (New York, NY: 2014a)

Worthington, I., 'From East to West: Alexander and the Exiles Decree', in E. Baynham (ed.), *East and West in the World of Alexander: Essays in Honour of A.B. Bosworth* (Oxford: 2014b), pp. 93–106

Worthington, I., *Ptolemy I: King and Pharaoh of Egypt* (New York, NY: 2016)

Worthington, I., 'Campaigns of Alexander the Great, 336–323 BC', in H. Sidebottom and M. Whitby (eds.), *Blackwell Encyclopaedia of Ancient Battles* (Malden: 2017), pp. 1–71

Worthington, I., 'Why Arrian Favoured Ptolemy in the Preface of His *Anabasis*: A Simple Solution', in R. Rollinger and J. Degen (eds.), *Contextualizing Arrian: The World of Alexander in Perspective* (Wiesbaden: 2022), pp. 231–241

Wrightson, G., 'The Nature of Command in the Macedonian Sarissa Phalanx', *AHB* 24 (2010), pp. 71–92

Xenophon, *Oeconomicus*, trans. H. Tredennick and R. Waterfield (London: 1990)

Xydopoulos, I.K., 'Upper Macedonia', in M. Tiverios, P. Nigdelis and P. Adam-Veleni (eds.), *Threpteria: Studies on Ancient Macedonia* (Thessaloniki: 2012), pp. 520–539

Yenne, B., *Alexander the Great: Lessons from History's Undefeated General* (New York, NY: 2010)

Modern War and National Security

Ackerman, E., 'Ukraine's Three-to-One Advantage', *The Atlantic*, 24 March 2022

Ackerman, S., 'A Decade Later, Pentagon Wants to Study Muslim World's Nuances', *Wired*, 21 July 2011

Afzal, M., 'Biden Was Wrong on Afghanistan', *Brookings Institution*, 9 November 2021

Agrawal, A., J. Gans and A. Goldfarb, *Prediction Machines: The Simple Economics of Artificial Intelligence* (Cambridge, MA: 2018)

Ahmadzai, S. and A. McKinna, 'Afghanistan Electrical Energy and Trans-Boundary Water Systems Analyses: Challenges and Opportunities', *Energy Reports* 4 (2018), pp. 435–469

Aikins, M., 'Times Investigation: In U.S. Drone Strike, Evidence Suggests No ISIS Bomb', *New York Times*, 10 September 2021

Albertini, R.V., 'The Impact of Two World Wars on the Decline of Colonialism', *Journal of Contemporary History* 4, no. 1 (January 1969), pp. 17–35

Allen, J.R. and A. Husain, 'The Next Space Race is Artificial Intelligence', *Foreign Policy*, 3 November 2017

Allison, G.T., *Destined for War: Can America and China Escape Thucydides's Trap?* (New York, NY: 2017)

Allison, G.T. and N. Ferguson, 'Why the U.S President Needs a Council of Historians', *The Atlantic*, 15 September 2016

Allison, W.T., *The Gulf War, 1990–91* (New York, NY: 2012)
Alterman, E., 'The Decline of Historical Thinking', *The New Yorker*, 4 February 2019
Anderson, B., *Imagined Communities* (London: 1983)
Andrew, C. and V. Mitrokhin, *The Sword and the Shield: The Mitrokhin Archive and the Secret History of the KGB* (New York, NY: 1999)
Anon, M., 'What Happened to Retention?', *Wavell Room*, 17 September 2019
Anthony, T., 'China Tells World Leaders "External Interference" on Taiwan Won't Be Tolerated', *Public Broadcasting System*, 24 September 2022
Applied Physics Laboratory, 'Johns Hopkins APL Bridges the Gap with Next Phase of DARPA's ACE Program', *Johns Hopkins University Applied Physics Laboratory*, 8 April 2021
Ardant du Picq, C.J.J.J., *Battle Studies* (Lawrence, KS: 2017)
Arendt, H., *The Human Condition* (Chicago: 1958)
Arendt, H., *The Origins of Totalitarianism* (New York, NY: 1966)
Armistead, L. (ed.), *Information Operations: Warfare and the Hard Reality of Soft Power* (Dulles, VA: 2004)
Ashley, R.P. Jr., *Defense Intelligence Agency: China Military Power, Modernizing a Force to Fight and Win* (Washington, DC: 2019)
Associated Press, 'Putin: Leader in Artificial Intelligence Will Rule the World', *Associated Press*, 1 September 2017
Atherton, K., 'DARPA Wants AI to Make Soldiers Fitter, Happier, More Productive', *C4ISRNET*, 2 May 2019
Atwan, A.B., *Islamic State: The Digital Caliphate* (University of California Press, Oakland, CA: 2015).
Austin, L.J. III, *Annual Report to Congress on Military and Security Developments Involving the People's Republic of China, 2021* (Washington, DC: 2021)
Austin, L.J. III, *2022 National Defense Strategy of the United States: Fact Sheet* (Washington, DC: 2022)
Avey, P.C., J.N. Markowitz and R.J. Reardon, 'Disentangling Grand Strategy: International Relations Theory and U.S. Grand Strategy', *Texas National Security Review* 2, no. 1 (November 2018), pp. 28–51
Bacevich, A.J., 'Why We Lost in Afghanistan', *The Nation*, 23 August 2021
Baptista, E. and R. Kasolowsky, 'Taiwan Is Not a Part of U.S. but Chinese Territory, Says Chinese Foreign Minister', *Reuters*, 7 August 2022
Barclay, D.A., *Disinformation: The Nature of Facts and Lies in the Post-Truth Era* (New York, NY: 2022)
Barnes, P., 'Learning the Wrong Lessons: Biases, the Rejection of History, and Single-Issue Zealotry in Modern Military Thought', *Modern War Institute*, 4 February 2022, https://mwi.usma.edu/learning-the-wrong-lessons-biases-the-rejection-of-history-and-single-issue-zealotry-in-modern-military-thought/
Barnwell, R. and G. Mohammad, 'China Undercover', *Public Broadcasting System*, 7 April 2020
Barrett, R.C., *Oman: The Present in the Context of a Fractured Past* (Tampa, FL: 2011)
Bayly, B.A., *Empire and Information: Intelligence Gathering and Social Communication in India, 1780–1870* (Cambridge: 2000)
Beaudette, F.M., *U.S. Army Special Operations Command: Army Special Operations Forces Strategy* (Fort Bragg, NC: 2021), www.soc.mil/AssortedPages/ARSOF_Strategy.pdf

Belasco, A., 'Troop Levels in the Afghan and Iraq Wars, FY2001–2012: Cost and Other Potential Issues', *Congressional Research Service*, 2 July 2009

Bennett, T.P.M., *The Pentagon's New Map: War and Peace in the Twenty-First Century* (New York, NY: 2004)

Bensouda, F., 'Statement of the Prosecutor, Fatou Bensouda, on the Conclusion of the Preliminary Examination of the Situation in Iraq/United Kingdom', *International Criminal Court*, 9 December 2020

Berger, D.H., *Force Design 2030* (Washington, DC: March 2020)

Berger, D.H. and R. Evans, 'A Chat with the Commandant: Gen. David H. Berger on the Marine Corps' New Direction', *War on the Rocks*, 6 April 2020

Berman, E., J.H. Felter and J.N. Shapiro, *Small Wars, Big Data: The Information Revolution in Modern Conflict* (Princeton: 2018)

Bernsen, D., 'War in All but Name', *The Strategy Bridge*, 26 April 2021

Bialik, K., 'U.S. Active Duty Military Presence Overseas is at its Smallest in Decades', *Pew Research Center*, 22 August 2017

Biddle, S., *Nonstate Warfare: The Military Methods of Guerrillas, Warlords, and Militias* (Princeton: 2021)

Biden, J., *2021 Interim National Security Guidance* (Washington, DC: 2021)

Biden, J., *2022 National Security Strategy of the United States* (Washington, DC: 2022)

Bird, K. and M.J. Sherwin, *American Prometheus: The Triumph and Tragedy of J. Robert Oppenheimer* (New York, NY: 2005)

Birtle, A.J., *U.S. Army Counterinsurgency and Contingency Operations Doctrine 1942–1976* (Washington, DC: 2007)

Blythe, W.C. Jr., 'A History of Operational Art', *Military Review* (November–December 2018), pp. 37–49

Bolger, D.P., *Why We Lost: A General's Inside Account of the Iraq and Afghanistan Wars* (New York, NY: 2014)

Bonn, K.E. and A.E. Baker, *Guide to Military Operations Other Than War: Tactics, Techniques, and Procedures for Stability and Support Operations* (Philadelphia, PA: 2000)

Boot, M., *War Made New: Technology, Warfare, and the Course of History* (New York, NY: 2006)

Boot, M., *Invisible Armies: An Epic History of Guerrilla Warfare from Ancient Times to the Present* (New York, NY: 2013)

Borghard, E., 'A Grand Strategy Based on Resilience', *War on the Rocks*, 4 January 2021

Boudali, L.K., *The GSPC: Newest Franchise in al-Qa'ida's Global Jihad* (West Point: 2007)

Boynton, H.M., 'Spirituality and Transcendent Meaning Making: Possibilities for Enhancing Posttraumatic Growth', *Journal of Religion & Spirituality in Social Work* 27, no. 1–2 (2008), pp. 69–86

Bracken, P. and R. Alcala, *Whither the RMA: Two Perspectives on Tomorrow's Army* (Carlisle Barracks, PA: 1994)

Brafman, O. and R.A. Beckstrom, *The Starfish and the Spider: The Unstoppable Power of Leaderless Organizations* (New York, NY: 2006)

Brands, H., *The Promise and Pitfalls of Grand Strategy* (Carlisle, PA: 2012)

Brands, H., *What Good Is Grand Strategy? Power and Purpose in American Statecraft from Harry S. Truman to George W. Bush* (Ithaca, NY: 2014)

Brands, H., 'American Grand Strategy in the Post-Cold War Era', in *New Directions in Strategic Thinking 2.0* (Acton, Australia: 2018), pp. 133–148

Brands, H., *The Twilight Struggle: What the Cold War Teaches Us About Great-Power Rivalry Today* (New Haven, CT: 2022)

Brands, H. and C. Edel, *The Lessons of Tragedy: Statecraft and World Order* (New Haven, CT: 2019)

Brands, H. and F.J. Gavin, 'The Historical Profession Is Committing Slow-Motion Suicide', *War on the Rocks*, 10 December 2018

Brennan, J., 'The Turmoil of Identity Crisis: Special Forces Organizational Culture', *War Room Podcast*, 4 August 2020, https://warroom.armywarcollege.edu/podcasts/sfcom-culture/

Broadway, C., 'DoD Official Highlights Value of Artificial Intelligence to Future Warfare', *Department of Defense*, 9 April 2018

Brose, C., 'The New Revolution in Military Affairs: War's Sci-Fi Future', *Foreign Affairs*, May–June 2019

Brose, C., *The Killchain: Defending America in the Future of High-Tech Warfare* (New York, NY: 2020)

Brown, C.Q. Jr., 'Accelerate Change or Lose', *U.S. Air Force*, August 2020, www.af.mil/Portals/1/documents/csaf/CSAF_22/CSAF_22_Strategic_Approach_Accelerate_Change_or_Lose_31_Aug_2020.pdf

Burdick, E. and W.J. Lederer, *The Ugly American* (New York, NY: 1958)

Burgos, R.A., 'Pushing the Easy Button: Special Operations Forces, International Security, and the Use of Force', *Special Operations Journal* 4, no. 2 (November 2018), pp. 109–128

Burke, E.M. and D.P. Wright, *Ensuring Success: Consolidation of Gains in Large-Scale Combat Operations* (Fort Leavenworth, KS: 2022)

Burkhard, T., *Strategic Vision of the Chief of the French Army* (Paris: 2020), pp. 1–20

Burr, R.M., *Army in Motion: Army's Contribution to Defence Strategy: Edition Two* (Canberra: 2020), pp. 1–61

Burton, R.A., *On Being Certain: Believing You Are Right Even When You're Not* (New York, NY: 2009)

Bush, G.W., 'U.S. Military Academy Commencement', *C-SPAN* (video), 1 June 2002, www.c-span.org/video/?170353-1/us-military-academy-commencement

Byman, D., 'The Limits of Air Strikes when Fighting the Islamic State', *Lawfare*, 5 December 2016

Calvan, B.C., 'Kerry Hits Romney on Foreign Policy', *Boston Globe*, 26 May 2012

Calvert, J., *Sayyid Qutb and the Origins of Radical Islamism* (New York, NY: 2010)

Carleton-Smith, M., Sir, *Future Soldier: Transforming the British Army* (London: 2021), pp. 1–53

Carter, N., *Integrated Operating Concept 2025* (London: 2021)

Carver, M., 'Conventional Warfare in the Nuclear Age', in P. Paret (ed.), *Makers of Modern Strategy: From Machiavelli to the Digital Age* (Princeton: 1986)

Catmull, E., *Creativity, Inc.: Overcoming the Unseen Forces That Stand in the Way of True Inspiration* (New York, NY: 2014)

Cavanaugh, M.L., 'It's Time to End the Tyranny of Ends, Ways, and Means', *Modern War Institute*, 24 July 2017

Cebrowski, A.K. and J.H. Garstka, 'Network-Centric Warfare – Its Origin and Future', *Proceedings* 124, no. 1 (January 1998)

Chandler, D.G., *The Campaigns of Napoleon* (New York, NY: 1966)
Chandrasekaran, R., 'U.S. Deploying Heavily Armored Battle Tanks for First Time in Afghan War', *The Washington Post*, 19 November 2010
Clark, C., *The Sleepwalkers: How Europe Went to War in 1914* (New York, NY: 2012)
Clarke, R.A., *Against All Enemies: Inside America's War on Terror* (New York, NY: 2004)
Clausewitz, C. V., *On War*, trans. M. Howard (Princeton, NJ: 1976).
Cleveland, C.T. and D. Egel, *The America Way of Irregular War: An Analytical Memoir* (Santa Monica: 2020)
Cohen, E.A., *Supreme Command: Soldiers, Statesmen, and Leadership in Wartime* (New York, NY: 2003)
Cohen, E.A., *The Big Stick: The Limits of Soft Power and the Necessity of Military Force* (New York, NY: 2017)
Cohen, E.A., 'Why Can't the West Admit That Ukraine Is Winning?" *The Atlantic*, 21 March 2022
Coker, C., *Waging War Without Warriors? The Changing Culture of Military Conflict* (Boulder: 2002)
Colby, E. A., *The Strategy of Denial: American Defense in an Age of Great Power Conflict* (New Haven, CT: 2021)
Coleman, J., 'Critical Thinking Is About Asking Better Questions', *Harvard Business Review*, 22 April 2022
Coles, I., 'Pompeo Urges Iraq to Act Against Killers of Top Security Analyst', *The Wall Street Journal*, 8 July 2020, www.wsj.com/articles/pompeo-urges-iraq-to-act-against-killers-of-top-security-analyst
Coll, S., *Ghost Wars: The Secret History of the CIA, Afghanistan, and Bin Laden, from the Soviet Invasion to September 10, 2001* (New York, NY: 2004)
Collins, L. and H. Morgan, 'Affordable, Abundant, and Autonomous: The Future of Ground Warfare', *War on the Rocks*, 21 April 2020
Collins, L. and J. Spencer, *Understanding Urban Warfare* (Havant, UK: 2022)
Collins, N.W., *Grey Wars: A Contemporary History of U.S. Special Operations* (New Haven, CT: 2021)
Colón-López, R., *Developing Enlisted Leaders for Tomorrow's Wars: Our Shared Vision for Enlisted Professional Military Education & Talent Management* (Washington, DC: 2021)
Combat Capabilities Development Command Chemical Biological Center, *Cyber Soldier 2050: Human/Machine Fusion and the Implications for the Future of the DOD* (Aberdeen Proving Ground, MD: 2019)
Committee on Foreign Relations in the United States Senate, 'Tora Bora Revisited: How We Failed to Get Bin Laden and Why It Matters Today', *111th Congress*, 1st Session, 30 November 2009
Committee on Foreign Relations in the United States Senate, 'Al Qaeda in Yemen and Somalia: A Ticking Time Bomb', *111th Congress*, 2nd Session, 21 January 2010
Copinger-Symes, T.R., 'Digital Disruption: Major General Copinger-Symes's Speech to the UK Strategic Command Inaugural Conference at RUSI', *The Wavell Room*, 24 February 2020
Coram, R., *Boyd: The Fighter Pilot Who Changed the Art of War* (New York, NY: 2004)

Corder, M., 'US Launches Artificial Intelligence Military Use Initiative', *Associated Press*, 16 February 2023, https://apnews.com/article/russia-ukraine-technology-china-the-hague-artificial-intelligence-d49c5fb442fa825e0a7a7419d6f04469

Creveld, M.V., *Technology and War: From 2000 B.C. to the Present, Revised and Expanded Edition* (New York, NY: 1991)

Crone, P., *God's Rule: Government and Islam* (Edinburgh: 2004)

Dahm, M., 'Chinese Debates on the Military Utility of Artificial Intelligence', *War on the Rocks*, 5 June 2020

Dalrymple, W., *Return of a King: The Battle for Afghanistan, 1839–42* (New York, NY: 2013)

Dalsjo, R., M. Jonsson and J. Norberg, 'A Brutal Examination: Russian Military Capability in Light of the Ukraine War', *Survival* 64, no. 3 (2022), pp. 7–28

Dalton, M. and H. Shah, 'Partners, Not Proxies: Capacity Building in Hybrid Warfare', *Center for Strategic and International Studies*, 27 May 2020, pp. 1–10

Daly, E., 'Talent Management Requires Continued Effort, Focus', *U.S. Army*, 24 February 2022

David, A., S.A. Acosta and N. Krohley, 'Getting Competition Wrong: The US Military's Looming Failure', *Modern War Institute at West Point*, 3 December 2021

Defense Advanced Research Projects Agency, 'DARPA Selects Teams to Further Advance Dogfighting Algorithms', *DARPA*, 11 November 2020

Defense Intelligence Agency of the United States, 'DIA's Vision of MARS: Decision Advantage for the 21st Century', *Defense Intelligence Agency*, 23 May 2019

Delaporte, M., 'France Wants to Transform Its "Beautiful" Army for High-Intensity Warfare', *Breaking Defense*, 16 December 2021

Demirjian, K., A. Horton, J. Wagner and F. Sonmez, 'Military Leaders, Refusing to Fault Biden, Say Troop Withdrawal Ensured Afghanistan's Collapse', *The Washington Post*, 28 September 2021

Department of State, 'Saddam's Chemical Weapons Campaign: 1988 Halabja Massacre', United States Department of State Archives, 20 January 2009

De Silva, S.J., 'The Formation of the Australian Space Command: The US Space Force as a Blueprint', *Journal of Indo-Pacific Affairs* (Maxwell AFB: 2022), pp. 1–10

De Witte, M., 'Special Forces Veteran and Stanford Scholar Applies Data and Scholarship to Conflict', *Stanford University News*, 10 November 2020

DeYoung, K., *Soldier: The Life of Colin Powell* (New York, NY: 2006)

Dickinson, P., 'Russian Army Faces Morale Problems as Putin's Ukraine Invasion Drags on', *The Atlantic Council*, 4 August 2022

Dixon, B., 'Trading Queens', *War Room – U.S. Army War College*, 4 May 2017

Doshi, R., *The Long Game: China's Grand Strategy to Displace American Order* (New York, NY: 2021)

Dower, J.W., *Embracing Defeat: Japan in the Wake of World War II* (New York, NY: 1999)

Downes, A.B. and L.A. O'Rourke, 'You Can't Always Get What You Want: Why Foreign-Imposed Regime Change Seldom Improves Interstate Relations', *International Security* 41, no. 2 (2016), pp. 43–89

Dubik, J.M. and G.R. Sullivan, *Envisioning Future Warfare* (Fort Leavenworth, KS: 1994)

Duffy, B. and M. Thain, 'Do We Have Your Attention? How People Focus and Live in the Modern Information Environment', *The Policy Institute at King's College London*, February 2022

Duggan, W., *Napoleon's Glance: The Secret of Strategy* (New York, NY: 2002)

Echevarria, A.J. II, *Reconsidering the American Way of War: U.S. Military Practice from the Revolution to Afghanistan* (Washington, DC: 2014)

Eckstein, M., 'Navy Betting Big on Unmanned Warships Defining Future of the Fleet', *US Naval Institute News*, 8 April 2019

Economist Editorial Board, 'The Study of History Is in Decline in Britain', *The Economist*, 18 July 2019

Economy, E.C., *The World According to China* (New York, NY: 2022)

Ehrhardt, A., 'Everyman His Own Philosopher of History: Notions of Historical Process in the Study and Practice of Foreign Policy', *Texas National Security Review* 5, no. 3 (Summer 2022), pp. 11–32

Eisenhower, D.D., *The Eisenhower Diaries*, ed. R.H. Ferrell (New York, NY: 1981)

Eisenhower, D. D., *Waging Peace: The White House Years, 1956–1961* (New York, NY: 1965)

Eliason, W.T., 'An Interview with Robert O. Work', *Joint Force Quarterly 84* (1st Quarter 2017), pp. 6–11

Elkus, A., '50 Shades of Gray: Why the Gray Wars Concept Lacks Strategy Sense', *War on the Rocks*, 15 December 2015

Ellis, D.C., C.N. Black and M.A. Nobles, 'Thinking Dangerously: Imagining United States Special Operations Command in the Post-CT World', *PRISM 6*, no. 3 (2016), pp. 111–129

Engels, D.W., *Alexander the Great and the Logistics of the Macedonian Army* (Berkeley: 1978)

Engstrom, J., *Systems Confrontation and Systems Destruction Warfare: How the Chinese People's Liberation Army Seeks to Wage Modern Warfare* (Santa Monica: 2018)

Enriquez, V., 'I Took Part in the Army's New Battalion Commander Assessment Program: Here's What I Learned', *Modern War Institute at West Point*, 2 July 2020

Eversden, A., 'At Project Convergence, Army "Struggling" to See Joint Battlefield as It Heeds "Hard" Lessons', *Breaking Defense*, 17 November 2021

Fairweather, J., *The Good War: Why We Couldn't Win the War or the Peace in Afghanistan* (New York, NY: 2014)

Fehrenbach, T.R., *This Kind of War: A Study in Unpreparedness* (New York, NY: 1963)

Feickert, A. and N.J. Lucas, 'Army Future Combat System (FCS) "Spin-Outs" and Ground Combat Vehicle (GCV): Background and Issues for Congress', *Congressional Research Service*, 30 November 2009

Ferguson, M., 'The Mission Command of Islamic State: Deconstructing the Myth of Lone Wolves in the Deep Fight', *Military Review* (September–October 2017), pp. 68–77

Ferguson, M., 'Don't Shoot the Messenger: Demosthenes, Churchill and the Consensus Delusion', *Joint Force Quarterly* 90 (July–September 2018a), pp. 78–85

Ferguson, M., 'Welcome to the Disinformation Game – You're Late', *The Strategy Bridge*, 29 August 2018b

Ferguson, M., 'The Digital Maginot Line: Autonomous Warfare and Strategic Incoherence', *PRISM* 8, no. 2 (2019), pp. 132–144

Ferguson, M., 'The Evolution of Disinformation: How Public Opinion Became Proxy', *The Strategy Bridge*, 14 January 2020

Ferguson, M., 'America's High-Tech Problem in Low-Tech Wars', *Small Wars Journal*, 8 September 2021a

Ferguson, M., 'Guarding Against an Exclusive Warrior Class', *Inkstick Media*, 28 October 2021b

Ferguson, M., 'Irregular Warfare Is Great Power Competition – Part 1', *War Room – U.S. Army War College*, 19 August 2021c

Ferguson, M., 'Irregular Warfare Is Great Power Competition – Part 2', *War Room – U.S. Army War College*, 20 August 2021d

Ferguson, M., 'Security Assistance in Africa Needs an Industrial Boost', *The Hill*, 20 November 2021e

Ferguson, M., 'Strategic Imperative: A Competitive Framework for U.S.-Sino Relations', *Strategic Studies Quarterly* 15, no. 1 (2021f), pp. 48–68

Ferguson, M., 'The Taliban Didn't Change – It Adapted to the (Dis)Information Age', *The Hill*, 27 September 2021g

Ferguson, M., 'Europe's Gordian Knot', *The Hill*, 19 February 2022a

Ferguson, M., 'Is Imperialism Negotiable?', *The Hill*, 14 July 2022b

Ferguson, M., 'Putin's Jedi Mind Trick in Ukraine: How Truth Decay Shapes the Operational Environment', *The Strategy Bridge*, 9 June 2022c

Ferguson, M., 'Sun Tzu's Trap: The Illusion of Perpetual Competition', *The Modern War Institute at West Point*, 10 February 2022d

Ferguson, M., 'The Nature of War Is Not Changing in Ukraine', *The Hill*, 16 June 2022e

Ferguson, M., J.R. Crifasi and N. Rife, 'The Human-Machine Paradox: A Balanced Approach to Finding and Fixing in 2035', *Military Review* (November–December 2020), pp. 38–47

Fitzsimonds, J.R. and J.M. Van Tol., 'Revolutions in Military Affairs', *Joint Force Quarterly* 4 (Spring 1994), pp. 24–31

Flannigan, W., 'Facts Over Fear; T-14 Armata', *Wavell Room*, 19 February 2019

Fortescue, J.W., Sir, *The Bloodiest Folly: The British Army in Afghanistan 1837–42* (East Yorkshire: 2016)

Franks, T., *American Soldier* (New York, NY: 2004)

Freddie, 'The Army Needs to Look Hard at Retention Not Just Recruitment', *Wavell Room*, 7 May 2019, https://wavellroom.com/2019/05/07/the-army-needs-to-look-hard-at-retention-not-just-recruitment/

Freedberg, S.J. Jr., 'Army Won't Repeat Mistakes of FCS: Gen. Murray Exclusive', *Breaking Defense*, 30 March 2021

Freedberg, S.J. Jr., 'Pentagon's AI Problem is 'Dirty' Data: Lt. Gen. Shanahan', *Breaking Defense*, 13 November 2019

Freedman, L., *Strategy: A History* (New York, NY: 2013)

Freedman, L., 'The First Two Generations of Nuclear Strategists', in P. Paret (ed.), *Makers of Modern Strategy: From Machiavelli to the Digital Age* (Princeton: 1986), pp. 735–778

Freedman, L., *The Future of War: A History* (New York, NY: 2017)

Freedman, L., *The Politics of Command* (Oxford: 2022)

Friedman, G., *Flashpoints: The Emerging Crisis in Europe* (New York, NY: 2015)

Friedman, G. and M. Friedman, *The Future of War: Power, Technology & American World Dominance in the 21st Century* (New York, NY: 1996)

Frieser, K., *The Blitzkrieg Legend: The 1940 Campaign in the West* (Annapolis, MD: 2005)

Fuchs, M.H., 'America Doesn't Need a Grand Strategy', *Foreign Policy*, 28 July 2019

Fukuyama, F., *The End of History and the Last Man* (New York, NY: 1992)

Fuller, J.F.C., *The Conduct of War, 1789–1961: A Study of the Impact of the French, Industrial, and Russian Revolutions on War and its Conduct* (New Brunswick, NJ: 1961)

Fussell, P., *The Great War and Modern Memory* (New York, NY: 1975)

Gaddis, J.L., *George F. Kennan: An American Life* (New York, NY: 2012)

Gaddis, J.L., *The Cold War: A New History* (New York, NY: 2005)

Gaddis, J.L., *On Grand Strategy* (New York, NY: 2018)

Galeotti, M., 'I'm Sorry for Creating the "Gerasimov Doctrine"', *Foreign Policy*, 5 March 2018

Galeotti, M., *The Weaponisation of Everything: A Field Guide to the New Way of War* (New Haven, CT: 2022)

Gans, J., 'AI Flies F-16-Inspired Jet for 17 Hours in First Test with Tactical Aircraft', *The Hill*, 14 February 2023

Gardner, J.W., *On Leadership* (New York, NY: 1990)

Garthoff, R.L., *Soviet Military Policy: A Historical Analysis* (New York, NY: 1996)

Gates, R.M., *Duty: Memoirs of a Secretary at War* (New York, NY: 2014)

Gates, R.M., *A Passion for Leadership: Lessons on Change and Reform from Fifty Years of Public Service* (New York, NY: 2017)

Gavin, F.J., 'Thinking Historically: A Guide for Strategy and Statecraft', *War on the Rocks*, 19 November 2019

Gaynor, J.M., *Inspector General of the Australian Defence Force: Afghanistan Inquiry Report* (Canberra: 2020)

Gerasimov, V., 'The Value of Science is in the Foresight: New Challenges Demand Rethinking the Forms and Methods of Carrying Out Combat Operations, trans. R. Coalson', *Military Review* (January–February 2016), pp. 23–29

Gerasimov, V., 'The Development of Military Strategy Under Contemporary Conditions: Tasks for Military Science, trans. Dr. Harold Orenstein and Timothy Thomas', *Military Review* (March 2019), pp. 1–10

Giles, M., 'The US and China Are in a Quantum Arms Race That Will Transform Warfare', *MIT Technology Review*, 3 January 2019

Golan, G., *Yom Kippur and After* (Cambridge, UK: 1977)

Gordon, M.R. and B.E. Trainor, *The Endgame: The Inside Story of the Struggle for Iraq, from George W. Bush to Barack Obama* (New York, NY: 2013)

Gordon, P.H., *Losing the Long Game: The False Promise of Regime Change in the Middle East* (New York, NY: 2020)

Government Accountability Office, *Defense Acquisitions: Opportunities for the Army to Position Its Ground Force Modernization Efforts for Success* (Washington, DC: 10 March 2010)

Grady, J., 'Russian Hypersonic Missiles Underperforming in Ukraine Conflict, NORTHCOM Say', *U.S. Naval Institute News*, 19 May 2022

Grau, L.W. and C.K. Bartles, *The Russian Way of War: Force Structure, Tactics, and Modernization of the Russian Ground Forces* (Fort Leavenworth, KS: 2016)

Grau, L.W. and M.A. Gress, *The Soviet-Afghan War: How a Superpower Fought and Lost: The Russian General Staff* (Lawrence, KS: 2002)

Gray, C.S., *Modern Strategy* (New York, NY: 1999)

Gray, C.S., *Another Bloody Century: Future Warfare* (London: 2005)

Gray, C.S., *Strategy and Defence Planning: Meeting the Challenge of Uncertainty* (Oxford, UK: 2014)

Gray, C.S., *The Future of Strategy* (Cambridge, UK: 2015)

Greenfield, N.M., 'Why Is Military History in Retreat at Universities?', *University World News*, 6 March 2021

Gronholt-Pedersen, J., 'Western Countries Pledge $1.55 bln in Military Aid to Ukraine', *Reuters*, 11 August 2022

Grossman, D., *On Killing: The Psychological Cost of Learning to Kill in War and Society* (New York, NY: 1995)

Guderian, H., *Panzer Leader*, trans. Constantine Fitzgibbon (Cambridge, MA: 1996)

Guriev, S., *Spin Dictators: The Changing Face of Tyranny in the 21st Century* (Princeton: 2022)

Haas, R., 'America's Withdrawal of Choice', *Council on Foreign Relations*, 15 August 2021

Hackett, J. Sir, et al., *The Third World War: A Future History* (London: 1978)

Hallex, M.A. and T.S. Cottom, 'Proliferated Commercial Satellite Constellations: Implications for National Security', *Joint Force Quarterly* 97 (2nd Quarter 2020), pp. 20–28

Hamburger, K.E., *Leadership in the Crucible: The Korean War Battles of Twin Tunnels and Chipyong-Ni* (College Station, TX: 2003)

Hammes, T.X., 'Key Technologies and the Revolution of Small, Smart, and Cheap in the Future of Warfare', in *Strategic Assessment 2020* (Washington, DC: 2020)

Hanson, V.D., *Carnage and Culture: Landmark Battles in the Rise of Western Power* (New York, NY: 2001)

Harari, Y.N., *Homo Deus: A History of Tomorrow* (New York, NY: 2017)

Hart, H., 'Don't Be So Sure: The Perils of Certainty', *Forbes*, 6 May 2019

Hasik, J., 'Beyond the Third Offset: Matching Plans for Innovation to a Theory of Victory', *Joint Force Quarterly* 91 (4th Quarter 2018), pp. 14–21

Haynes, W., 'The Hidden Cost of Strategy by Special Operations', *War on the Rocks*, 17 April 2019

Headrick, D.R., *The Tools of Empire: Technology and European Imperialism in the Nineteenth Century* (Oxford, UK: 1981)

Hodges, B., 'How We as a Nation – and I as a Military Officer – Failed in Afghanistan', *New York Post*, 24 August 2021

Hoffman, F.G., *Mars Adapting: Military Change During War* (Annapolis, MD: 2021)

Hoffman, F.G., 'Strategy as Appetite Suppressant', *War on the Rocks*, 3 March 2020a

Hoffman, F. G., 'The Missing Element in Crafting National Strategy: A Theory of Success', *Joint Force Quarterly* 97 (2nd Quarter 2020b), pp. 55–64

Holmes, J.R., 'The Tyranny of Distance', *Foreign Policy*, 18 January 2016

Hopkirk, P., *Setting the East Ablaze: Lenin's Dream of an Empire in Asia* (New York, NY: 1984)

Hopkirk, P., *The Great Game: The Struggle for Empire in Central Asia* (New York, NY: 1992)

Horne, A., *To Lose a Battle: France 1940* (London: 1969).
Horne, A., *Hubris: The Tragedy of War in the Twentieth Century* (New York, NY: 2015)
Howard, M., 'The Use and Abuse of Military History', *Parameters* 11, no. 1 (1981), pp. 9–14 (originally published by RUSI in 1961)
Howard, M., *The Lessons of History* (New Haven, CT: 1991)
Howard, M., *War in European History* (Oxford: 2009)
Human Rights Watch, 'Endless Torment: The 1991 Uprising in Iraq and Its Aftermath', *Human Rights Watch*, June 1992
Human Rights Watch, 'Ukraine: Apparent War Crimes in Russia-Controlled Areas', *Human Rights Watch*, 3 April 2022
Human Rights Watch, 'World Report 2013: Iraq, Events of 2012', *Human Rights Watch*, 2013
Huntington, S.P., *The Clash of Civilizations and the Remaking of the World Order* (London: 1996)
Huntington, S.P., *The Soldier and the State: The Theory and Politics of Civil-Military Relations* (Cambridge, MA: 1957)
Hybrid Conflict Project, 'Today's Wars Are Fought in the "Gray Zone": Here's Everything You Need to Know About It', *Atlantic Council*, 23 February 2022
James, D., 'Warfare, Dinner Jackets, Hammers and Nails', *Wavell Room*, 7 May 2020
Jeapes, T., *SAS Secret War: Codename Operation Storm* (London: 1996)
Johnson, D.E., *Fast Tanks and Heavy Bombers: Innovation in the U.S. Army, 1917–1945* (Ithaca, NY: 1998)
Johnson, R., *The Great War and the Middle East* (Oxford, UK: 2016)
Johnson, R., 'Internet of Things Cybersecurity Improvement Act, Report of the Committee on Homeland Security and Governmental Affairs', in *U.S. Senate, 116th Congress* (Washington, DC: 2019)
Jomini, A.H.D., *The Art of War*, trans. G.H. Mendell and W.P. Craighill (New Delhi, India: 2020, 1st edition 1862)
Jones, D., *Magna Carta: The Birth of Liberty* (New York, NY: 2015)
Jones, G., *Honor in the Dust: Theodore Roosevelt, War in the Philippines, and the Rise and Fall of America's Imperial Dream* (New York, NY: 2013)
Jones, S.G., *In the Graveyard of Empires: America's War in Afghanistan* (New York, NY: 2009)
Jones, S.G., *Hunting in the Shadows: The Pursuit of Al Qa'ida Since 9/11* (New York, NY: 2012)
Jones, S.G., 'Biden's Withdrawal from Afghanistan Was a Strategic Failure', *USA Today*, 29 November 2021a
Jones, S.G., *Three Dangerous Men: Russia, China, Iran, and the Rise of Irregular Warfare* (New York, NY: 2021b)
Jones, S.G., *Russia's Ill-Fated Invasion of Ukraine* (Washington, DC: 2022)
Joyner, J., 'Does the U.S. Military Really Need More Strategists?', *War on the Rocks*, 8 November 2018
Just, W., *Military Men* (New York, NY: 1970)
Kagan, K., 'The Anbar Awakening: Displacing al Qaeda from Its Stronghold in Western Iraq', *Institute for the Study of War*, 15 September 2009
Kagan, R., *The World American Made* (New York, NY: 2012)

Kagan, F.W., M. Clark, G. Barros and K. Stepanenko, *Putin's Likely Course of Action in Ukraine: Updated Course of Action Assessment*, Institute for the Study of War (Washington, DC: 2022), pp. 1–37

Kamphausen, R., *The People of the PLA 2.0* (Carlisle, PA: 2021)

Kanaan, M., *T-Minus AI: Humanity's Countdown to Artificial Intelligence and the New Pursuit of Global Order* (Dallas, TX: 2020)

Kane, G.C. (ed.), *The Technology Fallacy: How People are the Real Key to Digital Transformation* (Cambridge, MA: 2019)

Kania, E.B., 'Minds at War: China's Pursuit of Military Advantage Through Cognitive Science and Biotechnology', *PRISM* 8, no. 3 (January 2020), pp. 83–94

Kania, E.B. and E. Moore, 'Great Power Rivalry Is also a War for Talent', *Center for a New American Security*, 19 May 2019

Kaplan, L.S., *NATO Divided, NATO United: The Evolution of an Alliance* (Westport, CT: 2004)

Kaplan, R.D., *Warrior Politics: Why Leadership Demands a Pagan Ethos* (New York, NY: 2002)

Kaplan, R.D., *The Revenge of Geography: What the Map Tells Us About Coming Conflicts and the Battle Against Fate* (New York, NY: 2013)

Kaplan, R.D., *Asia's Cauldron: The South China Sea and the End of a Stable Pacific* (New York, NY: Random House, 2015)

Karlin, M.E., *The Inheritance: America's Military After Two Decades of War* (Washington, DC: 2022)

Karsh, E., *The Tail Wags the Dog: International Politics and the Middle East* (London: 2015)

Kaune, P.N., 'Analysis of US Army Preparation for Megacity Operations', in *Institute for National Security and Counterterrorism at the U.S. Army War College* (Carlisle, PA: April 2016)

Kavanaugh, J. and M.D. Rich, *Truth Decay: An Initial Exploration of the Diminishing Role of Facts and Analysis in American Public Life* (Santa Monica: 2018)

Keegan, J., *The Face of Battle: A Study of Agincourt, Waterloo and the Somme* (New York, NY: 1976)

Keegan, J., *A History of Warfare* (London: 1993)

Keegan, J., *Intelligence in War: The Value – and Limitations – of What the Military Can Learn About the Enemy* (London: 2002)

Kennan, G.F., (Mr. X), 'The Sources of Soviet Conduct', *Foreign Affairs*, July 1947

Kennan, G.F., 'Policy Planning Staff Memorandum', in C.T. Thorne Jr. and D.S. Patterson (eds.), *Foreign Relations of the United States, 1945–1950, Emergence of the Intelligence Establishment*, Document 269 (Washington, DC: 1996)

Kennedy, H., *The Great Arab Conquests: How the Spread of Islam Changed the World We Live in* (Philadelphia: 2007)

Kennedy, H., *Caliphate: The History of an Idea* (New York, NY: 2016)

Kennedy, P. (ed.), *Grand Strategies in War and Peace* (New Haven, CT: 1991)

Kern, P., et al., *Army Futures Command Research Program Realignment Study* (Washington, DC: 2022)

Kerr, J., 'Space Command Begins Operations', *Australian Defence Magazine*, 24 March 2022

Khan, S.W., *Haunted by Chaos: China's Grand Strategy from Mao Zedong to Xi Jinping* (Cambridge, MA: 2018)

Kilcullen, D., *Blood Year: The Unraveling of Western Counterterrorism* (New York, NY: 2016)

Kilcullen, D., *The Accidental Guerrilla: Fighting Small Wars in the Midst of a Big One* (New York, NY: 2009)

Kilcullen, D., *The Dragons and the Snakes: How the Rest Learned to Fight the West* (Oxford, UK: 2020)

King, A., *Command: The Twenty-First Century General* (Cambridge, UK: 2019)

King, I., 'Toward an Information Warfare Theory of Victory', *Modern War Institute at West Point*, 19 October 2020, https://mwi.usma.edu/toward-an-information-warfare-theory-of-victory/

Kipling, R., *Kim* (New York, NY: 2002)

Kirillova, K., 'Putin Is Losing the War, but Russians Have Stockholm Syndrome, The Jamestown Foundation', *Eurasia Daily Monitor* 19, no. 33 (10 March 2022)

Kirk-Wade, E., 'UK Defence Personnel Statistics', in *House of Commons Library of the United Kingdom Parliament* (London: 2022)

Knox, M. and W. Murray (eds.), *The Dynamics of Military Revolution, 1300–2050* (New York, NY: 2001)

Koch, O.W. and R.G. Hays, *G-2: Intelligence for Patton* (Philadelphia, PA: 1971)

Kofman, M., 'Putin's Wager in Russia's Standoff with the West', *War on the Rocks*, 24 January 2022

Kolenda, C. (ed.), *Leadership: The Warrior's Art* (Carlisle, PA: 2001)

Kolenda, C.D., *Zero-Sum Victory: What We're Getting Wrong About War* (Lexington, KY: 2021)

Kolodyazhnyy, A., T. Balmforth and M. Trevelyan, 'Russia's Lavrov Questions Ukraine's Right to Sovereignty', *Reuters*, 22 February 2022

Kone, K., 'A Southern View on the Tuareg Rebellions in Malie', *African Studies Review* 60, no. 1 (April 2017), pp. 53–75

Konaev, M., 'The Future of Urban Warfare in the Age of Megacities', *Focus Stratégique* 88 (March 2019), pp. 1–58

Kroenig, M., *The Return of Great Power Rivalry: Democracy Versus Autocracy from the Ancient World to the U.S. and China* (New York, NY: 2020)

Kube, C., C.E. Lee and D. De Luce, 'Iran-Backed Militias' Attacks Against U.S. Targets Are Up: The U.S. Hasn't Responded with Force Since Last Year', *NBC News*, 10 June 2022

Kuo, K., 'Dangerous Changes: When Military Innovation Harms Combat Effectiveness', *International Security* 47, no. 2 (2022), pp. 48–87

Lederer, E.M., 'US Envoy: Russia Intends to Dissolve Ukraine from the World Map', *Associated Press*, 29 July 2022

Lafontaine, D., 'Army Set to Modernize Blue Force Tracking Network', *U.S. Army*, 13 July 2018

Laqueur, W., *Putinism: Russia and Its Future with the West* (New York, NY: 2015)

Latiff, R.H., *Future Peace: Technology, Aggression, and the Rush to War* (Notre Dame, IN: 2022)

Latiff, R.H., *Future War: Preparing for the New Global Battlefield* (New York, NY: 2017)

Laver, H.S. and J.J. Matthews (eds.), *The Art of Command: Military Leadership from George Washington to Colin Powell* (Lexington, KY: 2008)

Lawrence, T.E. (Lawrence of Arabia), *Seven Pillars of Wisdom* (Middlesex: 1962)

Lee, K., *AI Superpowers: China, Silicon Valley, and the New World Order* (New York, NY: 2018)

Lee, W., 'Cultural Analysis in American Military History', *The Journal of American History* (March 2017), pp. 1116–1142

Lenczowski, G., *American Presidents in the Middle East* (Durham: 1990)

Liang, Q. and W. Xiangsui, *Unrestricted Warfare* (Beijing: 1999)

Liddell Hart, B.H., *The Defence of the West* (New York, NY: 1950)

Liddell Hart, B.H., *Strategy* (New York, NY: 1991, first edition Faber & Faber Ltd., London: 1954).

Liddell Hart, B.H., *Why Don't We Learn from History?* ed. G. Laurén (Columbia, SC: 2019)

Linn, B.M., 'A Historical Perspective on Today's Recruiting Crisis', *Parameters* 53, no. 3 (2023), pp. 5–18

Liotta, P.H., 'Chaos as Strategy', *Parameters* 32, no. 2 (Summer 2002), pp. 47–56

Lonsdale, D.J., *The Nature of War in the Information Age: Clausewitzian Future* (Oxford, UK: 2004)

Lonsdale, D.J., 'Alexander the Great and the Art of Adaptation', *Journal of Military History* 77, no. 3 (2013), pp. 817–835

Lonsdale, D.J. and T.M. Kane, *Understanding Contemporary Strategy: Second Edition* (Oxford, UK: 2020)

Luft, A., 'The OODA Loop and the Half-Beat', *The Strategy Bridge*, 17 March 2020

Luhnow, D. and G.F. Seib, 'A Farewell to Nation-Building', *Wall Street Journal*, 3 September 2021

Lushenko, P., 'Warfighters in Ivory Towers: Does the US Army Need Officers with Doctoral Degrees?', *Modern War Institute at West Point*, 7 August 2020

Luttrell, M. and P. Robinson, *Lone Survivor: The Eyewitness Account of Operation Redwing and the Lost Heroes of SEAL Team 10* (New York, NY: 2007)

Luttwak, E.N., *Strategy: The Logic of War and Peace* (Cambridge, MA: 2001)

Luzin, P., 'Russia's Military Manpower Crunch Will Worsen', *CEPA*, 21 September 2022

Lynn, J.A., *Battle: A Cultural History of Combat and Culture* (Boulder: 2003)

Macfarlane, R., 'The Invisible City Beneath Paris', *The New Yorker*, 23 May 2019

Machiavelli, N., *The Prince*, trans. Tim Parks (New York, NY: 2014)

MacMillan, M., *Dangerous Games: The Uses and Abuses of History* (New York, NY: 2008)

MacMillan, M., *War: How Conflict Shaped Us* (New York, NY: 2020)

Maguire, S., 'Professional Military Education Needs Reform: Here's Why and What to Do', *Wavell Room*, 13 October 2021

Maher, S., *Salafi-Jihadism: The History of an Idea* (New York, NY: 2016)

Maizland, L., 'China's Modernizing Military', *Council on Foreign Relations*, 5 February 2020

Malkasian, C., 'How the Good War Went Bad', *Foreign Affairs*, March–April 2020

Malkasian, C., *Illusions of Victory: The Anbar Awakening and the Rise of the Islamic State* (New York, NY: 2017)

Mansoor, P.R., *Surge: My Journey with General David Petraeus and the Remaking of the Iraq War* (New Haven, CT: 2013)

Mansoor, P.R. and W. Murray (eds.), *The Culture of Military Organizations* (Cambridge: 2019)

Marson, J., 'The Ragtag Army That Won the Battle of Kyiv and Saved Ukraine', *Wall Street Journal*, 20 September 2022

Mashal, M. and T. Gibbons-Neff, 'How a Taliban Assassin Got Close Enough to Kill a General', *The New York Times*, 2 November 2018

Massicot, D., 'What Russia Got Wrong: Can Moscow Learn From Its Failures in Ukraine?,' *Foreign Affairs*, March–April 2023

Matsakis, L., 'Artificial Intelligence May Not "Hallucinate" After All', *Wired*, 8 May 2019

Matthews, J. J., 'Exemplary Followership', in H.S. Laver and J.J. Matthews (eds.), *The Art of Command* (Lexington, KY: 2008), pp. 231–264

Mattis, J.N., *Summary of the 2018 National Defense Strategy of the United States of America* (Washington, DC: 2018)

Mattis, J.N. and F.J. West, *Call Sign Chaos: Learning to Lead* (New York, NY: 2019)

May, E.R. and P.D. Zelikow, *The 9/11 Commission Report* (Washington, DC: 2004)

Mazarr, M.J., *Leap of Faith: Hubris, Negligence, and America's Greatest Foreign Policy Tragedy* (New York, NY: 2019)

Mazarr, M.J., *Mastering the Gray Zone: Understanding the Changing Era of Conflict* (Carlisle, PA: 2015)

McChrystal, S., *Team of Teams: New Rules of Engagement for a Complex World* (New York, NY: 2015)

McChrystal, S., *Leaders: Myth and Reality* (New York, NY: 2018)

McClintock, B., 'Space Safety Coordination a Norm for All Nations', *Small Wars Journal*, 16 April 2019

McConville, J.C. and J.P. McGee, 'Battalion Commanders Are the Seed Corn of the Army', *War on the Rocks*, 23 December 2019

McDevitt, M.A., W.E. Cobble, H.H. Gaffney and K.E. Gause, *The Changing Nature of Warfare: Transcript and Summary of a Conference, 25–26 May 2004 at the CAN Corporation* (Alexandria, VA: 2004)

McFate, M., *Military Anthropology: Soldiers, Scholars and Subjects at the Margins of Empire* (New York, NY: 2018)

McFate, M. and J.H. Laurence (eds.), *Social Science Goes to War: The Human Terrain System in Iraq and Afghanistan* (Oxford: 2015)

McFate, S., *Goliath: Why the West Doesn't Win Wars. And What We Need to Do About It* (New York, 2020)

McFate, S., 'An Expert Explains Why Putin Seems to Be Using an Outdate Military Manual', *NPR*, 13 March 2022a

McFate, S., 'The Mercenaries Behind the Bucha Massacre', *Wall Street Journal*, 12 April 2022b

McFate, S., *The New Rules of War: How America Can Win – Against Russia, China, and Other Threats* (New York, NY: 2019)

McLaughlin, E., H. Abbasi and B. O'Reilly, 'In a Ukrainian Forest, Russian Retreat Means Digging Up the Dead', *NBC News*, 19 September 2022

McMaster, H.R., *Dereliction of Duty: Johnson, McNamara, the Joint Chiefs of Staff, and the Lies That Led to Vietnam* (New York, NY: 1997)

McMaster, H.R., 'Continuity and Change: The Army Operating Concept and Clear Thinking About Future War', *Military Review* (March–April 2015), pp. 6–20

McMaster, H.R., *Battlegrounds: The Fight to Defend the Free World* (New York, NY: 2020a)

McMaster, H.R., 'How China Sees the World', *The Atlantic*, April 2020b
Mead, N.V., 'China in Africa: Win-Win Development, or a New Colonialism?', *The Guardian*, 31 July 2018
Meijer, H. and S.G. Brooks, 'Illusions of Autonomy: Why Europe Cannot Provide for Its Security if the United States Pulls Back', *International Security* 45, no. 4 (2021), pp. 7–43
Meiser, J., 'Ends+Ways+Means=(Bad) Strategy', *Parameters* 46, no. 4 (2016), pp. 81–91
Melton, S.L., *The Clausewitz Delusion: How the American Army Screwed Up the War in Iraq and Afghanistan (A Way Forward)* (Minneapolis, MN: 2009)
Menon, R. and E. Rumer, *Conflict in Ukraine: The Unwinding of the Post-Cold War Order* (Cambridge, MA: 2015)
Metz, S. and R. Millen, *Insurgency and Counterinsurgency in the 21st Century: Reconceptualizing Threat and Response* (Carlisle, PA: 2004)
Miller, B., 'Explaining Changes in US Grand Strategy: 9/11, the Rise of Offensive Liberalism, and the War in Iraq', *Security Studies* 19, no. 1 (2010), pp. 26–65
Millett, A.R., 'Patterns of Military Innovation in the Interwar Period', in W. Murray and A.R. Millett (eds.), *Military Innovation in the Interwar Period* (Cambridge: 1996), pp. 329–368
Milley, M.A., *Developing Today's Joint Officers for Tomorrow's Ways of War: The Joint Chiefs of Staff Vision and Guidance for Professional Military Education and Talent Management* (Washington, DC: 2020)
Milley, M.A., 'West Point Graduates Are What Is Inherent in the U.S. Military, Milley Says', *U.S. Department of Defense*, 21 May 2022
Milner, H.V. and D. Tingley, *Sailing the Water's Edge: The Domestic Politics of American Foreign Policy* (Princeton: 2015)
Ministry of Defence of the United Kingdom, 'British Army Unveils Most Radical Transformation in Decades', 25 November 2021
Montgomery, N., 'Study Finds 37% Greater Veteran Suicide Rate Than Reported by VA', *Stars and Stripes*, 17 September 2022.
Morrison, S. and L. Reynolds, *2020 Defence Strategic Update* (Canberra: 2020), pp. 1–68
Murray, W., 'Innovation: Past and Future', in *Military Innovation in the Interwar Period* (Cambridge: 1996), pp. 300–328
Murray, W., 'Clausewitz Out, Computer in: Military Culture and Technological Hubris', *The National Interest*, 1 June 1997a
Murray, W., 'Thinking About Revolutions in Military Affairs', *Joint Force Quarterly* 16 (1997b), pp. 68–76
Murray, W., 'Professionalism and Professional Military Education in the Twenty-First Century', in S.C. Nielson and D.M. Snider (eds.), *American Civil-Military Relations: The Soldier and the State in a New Era* (Baltimore, MD: 2009), pp. 133–148
Murray, W. and A.R. Millett (eds.), *Military Innovation in the Interwar Period* (Cambridge: 1996)
Murray, W. and K.M. Woods, *The Iran-Iraq War: A Military and Strategic History* (Cambridge: 2014)
Murray, W. and R.H. Sinnreich (eds.), *The Past as Prologue: The Importance of History to the Military Profession* (New York, NY: 2006)

Nagl, J.A., *Knife Fights: A Memoir of Modern War in Theory and Practice* (New York, NY: 2014)

National Intelligence Council of the United States, *Global Trends 2030: Alternative Worlds* (Washington, DC: December 2012), pp. 1–160

National Intelligence Council of the United States, *The Future of the Battlefield* (Washington, DC: April 2021), pp. 1–12

National Security Council of the United States, *Final Report of the National Security Commission on Artificial Intelligence* (Washington, DC: 2021), www.nscai.gov/wp-content/uploads/2021/03/Full-Report-Digital-1.pdf

Nelson, A.J. and A.H. Montgomery, 'Is the U.S. Military's Futurism Obsession Hurting National Security?', *Brookings Institution*, 18 January 2022

Neustadt, R.E. and E.R. May, *Thinking in Time: The Uses of History for Decision Makers* (New York, NY: 1986)

Newcomb, T., 'A Secret, Shady Russian Satellite Just Broke Apart in Earth's Orbit', *Popular Mechanics*, 10 February 2023

Newman, L.H., 'Europe's Weeklong Outage Is Over, But Still Serves as a Warning', *Wired*, 18 July 2019

Nielsen, S.C. and D.M. Snider (eds.), *American Civil-Military Relations: The Soldier and the State in a New Era* (Baltimore, MD: 2009)

Noonan, M., *RAS-AI Strategy 2040: Warfare Innovation Navy* (Canberra: 2020), pp. 1–28

Nye, J.S., Jr., *The Future of Power* (New York, NY: 2011)

Oakley, S.S., 'DOD Acquisition Reform', *U.S. Government Accountability Office*, 26 April 2021

O'Brien, P.P., 'Ukraine Has Exposed Russia as a Not-So-Great Power', *The Atlantic*, 1 July 2022

O'Hanlon, M.E., 'America's History of Counterinsurgency', *Brookings Institution*, 18 June 2009

O'Hanlon, M.E., 'Beware the "RMA'nia!"', *Brookings Institution*, 9 September 1998

O'Hanlon, M.E., *Technological Change and the Future of Warfare* (Washington, DC: 2000)

O'Hanlon, M.E., *The Future of Land Warfare* (Washington, DC: 2015)

O'Hanlon, M.E., *The Senkaku Paradox: Risking Great Power War Over Small Stakes* (Washington, DC: 2019)

O'Hara, W., 'How China Masters the Art of Propaganda', *The Cipher Brief*, 21 September 2020

Oller, J., *The Swamp Fox: How Francis Marion Saved the American Revolution* (Boston, MA: 2016)

Oppenheimer, J.R., 'Oppenheimer's Farewell Speech', *The Atomic Heritage Foundation*, accessed 19 October 2022

Oren, M.B., *Power, Faith, and Fantasy: America in the Middle East, 1776 to the Present* (New York, NY: 2007)

Ostovar, A., *Vanguard of the Imam: Religion, Politics, and Iran's Revolutionary Guards* (New York, NY: 2016)

Ostrovsky, A., *The Invention of Russia: The Rise of Putin and the Age of Fake News* (New York, NY: 2015)

Owen, M. and K. Maurer, *No Easy Day: The Firsthand Account of the Mission That Killed Osama Bin Laden* (New York, NY: 2012)

Owen, W., 'Dulce et Decorum Est', in *Poems* (New York, NY: 1921)
Oxford New Desk Dictionary and Thesaurus: Third Edition (New York, NY: 2009)
Paret, P. (ed.), *Makers of Modern Strategy: From Machiavelli to the Digital Age* (Princeton: 1986)
Parker, K., R. Igielnik, A. Barroso and A. Cilluffo, 'The American Veteran Experience and the Post-9/11 Generation', *Pew Research Center*, 10 September 2019, www.pewsocialtrends.org/2019/09/10/the-american-veteran-experience-and-the-post-9-11-generation/
Patton, G.S., *War as I Knew It* (New York, NY: 1947)
Perez, C. Jr., 'What Military Education Forgets: Strategy Is Performance', *War on the Rocks*, 7 September 2018
Phelps, W., *On Killing Remotely: The Psychology of Killing with Drones* (New York, NY: 2021)
Pherson, R.H., P.M. Ranta and C. Cannon, 'Strategies for Combating the Scourge of Digital Disinformation', *International Journal of Intelligence and Counterintelligence* 34, no. 2 (2021), pp. 316–341
Philipps, D., *Alpha: Eddie Gallagher and the War for the Soul of the Navy SEALs* (New York, NY: 2021)
Phillips, A., 'The Anbar Awakening: Can It Be Exported to Afghanistan?', *Security Challenges* 5, no. 3 (Spring 2009), pp. 27–46
Plokhy, S., *The Gates of Europe: A History of Ukraine* (New York, NY: 2015)
Polyakova, A. and J. Herbst, 'Ukraine Can Win', *Foreign Affairs*, 22 April 2022
Pontin, M.W., 'Technology and the Future of Warfare', *MIT Technology Review*, 23 March 2006
Posen, B., *Restraint: A New Foundation for U.S. Grand Strategy* (Ithaca, NY: 2014)
Powell, C., *It Worked for Me: In Life and Leadership* (New York, NY: 2014)
Powell, C., *My American Journey* (New York, NY: 2003)
Public Broadcasting System, 'Military Investigation into 05 Haditha Killings Raises Questions', *Public Broadcasting System*, 2 January 2008
Puckett, R., *Words for Warriors: A Professional Soldier's Notebook* (Tucson, AZ: 2007)
Putin, V., 'Speech and the Following Discussion at the Munich Conference on Security Policy', *The Kremlin*, 10 February 2007
Putin, V., 'State of the Nation 2017', *The Kremlin* (Moscow: 2017)
Quadrennial Defense Review, *U.S. Department of Defense* (Washington, DC: February 2006)
Quataert, D., *The Ottoman Empire 1700–1922* (Cambridge, UK: 2000)
Qutb, S., *Milestones* (New Delhi, India: 2002)
Rabinovich, A., *The Yom Kippur War: The Epic Encounter That Changed the Middle East* (New York, NY: 2004)
Rabinowitz, B. and P. Jargowsky, 'Rethinking Coup Risk: Rural Coalitions and Coup-Proofing in Sub-Saharan Africa', *Armed Forces & Society* 44, no. 2 (April 2018), pp. 322–346
Radin, A., et al., *The Future of the Russian Military: Russia's Ground Combat Capabilities and Implications for U.S.-Russia Competition* (Santa Monica: 2019)
Ramani, S., 'Russia Has Big Plans for Africa', *Foreign Affairs*, 17 February 2022
Rashid, A., *Taliban: Militant Islam, Oil and Fundamentalism in Central Asia* (New Haven, CT: 2000)

Ravitch, D., 'Decline and Fall of Teaching History', *New York Times Magazine*, 17 November 1985

Reardon, C., *Soldiers and Scholars: The U.S. Army and the Uses of Military History, 1865–1920* (Lawrence, KS: 1990)

Reynolds, L., *Lead the Way: Defence Transformation Strategy* (Canberra: 2020), pp. 1–88

Rice, C., *No Higher Honor: A Memoir of My Years in Washington* (New York, NY: 2011)

Richards, T., *Imperial Archives: Knowledge and the Fantasy of Empire* (London: 1993)

Ricks, T.E., *Fiasco: The American Military Adventure in Iraq* (New York, NY: 2007)

Ricks, T.E., *The Generals: American Military Command from World War II to Today* (New York, NY: 2012)

Rid, T., *Cyber War Will Not Take Place* (New York, NY: 2013)

Rid, T., *Rise of the Machines: A Cybernetic History* (New York, NY: 2016)

Rid, T., *Active Measures: The Secret History of Disinformation and Political Warfare* (New York, NY: 2020)

Riedel, B. and B.Y. Saab, 'Al Qaeda's Third Front: Saudi Arabia', *The Washington Quarterly* 31, no. 2 (Spring 2008), pp. 33–46

Risch, J.E., 'Left Behind: A Brief Assessment of the Biden Administration's Strategic Failures During the Afghanistan Evacuation', *United States Senate Committee on Foreign Relations Minority Report* (February 2022), pp. 1–77

Riza, M.S., *Killing Without Heart: Limits on Robotic Warfare in an Age of Persistent Conflict* (Dulles, VA: 2013)

Roberts, A., *Leadership in War: Essential Lessons from Those Who Made History* (New York, NY: 2020)

Roberts, B., 'On the Need for a Blue Theory of Victory', *War on the Rocks*, 17 September 2020

Roberts, H., J. Cowls, J. Morley, M. Taddeo, V. Wang and L. Floridi, 'The Chinese Approach to Artificial Intelligence: An Analysis of Policy, Ethics, and Regulation', *AI & Society* 36 (2021), pp. 59–77

Roberts, I., 'Poland Is Now the Rising Power in Europe', *The Telegraph*, 17 February 2023

Roggio, B. and L. Lundquist, 'Green-on-Blue Attacks in Afghanistan: The Data', *Foundation for the Defense of Democracy's Long War Journal*, 17 June 2017

Roisman, J., *The Classical Art of Command: Eight Greek Generals Who Shaped the History of Warfare* (Oxford, UK: 2017)

Roll, D.L., *George Marshall: Defender of the Republic* (New York, NY: 2019)

Romo, V., 'No U.S. Troops Behind Drone Strike That Killed Civilians Will Be Punished', *National Public Radio*, 13 December 2021

Roth, A., S. Walker, J. Rankin and J. Borger, 'Putin Signals Escalation as He Puts Russia's Nuclear Force on High Alert', *The Guardian*, 27 February 2022

Roth, K., 'Africa Must Do Its Part to Break Ethiopia's Abusive Tigray Siege', *Foreign Policy*, 31 August 2022

Rothenberg, G., 'Maurice of Nassau, Gustavus Adolphus, Raimondo Montecuccoli, and the "Military Revolution" of the Seventeenth Century', in P. Paret (ed.), *Makers of Modern Strategy: From Machiavelli to the Digital Age* (Princeton: 1986), pp. 32–63

Roulette, J., 'Debris from Test of Russian Antisatellite Weapon Forces Astronauts to Shelter', *New York Times*, 15 November 2021

Rozman, J., 'Urbanization and Megacities: Implications for the U.S. Army', *The Institute of Land Warfare* (2019), pp. 1–12

Rumsfeld, D., *Known and Unknown: A Memoir* (New York, NY: 2011)

Russia Monitor, 'Putin (Again) Announces End of Compulsory Military Service in Russia', *The Warsaw Institute*, 19 April 2019

Ryan, M., *War Transformed: The Future of Twenty-First-Century Great Power Competition and Conflict* (Annapolis, MD: 2022)

Sada, G.H., *Saddam's Secrets: How an Iraqi General Defied and Survived Saddam Hussein* (Nashville, TN: 2006)

Said, E.W., *Orientalism* (New York, NY: 1979)

Salzman, P.C., *Culture and Conflict in the Middle East* (Amherst, NY: 2008)

Sanger, D.E. and W.J. Broad, 'China's Weapon Tests Close to a "Sputnik Moment", U.S. General Says', *New York Times*, 27 October 2021

Sarotte, M.E., *Not One Inch: America, Russia, and the Making of the Post-Cold War Stalemate* (New Haven, CT: 2021)

Saunders, P.C., A.S. Ding, A. Scobell, A.N.D. Yang and J. Wuthnow, *Chairman Xi Remakes the PLA: Assessing Chinese Military Reforms* (Washington, DC: 2019)

Sayler, K.M., 'Artificial Intelligence and National Security', *Congressional Research Service Report* (10 November 2020), pp. 1–48

Scales, R., 'Too Busy to Learn', *Proceedings* 136, no. 2 (February 2010)

Scarborough, R., 'Pentagon's Top Brass Explores Islamic Ideology's Ties to Terror Behind the Scenes', *The Washington Times*, 25 September 2016

Scharre, P., *Army of None: Autonomous Weapons and the Future of War* (New York, NY: 2018)

Scherer, S., 'Canada's Parliament Passes Motion Saying China's Treatment of Uighurs Is Genocide', *Reuters*, 23 February 2021

Schinella, A.M., *Bombs Without Boots: The Limits of Airpower* (Washington, DC: 2019)

Schmidt, E., N. Schadlow, R.O. Work, W. Thornberry III and M. Flournoy, *Mid-Decade Challenges to National Competitiveness: The Special Competitive Studies Project* (Arlington, VA: September 2022)

Schneaubelt, C.M., 'Whither the RMA?', *Parameters* 37, no. 3 (2007), pp. 95–107

Schneider, P., 'The Plight of the Green Beret: Why Special Forces Is Still Losing Most of Its Junior Leaders and Its Survivors are Forced to Contend with a Cultural Crisis', *Small Wars Journal*, 20 January 2022, https://smallwarsjournal.com/jrnl/art/plight-green-beret-why-special-forces-still-losing-most-its-junior-leaders-and-its

Schogol, J., 'The War in Afghanistan Is Over but Military Leaders Are Still Trying to Hide Their Failures', *Task & Purpose*, 9 September 2021

Schroden, J., 'Who Is to Blame for the Collapse of Afghanistan's Security Forces?', *War on the Rocks*, 24 May 2022

Schultz, K., *Being Wrong: Adventures in the Margin of Error* (New York, NY: 2011)

Schuman, M., *Superpower Interrupted: The Chinese History of the World* (New York, NY: 2020)

Sciutto, J., 'A Vulnerable U.S. Really Does Need a Space Force', *The Wall Street Journal*, 10 May 2019

Searls, D., *The Inkblots: Hermann Rorschach, His Iconic Test, and the Power of Seeing* (New York, NY: 2017)
Shaker, S.M. and A.R. Wise, *War Without Men: Robots on the Future Battlefield* (London: 1988)
Shamir, E., *Transforming Command: The Pursuit of Mission Command in the U.S., British, and Israeli Armies* (Stanford, CA: 2011)
Shanahan, J., 'Statement Before the Senate Armed Services Committee Subcommittee on Emerging Threats and Capabilities: Artificial Intelligence Initiatives', *116th Congress*, 12 March 2019a
Shanahan, J., 'Lt. Gen. Jack Shanahan Media Briefing on A.I.-Related Initiatives Within the Department of Defense', *Department of Defense*, 30 August 2019b
Sharma, P., 'Role of Religion in Afghan Politics: Evolution and Key Trends', *Islam and Politics: Renewal and Resistance in the Muslim World*, Stimson Center (1 January 2009), pp. 33–42
Shaw, G.B., *Man and Superman: A Comedy and a Philosophy* (New York, NY: 1967)
Shulman, L.S., 'Those Who Understand: Knowledge Growth in Teaching', *Educational Researcher* 15, no. 2 (February 1986), pp. 4–11
Shurkin, M., 'French Army Approaches to High Intensity Warfare in the 21st Century', *Wavell Room*, 22 June 2022
Silva, P.J., 'Prologue', *PRISM* 7, no. 2 (December 2017), p. 3.
Silverstone, S.A., 'Educating Strategic Lieutenants at West Point', *Parameters* 49, no. 4 (Winter 2019), pp. 65–76
Sims, C., *The Human Terrain System: Operationally Relevant Social Science Research in Iraq and Afghanistan* (Carlisle, PA: 2015)
Sims, C., 'Academics in Foxholes: The Life and Death of the Human Terrain System', *Foreign Affairs*, 4 February 2016
Singer, P.W., *Wired for War: The Robotics Revolution and Conflict in the 21st Century* (New York, NY: 2009)
Singer, P.W. and A. Cole, *Ghost Fleet: A Novel of the Next World War* (New York, NY: 2016)
Sitaraman, G., 'A Grand Strategy of Resilience', *Foreign Affairs*, September–October 2020
Sloan, E.C., *The Revolution in Military Affairs* (Montreal: 2002)
Smith, N. and S. MacFarland, 'Anbar Awakens: The Tipping Point', *Military Review* (March–April 2008), pp. 41–52
Smith, R., *The Utility of Force: The Art of War in the Modern World* (New York, NY: 2007)
Snyder, T., *Bloodlands: Europe Between Hitler and Stalin* (New York, NY: 2010)
South, T., 'Four Takeaways from the 4-Star General at Army Futures Command', *Army Times*, 7 May 2019
South, T., 'Goodbye, Tanks: How the Marine Corps Will Change, and What It Will Lose, by Ditching Its Armor', *Marine Corps Times*, 22 March 2021
Special Inspector-General for Afghanistan Reconstruction, 'Collapse of the Afghan National Defense and Security Forces: An Assessment of the Factors That Led to Its Demise', *Interim Report* (May 2022), pp. 1–70
Spencer, J., *Connected Soldiers: Life, Leadership, and Social Connections in Modern War* (Dulles, VA: 2022)

Stanton, D., *Horse Soldiers: The Extraordinary Story of a Band of U.S. Soldiers Who Rode to Victory in Afghanistan* (New York, NY: 2009)
Stark, R., *God's Battalion's: The Case for the Crusades* (New York, NY: 2009)
Stiennon, R., *There Will Be Cyber War: How the Move to Network-Centric War Fighting Has Set the Stage for Cyber War* (Birmingham, MI: 2015)
Stoker, D. and C. Whiteside, 'Blurred Lines: Gray-Zone Conflict and Hybrid War – Two Failures of American Strategic Thinking', *Naval War College Review* 73, no. 1 (Winter 2020), Article 4.
Stoker, D., *Clausewitz: His Life and Work* (New York, NY: Oxford University Press, 2014).
Stoker, D., *Why America Loses Wars: Limited War and US Strategy from the Korean War to the Present* (Cambridge, UK: 2019)
Storr, J., *Something Rotten: Land Command in the 21st Century* (Havant, UK: 2022)
Strachan, H., *The Direction of War: Contemporary Strategy in Historical Perspective* (Cambridge, UK: 2013)
Strachan, H., *The First World War in Africa* (Oxford, UK: 2004)
Strauss, B.S., *Masters of Command: Alexander, Hannibal, Caesar, and the Genius of Leadership* (New York, NY: 2012)
Strout, N., 'The Pentagon Now Has 5 Principles for Artificial Intelligence', *C4ISR*, 24 February 2020
Sullivan, J.F., 'Sun Tzu's Fighting Words', *The Strategy Bridge*, 15 June 2020
Summary of the Irregular Warfare Annex to the 2018 National Defense Strategy of the United States (Washington, DC: 2020)
Taleb, N.N., *The Black Swan: The Impact of the Highly Improbable, Second Edition* (New York, NY: 2010)
Tanner, S., *Afghanistan: A Military History from Alexander the Great to the War Against the Taliban* (Philadelphia, PA: 2002)
Taylor, R., *The Macedonian Phalanx: Equipment, Organization and Tactics from Philip and Alexander to the Roman Conquest* (Barnsley: 2020)
Terino, J.G. Jr., 'Cultivating Future Airpower Strategists', *Strategic Studies Quarterly* 15, no. 4 (Winter 2021), pp. 101–105
Thorne, D., 'AI-Powered Propaganda and the CCP's Plans for Next-Generation "Thought Management"', *The Jamestown Foundation China Brief* 20, no. 9 (15 May 2020), pp. 25–30
Thornhill, P., 'More Military Education Should Be Like the "Strategic Thinkers Program"', *Defense One*, 2 June 2022
Tingley, B., 'A Chinese Satellite Just Grappled Another and Pulled It Out of Orbit', *The Warzone*, 27 January 2022
Tobin, D., 'How Xi Jinping's 'New Era' Should Have Ended U.S. Debate on Beijing's Ambitions', *Testimony Before the U.S.-China Economic and Security Review Commission*, 13 March 2020
Tocqueville, A.D., *Democracy in America*, trans. G. Bevan (London: 2003)
Toffler, A., *Future Shock* (New York, NY: 1970)
Toffler, A., T. Johnson and L. Benningson, 'Riding the Third Wave: A Conversation with Alvin Toffler, Tom Johnson, and Lawrence Bennignso', *Strategy & Leadership* 27, no. 4–5 (1999), pp. 4–10
Townsend, S.J., *TRADOC Pamphlet 525–3–1: The U.S. Army in Multi-Domain Operations 2028* (Washington, DC: 2018)

Townsend, S.J., D.C. Crissman, J.C. Slider and K. Nightingale, 'Reinvigorating the Army's Approach to Mission Command: It's Okay to Run with Scissors (Part 1)', *Military Review* (April 2019), pp. 1–9

Trevett, J., *The Oratory of Classical Greece: Demosthenes, Speeches 1–17* (Austin, TX: 2011)

Trinquier, R., *Modern Warfare: A French View of Counterinsurgency*, trans. Daniel Lee (Westpoint, CT: 2006 1st Edition 1964).

Troianovski, A., 'Putin Invokes Nazis to Justify His Invasion of Ukraine', *New York Times*, 17 March 2022

Tse-Tung, M., *On Guerrilla Warfare*, trans. S.B. Griffith (New York, NY: 1961)

Turek, M., 'Explainable Artificial Intelligence (XAI)', *Defense Advanced Research Projects Agency*, 2022 (accessed 20 October 2022)

Tzu, S., *Art of War*, trans. J. Minford (New York, NY: 2002)

Ucko, D.H. and R.C. Engell, 'Options for Avoiding Counterinsurgencies', *Parameters* 44, no. 1 (2014), pp. 11–22

United Nations, 'Operational Data Portal: Ukraine Refugee Situation', *United Nations High Commissioner for Refugees*, 2022 (accessed 16 October 2022)

United Nations, '68% of the World Population Projected to Live in Urban Areas by 2050, Says UN', *The United Nations*, www.un.org/development/desa/en/news/population/2018-revision-of-world-urbanization-prospects.html

Venable, J., 'U.S. Space Force', *The Heritage Foundation 2022 Index of U.S. Military Strength*, 20 October 2022

Vencil, T., 'New Critical Thinking Course Responds to DOD's Latest Guidance', *U.S. Naval Postgraduate School*, 14 October 2020

Vincent, I., 'Decorated Green Beret Known as 'Captain America" Commits Suicide', *New York Post*, 11 July 2020

Wakabayashi, D. and S. Shane, 'Google Will Not Renew Pentagon Contract That Upset Employees', *New York Times*, 1 June 2018

Walberg, E., *Postmodern Imperialism: Geopolitics and the Great Games* (Atlanta, GA: 2011)

Wall Street Journal Editorial Board, 'The History Major Won't Go the Way of the Dodo', *Wall Street Journal*, 14 May 2019

Wall Street Journal Editorial Board, 'The U.S. Is Losing the Information War With China', *Wall Street Journal*, 16 June 2020, www.wsj.com/articles/the-u-s-is-losing-the-information-war-with-china-11592348246

Wall Street Journal Editorial Board, 'Ukraine Leads the World', *The Wall Street Journal*, 27 February 2022

Wallace, B., *Defence Artificial Intelligence Strategy* (London: 2022), pp. 1–72

Waller, D., *Wild Bill Donovan: The Spymaster Who Created the OSS and Modern American Espionage* (New York, NY: 2011)

Wang, L., 'The Century of Humiliation and the Politics of Memory in China', *Leviathan* 11, no. 1 (2020), pp. 38–42

Warraq, I., *Defending the West: A Critique of Edward Said's Orientalism* (Amherst, NY: 2007)

Warrick, J., E. Nakashina and D. Lamonthe, 'Islamic State Defector Inside Baghdadi's Hideout Critical to Success of Raid, Officials Say', *The Washington Post*, 29 October 2019

Waterman, S. and G. Hadley, 'Fix My Computer', *Air & Space Forces Magazine*, 17 February 2022

Webster, G., R. Creemers, E. Kania and P. Triolo, 'Full Translation: China's "New Generation Artificial Intelligence Plan"', *DigiChina at Stanford University*, 1 August 2017

Weeks, A.L., *The Choice of War: The Iraq War and the Just War Tradition* (Santa Barbara, CA: 2010)

Weigley, R.F., *The American Way of War: A History of United States Military Strategy and Policy* (Bloomington, IN: 1973)

Weinberger, C.W., *Fighting for Peace: Seven Critical Years in the Pentagon* (New York, NY: 1990)

Weinberger, C.W., *In the Arena: A Memoir of the 20th Century* (Washington, DC: 2001)

West, B., *No True Glory: A Frontline Account of the Battle for Fallujah* (New York, NY: 2005)

Wexler, N., 'Why Kids Know Even Less About History Now – And Why It Matters', *Forbes*, 24 April 2020

Weyl, G. and J. Lanier, 'AI Is an Ideology, Not a Technology', *Wired*, 15 March 2020

Whitlock, C., *The Afghanistan Papers: A Secret History of the War* (New York, NY: 2021)

Wilford, H., *America's Greatest Game: The CIA's Secret Arabists and the Shaping of the Modern Middle East* (New York, NY: 2013)

Williams, G., *SEAL of Honor: Operation Red Wings and the Life of Lt. Michael P. Murphy, USN* (Annapolis, MD: 2011)

Williams, T.P., 'Exercise Defender-Europe 20: Enablement of Resilience in Action', *NATO Review*, 16 June 2020

Williams, T.S. and N.J. Schlosser, *U.S. Marines in Battle: Fallujah, November–December 2004* (Quantico, VA: 2014)

Wired Magazine, 'Mimicking a Cybersecurity Analyst's Intuition with AI', *Wired*, September 2019

Wong, E. and C. Buckley, 'U.S. Says China's Repression of Uighurs Is "Genocide"', *New York Times*, 27 July 2021

Wong, L., 'Fashion Tips for the Field Grade', in *Strategic Studies Institute* (Carlisle, PA: 2006)

Wong, Y.H., J. Yurchak, R.W. Button, A.B. Frank, B. Laird, O.A. Osoba, R. Steeb, B.N. Harris and S.J. Bae, *Deterrence in the Age of Thinking Machines* (Santa Monica, CA: 2020)

Woodward, B., *Plan of Attack* (New York, NY: 2004)

Worthington, I., *The Last Kings of Macedonia and the Triumph of Rome* (New York, NY: 2023)

Wright, L., *The Looming Tower: Al-Qaeda and the Road to 9/11* (New York, NY: 2006)

Yoshitani, G.E.S., *Reagan at War: A Reappraisal of the Weinberger Doctrine, 1980–1984* (College Station, TX: 2012)

Zegart, A., 'Intelligence isn't Just for Government Anymore', *Foreign Affairs*, 2 November 2020

Zegart, A., *Spies, Lies, and Algorithms: The History and Future of American Intelligence* (Princeton, NJ: 2022)

Index

173rd Airborne Brigade (Vicenza, Italy) 168
3,000-mile screwdriver 41, 161
9/11/2001 attacks 6, 37, 44, 163–164, 297; influence on western military thought 44–45, 292; military response to 6, 237, 296

Abulites 148
Afghanistan, modern 6–8, 12, 22, 35, 43–44, 46, 48, 93, 101, 109, 127, 132, 148, 168, 179, 240, 242, 247, 249, 251, 261, 284, 286; 2021 withdrawal of U.S. forces from 7, 137, 247, 287, 308; British Empire's occupation of 232; early victories in 174, 296–297; geography in relation to the ancient world 181; green-on-blue attacks in 239; Helmand 231; major cities in 237; post 9/11 political movements in 238; Tora Bora 164; tribal culture in 237; troop surge in 239; U.S. invasion of 160; U.S. planning for invasion of 163–164; U.S. reluctance to nation build in 236; western ignorance of 241; Whitlock's book on 233; *see also* Britain/British, military operations in Afghanistan; Operation Enduring Freedom (OEF)
Africa 43, 65, 235, 252, 290; Patton takes command in Tunisia 292; projected population growth in 244; sub-Saharan 236; Tuaregs in 237; U.S. SOF presence in 287
Agis III 126, 269; cf. 109
Ahura Mazda 131, 221

Ai-Khanoun 221, 227
air strikes/aerial bombing 19, 34, 82, 88, 137, 245; assumed effectiveness of 164
alcohol 22, 124, 190, 270; Alexander's abuse of 189–190, 213; Macedonian consumption of 21–22, 210, 212; modern abuse of 247, 250; Philip's abuse of 22, 29
Alda, Alan 308
Alexander I 57, 58
Alexander II 58, 59
Alexander III ('The Great'), and administration 218–221, 223, 277, 285; death of 212–213; divinity of 27, 141, 143, 197, 211, 225–226, 227–228, 263; early campaigns (335) 63, 103–106; cf. 34, 43; emulates Achilles/Homeric heroes 30–31, 116, 141, 212, 265, 266; fleet of 76–77, 94, 126–127, 268; generalship and strategic skills of 2–5, 19, 34, 68–69, 76–77, 94, 104, 105, 106–107, 117–118, 120, 123, 126–127, 131, 145, 150–151, 153–154, 159, 163, 191, 200–201, 206, 209, 231, 233, 263–275, 276–307; 'greatness' of (?) 110, 112, 160, 227–228, 270–273, 281, 290, 294–295, 296, 297, 299–301; and honour 30–31, 109, 131, 153, 238–239, 266; 'King of Asia', 131, 152, 221–222, 267; leadership of 2–5, 11–12, 19, 68–69, 75–76, 106–107, 110, 115–116, 119, 129, 130, 136, 141, 143, 148, 150, 151, 153–154, 160, 181–182, 193, 201, 204, 206, 207, 209, 213, 222,

227–228, 247, 248–249, 250, 264–269, 272–273, 277–278, 281, 282, 293; as a man 4–5, 22, 23, 27, 28–31, 75, 108–109, 110, 116, 127, 130–131, 139, 141, 153, 181–182, 189–190, 198, 212, 238, 242, 250, 265, 266, 281, 282, 290, 291, 294–295, 298, 299–301; relations with his commanders 75–76, 158, 268–271; relations with Philip II 28–30, 130–131, 291; and unity of mankind 223–225; youth 26–27; *see also* Aristotle; army, Macedonian; Bactria/Bactrians; Egypt/Egyptians; Gaugamela; Granicus River; history; Hydaspes River; Hyphasis River; India/Indians; Issus; leadership; Macedonia/Macedonians; Parmenion; Persepolis; Persia/Persians; Persian Gates; Philip II; religion; Roxane; social customs; sources

Alexander IV 110, 222, 272
Alexander Mosaic 130
Alexandria 141, 220, 272; *see also* Egypt/Egyptians
Al-Hashimi, Hisham 242
al-Qaeda 6, 45, 228, 251; affiliate in the Arabian Peninsula 237; al-Qaeda in Iraq (AQI) 45; defeat in Afghanistan 296; ideology of 168; leader of 164; as precursor to ISIS 45, 167; strategy in Iraq 167
Al-Zarqawi, Ayman 45
Amazon Corporation 63, 85, 288
Anbar Awakening 45, 169; *see also* Ramadi
Anderson, Benedict 236
anti-access and area denial (A2/AD) 83
Antipater 27, 66, 67, 109, 213, 268, 269, 281
April Fool (codename) 168
Arabia 211, 212; *see also* al-Qaeda affiliate in Saudi Arabia; Lawrence of Arabia
Archelaus 57, 58
Ariamazes 190, 191
Ariobarzanes 149, 150, 157, 184; *see also* Persian Gates
Aristotle 5, 21, 23, 26, 28, 74, 197, 221, 282, 289, 291–292
army, Macedonian 4, 19, 23, 24, 57–69, 82, 116, 119, 145, 148, 181, 184, 197, 200, 207, 211, 224, 243–244, 247, 248–249, 264, 281, 285, 299; under Alexander III 11–12, 21, 66–68, 148, 181, 184, 224, 264, 281; cavalry 59–60, 66–67; composition under Alexander III 66–68, 148, 197; phalanx 60–62, 63–64, 67, 280; reforms of Philip II 59–65; cf. 68; sarissa 61–62; size of Alexander III's 66, 68, 103, 116, 117, 143, 148, 200, 207, 264, 267–268; *see also* Alexander III; army, Persian; Macedonia/Macedonians; Persia/Persians; sources

army, Persian 117, 127, 130, 142, 143, 145, 147; *see also* army, Macedonian; Persia/Persians; sources
army, U.S. 75, 234; Futures Command 87
Arsaces 183, 184
Arsites 116, 117, 119
Artacoana 182
artificial intelligence 8, 19, 38–39, 48, 78–79, 85, 87–88, 171; ATLAS system's use of 87; difference between types of 80; in national strategies 46; risk of 89–92; U.S. Navy's Aegis gun's use of 87; weaponization of 8, 39, 72, 80, 85–86
artillery 47, 82, 252, 286
Aspendus 121, 124–125, 219
Assaceni 198–199; *see also* India/Indians
Athens/Athenians 23, 24–25, 60, 124, 142, 151–152, 213, 220, 227, 278
Attalus 29, 30
Australia 58, 240; approach to space 89; defence forces of 168; investigations into war crimes 247; strategies from 9, 45, 73, 79

Babylon 147, 212, 213, 219, 221, 226
Bacevich, Andrew 232
Bactria/Bactrians 2, 43, 132, 152, 153, 181–196, 211, 220–221, 222–223, 224–225, 227, 286; *see also* social customs
Bagoas 131, 182
Barsaentes 152, 183
Barsine 130, 192
Batis 140, 141
Battalion Commander Assessment Program (BCAP) 75

Bazira 198, 199, 243
Begram 221
Bei-Dou (Chinese satellites) 88
Bekovich, Alexander 238
Berenhorst, George Heinrich von 282
Berger, David H., Gen. 92
Bessus 145, 146, 147, 152, 153, 182, 184, 185; cf. 233, 238
Biden, Joe (Joseph) R., President 232
Bin Laden, Osama 6, 158, 164
Blitzkrieg (1940) 38
Boeing 88
Bolger, Daniel P., Lt. Gen. 297
Borghard, Erica 285
Boyd, John 170–171
Brahmans 208, 223; *see also* India/Indians
Branchidae 185–186
Bremer III, Paul 160
Britain/British 73, 78, 137, 161, 231, 234, 247, 286; empire in central Asia 231–232, 241–242; military operations in Afghanistan 35, 232, 238; officers' views of T. E. Lawrence 239; operation in Oman 239; in the Opium Wars 298
Bucephalas 130, 204
Burkhard, Thierry, Gen. 288
Bush, George H. W., President 166, 266
Bush, George W., President 164, 167, 232; 2002 speech at West Point 235; views on nation building 236

Caesar, Julius 110, 264
Calanus 205, 210
Callisthenes 192, 193–194, 206, 269
Camp David 164–166
Card, Andy 164
Carlyle, Thomas 11, 49
Carthage 137, 139, 140, 212, 285
Celaenae 125
Center of Gravity (COG) 4, 129, 136, 261, 282
Central Command, U.S. (CENTCOM) 6, 159–160, 163, 166, 168, 287
Central Intelligence Agency (CIA) 159
Chaeronea, Battle of 25, 27, 28, 30, 59, 103, 107, 189
Chalabi, Ahmed 164, 252
Châteaux generalship 41, 50; *see also* 3,000-mile screwdriver
China 46, 65, 68, 72, 82; civil-military fusion in 93; involvement in space 88–89; lasting influence of opium wars on 298; military buildup in 286, 308; military education in 75; modernization of military in 82, 87–88, 288; on reunification with Taiwan 82; Uighurs in Xinjiang 86, 252; U.S. in competition with 79, 92, 252, 264, 299, 308; way of war 82, 161, 172, 278–279; *see also* Jinping, Xi
Clark, Ronald P., Lt. Gen. 294
Clausewitz, Carl von 4, 5, 266, 267, 271; definition of war 279; essence of strategy and war 276, 278–279; on genius 281–282; influence on Fuller 276; influence on Liddell Hart 42, 299; relationship with Scharnhorst 291; on the value of ancient history 35; views on the moral element in war 35, 93; ways, means, and ends 38, 281
Cleitus 120, 184, 265, 266, 268, 270; murder of 189–190
Clinton, Bill J., President 37–38, 44, 137
Coenus 139, 192, 198, 202, 205–206, 239, 253, 269, 270, 295
Cohen, Eliot 75
Cold War 17, 46–47, 84, 234, 289, 291; forgetting lessons learned during 240, 297; the new 252; U.S. containment strategy during 276, 293; U.S. foreign policy and assumptions after 44, 82, 221, 251, 296, 308
conscription 38, 58, 60, 68, 80, 83
Copinger-Symes, Thomas, Maj. Gen. 170–171
Cossaeans 212
Counterinsurgency (COIN) 44–46, 81, 174, 235, 238, 252, 284–285; *see also* counterterrorism; insurgency
Coup d'oeil 281–282
coup-proofing 270–271
Craterus 149, 150, 157, 163, 199, 201, 202, 206, 207, 211, 212
Creveld, Martin van 7, 90, 162
cyber, attacks 35–36, 42, 89; cyberspace 78; cyber-war 82
Cydnus, cf. 268
Cyropolis 187

Dahae 145
Daoud, Haji 237
Darius III 116, 127, 128, 129, 130, 131, 142, 147, 151, 210, 238, 264, 266,

267, 268, 282, 297; cf. 94; death of 152–153; *see also* Alexander III; army, Persian; Gaugamela; Hecatompylus; Issus; Persia/Persians
Darktrace Antigena (program) 89
DARPA (defense advanced research projects agency) 86–88
Dataphernes 185, 186, 192
D-Day 1945 191
Defense Innovation Unit, U.S. 80
Defense Intelligence Agency (DIA) 86
Demosthenes 22, 25, 103, 278
disinformation 47, 168, 171, 279, 283; misinformation in the news 168; *see also* information, as operations; propaganda
Dissolution Decree 210, 220
Dixon, Robert, Col. 92
Drucker, Peter 9

Ecbatana 2, 115, 157, 183, 212; *see also* Parmenion
Echevarria II, Antulio 173, 284
Egypt/Egyptians 2, 27, 141–142, 220, 224, 226, 282
Eisenhower, Dwight, President & Gen. 169, 172, 292–293; on leadership 12; policy toward middle east 239; reading habits of 291; on selective service 84; on unity of command 159
Engineer corps, Macedonian 19, 38, 64, 77, 137, 243
Epaminondas 59, 289
Ephesus 27, 121, 127, 219, 231
Epirus 23, 24, 26
Ethiopia 109, 252
Euphrates River 131, 142, 166
Exiles Decree 210–211, 212

Fairweather, Jack 237
Fedayeen 166; *see also* Iraq
Ferguson, Michael P. 41, 241, 249, 308
Fog of War 39, 158–159, 167–168, 170–173
Fortescue, John W. 232
Fort Liberty, North Carolina (formerly Fort Bragg) 285
France 9, 35, 74, 231, 234–235, 285–286, 288; high command asking Napoleon to share power 159; revolution in 38; *see also* Montclar, Ralph; Napoleon; Voltaire, Francois
Franks, Tommy, Gen. 6, 159, 163–166, 168; views on modern warfare 166, 173, 297
Freedman, Lawrence 39, 281, 295
Fukuyama, Francis 37
Fuller, J.F.C., Maj. Gen. 3, 4, 19, 128, 150, 188, 263, 264, 266, 277, 278
futurism 6, 83, 278

Gaddis, John Lewis 279, 281, 296–297
Galeotti, Mark 79
Galileo Satellites 88
Gardner, John, W. 8–9, 49
Garthoff, Raymond 41
Gates, Robert, Gen. 9, 241
Gaugamela 142; battle of 143–147; cf. 264–265, 268, 283
Gavin, Francis 75
Gaza 140–141, 243; cf. 243, 267
Gedrosian Desert 209, 263, 265
Gerasimov, Valery, Gen. 79, 83
global positioning system (GPS) 41, 88
GLONASS 88
Google 85, 288
Gordian knot 125–126, 127, 131, 170, 267
Granicus River, battle of 116–120, 265; cf. 5, 76, 268
Gray, Colin S. 5, 277, 295
Greece/Greeks 20, 21, 23, 24, 27–28, 59–60, 61, 63, 107, 109, 210, 213, 220, 225, 227, 269
Grossman, Dave, Lt. Col. 247
Guerilla Warfare 2, 43, 66, 181, 186, 189, 194, 266, 271; modern use of 245
Gulf War (1990–1991) 43, 165–166, 240, 266, 287, 296

Hadley, Stephen 236
Hague, Netherlands 80
Halicarnassus 121, 126, 219; siege of 123–124
Hanson, Victor Davis 163
Harpalus 210, 220
Harvard University 86
Headrick, Daniel 235
Hecatompylus 152, 153, 233
Hegesistratus 121, 122
Hephaestion 131, 145, 184, 197, 199, 206, 207, 210, 212, 213, 226, 270
Hindu Kush 184–185

history, value of 5–8; of a historical mind 74–76; Alexander as student of 291; discontinuity in 40; father of 123; the importance of teaching 309; as non-linear 47; uses of 35–36
Hitler, Adolf 278, 286
Hoffman, Frank x, 278
Homer 227, 291; Iliad 291
Hopkirk, Peter 231
Horace 250
Horne, Alistair 284
Howard, Michael, Sir 36, 48, 78
Hubris 4, 7, 261, 284, 295, 297–298
human intelligence 1, 41, 168, 231–232
Huntington, Samuel 11
Hussein, Saddam, President 37–38, 91, 152, 160, 166, 240, 251–252, 266, 293, 296, 308
Hydaspes River 199, 200, 201; battle of 202–204; cf. 157, 163, 264, 268
hypersonic missiles 8, 39, 42, 89, 93
Hyphasis River 2, 153, 205; mutiny at 2–3, 205–206; cf. 211, 248

Illyria/Illyrians 23, 24, 29, 59, 63, 65; Alexander campaigns in 105–106
imperialism 37, 65; colonialism 234–235; European imperialism 232, 234, 242; neo-imperialism 168, 233; soft or post-modern imperialism 235
India/Indians 1, 2, 12, 57, 67, 68, 143, 147, 157, 197–209, 223, 234, 236, 238, 242–244, 248
Indus River 197, 199, 200, 206, 208, 235
information 80, 116, 174, 232, 272; bad forms of 167, 170; fatigue or overload from 47, 73, 166, 169, 171; importance of 85, 159–160, 300; as operations 42, 82, 90, 168, 171, 283; as part of DIME 82, 235, 279–280; role in modern warfare 43, 48, 83, 167–172, 234; *see also* disinformation
insurgency 40, 42, 166–167, 169, 287; controversy over use of the term in Alexander's time 186–187; *see also* counterinsurgency
Integrated Joint Operational Platform (in China) 86
intelligence, military 1, 40, 48, 93, 150, 163, 168, 231–232; hybrid 88;

open-source 170; *see also* human intelligence
internet 170, 289
Iran/Iranians 37, 46, 140, 151, 184, 228, 235; influence in modern Iraq 252; in relation to Alexander's era 2, 115, 125, 148, 152, 182, 265, 272
Iran-Iraq War (1979–1989) 91, 296
Iraq 6, 8, 12, 22, 37, 40, 101, 173–174, 179, 232, 236, 247, 249, 251–252, 261, 296–297, 308; 2003 invasion of 43–44, 159–161, 166–167, 228; city of Fallujah 45–46; city of Ramadi 41, 45, 228; deception operations in 168; drawdown of troops from 46, 284; ignorance going into 240–241; Mosul 142; number of troops in 164–166; President Clinton missile strikes on 137; in relation to Alexander's era 142; *see also* Anbar Awakening; Iran-Iraq War; Nation building; Operation Iraqi Freedom; Saddam Hussein
Irregular Warfare 83, 186, 239, 284, 296; forces 47
Islamic State (ISIS) 167, 228
Israel 46, 87, 161
Issus 127–128, 226, 264; battle of 128–130; cf. 268

James, Denis, Col. 287
Japan 46, 247, 265, 298
Jeapes, Tony, Gen. 239
Jinping, Xi, Chairman 74–75, 298
Johnson, David E. 74
Joint All Domain Command and Control (JADC2) 171
Joint Artificial Intelligence Center (JAIC) 72, 85
Joint Force Quarterly (periodical) x
Joint Special Operations Command (JSOC), U.S. 148, 159; team from 164
Joint Task Force IV 166
Jomini, Antoine Henri de 81, 159
Just, Ward 289–290

Kandahar 220, 237
Kant, Immanuel 37
Kaplan, Robert D. 39

Keegan, John 41, 272
Kellerman, François-Christophe de, Gen. 159
Kennan, George 276, 293
Khodjend 221
killing, Alexander forbids 231; of civilians in war 83, 108–109, 139, 151, 167, 169, 198, 207, 223, 246–247, 252, 271; effects on U.S. policy in Iraq 168–169; of family members as Indian custom 223; group absolution for 247; psychology and psychological impact of 247–250
King, Anthony 10
King of Asia 131, 152, 221–222, 267; *see also* Alexander III
Kipling, Rudyard 231
Knox, MacGregor 84
Korean War (1950–1953) 40–41, 170, 284
Koster, Samuel, Maj. Gen. 289
Kurds/Kurdish 142, 168, 251
Kurtz, Walter (from the motion picture Apocalypse Now) 281
Kuwait 37, 38, 160, 163, 166, 240, 266, 293, 296

Lawrence of Arabia, Col. T. E. Lawrence 239, 250, 282
leadership 8–11, 48–50, 174; crisis of 5, 10, 73; definition of 9; difference between a leader and leadership 8–9; leader development and assessment 75–76; the true test of 115; *see also* Alexander III
League of Corinth 25–26, 27–28, 30, 103, 108, 109, 120, 121, 136, 152, 153, 186, 213, 223, 269, 271
Lee, Kai-Fu 85
Leonidas 282, 294
Lethal Autonomous Weapons Systems (LAWS) 8, 80; *see also* artificial intelligence
Levee en mass see Napoleon
Liddell Hart, B. H., Capt. 7, 38, 42, 173, 276, 278, 280, 285, 299
Lloyd, Henry 282
Lonsdale, David 129
Lorenz, Konrad 247
Luttrell, Marcus, U.S. Navy SEAL 237
Luttwak, Edward 299

Macedonia/Macedonians 20–23, 24, 25, 26, 28, 65, 225, 228, 233, 272, 299, 301; *see also* Alexander III; army, Macedonian; Philip II
Machiavelli 39
Machine-Assisted Analytic Rapid-Repository System (MARS) 86; *see also* artificial intelligence
MacMillan, Margaret 247–248
Macnaughten, William H., Gen. 238
Mali (Africa) 237, 252
Malli/Mallians 206–207, 213, 265; cf. 247, 268
Maracanda 115, 186, 187, 188, 189, 192, 222, 231, 270
Marine Corps, U.S. 8, 41, 160, 164, 166–167, 169; decommissioning its tanks 286; force design 2030 92; *see also* Berger, David H.; Iraq, Fallujah; Mattis, James, J.
Marshall, George C., Gen. 8, 276, 284, 291–293
Massachusetts Institute of Technology (MIT) 86
Massaga 198, 199, 243
Massagetae 145, 192, 198
Mattis, James, J., Gen., 8, 46, 75, 160–161, 168, 169, 171, 246; invasion of Iraq 166–167; task force in Afghanistan 163–164
Mazaces 141
Mazaeus 143, 145, 146, 147, 219
Mazarr, Michael J. 280
McConville, James C., Gen. 75
McKinley, William, President 241
McMaster, H. R., Lt. Gen., 293
Megacity Warfare 2, 47, 245–246
Memaceni 187
Memnon 117, 119, 123–124, 126
mentorship 282–283, 289, 291–292, 295, 300; *see also* leadership
mercenaries 25, 57–58, 65, 83, 115, 117, 119, 122, 124–127, 129–130, 145–146, 148, 153, 198–199, 201, 210, 220
Microsoft 288
Miletus 76–77, 121–122, 123, 268
Miller, Scott, Gen. 148
Millet, Alan R. 90
Milley, Mark A., Gen. 246
Mission Command (*auftragstaktik*), philosophy of 101, 160–161, 163, 173–174
Mithrenes 121
Monclar, Ralph 48

Murray, John, Gen. 87
Murray, Williamson 6, 7, 11–12, 38, 84
Musicanus 208
Musk, Elon 278
Myndus 243

Nabarzanes 152, 182
Napoleon 11, 77, 148, 159, 161–162, 209, 264, 266, 276, 280; mobilization of French society by 35, 38
nation building 174, 218, 221, 223, 235–236
nature of war 4, 6–7, 12, 19, 41, 48, 160, 285, 309; hopes of changing 90, 250, 254; in relation to the character of war 38–39
navy/naval forces, China's 308; America's 87, 237; Macedonia's 76–77, 127; Persia's 77, 94, 122–123, 126, 131, 136, 139; Phoenician 282
Nearchus 207, 208, 210
News media 82, 168–169; CNN effect 168; fake news 107; social media 170
New York City 6, 163
Nigeria 244
Noncommissioned officer (NCO) corps, U.S. 83
North Atlantic Treaty Organization (NATO) 46–47, 74, 80, 83, 88–89, 223, 232–236, 241, 250, 284, 287, 296, 308; Invokes Article 5, 237
Northern Alliance (Afghan) 164
North Korea 37, 40; *see also* Korean War (1950–1953)
Novel Coronavirus (COVID-19) 82
nuclear weapons 38, 40–42, 49, 80, 89, 308; as deterrent 286; development of 87; nuclear war 37, 47, 90; use of 40
Nysa 225–226

Obama, Barrack, President 236, 239, 241
O'Hanlon, Michael 46, 288
Olympias 26, 28, 29, 30, 131
Oman 236; Dhofar Rebellion in 239
OODA Loop 170
open-source intelligence 170
operational art 159, 161, 294, 299
Operation Desert Storm 37, 173; *see also* Gulf War
Operation Enduring Freedom (OEF) 240; achievement of early objectives in 296; culture shock of 237–240; planning for 163–164; *see also* Afghanistan; nation building
Operation Iraqi Freedom (OIF), achievement of early objectives in 296; execution of 166–169; influence on western military thinking 45, 286, 299; OPLAN 1003V 168; planning for 163–166; *see also* Iraq
Opis 3, 68, 141, 181, 211, 224; banquet at 212, 224–225; mutiny at 3, 211–212; cf. 141, 181
Oppenheimer, Robert J. 40, 87
Owen, Wilfred 250
Oxford University 36
Oxicanus 286
Oxyartes 190, 192, 222; cf. 270; *see also* Roxane

Paeonia/Paeonians 23, 24, 59, 65
pages 64–65, 74; conspiracy of 193–194; cf. 270
Pakistan 1–2, 20, 57, 115, 197, 218, 272; 2011 Abbottabad raid in 158; Osama bin Laden escapes into 164
Parmenion 29, 76–77, 94, 117, 118, 119, 120, 121, 122, 129, 130, 142, 146–147, 149, 152, 183, 184, 268, 269–270; *see also* Alexander III; Philotas
Pasargadae 210
Patala 208
Patton, George S., Gen. 77, 169, 292
Paullus, Lucius Aemilius 78
Pelopidas 59, 289
Pentagon, U.S. Department of Defense 6, 37–38, 40, 46, 72, 80, 85, 92, 160, 164
People's Republic of China (PRC) *see* China
Perdiccas 108, 112, 124, 197, 199
Persepolis 2, 115, 136, 147, 148, 149, 150, 151–152, 153, 157, 210, 267, 269, 270, 272, 281, 283
Pershing, John J., Gen. 292
Persia/Persians 1–2, 25–26, 27, 115–156, 218–220, 221–222, 224–225, 226; fleet 76–77, 121–122, 123, 126–127, 138; cf. 94; *see also* Alexander III; army, Persian; Darius III
Persian Gates 149; battle of 149–151, 157; cf. 157, 159, 162, 267, 268

Peucelaotis 197–198
Peucestas 207, 227
Pharnuches 115, 187, 188, 231, 233
Philip II 2, 3, 19, 21, 22, 23–26, 27, 58, 65–66, 68, 69, 74, 104, 107, 130, 131, 136, 184, 213, 228, 266, 272, 273, 282, 289; cf. 280, 282; army reforms of 59–65, 68; relations with Alexander 28–30, 130–131, 291; *see also* Macedonia/Macedonians
Philip III 272
Philippines 241
Philotas 29, 30, 106, 119, 150, 194, 268; conspiracy of 183–184; cf. 270; *see also* Alexander III; Parmenion
Phrada 183, 184, 270
Pisidia 124, 125
Pixodarus 29, 30, 184
Plato 23, 160
Point du Hoc 191
Poland 74; increased ground forces in 82
Porus 199, 200, 201, 202, 204, 205, 208, 223; medallion 204
Porus (cousin) 205
Posen, Barry 285
post-traumatic stress disorder (PTSD) 249
Powell, Colin, Gen. 164–165, 240, 251, 287, 293; *see also* Weinberger-Powell Doctrine
Precision Munitions (PGM) 6, 37, 38, 40, 43, 79, 84, 165, 251, 287
Professional Military Education (PME) 31, 55, 74–76
Project Maven 85
propaganda 27, 90, 120–121, 125, 130, 167, 185, 204
Proskynesis 192–193, 194, 224
psychological warfare 68, 116, 125, 191, 263
Ptolemy 108, 124, 130, 141, 150, 157, 185, 189, 191, 199, 204, 207, 221, 226, 273; source for Alexander 111–112, 130; *see also* sources
Puckett, Ralph, Col. 40
Pura 209
Putin, Vladimir, President 37, 43, 79, 233, 252

Qaboos bin Said 239
Quadrennial Defense Review, U.S. 45

Ramadi *see* Anbar Awakening; Iraq, city of Ramadi
Rangers, U.S. Army 191
Raytheon Corporation 63, 89
Raziq, Abdul 242
Reagan, Ronald, President 167
religion 20, 109, 126, 131, 137, 139, 182, 189, 225–226; secular militaries in religious countries 238, 241; *see also* Afghanistan; Alexander III; social customs
Revolutions in Military Affairs (RMA) 6, 7, 17, 37–43, 49, 74, 78, 90, 101, 106, 161
Rice, Condoleezza, Secretary 164
Ricks, Thomas E. 10, 74
Roberts, Andrew 5, 12
Roberts, Brad 278
robotics 78–80, 82; *see also* artificial intelligence; technology
Rock of Aornus 197–199; cf. 243
Rock of Chorienes 191–192; cf. 199
Rorschach, Herman 44–45
Rothenberg, Gunther 39
Roxane 110, 130, 190, 192, 213, 222, 223, 224, 270, 272, 277; *see also* Alexander III
Royal United Services Institute (RUSI) 170
Rumsfeld, Donald, Secretary 163–164, 166
Russia 37, 46, 58, 68, 72, 79, 161, 246, 278–279, 288, 298, 308; army of 50, 73; conscription in 68, 83; invasions of Ukraine by 35, 43, 44–47, 49, 82–83, 91, 109, 170, 173, 232–233, 236; promotion rate of officers in 294; space weapons of 88–89; Tsarist empire of 231, 238, 241; war crimes of 252; *see also* Gerasimov, Valery; Putin, Vladimir; Soviet Union

Sacae 187–188; *see also* Scythia/Scythians
Said, Edward 240
Salafism 168, 241–242
Salmus 210
Sambus 208
Sangala 205
Sardis 2, 115, 121, 125, 218, 268, 272
Satibarzanes 74, 152, 182, 183, 184
Saudi Arabia (modern) 237
Scales, Robert, Maj. Gen. 292
Scharnhorst, Gerhard von 282, 291

Scythia/Scythians 60, 61, 62, 188, 243
Shanahan, Jack, Lt. Gen. 72, 78, 92
Shaw, George Bernard 292
Shelton, William, Gen. 89
Shia Muslims 251–252
Showalter, Dennis 309
sieges 1–2, 19; *see also* Halicarnassus, siege of; Rock of Chorienes; Sogdian Rock; Tyre, siege of
Sillyum 124
Sisimithres 191, 192, 199
Sitaraman, Ganesh 285
slaughter *see* killing
social customs 221–225, 238–239, 242; cf. 243
Sogdian Rock 190–191; cf. 243
Sources, on Alexander 110–112; on his battles 104–105 (in 335) 117, 120 (Granicus River); 127, 130 (Issus); 143, 147 (Gaugamela); 203–204 (Hydaspes River)
South Korea 82, 247
Soviet Union 36–38, 43, 47, 84, 298, 308; U.S. containment policy toward 276, 291; war in Afghanistan (1979–1989) 35, 164, 234, 241; *see also* Russia
space (outer) 79, 85; abundance of satellites in 88; counter weapons 39, 40, 47, 89; as a domain of warfare 78; International Space Station 89; military reliance upon 39, 73, 88, 92; U.S. Space Force 89; vulnerabilities in 88–89
Space X (company) 88
Sparta/Spartans 22, 25, 109, 126, 220, 223, 248, 269, 282, 290
Special Forces, U.S. (green berets) 9–10, 168; mountain warfare school of 191
Special Operations Command, U.S. (SOCOM) 287
Special Operations Forces (SOF) 42, 45, 164, 239, 246, 287, 296; Macedonian equivalent 58, 61; *see also* Joint Special Operations Command; Special Operations Command; Special Forces
Spitamenes 185, 186, 187, 188, 189, 192, 231, 271
Spithridates 120, 265
stability operations 42, 252, 296

stealth technology 37–38, 296
Stogdill, Ralph 11
Storr, Jim 10
Strachan, Hew 276
strategy 78; Alexander's flaws in 299–301; definitions of 276–278; grand 276–280, 299; object of 285; as a policy 37, 46, 72, 78–79, 241, 286; strategic education 7, 289–295; as a theory 173, 277; *see also* Alexander III; Clausewitz, Carl von; Freedman, Lawrence; Gaddis, John Lewis; Gray, Colin S.; Liddell Hart, B. H.; Weinberger-Powell Doctrine
Strauss, Barry 4
successors 68, 116, 125, 272–273, 294
Sunni Muslims 45, 166, 252, 296
Sun Tzu 171
Susa 147, 148, 210, 211, 224, 277
Sweden 68, 83

Taiwan *see* China
Taleb, Nassim Nicholas 43, 81
Taliban 6–7, 109, 137, 164, 174, 233, 236–237, 242, 251, 287, 296, 308; *see also* Afghanistan
Tarsus 127
Taxila 198, 199, 200
Taxiles 198, 199, 205
technology 7, 19, 64, 67, 68–69, 139, 157–158, 280; culture of 10; cf. 43; *see also* army, Macedonian; artificial intelligence; cyber; Revolutions in Military Affairs (RMA)
telegraph (optical) 159
Termessus 125
Thalestris 131, 182
Thebes/Thebans 23, 25, 27–28, 59, 106, 112, 139, 182, 289, 290; revolt of 107–109; cf. 290
Thomas-Greenfield, Linda 252
Thrace/Thracians 23, 24, 27, 28, 34, 43, 103–104
Thucydides 9, 36, 81
Tiridates 151
Toffler, Alvin 278, 296
Treaty of Westphalia 236
tribal culture 24; in modern war 167, 236–241, 286
Triballi 104–105
Trump, Donald, President 46, 236, 293; administration of 232

Tyre/Tyrians 67, 140, 142, 225, 227, 269, 282–283, 293, 301; siege of 136–139; cf. 243, 267

Uighurs *see* China
Ukraine 37, 40, 43, 46–47, 49–50, 82–83, 91, 109, 170, 232–233, 245–246, 252, 288–289, 294; *see also* Russia, invasion of
United Kingdom 9–10, 89, 166, 170, 172, 240, 247, 285–286
United Nations (UN) 80, 244
unmanned weapons/vehicles 19, 34, 42, 48, 72, 84, 87; drones 85, 158, 247; drone swarming 89
Unrestricted Warfare (book published in China) 82, 161; *see also* China
urban warfare 43, 169, 233, 244–246, 253
Uxiana/Uxians 148–149, 150, 157

Vietnam Wars 6, 41, 234–235, 240, 261, 266, 285, 289–290, 293, 309
Voltaire, Francois 169

War on Terror (Global War on Terrorism) 43, 74, 233, 292; effect on strategic forecasting 45
Warsaw Pact 46
Washington, D.C. 161, 163, 166–167, 293
Weber, Max 39
Weigley, Russell 173
Weinberger-Powell Doctrine 240, 287
West, Bing 167
West Point, U.S. Military Academy at 235, 289–290
White House 158, 164, 167, 236
Whitlock, Craig 233
wine *see* alcohol
Wolfowitz, Paul 164
World War I 284
World War II 38, 74, 84, 89, 234, 288, 291, 293

Zadracarta 182, 184
Zagros Mountains 146, 148, 212
Zelensky, Volodymyr, President 49–50
Zinni, Anthony, Gen. 166

For Product Safety Concerns and Information please contact our EU
representative GPSR@taylorandfrancis.com
Taylor & Francis Verlag GmbH, Kaufingerstraße 24, 80331 München, Germany

www.ingramcontent.com/pod-product-compliance
Lightning Source LLC
Chambersburg PA
CBHW071358300426
44114CB00016B/2105